Skip·Beat!

Shojo Beat

Skip·Beat!

2

Story & Art by Yoshiki Nakamura

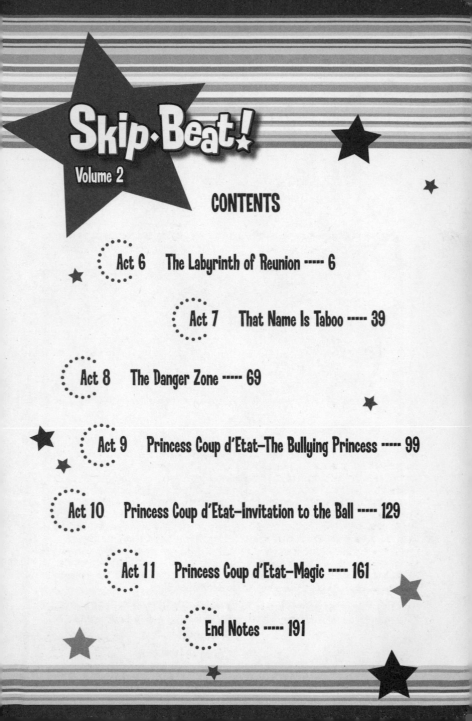

Skip·Beat!
Volume 2

CONTENTS

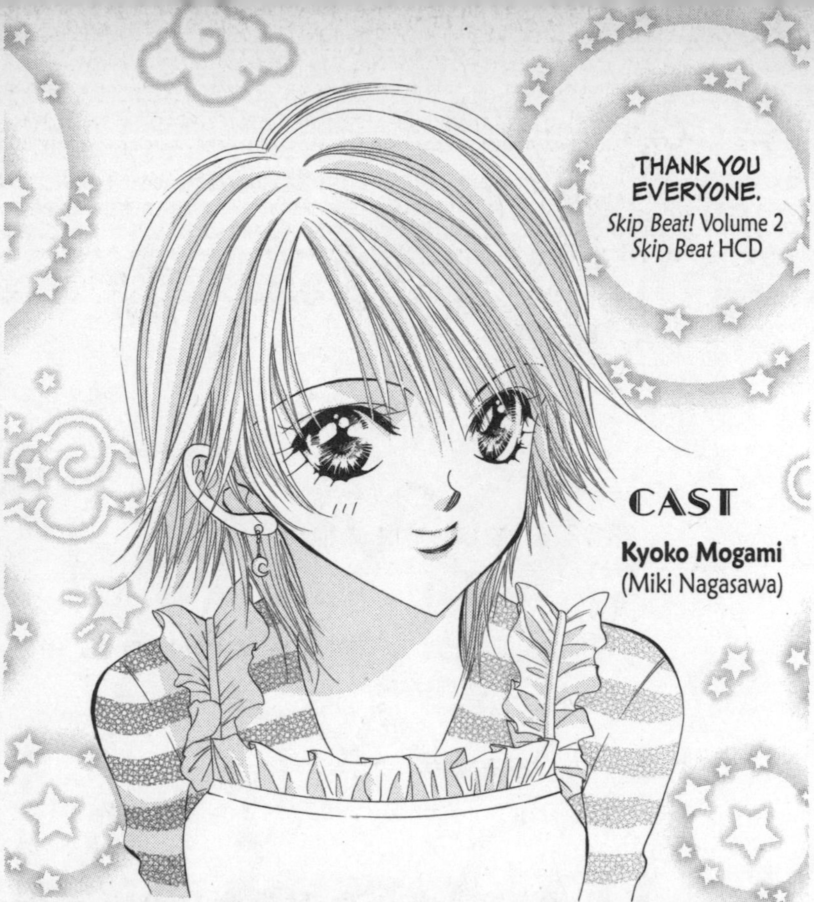
THANK YOU EVERYONE.
Skip Beat! Volume 2
Skip Beat HCD
CAST
Kyoko Mogami
(Miki Nagasawa)

Hello. I'm Nakamura. This is the second volume of the *Skip Beat!* manga. I started a series about "showbiz," and I was pretty worried. But I was able to bring the story this far, and I'm relieved. No, not about Kyoko's barging into showbiz... Her revenge against Shotaro has just started, but *Skip Beat!* itself wasn't originally a showbiz story, so it I hadn't decided specifically how Kyoko would join showbiz (we later decided on Kyoko failing the first audition and joining the Love Me Section). After that, now I go with whatever I think up in the moment. I know that doesn't sound like a good thing to say, and I'm having trouble effectively developing and bringing together the story I just thought up. Doing my storyboards is taking so much time, I feel like I'm in a crisis, and I feel a little disgusted with myself. What am I doing? The longer I am a mangaka, the longer it takes me to do storyboards!

I've been doing storyboards slowly, like a snail, and *Skip Beat!* has still managed to come this far... Amazingly, thankfully, HCD put out a *Skip Beat!* drama CD!!

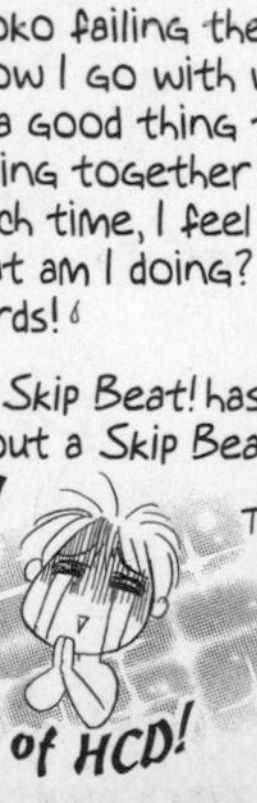
I'm happy!
Finally!
A member of HCD!

Tokyo Crazy Paradise wasn't an HCD, so it wasn't even included in the list of HCD advertisements!

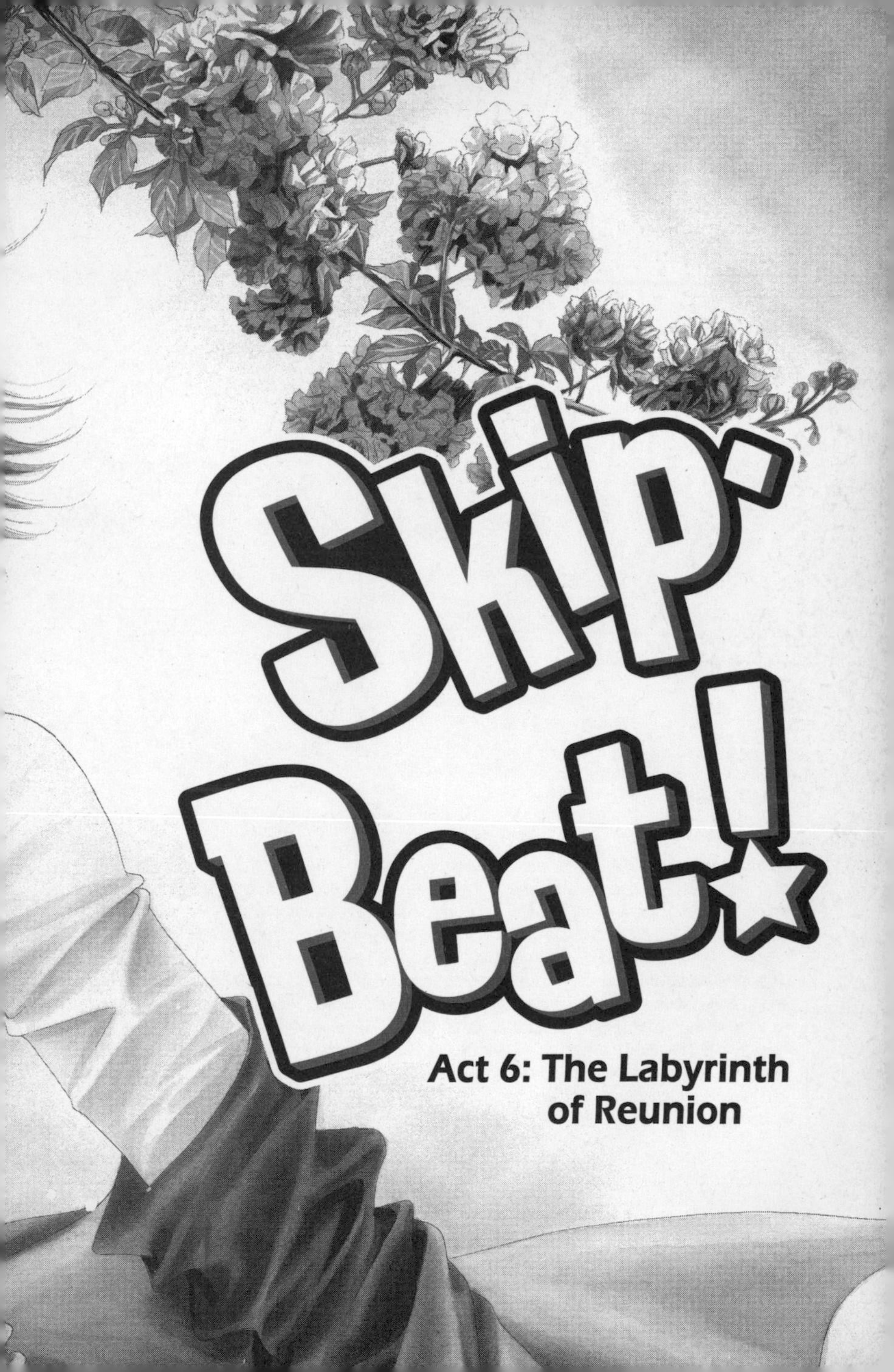
Skip Beat!
Act 6: The Labyrinth of Reunion

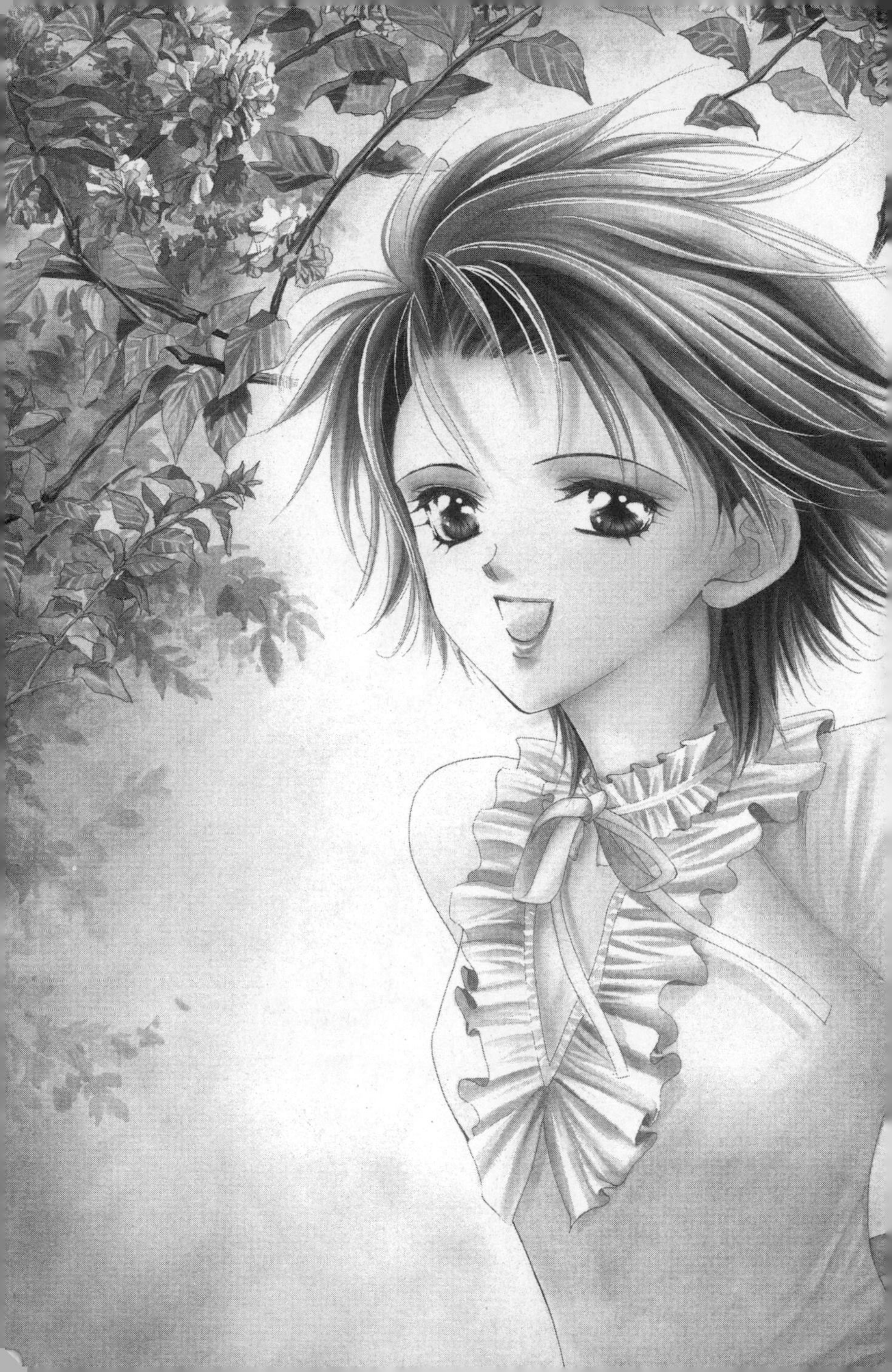

I heard about making *Skip Beat!* into an HCD in June. Volume 1 of the manga hadn't even come out yet (since it was coming out in July.) I was thankful for the offer, but I was very worried... The contents of the CD was going to be the volume 1 story, and there are no scenes to soften the hearts of shojo manga readers, like Sho and Kyoko being lovey-dovey, or Ren and Kyoko being lovey-dovey... (Since it just started, it can't be helped.) Moreover, the personalities of the characters other than Kyoko haven't been delved into yet (Both Sho and Ren don't appear enough...) What is really fatal is that *Skip Beat!* isn't known widely enough... So even if an HCD comes out, it might not sell. I understand that, but I decided to go with Hakusensha's generous offer.

...Because, if I refused the offer, another might never come...

I have no confidence...

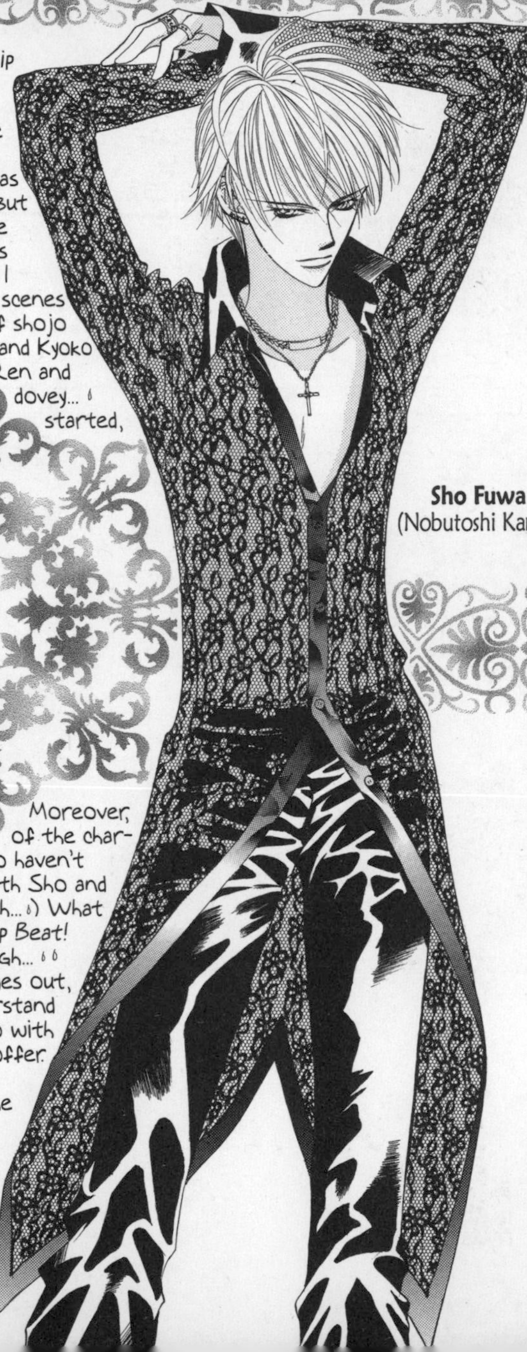

Sho Fuwa
(Nobutoshi Kanna)

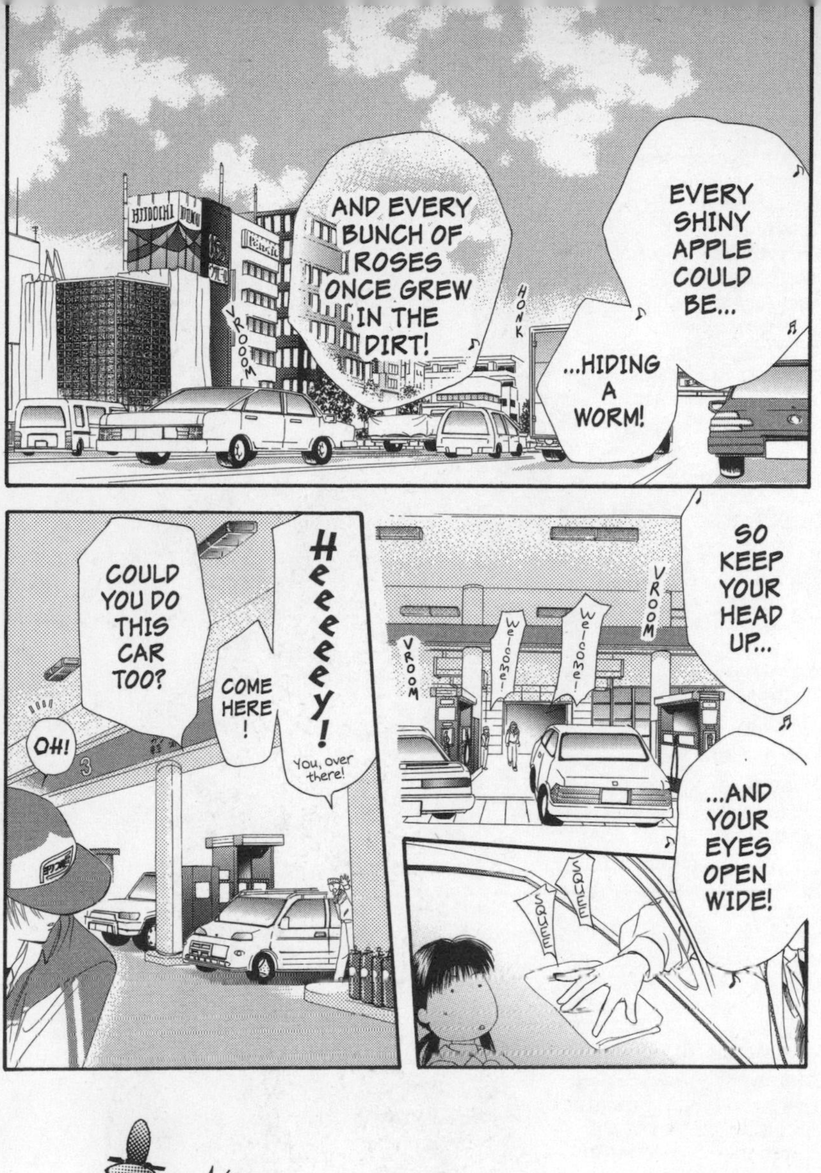
EVERY SHINY APPLE COULD BE...
...HIDING A WORM!
HONK
AND EVERY BUNCH OF ROSES ONCE GREW IN THE DIRT!
VROOOM
SO KEEP YOUR HEAD UP...
VROOM
Welcome!
Welcome!
VROOM
...AND YOUR EYES OPEN WIDE!
SQUEE
SQUEE
Heeeeey!
You, over there!
COME HERE!
COULD YOU DO THIS CAR TOO?
OH!

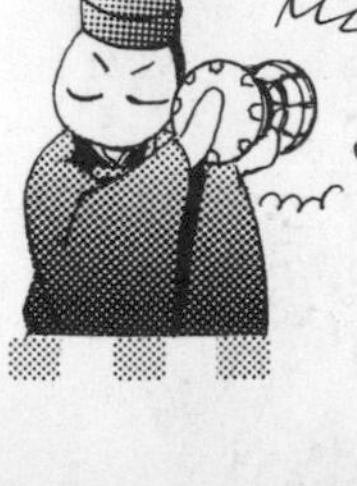

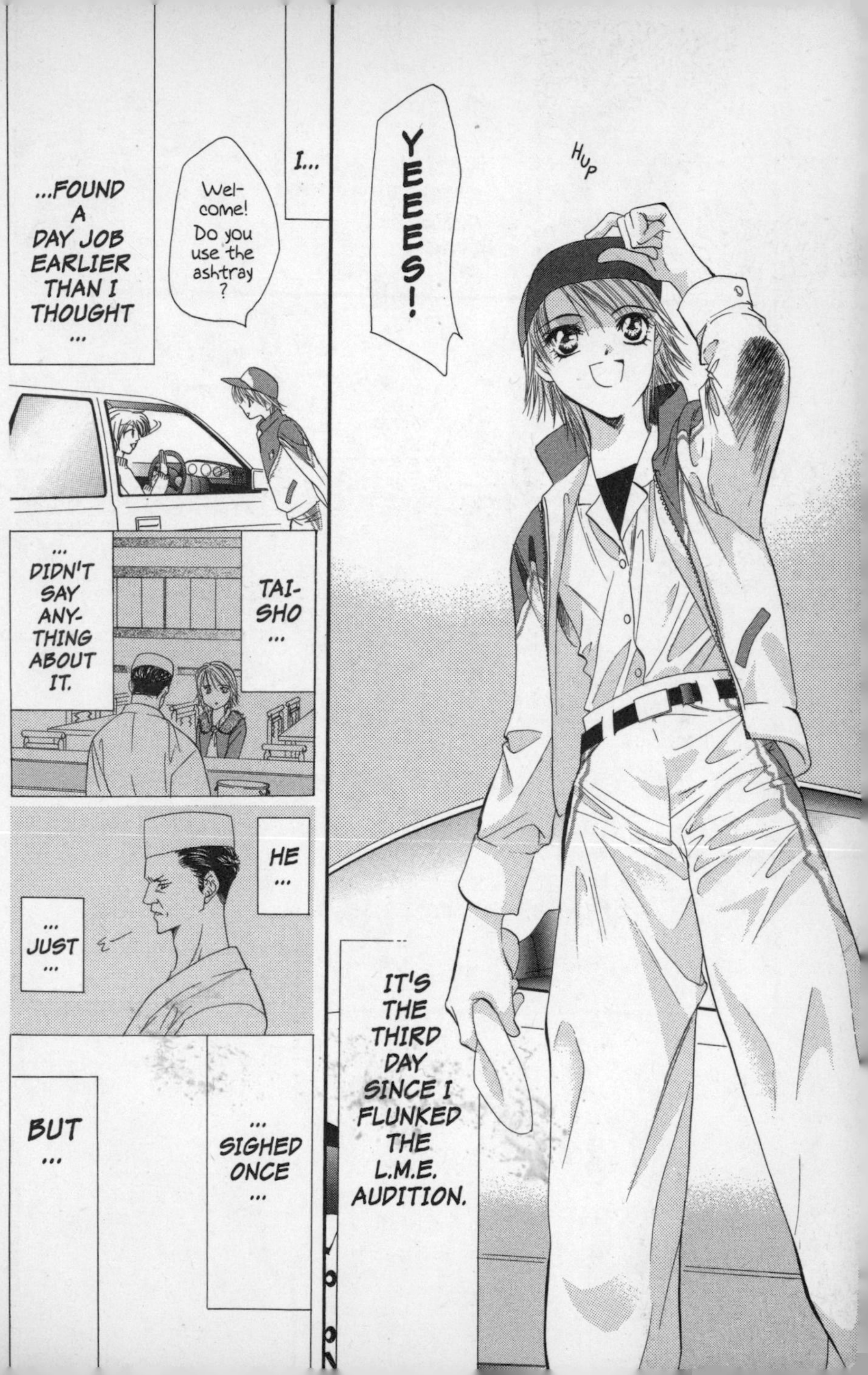

HUP
YEEEES!
IT'S THE THIRD DAY SINCE I FLUNKED THE L.M.E. AUDITION.
I...
Wel-come! Do you use the ashtray?
...FOUND A DAY JOB EARLIER THAN I THOUGHT...
TAI-SHO...
...DIDN'T SAY ANYTHING ABOUT IT.
HE...
...JUST...
...SIGHED ONCE...
BUT...

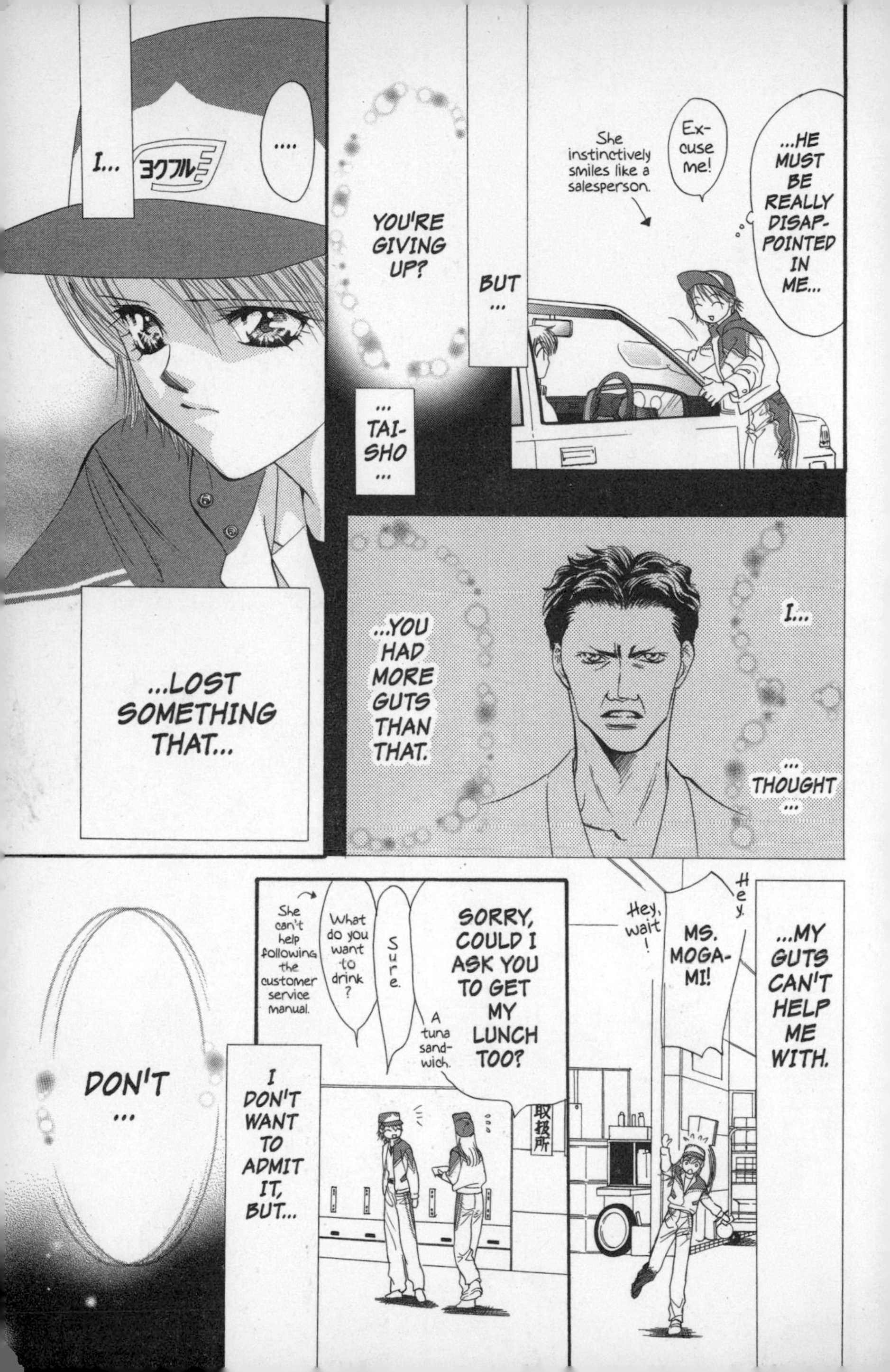
...HE MUST BE REALLY DISAPPOINTED IN ME...
Ex-cuse me!
She instinctively smiles like a salesperson.
BUT ...
YOU'RE GIVING UP?
... TAI-SHO ...
I...
... THOUGHT ...
...YOU HAD MORE GUTS THAN THAT.
....
I...
ヨクフル
...LOST SOMETHING THAT...
...MY GUTS CAN'T HELP ME WITH.
Hey.
Hey, wait!
MS. MOGAMI!
SORRY, COULD I ASK YOU TO GET MY LUNCH TOO?
A tuna sandwich.
Sure.
What do you want to drink?
She can't help following the customer service manual.
取扱所
I DON'T WANT TO ADMIT IT, BUT...
DON'T ...

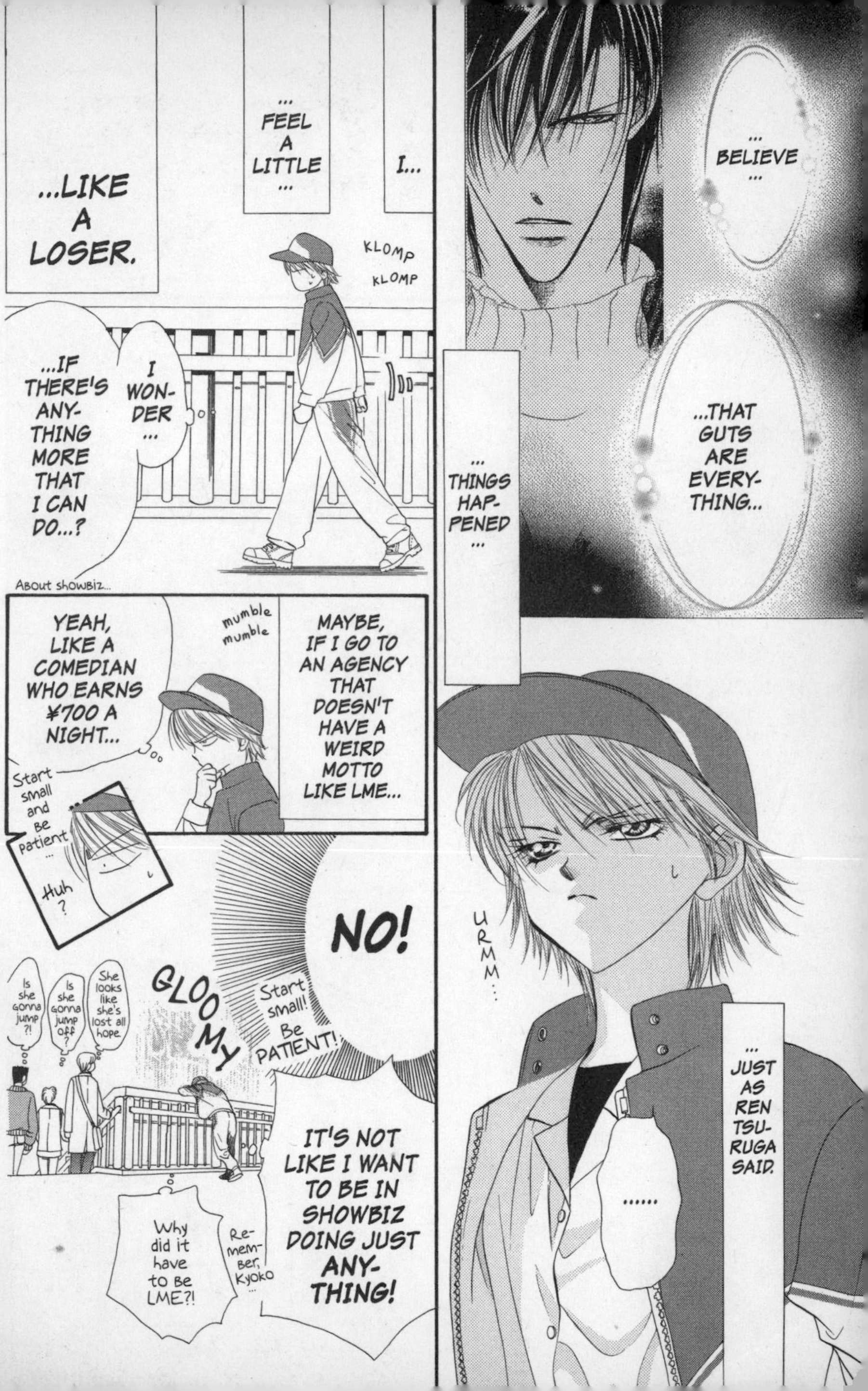

... BELIEVE ...
...THAT GUTS ARE EVERY-THING...
... THINGS HAP-PENED ...
URMM...
... JUST AS REN TSU-RUGA SAID.
......
I...
... FEEL A LITTLE ...
...LIKE A LOSER.
KLOMP KLOMP
I WON-DER ...
...IF THERE'S ANY-THING MORE THAT I CAN DO...?
About showbiz...
MAYBE, IF I GO TO AN AGENCY THAT DOESN'T HAVE A WEIRD MOTTO LIKE LME...
mumble mumble
YEAH, LIKE A COMEDIAN WHO EARNS ¥700 A NIGHT...
Start small and Be patient ...
Huh?
NO!
Start small! Be PATIENT!
GLOOMY
She looks like she's lost all hope
Is she gonna jump off?
Is she gonna jump?!
IT'S NOT LIKE I WANT TO BE IN SHOWBIZ DOING JUST ANY-THING!
Re-mem-Ber, Kyoko ...
Why did it have to Be LME?!

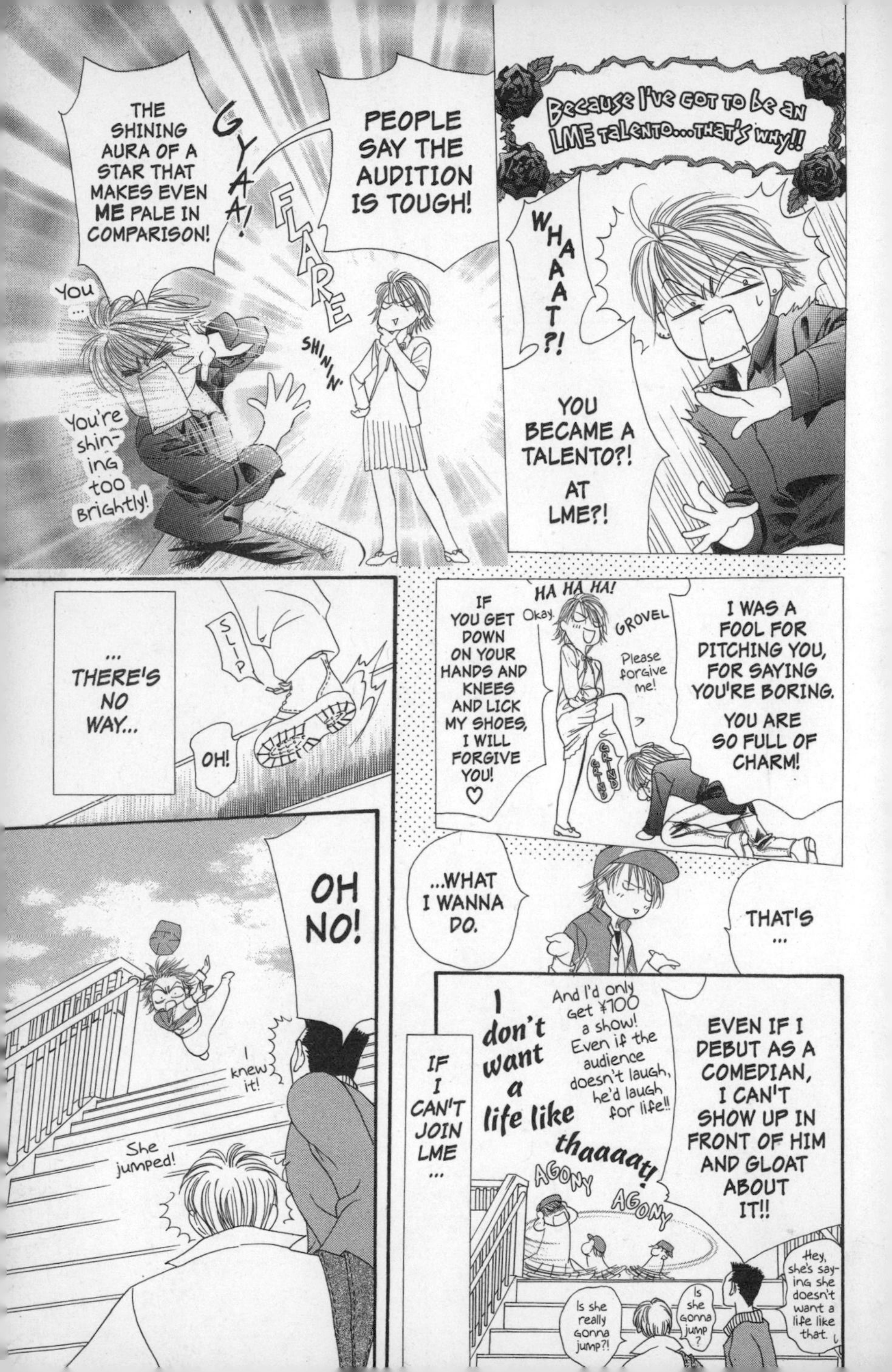
Because I've got to be an LME talento...that's why!!
WHAAAT?!
YOU BECAME A TALENTO?!
AT LME?!
PEOPLE SAY THE AUDITION IS TOUGH!
FLARE
SHININ'
THE SHINING AURA OF A STAR THAT MAKES EVEN ME PALE IN COMPARISON!
GYAA!
You...
You're shining too brightly!
I WAS A FOOL FOR DITCHING YOU, FOR SAYING YOU'RE BORING.
YOU ARE SO FULL OF CHARM!
GROVEL
Please forgive me!
HA HA HA!
Okay.
IF YOU GET DOWN ON YOUR HANDS AND KNEES AND LICK MY SHOES, I WILL FORGIVE YOU! ♡
GRIND GRIND
... THERE'S NO WAY...
SLIP
OH!
THAT'S ...
...WHAT I WANNA DO.
EVEN IF I DEBUT AS A COMEDIAN, I CAN'T SHOW UP IN FRONT OF HIM AND GLOAT ABOUT IT!!
And I'd only get ¥100 a show! Even if the audience doesn't laugh, he'd laugh for life!!
I don't want a life like thaaaat!
IF I CAN'T JOIN LME ...
AGONY
AGONY
Hey, she's saying she doesn't want a life like that.
Is she gonna jump?
Is she really gonna jump?!
OH NO!
I knew it!
She jumped!

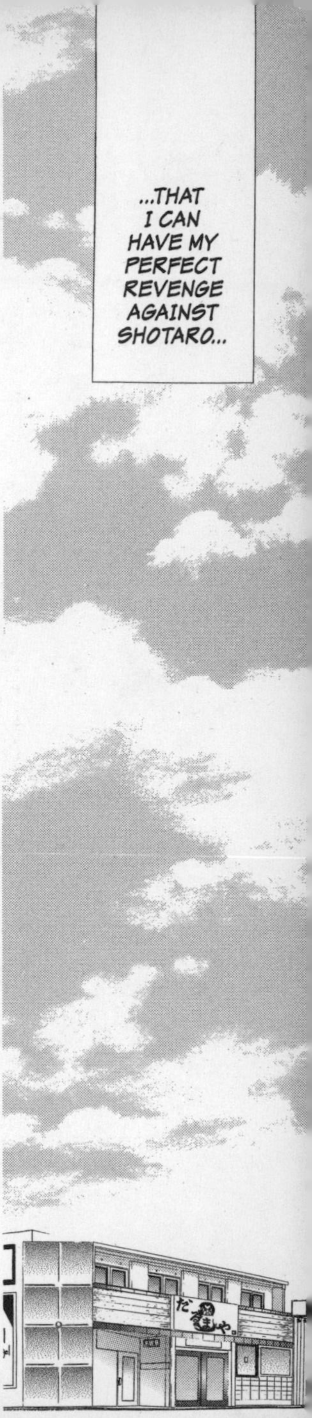
...THAT I CAN HAVE MY PERFECT REVENGE AGAINST SHOTARO...

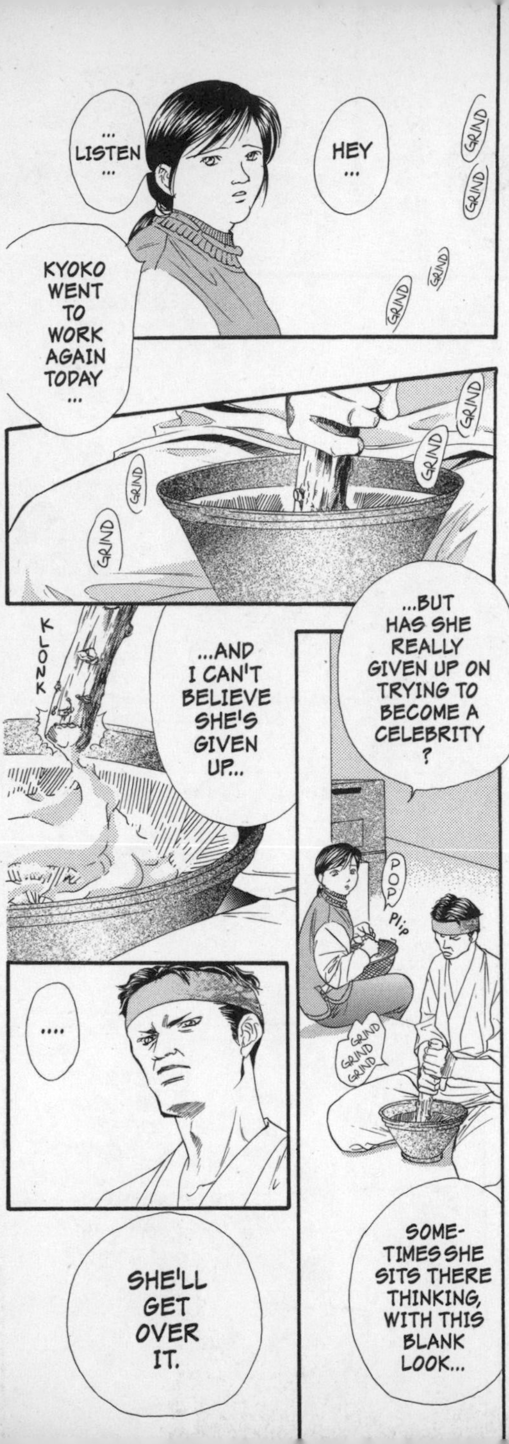
HEY ...
... LISTEN ...
GRIND GRIND
GRIND GRIND
KYOKO WENT TO WORK AGAIN TODAY ...
GRIND GRIND GRIND GRIND GRIND
...BUT HAS SHE REALLY GIVEN UP ON TRYING TO BECOME A CELEBRITY ?
POP
PLIP
GRIND GRIND GRIND
SOME-TIMES SHE SITS THERE THINKING, WITH THIS BLANK LOOK...
KLONK
...AND I CAN'T BELIEVE SHE'S GIVEN UP...
....
SHE'LL GET OVER IT.

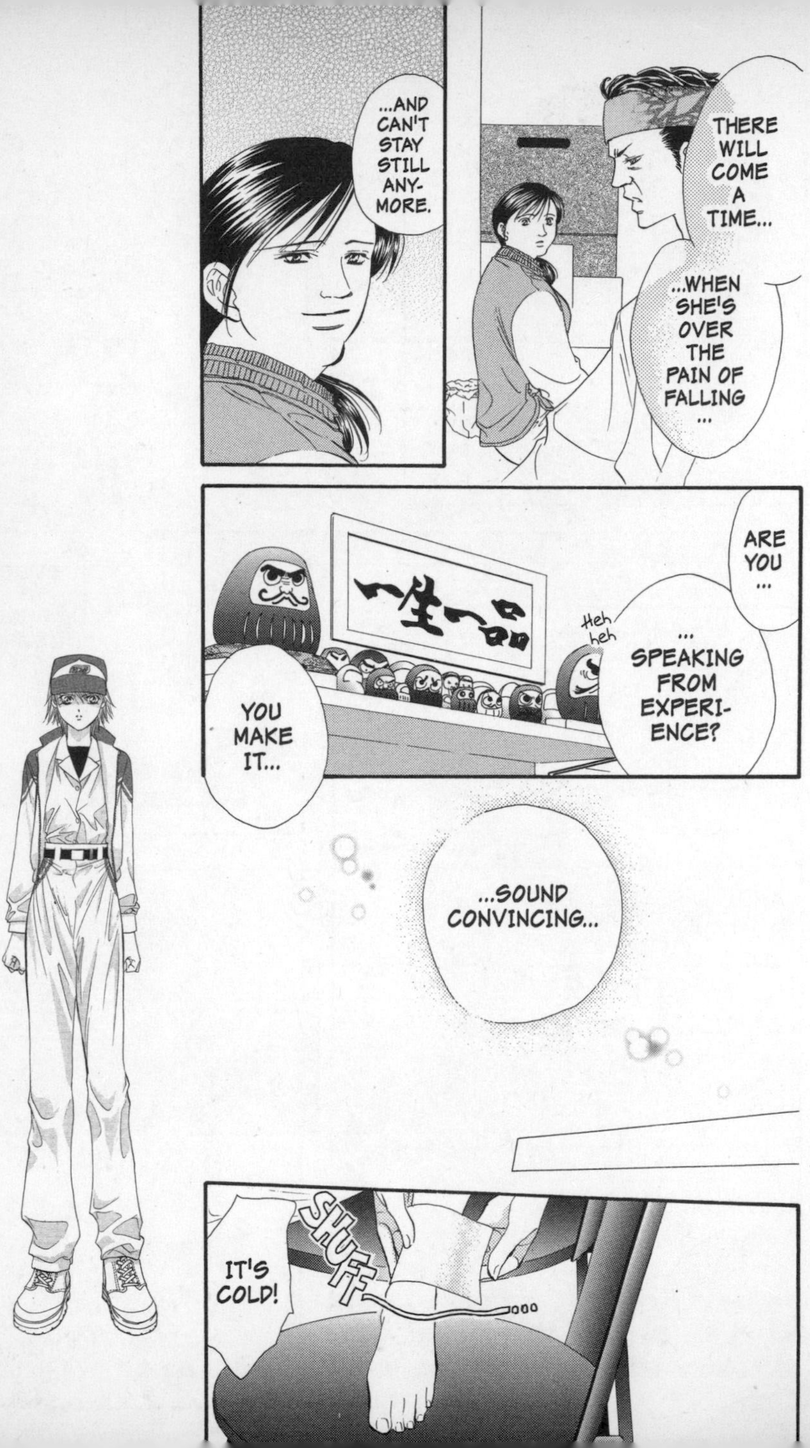
THERE WILL COME A TIME...
...WHEN SHE'S OVER THE PAIN OF FALLING ...
...AND CAN'T STAY STILL ANYMORE.
ARE YOU ...
... SPEAKING FROM EXPERIENCE?
Heh heh
一生一品
YOU MAKE IT...
...SOUND CONVINCING...
SHUFF
IT'S COLD!

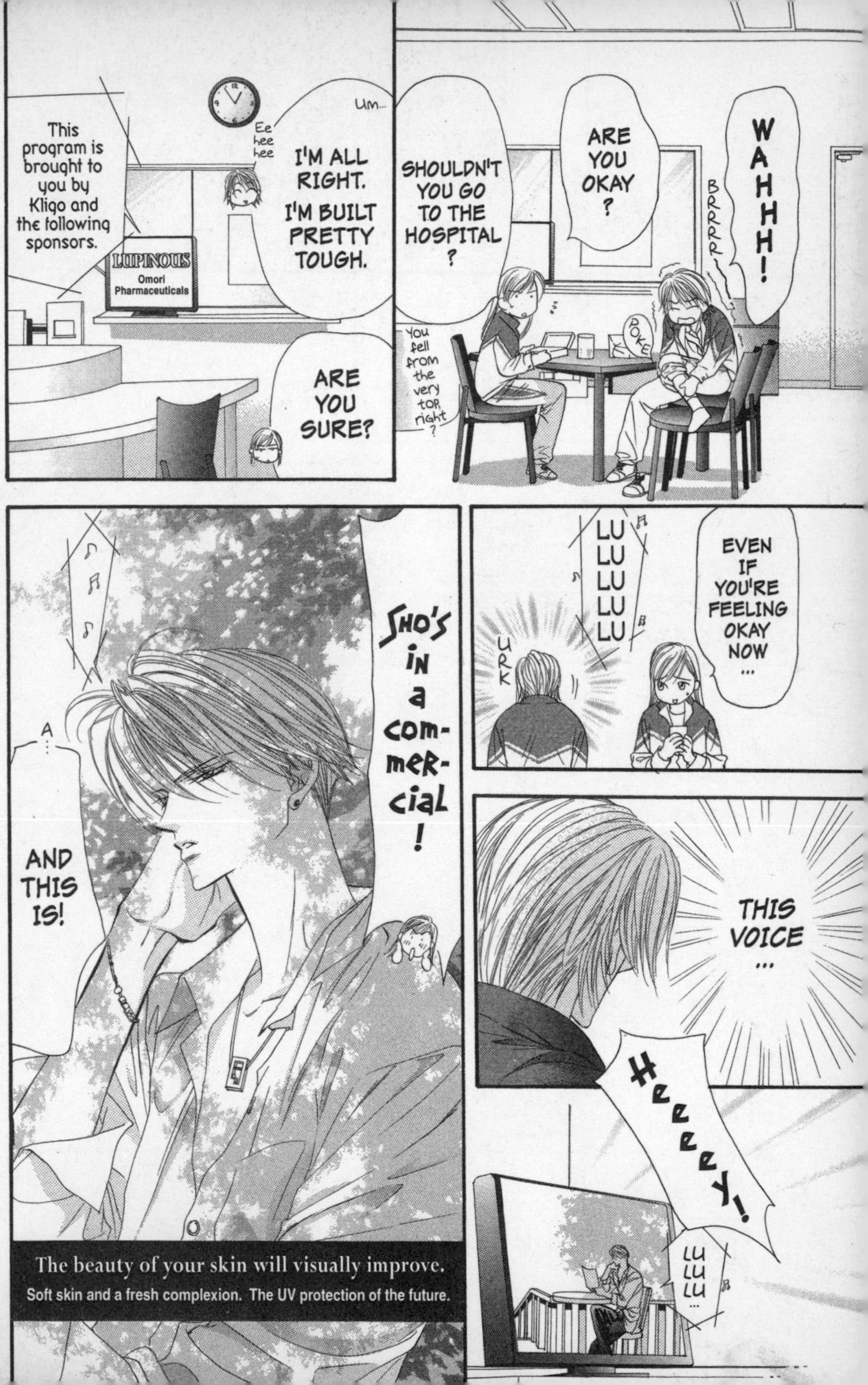
WAHHH!
BRRRRR
ARE YOU OKAY?
SHOULDN'T YOU GO TO THE HOSPITAL?
POKE
You fell from the very top, right?
Um...
I'M ALL RIGHT. I'M BUILT PRETTY TOUGH.
Ee hee hee
This program is brought to you by Kligo and the following sponsors.
LUPINOUS
Omori Pharmaceuticals
ARE YOU SURE?
EVEN IF YOU'RE FEELING OKAY NOW...
LU LU LU LU LU
URK
THIS VOICE...
Heeeey!
LULULU...
SHO'S in a commercial!
A...
AND THIS IS!
The beauty of your skin will visually improve.
Soft skin and a fresh complexion. The UV protection of the future.

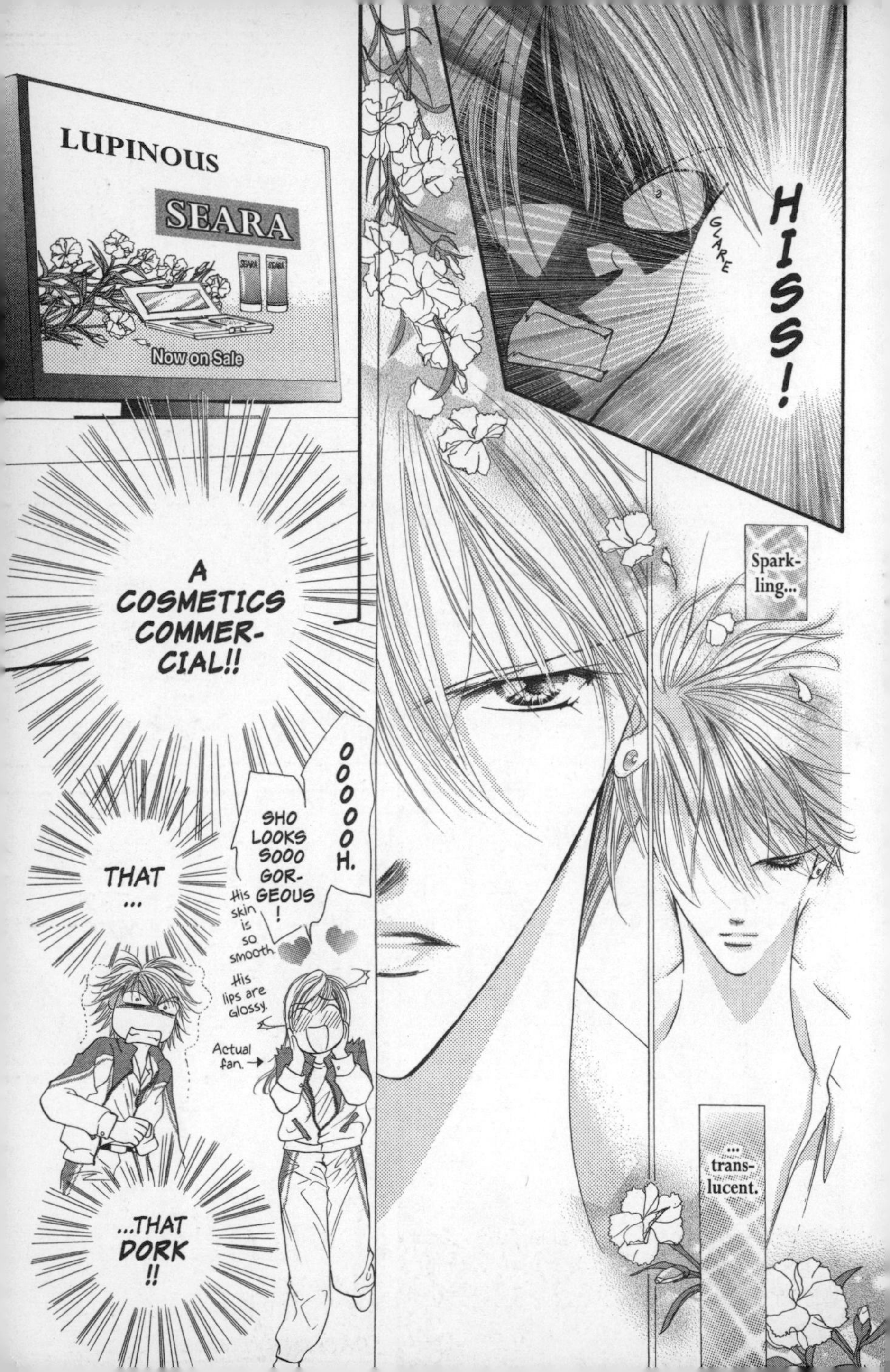
GLARE
HISS!
Spark-ling...
... trans-lucent.
LUPINOUS
SEARA
SEARA SEARA
Now on Sale
A COSMETICS COMMER-CIAL!!
OOOOOOH.
SHO LOOKS SOOO GOR-GEOUS!
His skin is so smooth.
His lips are glossy.
THAT ...
Actual fan.
...THAT DORK!!

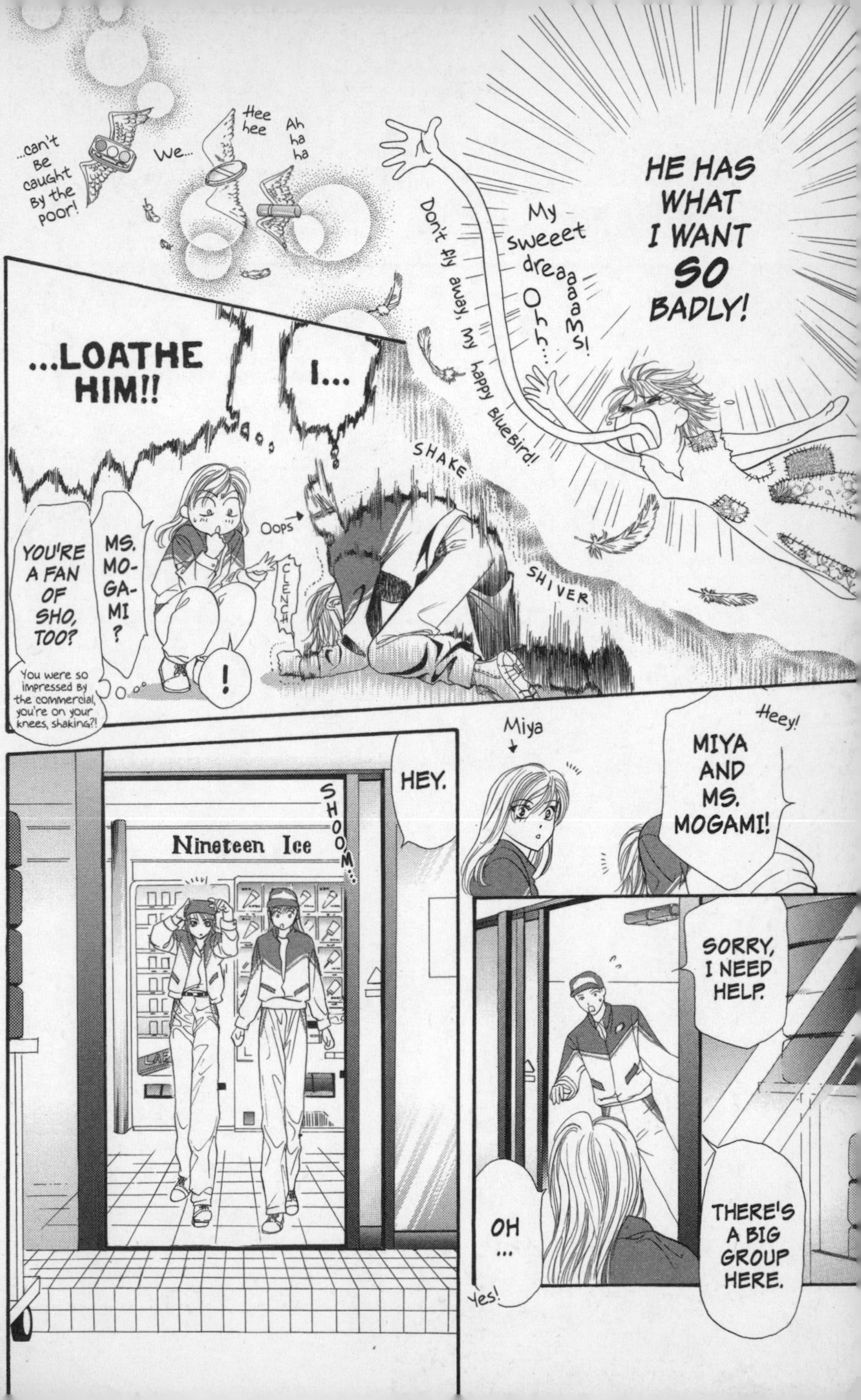
HE HAS WHAT I WANT SO BADLY!
My sweeet dreaaaaams!
Ohh...
Don't fly away, my happy BlueBird!
Ah ha ha
Hee hee
We...
...can't be caught by the poor!
I...
...LOATHE HIM!!
SHAKE
SHIVER
Oops
CLENCH
!
MS. MOGAMI?
YOU'RE A FAN OF SHO, TOO?
You were so impressed by the commercial, you're on your knees, shaking?!
Heey!
MIYA AND MS. MOGAMI!
Miya
SORRY, I NEED HELP.
THERE'S A BIG GROUP HERE.
OH ...
Yes!
HEY.
SHOOOM...
Nineteen Ice

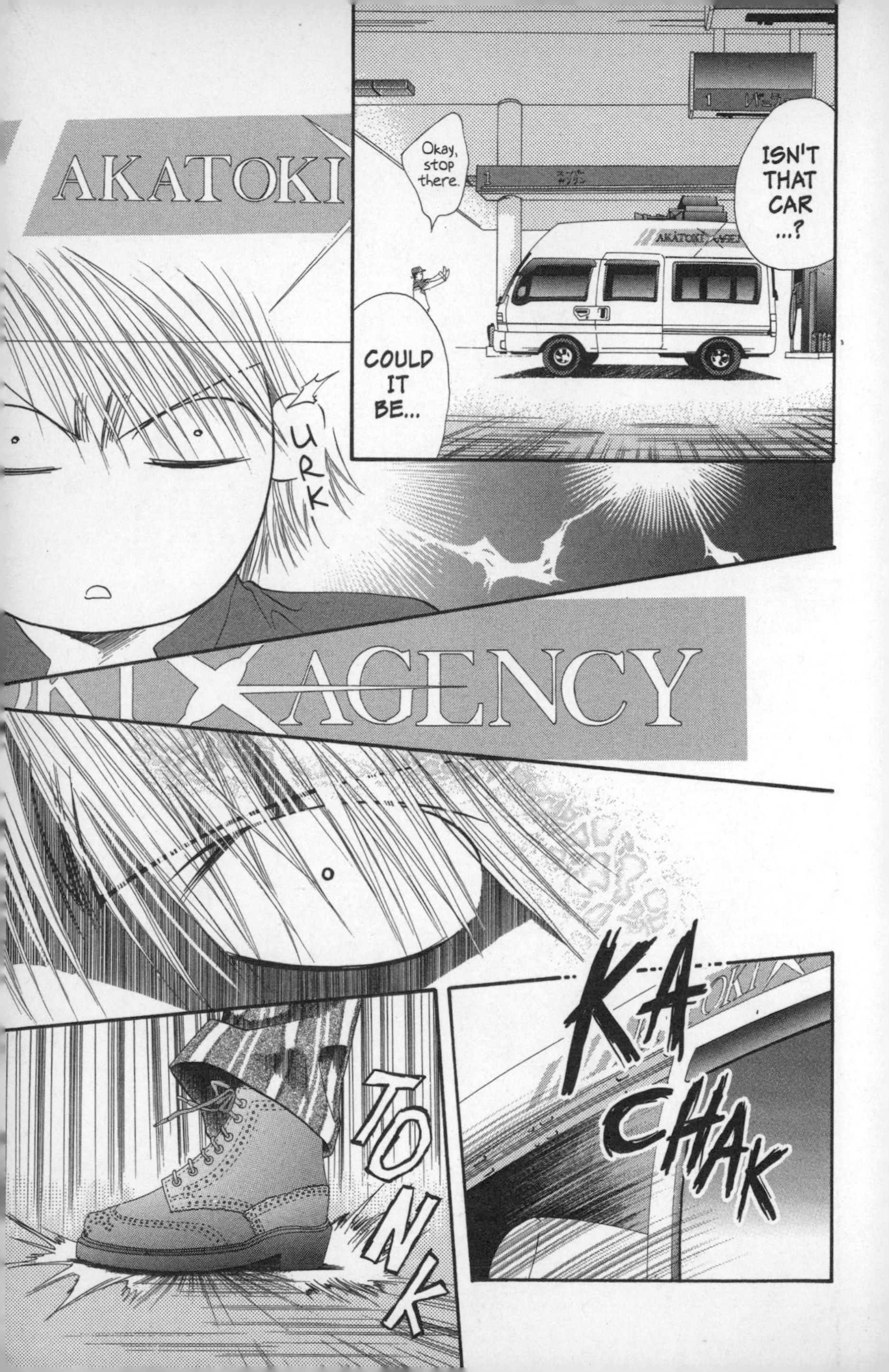
ISN'T THAT CAR ...?
Okay, stop there.
AKATOKI AGENCY
COULD IT BE...
AKATOKI
URK
AGENCY
KA CHAK
TONK

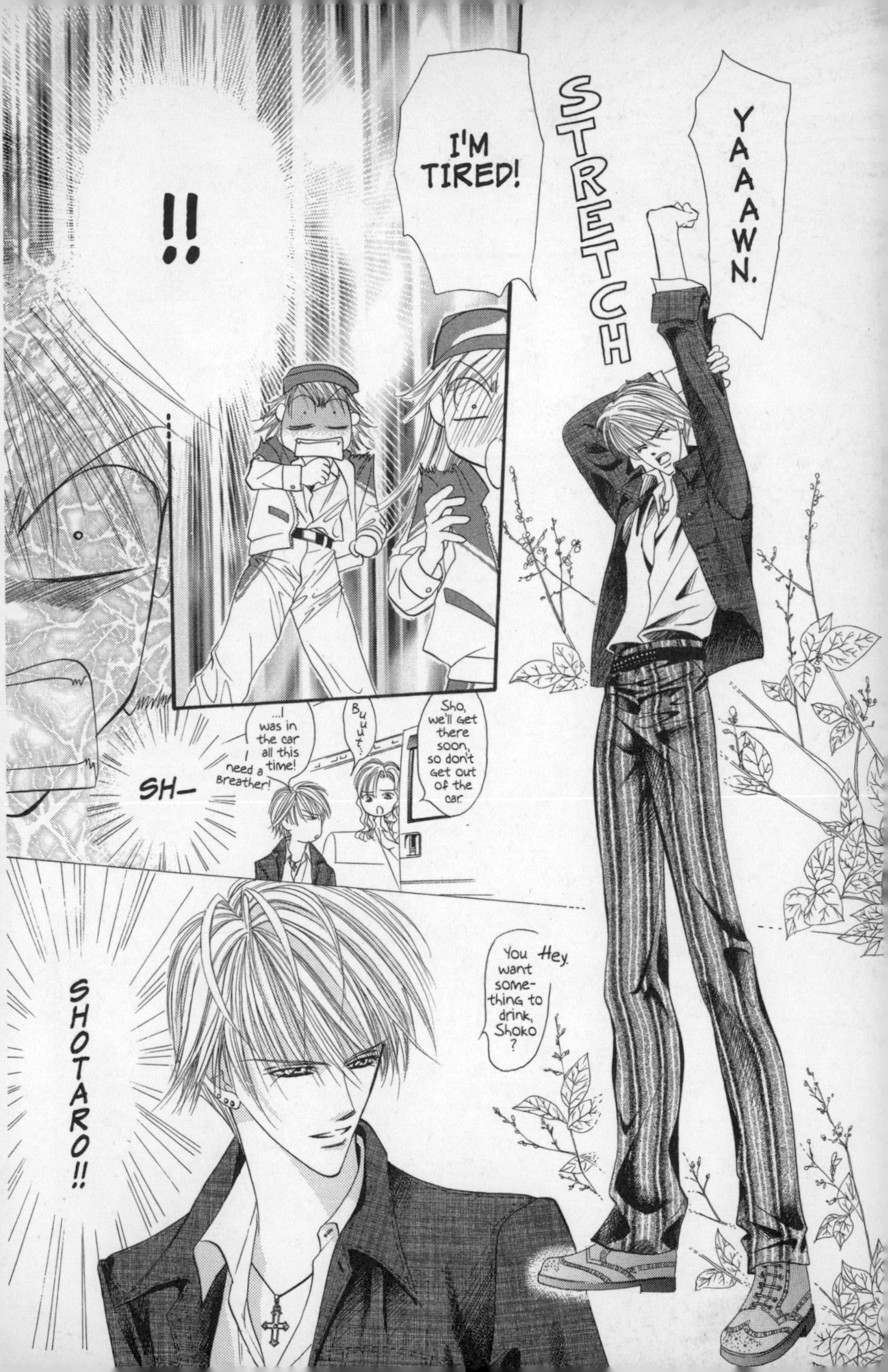

YAAAWN.
STRETCH
I'M TIRED!
Hey. You want something to drink, Shoko?
!!
Sho, we'll get there soon, so don't get out of the car.
Buuut...
...I was in the car all this time! I need a Breather!
SH—
SHOTARO!!

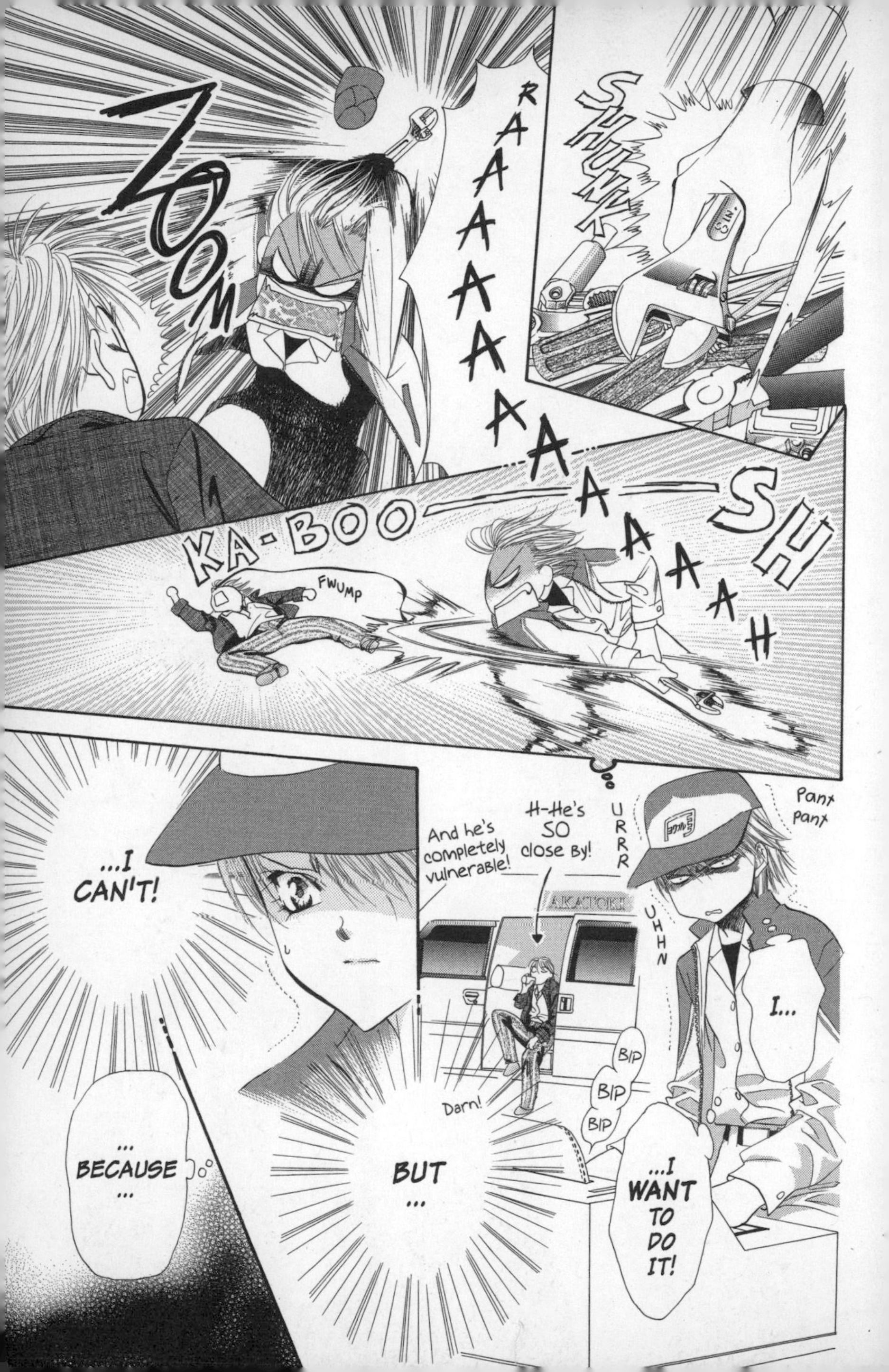
SHUNK
ZOOM
RAAAAAAAAAAAH
KA-BOOSH
FWUMP
Pant pant
URRR
H-He's SO close by!
And he's completely vulnerable!
UHHN
I...
BIP
BIP
BIP
Darn!
...I WANT TO DO IT!
...I CAN'T!
BUT ...
... BECAUSE ...

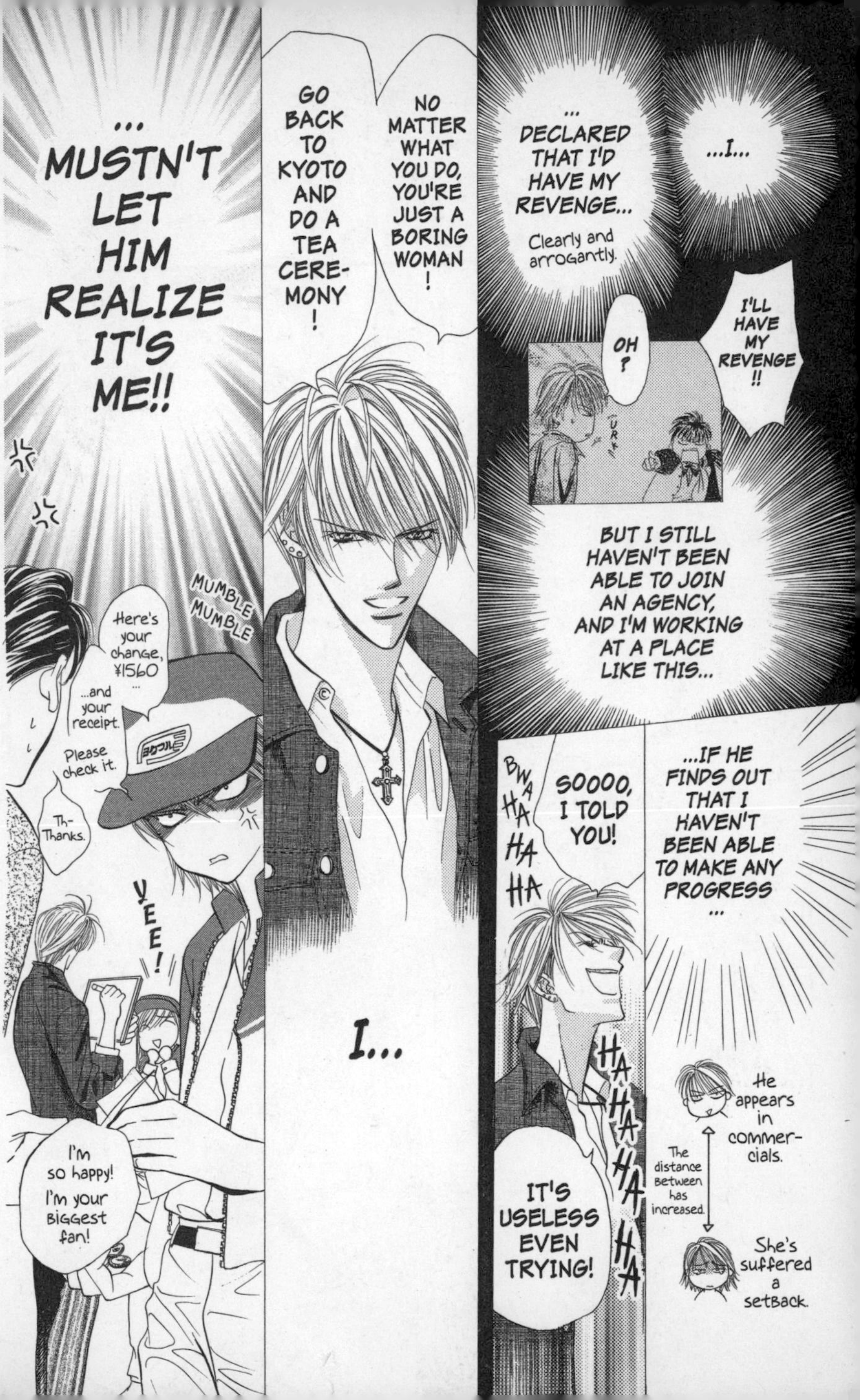
...I...
...DECLARED THAT I'D HAVE MY REVENGE...
Clearly and arrogantly.
I'LL HAVE MY REVENGE!!
OH?
BUT I STILL HAVEN'T BEEN ABLE TO JOIN AN AGENCY, AND I'M WORKING AT A PLACE LIKE THIS...
...IF HE FINDS OUT THAT I HAVEN'T BEEN ABLE TO MAKE ANY PROGRESS...
He appears in commercials.
The distance between has increased.
She's suffered a setback.
BWAHAHAHA
SOOOO, I TOLD YOU!
IT'S USELESS EVEN TRYING!
HAHAHAHAHAHA
NO MATTER WHAT YOU DO, YOU'RE JUST A BORING WOMAN!
GO BACK TO KYOTO AND DO A TEA CEREMONY!
I...
...MUSTN'T LET HIM REALIZE IT'S ME!!
MUMBLE MUMBLE
Here's your change, ¥1560...
...and your receipt.
Please check it.
Th-Thanks.
VEEE!
I'm so happy! I'm your biggest fan!

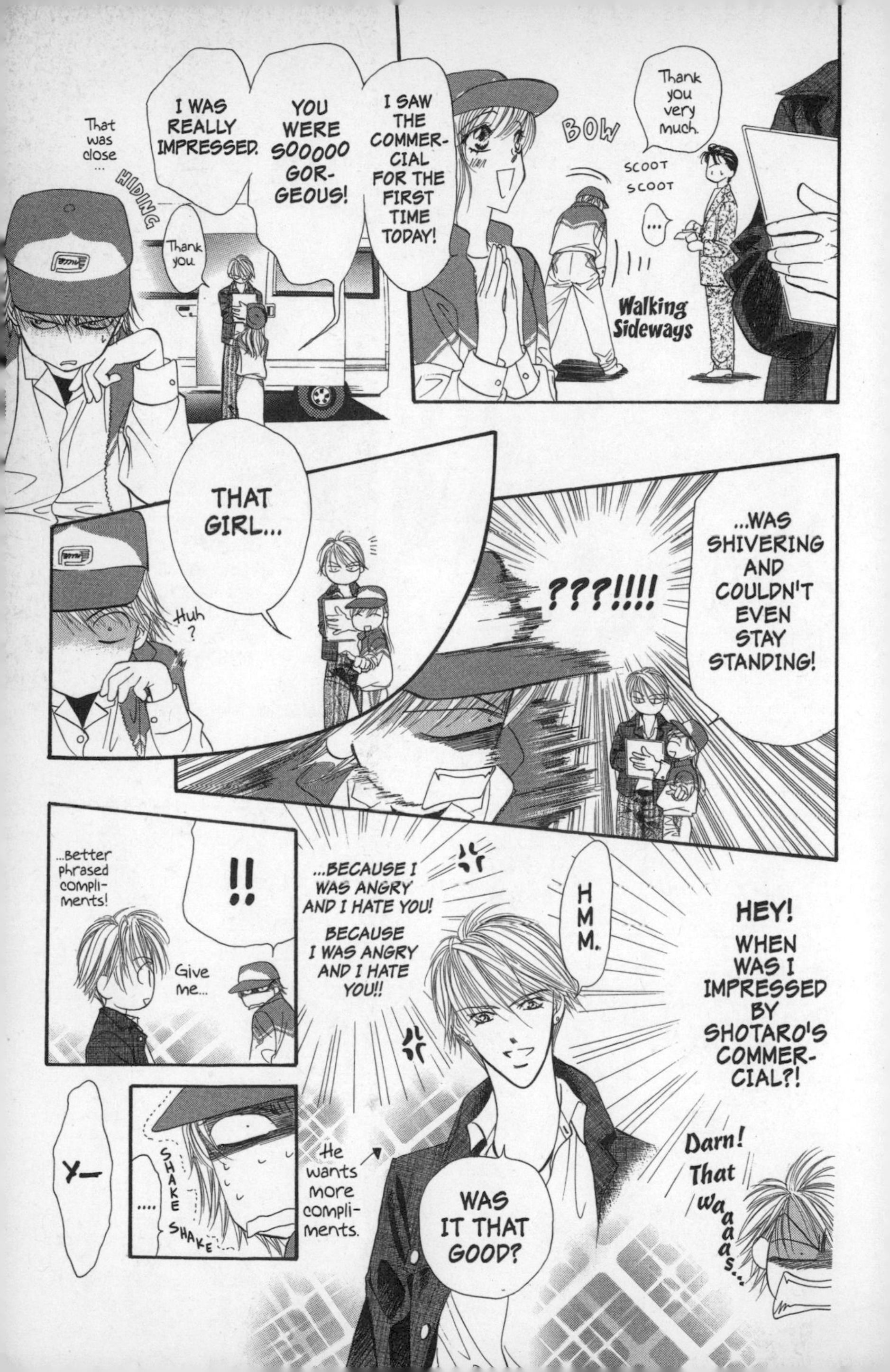
Thank you very much.
BOW
SCOOT SCOOT
...
Walking Sideways
I SAW THE COMMERCIAL FOR THE FIRST TIME TODAY!
YOU WERE SOOOOO GORGEOUS!
I WAS REALLY IMPRESSED.
Thank you.
That was close ...
HIDING
...WAS SHIVERING AND COULDN'T EVEN STAY STANDING!
???!!!!
THAT GIRL...
Huh?
HEY! WHEN WAS I IMPRESSED BY SHOTARO'S COMMERCIAL?!
HMM.
...BECAUSE I WAS ANGRY AND I HATE YOU!
BECAUSE I WAS ANGRY AND I HATE YOU!!
!!
Give me...
...Better phrased compliments!
Darn! That waaaas...
WAS IT THAT GOOD?
He wants more compliments.
SHAKE SHAKE
....
Y—

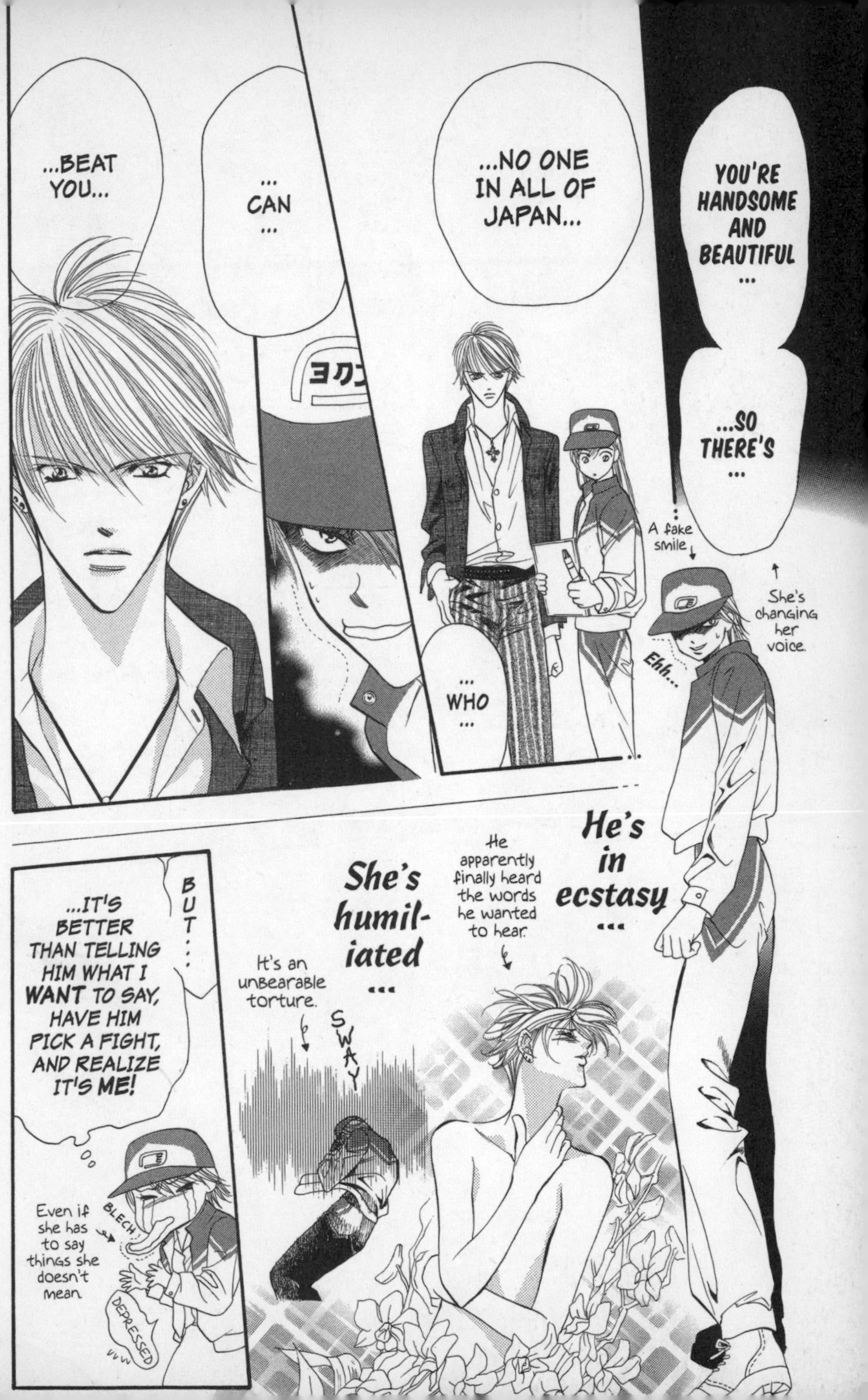
YOU'RE HANDSOME AND BEAUTIFUL...
...SO THERE'S...
A fake smile
She's changing her voice.
Ehh...
...NO ONE IN ALL OF JAPAN...
...WHO...
...CAN...
...BEAT YOU...
He's in ecstasy...
He apparently finally heard the words he wanted to hear.
She's humiliated...
It's an unbearable torture.
SWAY
BUT...
...IT'S BETTER THAN TELLING HIM WHAT I WANT TO SAY, HAVE HIM PICK A FIGHT, AND REALIZE IT'S ME!
BLECH
Even if she has to say things she doesn't mean.
DEPRESSED

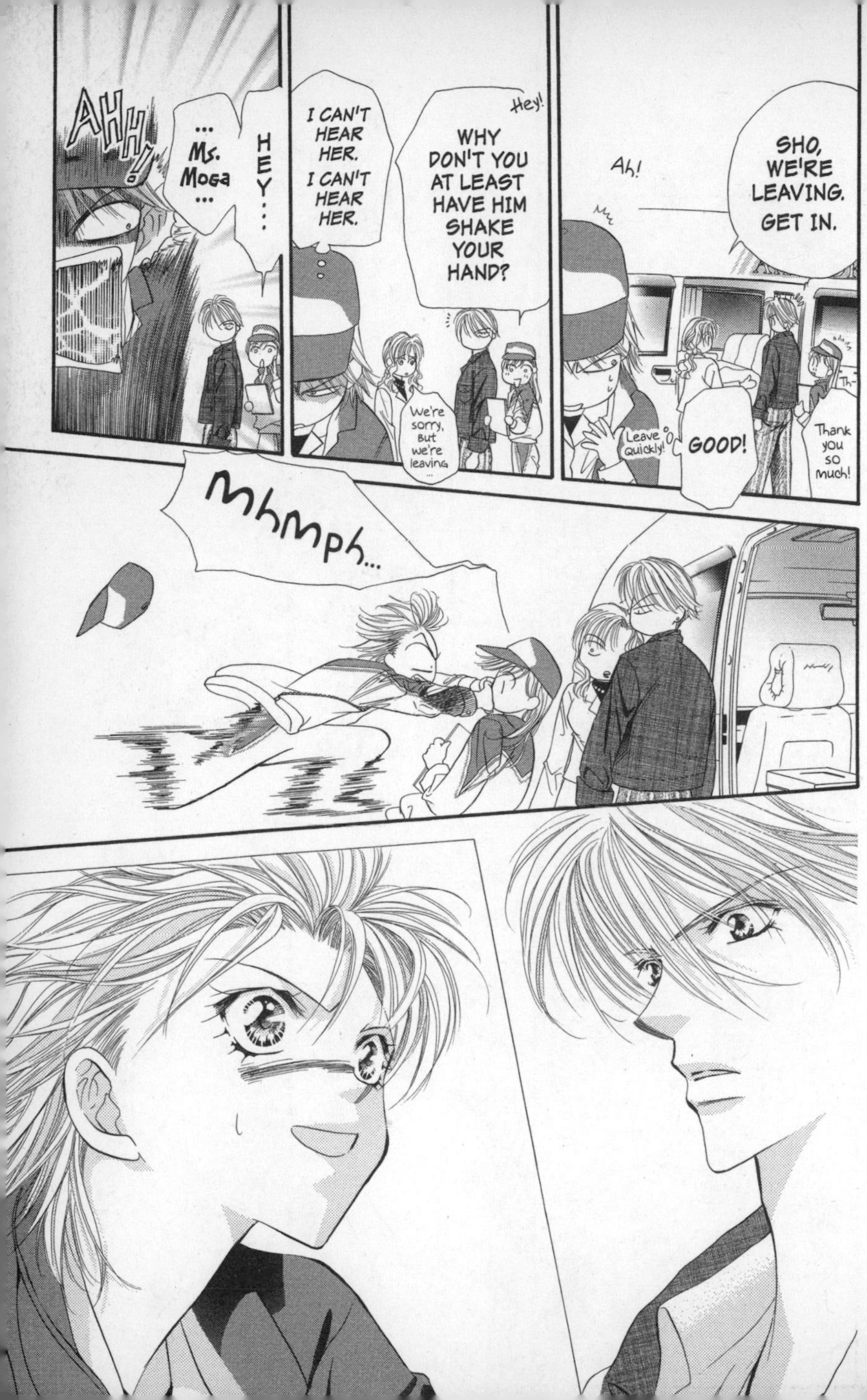
SHO, WE'RE LEAVING. GET IN.
Ah!
Th-
Thank you so much!
GOOD!
Leave quickly!
Hey!
WHY DON'T YOU AT LEAST HAVE HIM SHAKE YOUR HAND?
I CAN'T HEAR HER. I CAN'T HEAR HER.
We're sorry, but we're leaving...
HEY...
...Ms. Moga...
AHH!
Mhmph...

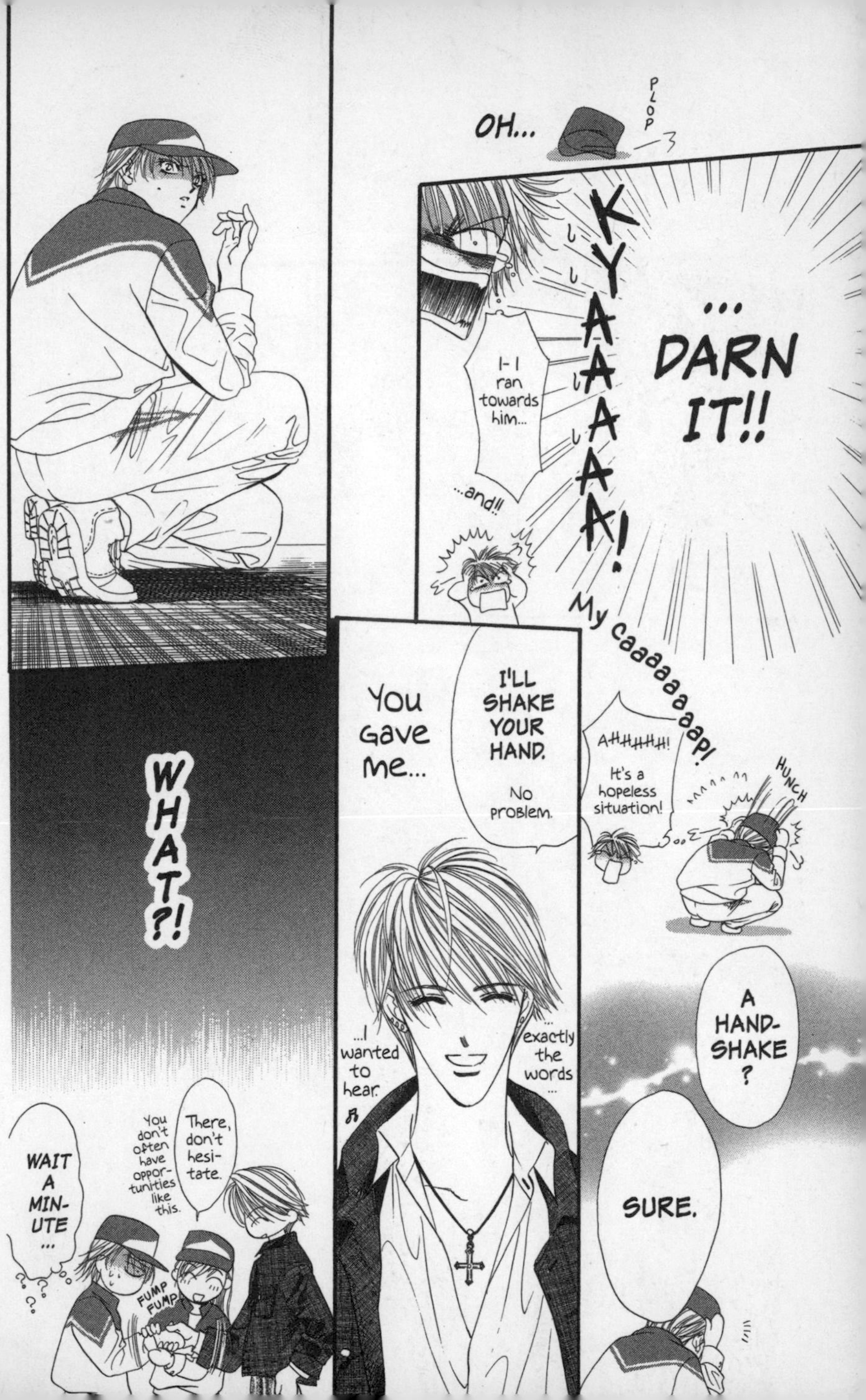
OH...
PLOP
KYAAAAA!
... DARN IT!!
I-I ran towards him...
...and!!
My caaaaaaaap!
AHHHHH!
It's a hopeless situation!
HUNCH
A HANDSHAKE?
SURE.
I'LL SHAKE YOUR HAND.
No problem.
You Gave me...
...exactly the words...
...I wanted to hear.
WHAT?!
There, don't hesi-tate.
You don't often have oppor-tunities like this.
WAIT A MIN-UTE...
FUMP FUMP

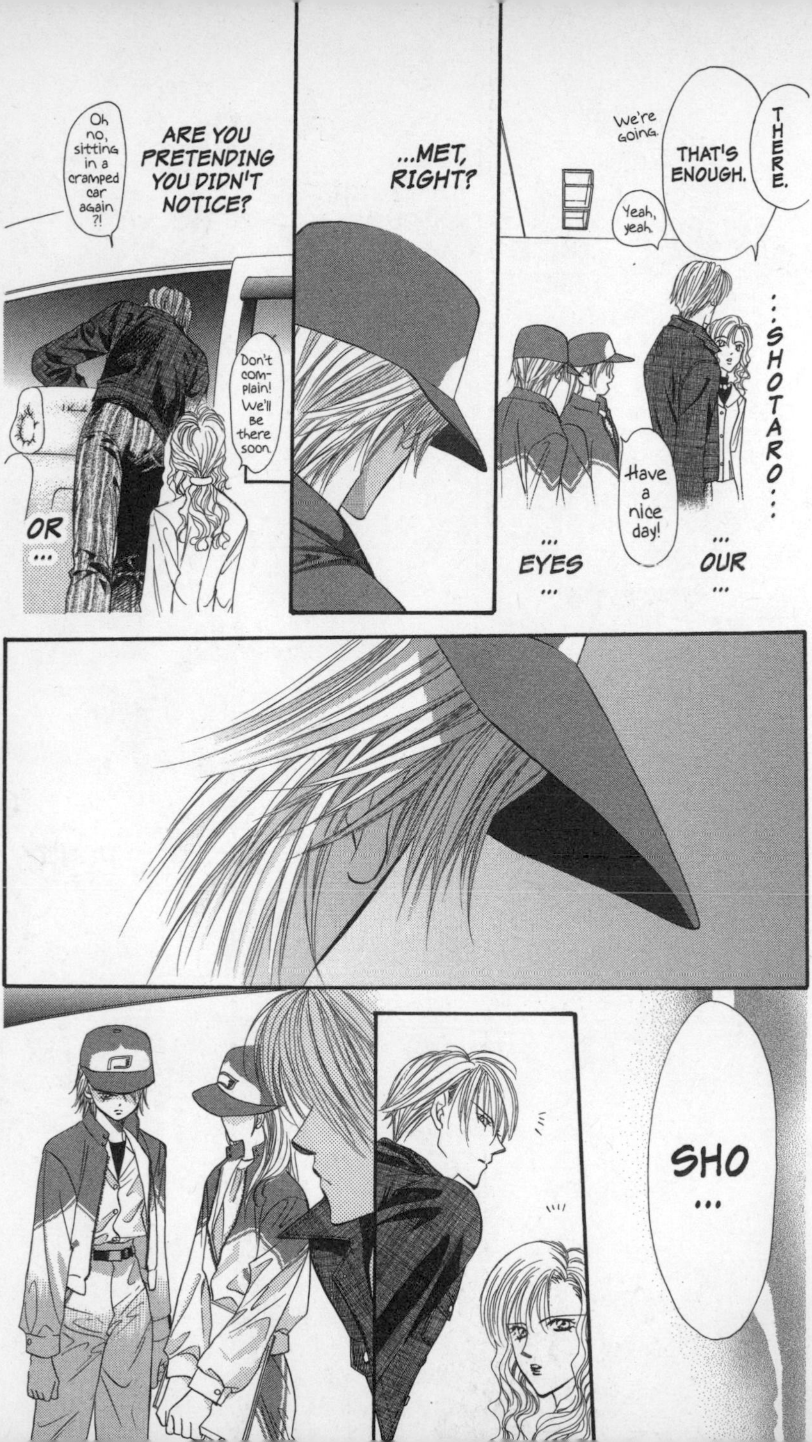
THERE.
THAT'S ENOUGH.
We're going.
Yeah, yeah.
...SHOTARO...
...OUR...
Have a nice day!
...EYES...
...MET, RIGHT?
ARE YOU PRETENDING YOU DIDN'T NOTICE?
Oh no, sitting in a cramped car again?!
Don't complain! We'll be there soon.
OR...
SHO...

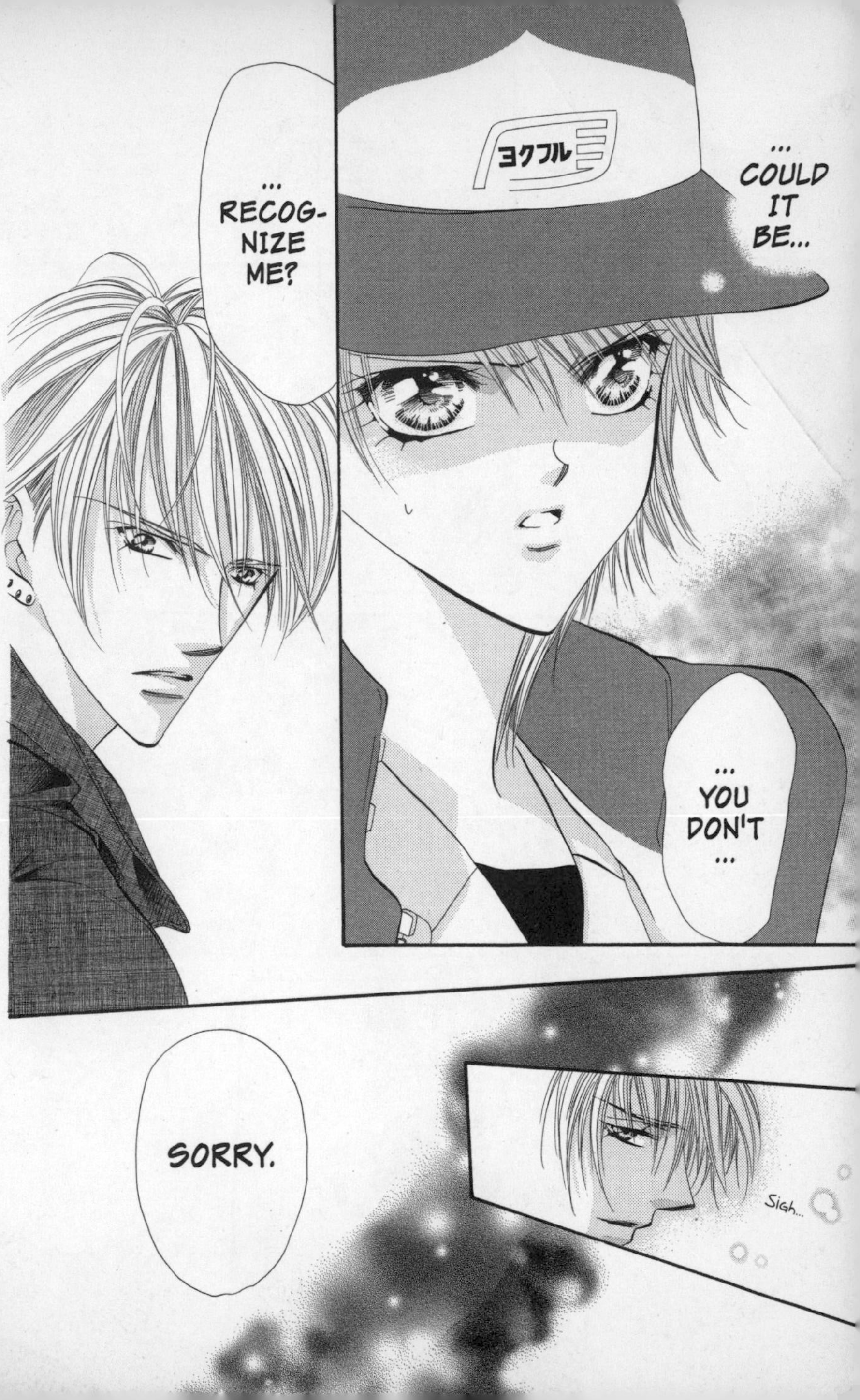

... COULD IT BE...
... YOU DON'T ...
... RECOG-NIZE ME?
Sigh...
SORRY.

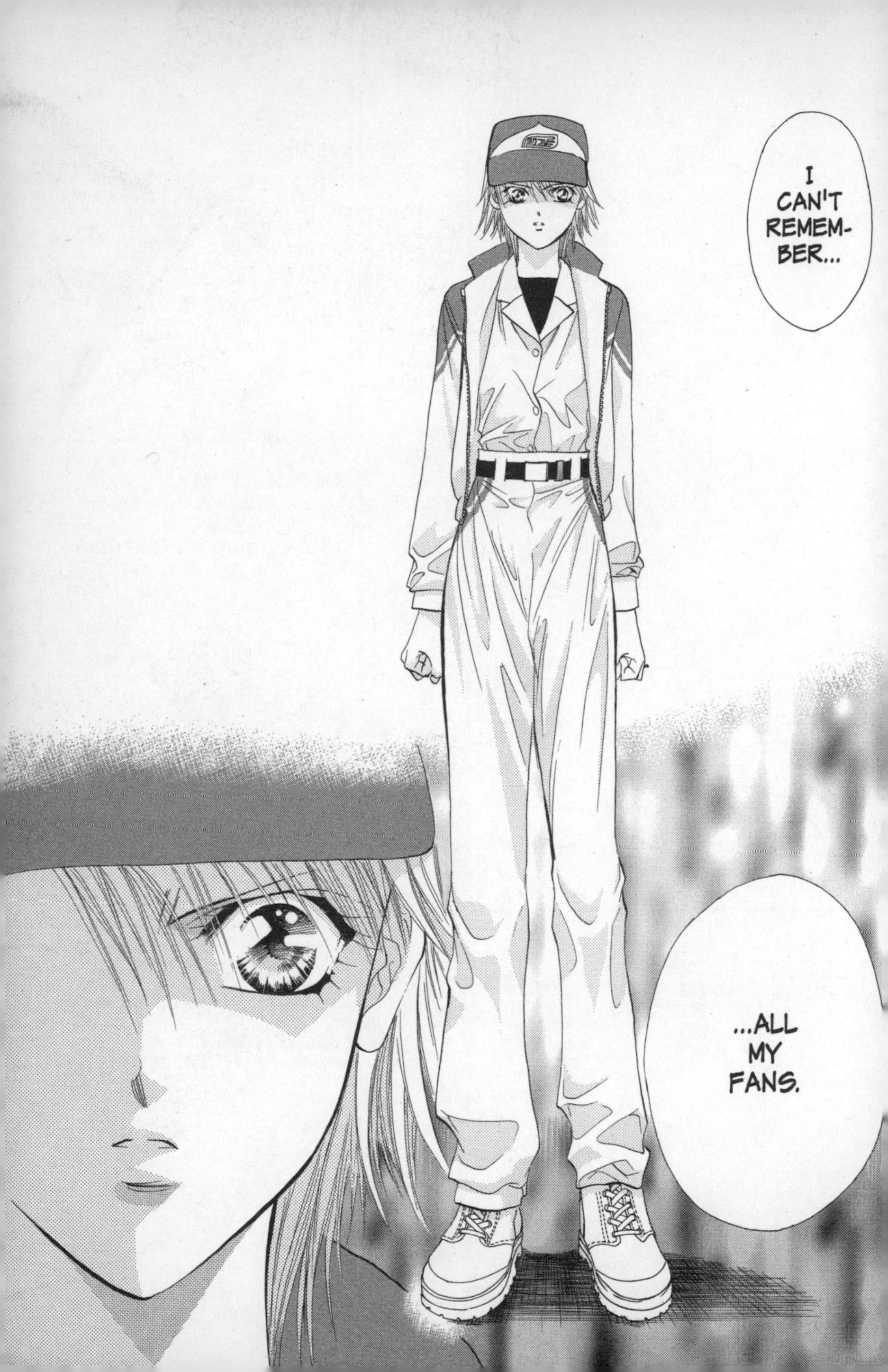
I CAN'T REMEMBER...
...ALL MY FANS.

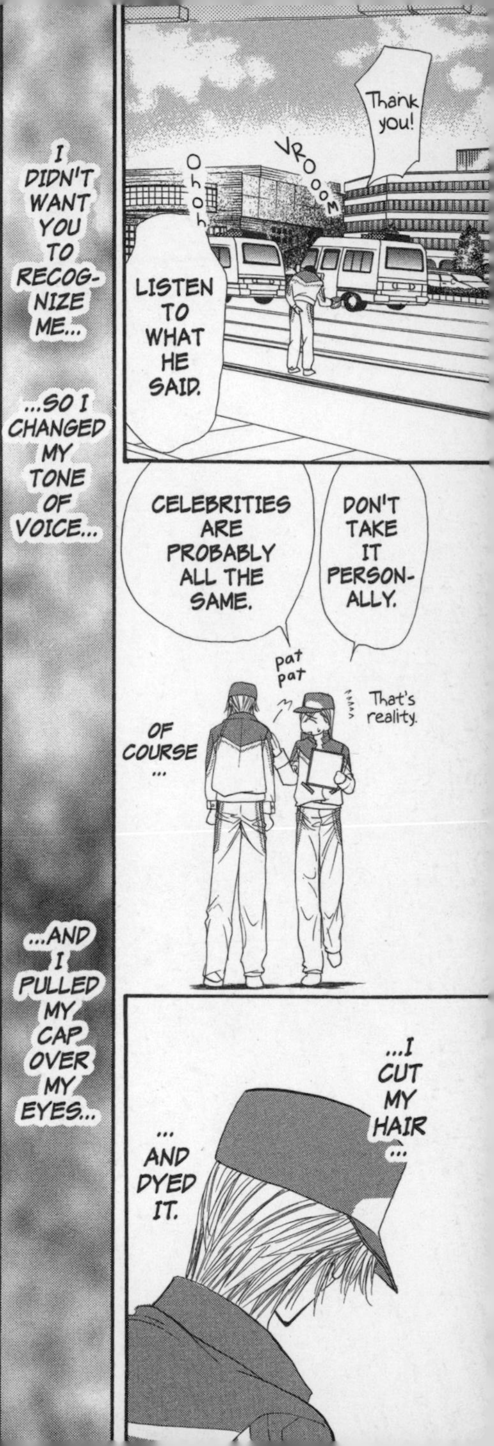
Thank you!
VROOOOM
Oh oh
LISTEN TO WHAT HE SAID.
DON'T TAKE IT PERSONALLY.
CELEBRITIES ARE PROBABLY ALL THE SAME.
pat pat
That's reality.
OF COURSE...
I DIDN'T WANT YOU TO RECOGNIZE ME...
...SO I CHANGED MY TONE OF VOICE...
...AND I PULLED MY CAP OVER MY EYES...
...I CUT MY HAIR...
...AND DYED IT.

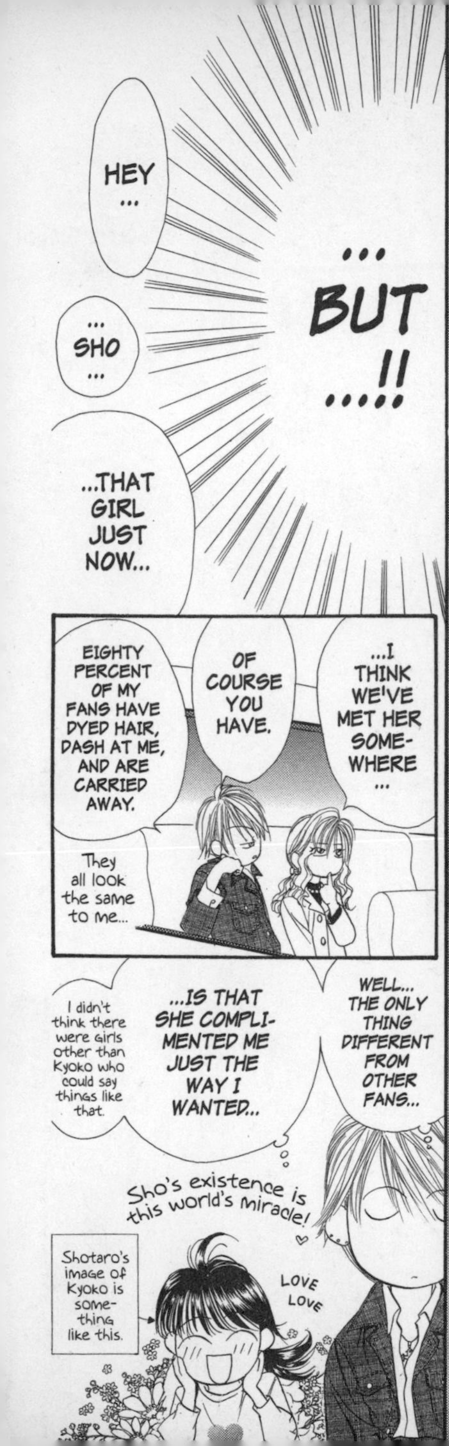
HEY...
...SHO...
...BUT ....!!
...THAT GIRL JUST NOW...
...I THINK WE'VE MET HER SOMEWHERE...
OF COURSE YOU HAVE.
EIGHTY PERCENT OF MY FANS HAVE DYED HAIR, DASH AT ME, AND ARE CARRIED AWAY.
They all look the same to me...
WELL... THE ONLY THING DIFFERENT FROM OTHER FANS...
...IS THAT SHE COMPLIMENTED ME JUST THE WAY I WANTED...
I didn't think there were girls other than Kyoko who could say things like that.
Sho's existence is this world's miracle!
LOVE LOVE
Shotaro's image of Kyoko is something like this.

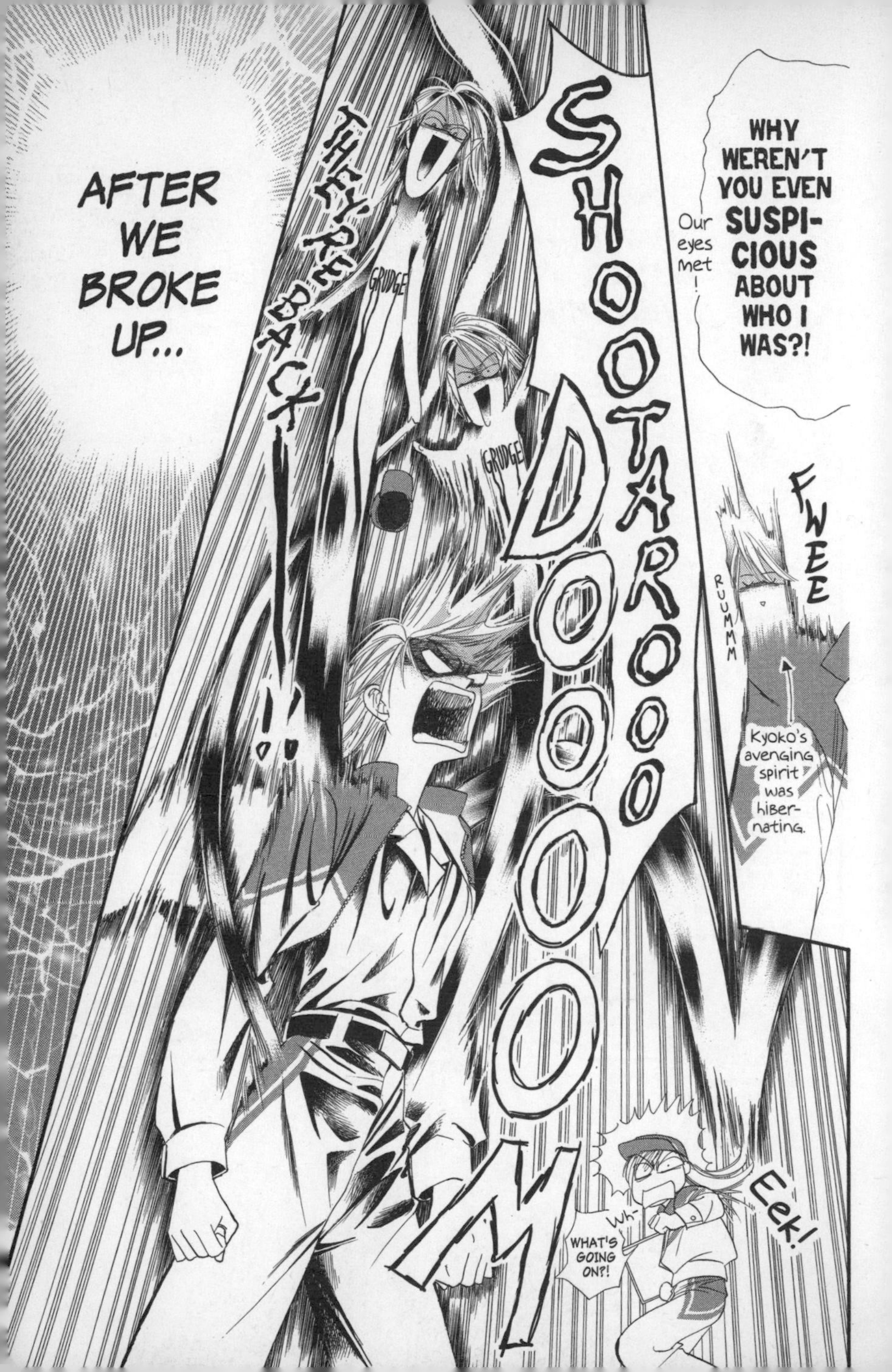

WHY WEREN'T YOU EVEN SUSPICIOUS ABOUT WHO I WAS?!
Our eyes met!
SHOOOTAROOOO
THEY'RE BACK!!
GRUDGE
GRUDGE
AFTER WE BROKE UP...
FWEE
RUUMMM
Kyoko's avenging spirit was hibernating.
DOOOOOOOM
Eek!
Wh-
WHAT'S GOING ON?!

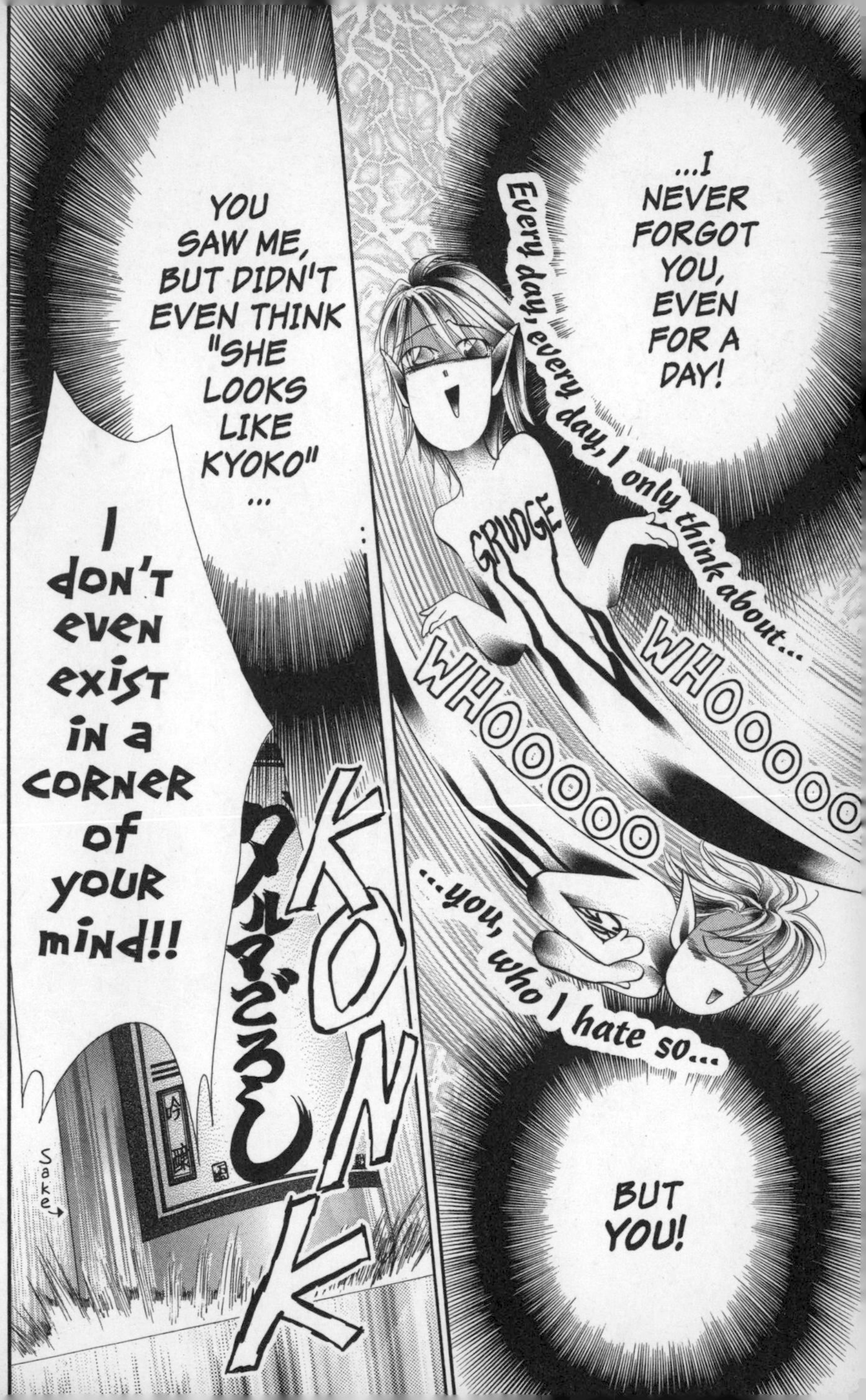
...I NEVER FORGOT YOU, EVEN FOR A DAY!
Every day, every day, I only think about...
GRUDGE
WHOOOOOO
WHOOOOOO
...you, who I hate so...
BUT YOU!
YOU SAW ME, BUT DIDN'T EVEN THINK "SHE LOOKS LIKE KYOKO" ...
I don't even exist in a corner of your mind!!
KONK
吟醸
Sake

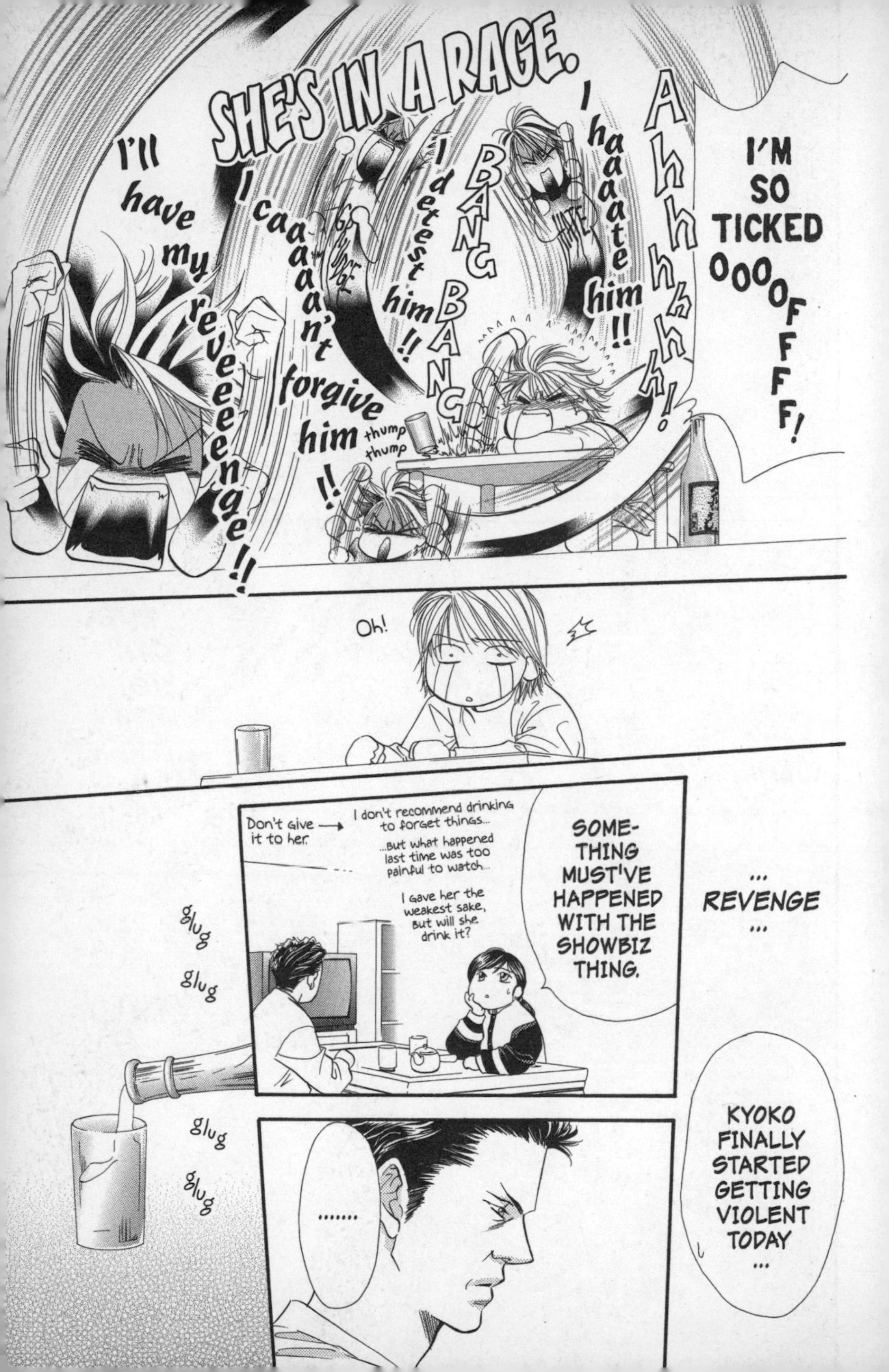
I'M SO TICKED OOOOFFFF!
Ahhhhhh!
I haaaate him!!
BANG BANG
I detest him!!
I caaaaaan't forgive him!!
thump thump
SHE'S IN A RAGE.
I'll have my reveeeeenge!!
Oh!
... REVENGE ...
SOME-THING MUST'VE HAPPENED WITH THE SHOWBIZ THING.
I don't recommend drinking to forget things...
...But what happened last time was too painful to watch...
I gave her the weakest sake, but will she drink it?
Don't give it to her.
glug
glug
KYOKO FINALLY STARTED GETTING VIOLENT TODAY ...
....
glug
glug

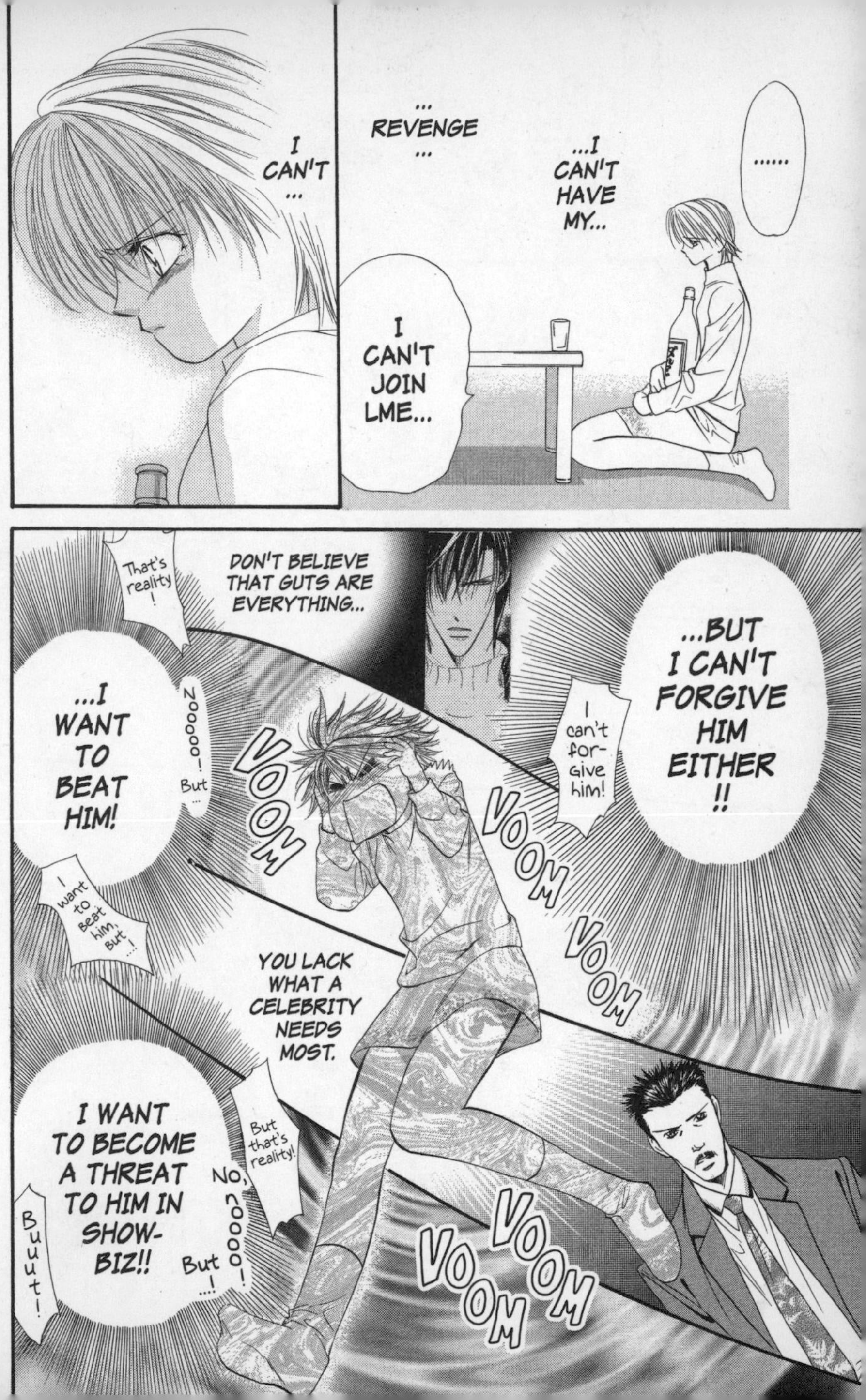
......
...I CAN'T HAVE MY...
... REVENGE ...
I CAN'T JOIN LME...
I CAN'T ...
...BUT I CAN'T FORGIVE HIM EITHER!!
I can't for-give him!
DON'T BELIEVE THAT GUTS ARE EVERYTHING...
That's reality!
VOOM VOOM
Nooooo! But...
...I WANT TO BEAT HIM!
VOOM
I want to beat him, but...!
YOU LACK WHAT A CELEBRITY NEEDS MOST.
VOOM VOOM
But that's reality!
No, noooo!
But...!
I WANT TO BECOME A THREAT TO HIM IN SHOW-BIZ!!
Buuut!

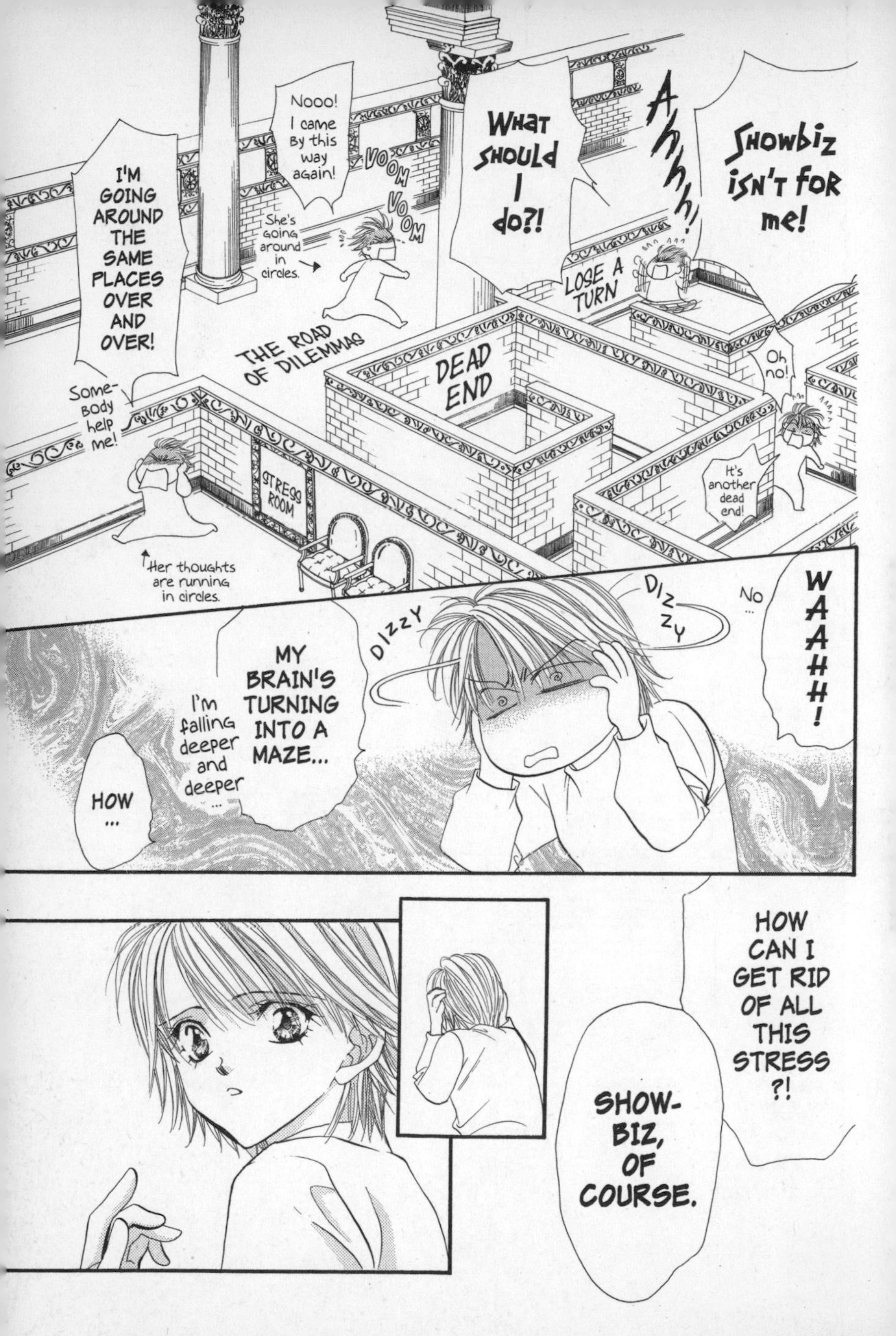

Showbiz isn't for me!
Ahhh!
What should I do?!
Nooo! I came by this way again!
VOOM VOOM
She's going around in circles.
I'M GOING AROUND THE SAME PLACES OVER AND OVER!
LOSE A TURN
Oh no!
It's another dead end!
DEAD END
THE ROAD OF DILEMMAS
Somebody help me!
STRESS ROOM
Her thoughts are running in circles.
WAAHH!
No...
DIZZY DIZZY
MY BRAIN'S TURNING INTO A MAZE...
I'm falling deeper and deeper...
HOW...
HOW CAN I GET RID OF ALL THIS STRESS?!
SHOW-BIZ, OF COURSE.

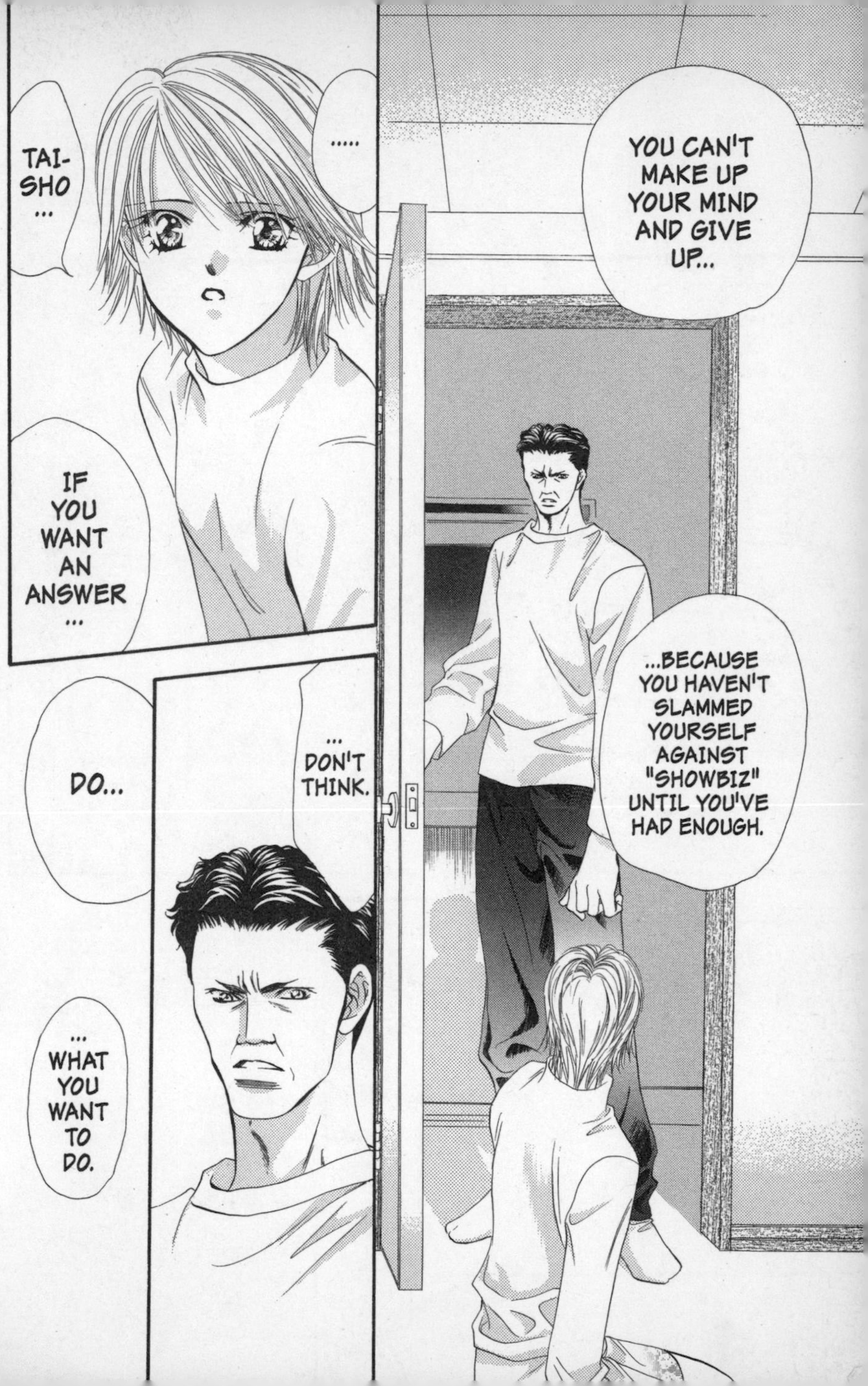
YOU CAN'T MAKE UP YOUR MIND AND GIVE UP...
...BECAUSE YOU HAVEN'T SLAMMED YOURSELF AGAINST "SHOWBIZ" UNTIL YOU'VE HAD ENOUGH.
.....
TAI-SHO ...
IF YOU WANT AN ANSWER ...
... DON'T THINK.
DO...
... WHAT YOU WANT TO DO.

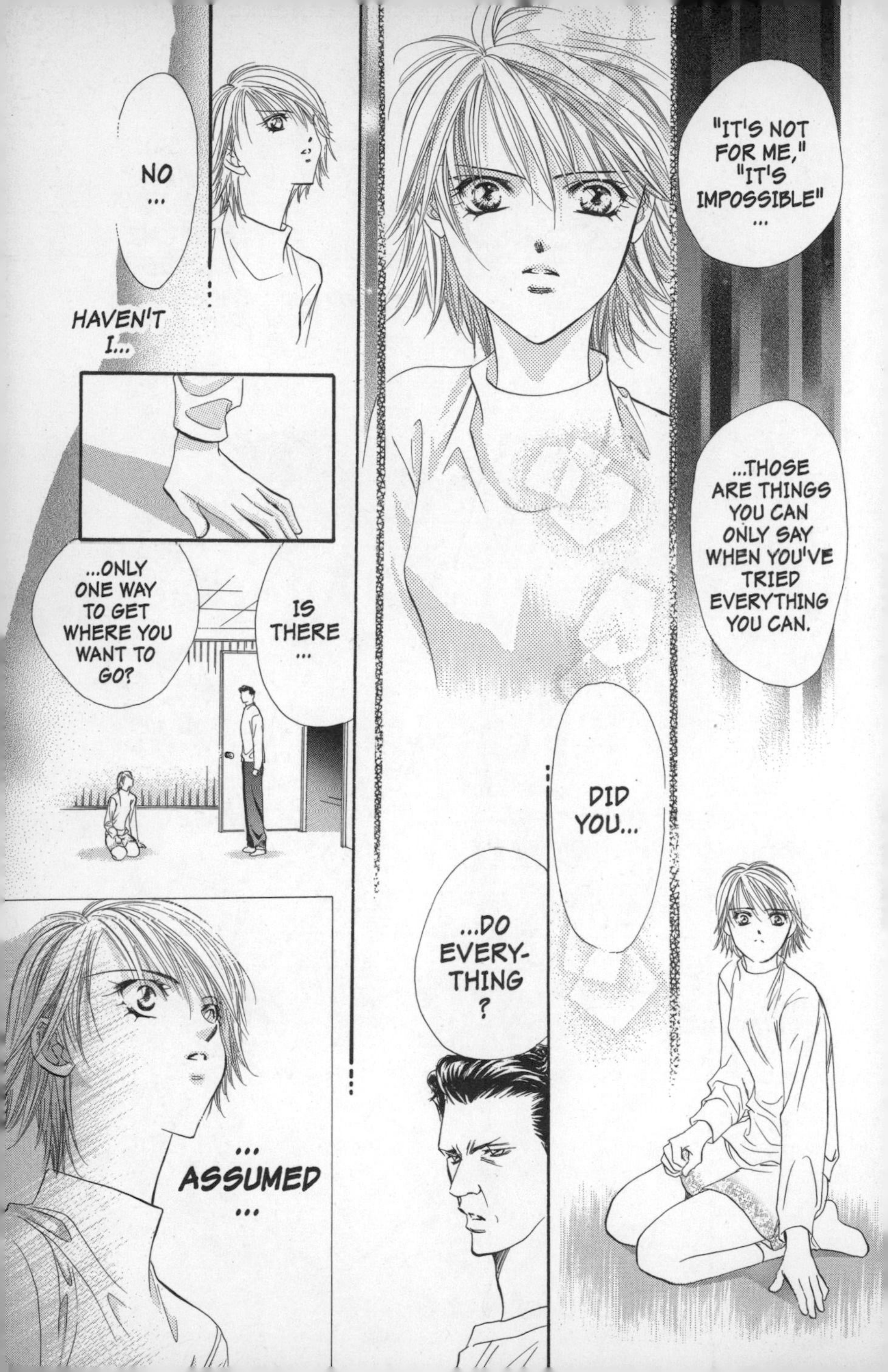
"IT'S NOT FOR ME," "IT'S IMPOSSIBLE" ...
...THOSE ARE THINGS YOU CAN ONLY SAY WHEN YOU'VE TRIED EVERYTHING YOU CAN.
DID YOU...
...DO EVERY-THING?
NO ...
HAVEN'T I...
IS THERE ...
...ONLY ONE WAY TO GET WHERE YOU WANT TO GO?
... ASSUMED ...

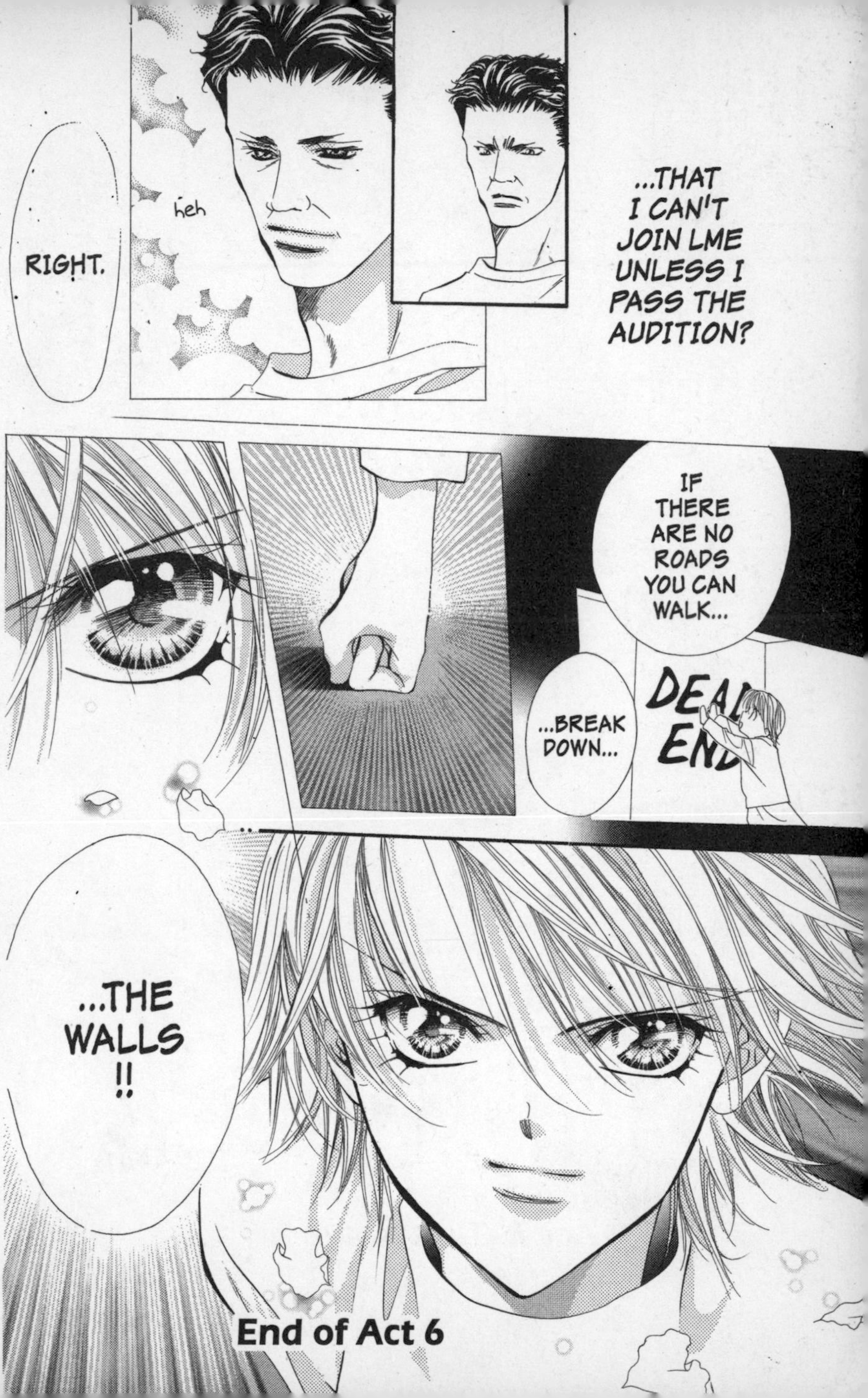
...THAT I CAN'T JOIN LME UNLESS I PASS THE AUDITION?
heh
RIGHT.
IF THERE ARE NO ROADS YOU CAN WALK...
DEAD END
...BREAK DOWN...
...THE WALLS !!
End of Act 6

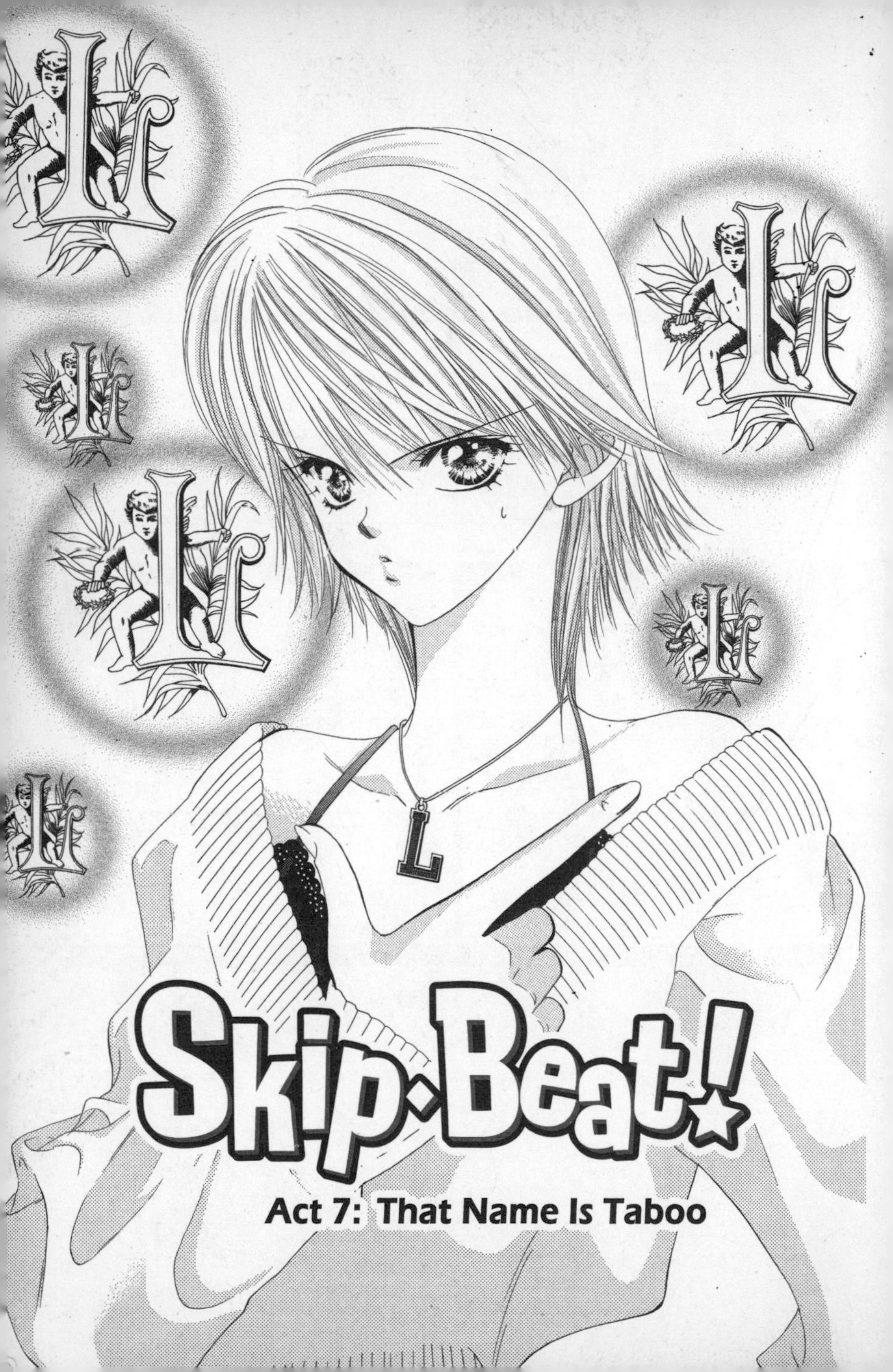
Skip·Beat!
Act 7: That Name Is Taboo

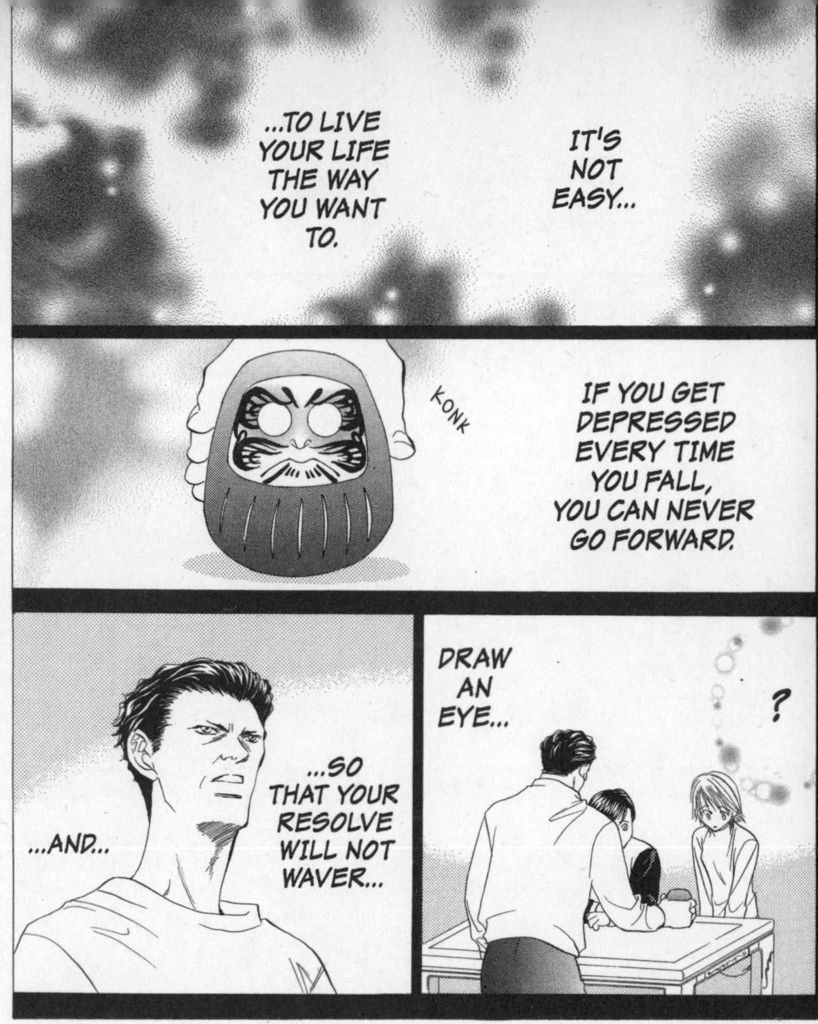
IT'S NOT EASY...
...TO LIVE YOUR LIFE THE WAY YOU WANT TO.
IF YOU GET DEPRESSED EVERY TIME YOU FALL, YOU CAN NEVER GO FORWARD.
KONK
?
DRAW AN EYE...
...SO THAT YOUR RESOLVE WILL NOT WAVER...
...AND...

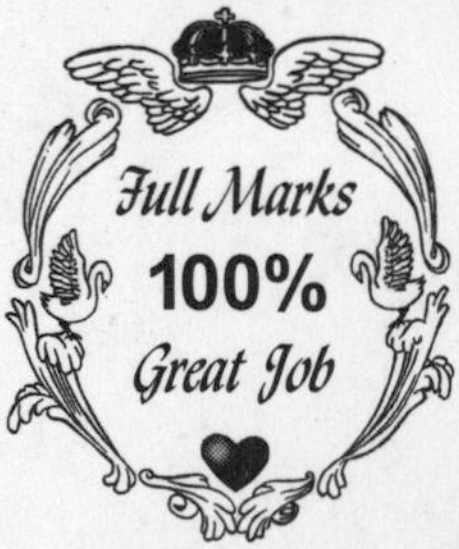
Full Marks
100%
Great Job

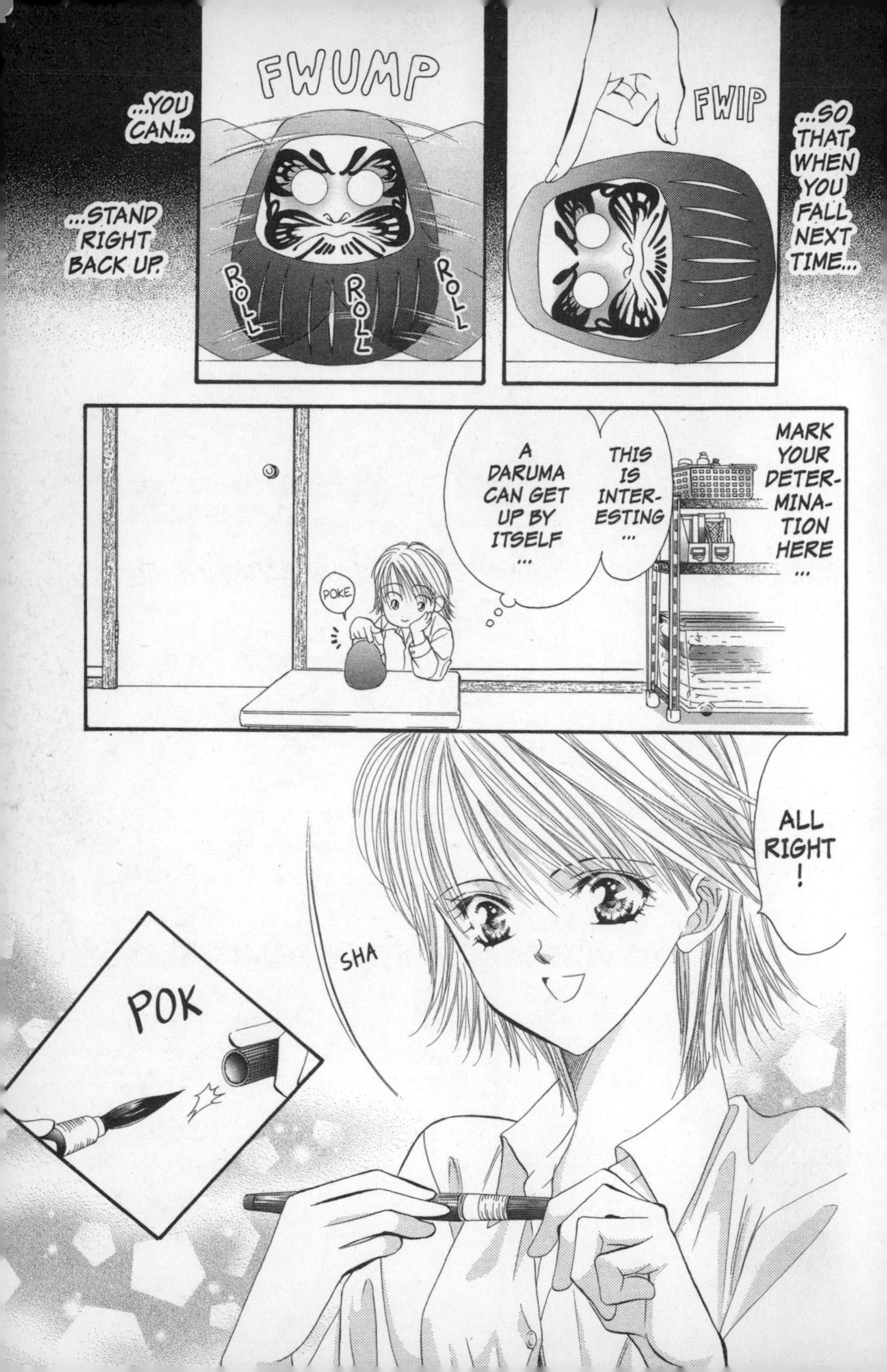

FWIP
...SO THAT WHEN YOU FALL NEXT TIME...
FWUMP
...YOU CAN...
...STAND RIGHT BACK UP.
ROLL
ROLL
ROLL
MARK YOUR DETERMINATION HERE...
THIS IS INTERESTING...
A DARUMA CAN GET UP BY ITSELF...
POKE
ALL RIGHT!
SHA
POK

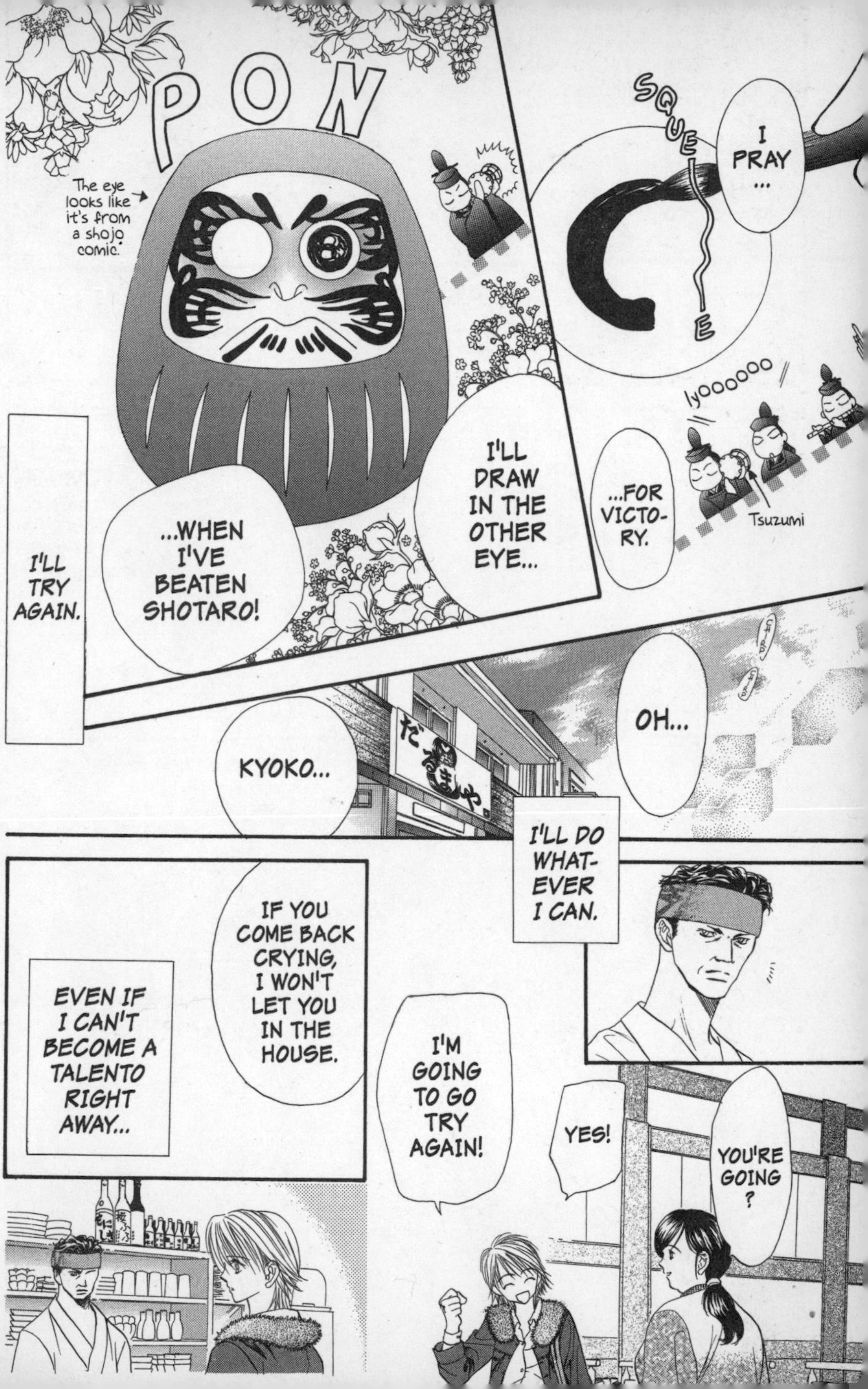
I PRAY ...
SQUEEE
...FOR VICTORY.
Iyoooooo
Tsuzumi
PON
I'LL DRAW IN THE OTHER EYE...
...WHEN I'VE BEATEN SHOTARO!
The eye looks like it's from a shojo comic.
I'LL TRY AGAIN.
OH...
KYOKO...
I'LL DO WHATEVER I CAN.
IF YOU COME BACK CRYING, I WON'T LET YOU IN THE HOUSE.
EVEN IF I CAN'T BECOME A TALENTO RIGHT AWAY...
YOU'RE GOING ?
YES!
I'M GOING TO GO TRY AGAIN!

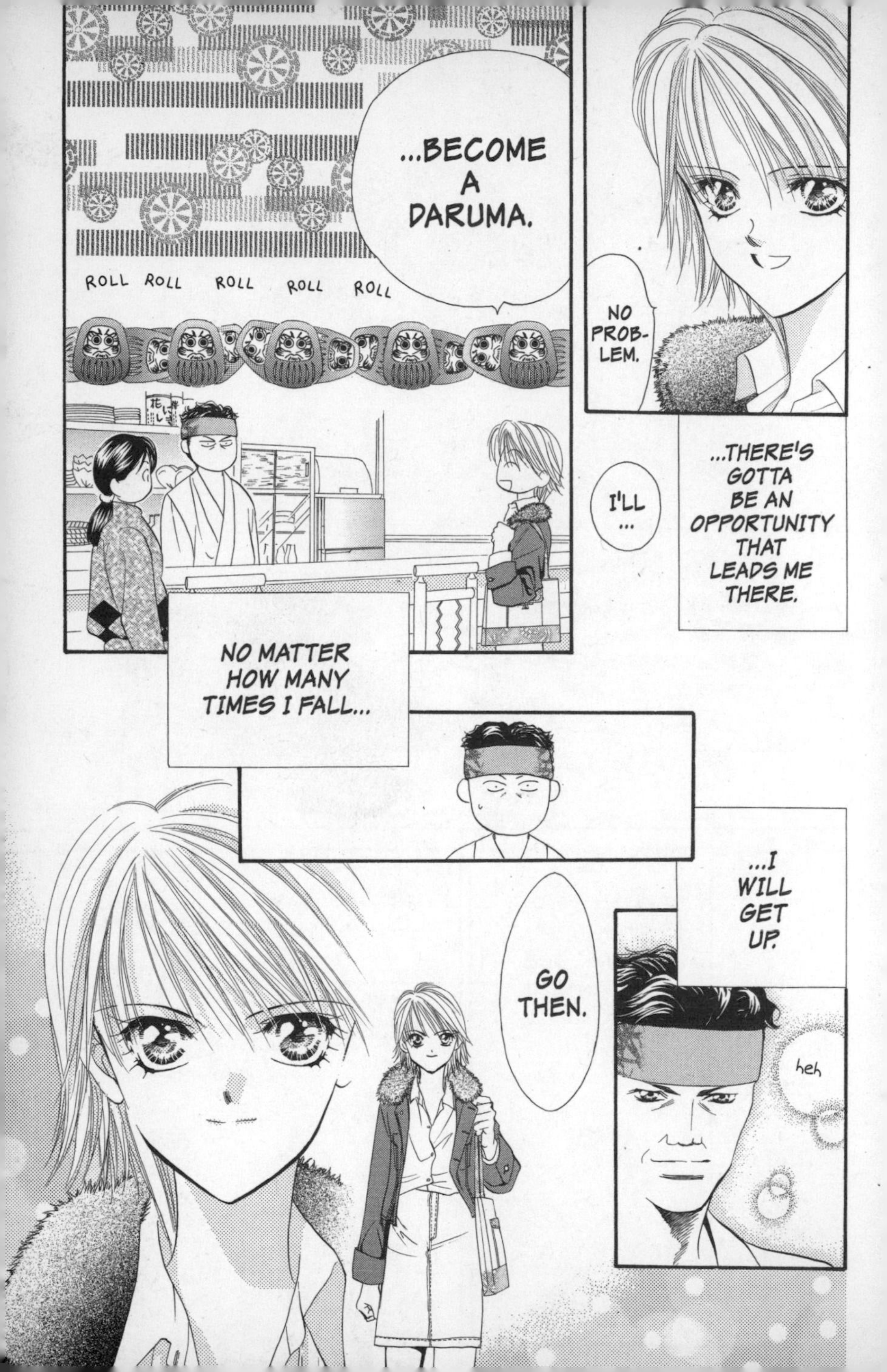
NO PROBLEM.
...THERE'S GOTTA BE AN OPPORTUNITY THAT LEADS ME THERE.
I'LL...
...BECOME A DARUMA.
ROLL ROLL ROLL ROLL ROLL
NO MATTER HOW MANY TIMES I FALL...
...I WILL GET UP.
heh
GO THEN.

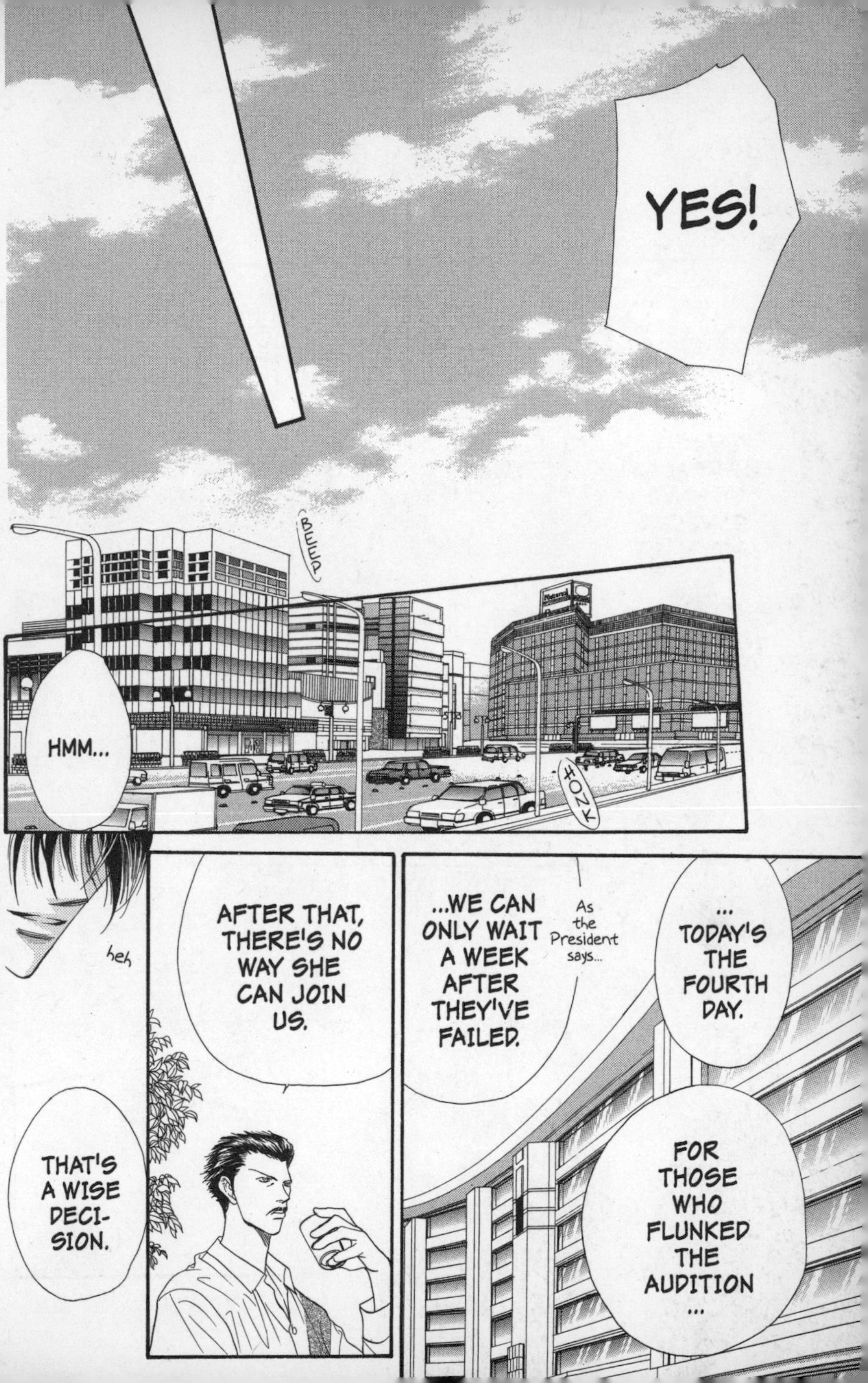
YES!
BEEP
HONK
HMM...
... TODAY'S THE FOURTH DAY.
As the President says...
...WE CAN ONLY WAIT A WEEK AFTER THEY'VE FAILED.
FOR THOSE WHO FLUNKED THE AUDITION ...
AFTER THAT, THERE'S NO WAY SHE CAN JOIN US.
heh
THAT'S A WISE DECI-SION.

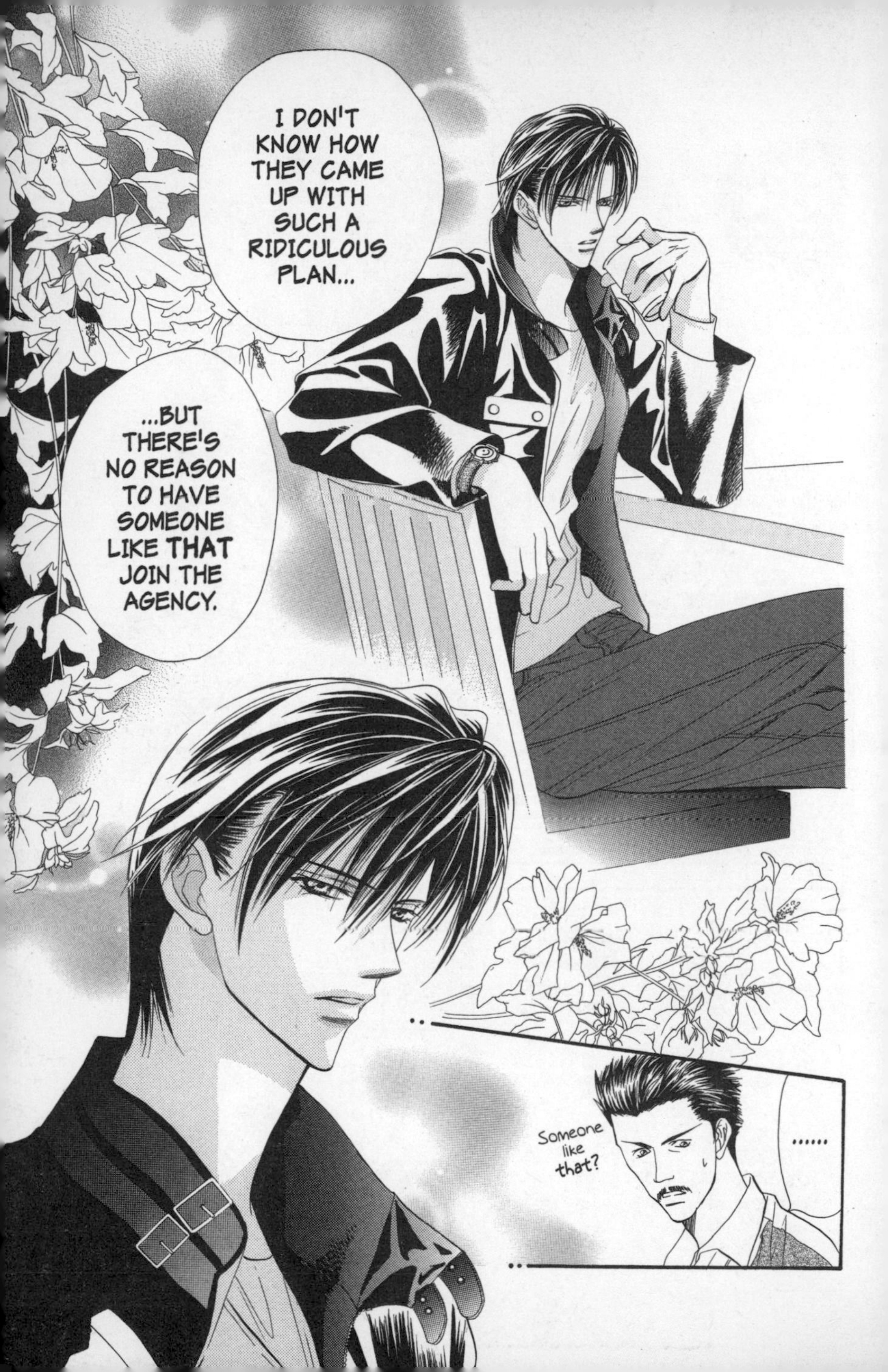
I DON'T KNOW HOW THEY CAME UP WITH SUCH A RIDICULOUS PLAN...
...BUT THERE'S NO REASON TO HAVE SOMEONE LIKE THAT JOIN THE AGENCY.
......
Someone like that?

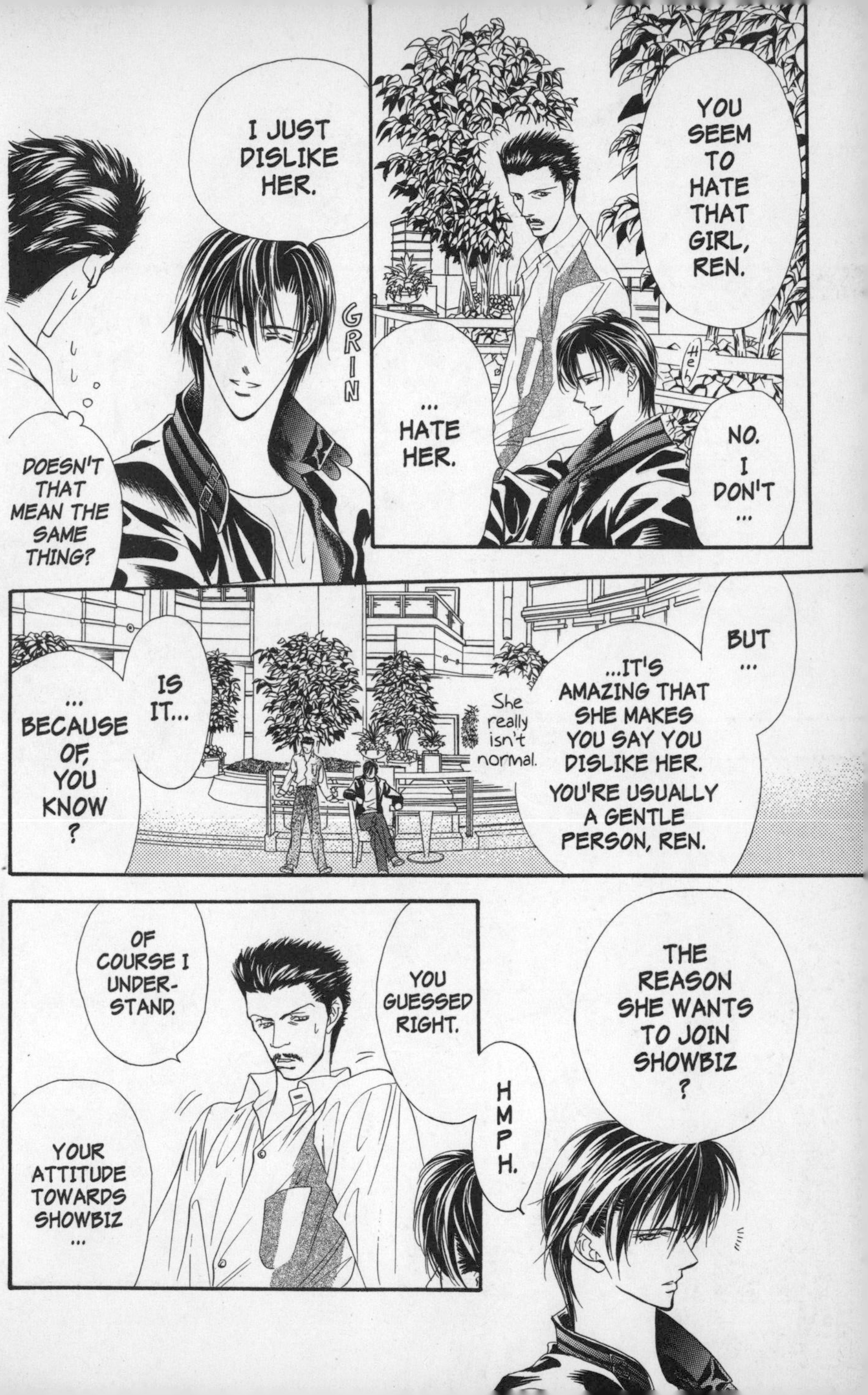
YOU SEEM TO HATE THAT GIRL, REN.
Heh
NO. I DON'T ...
... HATE HER.
I JUST DISLIKE HER.
GRIN
DOESN'T THAT MEAN THE SAME THING?
BUT ...
...IT'S AMAZING THAT SHE MAKES YOU SAY YOU DISLIKE HER. YOU'RE USUALLY A GENTLE PERSON, REN.
She really isn't normal.
IS IT...
... BECAUSE OF, YOU KNOW ?
THE REASON SHE WANTS TO JOIN SHOWBIZ ?
YOU GUESSED RIGHT.
HMPH.
OF COURSE I UNDERSTAND.
YOUR ATTITUDE TOWARDS SHOWBIZ ...

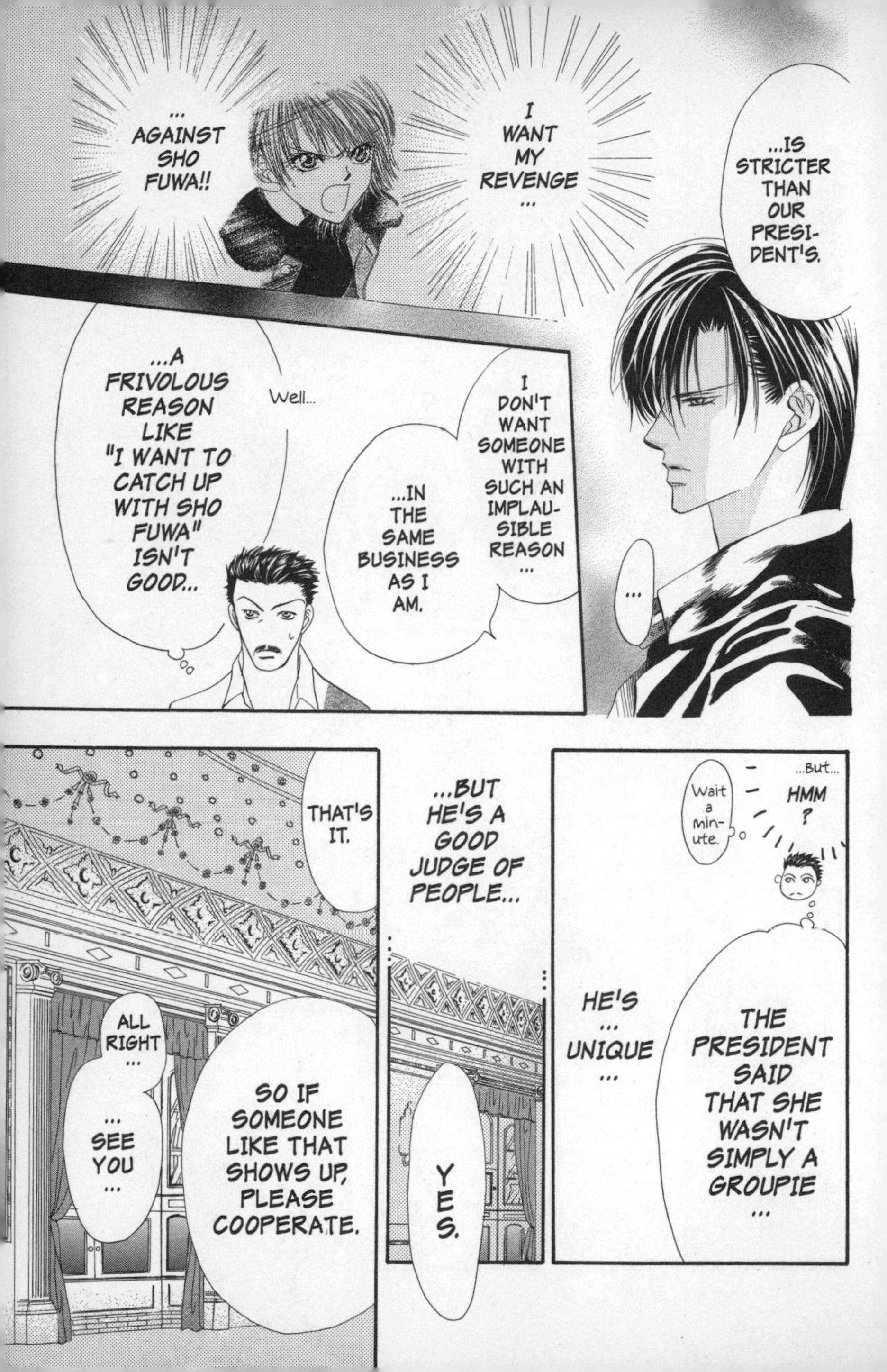

I WANT MY REVENGE...
...AGAINST SHO FUWA!!
Well...
I DON'T WANT SOMEONE WITH SUCH AN IMPLAUSIBLE REASON...
...IN THE SAME BUSINESS AS I AM.
...A FRIVOLOUS REASON LIKE "I WANT TO CATCH UP WITH SHO FUWA" ISN'T GOOD...
...
...IS STRICTER THAN OUR PRESIDENT'S.
...But...
HMM?
Wait a minute.
THE PRESIDENT SAID THAT SHE WASN'T SIMPLY A GROUPIE...
HE'S... UNIQUE...
...BUT HE'S A GOOD JUDGE OF PEOPLE...
THAT'S IT.
SO IF SOMEONE LIKE THAT SHOWS UP, PLEASE COOPERATE.
YES.
ALL RIGHT...
...SEE YOU...

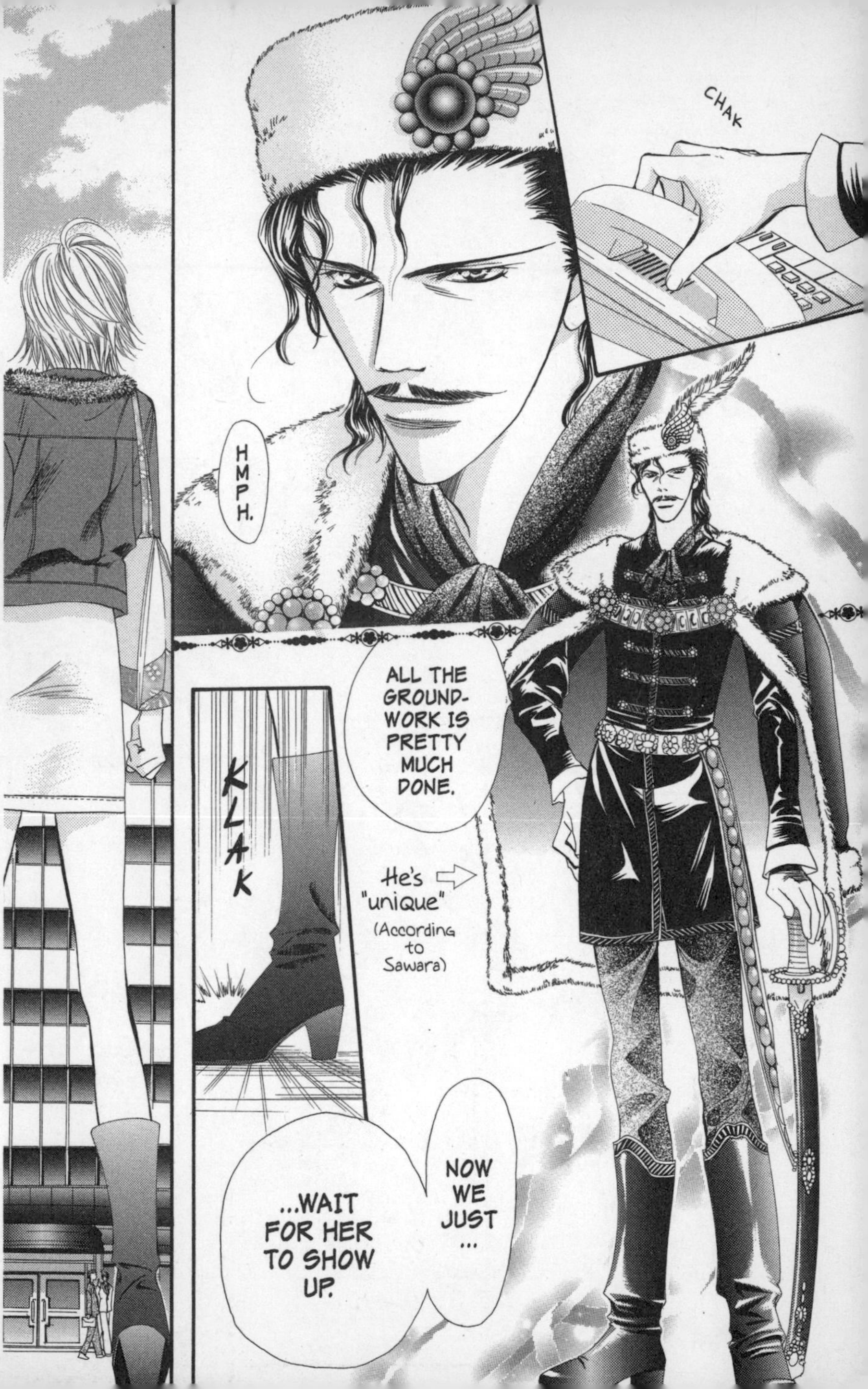
CHAK
HMPH.
ALL THE GROUND-WORK IS PRETTY MUCH DONE.
He's "unique" (According to Sawara)
KLAK
NOW WE JUST ...
...WAIT FOR HER TO SHOW UP.

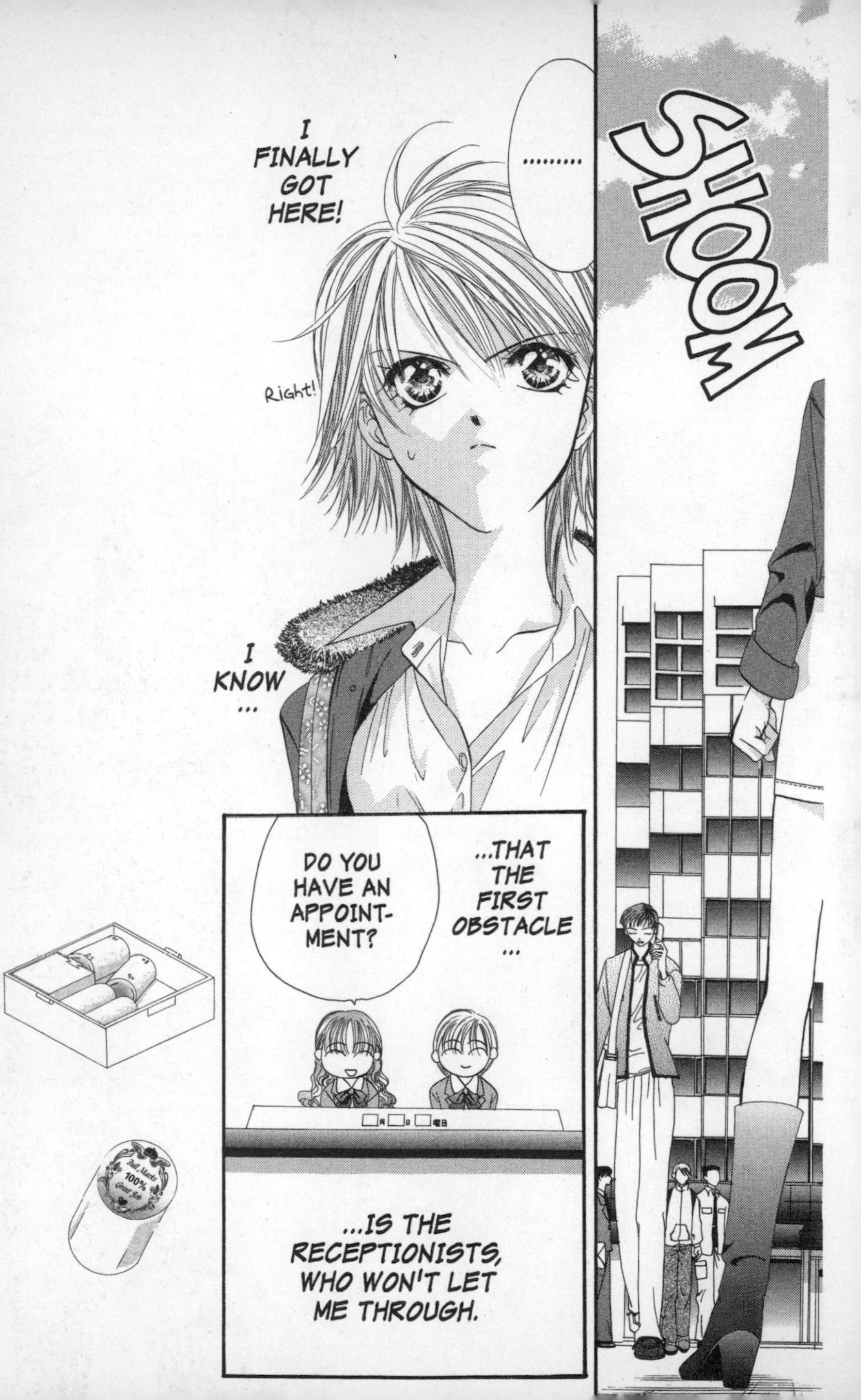
SHOOM
....
I FINALLY GOT HERE!
Right!
I KNOW ...
...THAT THE FIRST OBSTACLE ...
DO YOU HAVE AN APPOINTMENT?
...IS THE RECEPTIONISTS, WHO WON'T LET ME THROUGH.
Full Marks 100% Great Job

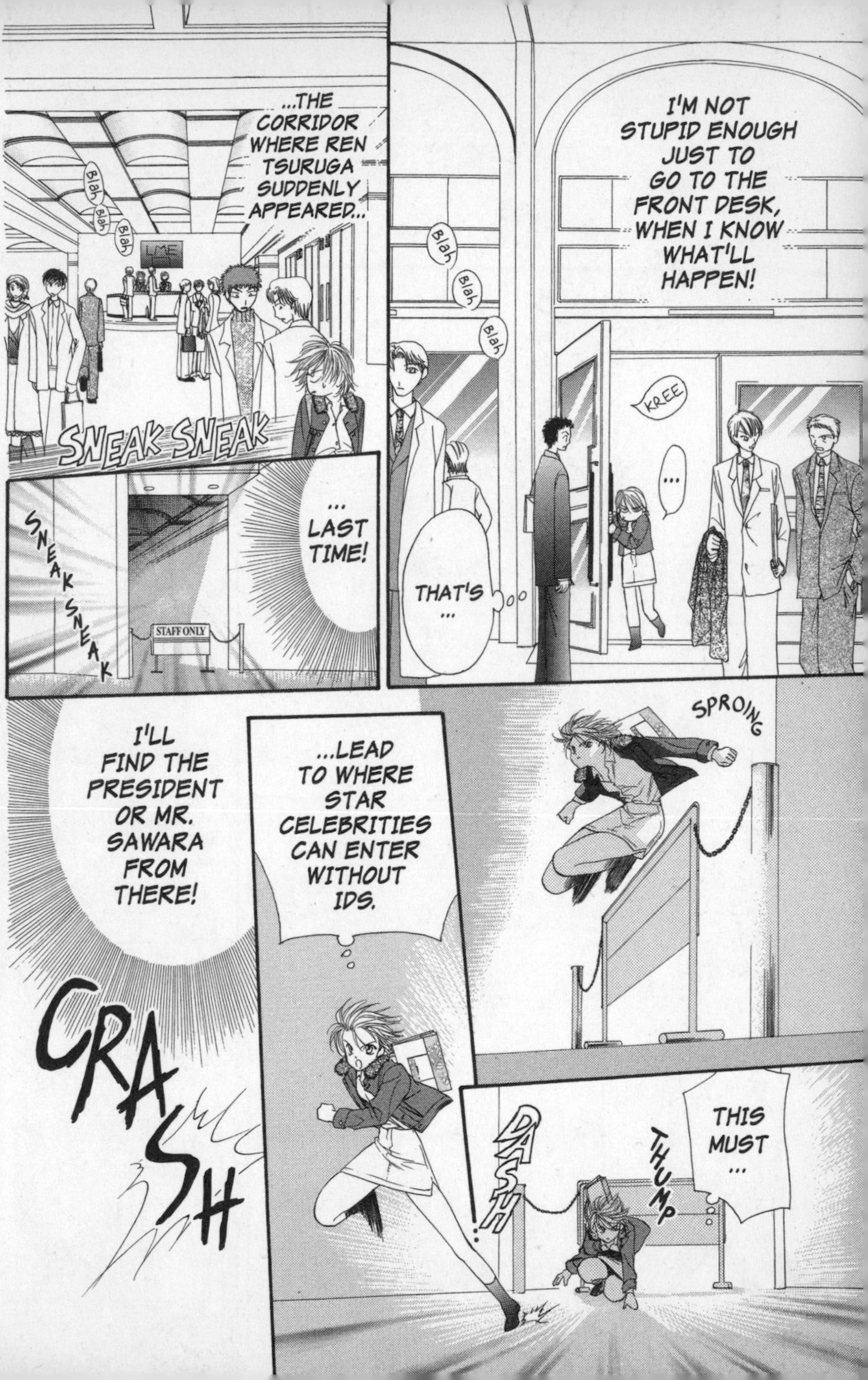

I'M NOT STUPID ENOUGH JUST TO GO TO THE FRONT DESK, WHEN I KNOW WHAT'LL HAPPEN!
Blah
Blah
Blah
KREE
...
THAT'S ...
...THE CORRIDOR WHERE REN TSURUGA SUDDENLY APPEARED...
Blah
Blah
Blah
LME
SNEAK SNEAK
... LAST TIME!
SNEAK SNEAK
STAFF ONLY
SPROING
THIS MUST ...
DASH
THUMP
...LEAD TO WHERE STAR CELEBRITIES CAN ENTER WITHOUT IDS.
I'LL FIND THE PRESIDENT OR MR. SAWARA FROM THERE!
CRASH

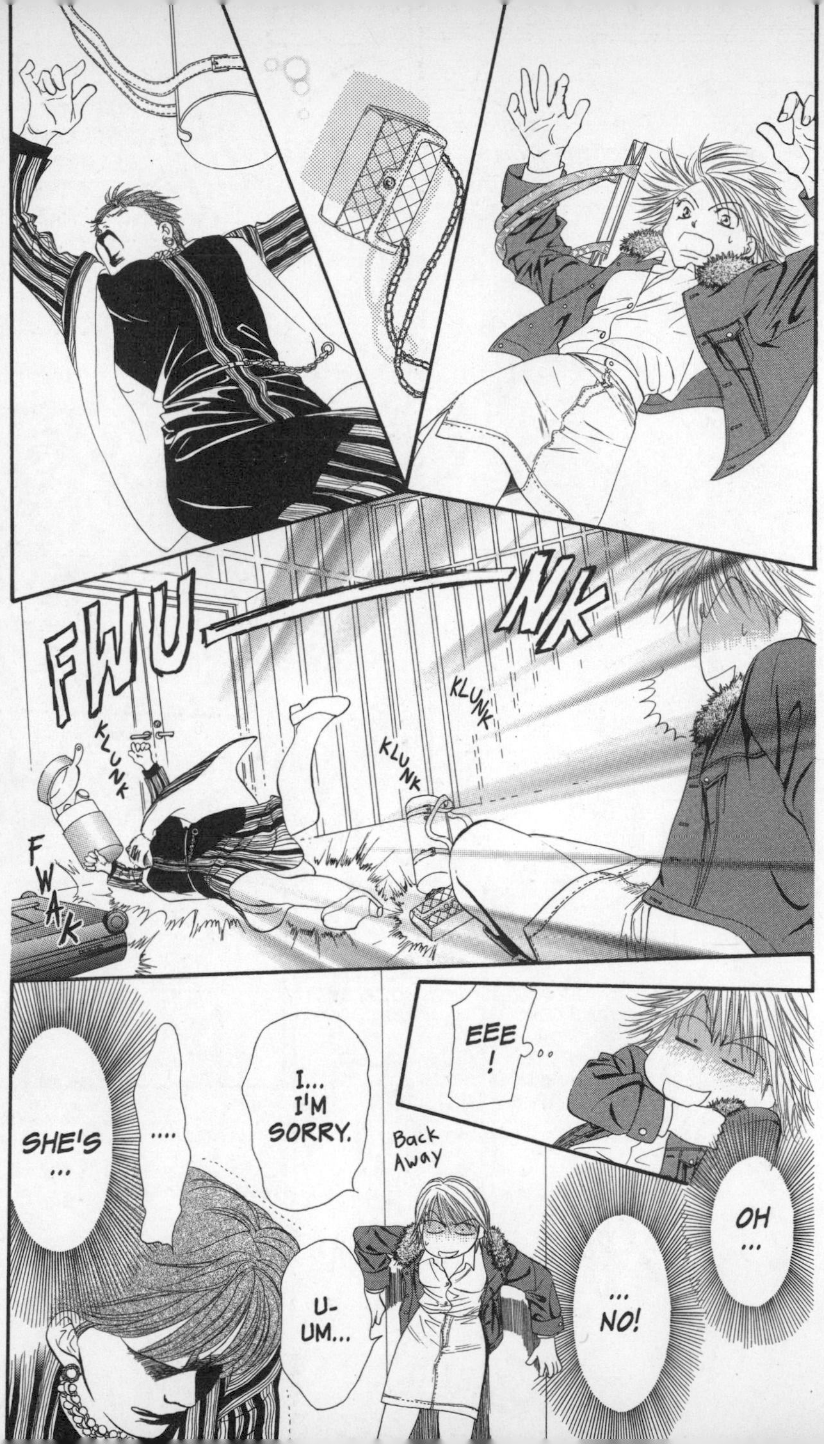
FWU—NK
KLUNK
KLUNK
KLUNK
FWAK
EEE!...
OH...
...NO!
Back Away
I... I'M SORRY.
U-UM...
....
SHE'S...

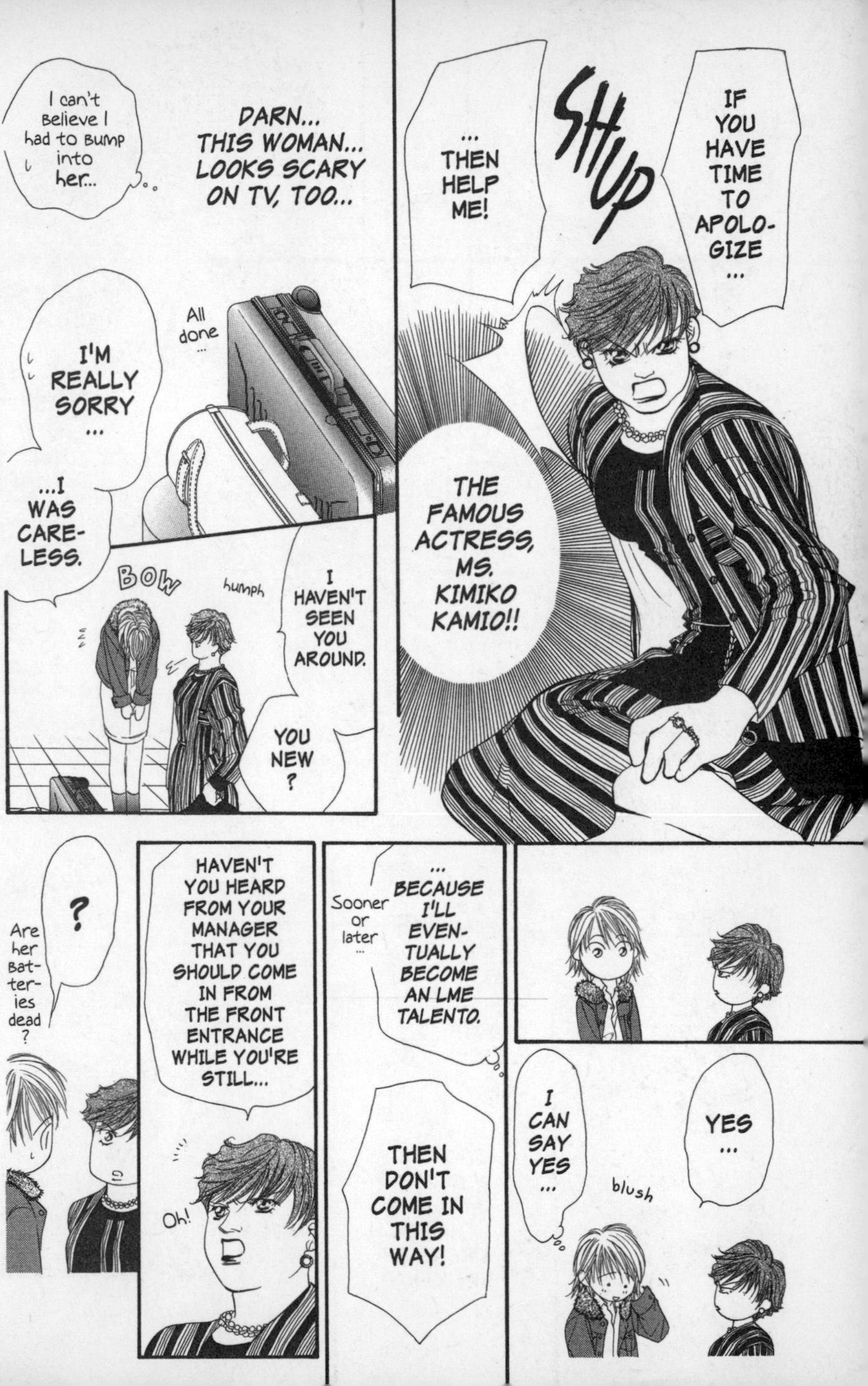

IF YOU HAVE TIME TO APOLOGIZE...
SHUP
...THEN HELP ME!
THE FAMOUS ACTRESS, MS. KIMIKO KAMIO!!
DARN... THIS WOMAN... LOOKS SCARY ON TV, TOO...
I can't believe I had to bump into her...
All done...
I'M REALLY SORRY...
...I WAS CARELESS.
BOW
humph
I HAVEN'T SEEN YOU AROUND.
YOU NEW?
YES...
I CAN SAY YES...
blush
...BECAUSE I'LL EVENTUALLY BECOME AN LME TALENTO.
Sooner or later...
THEN DON'T COME IN THIS WAY!
HAVEN'T YOU HEARD FROM YOUR MANAGER THAT YOU SHOULD COME IN FROM THE FRONT ENTRANCE WHILE YOU'RE STILL...
Oh!
?
Are her Batteries dead?

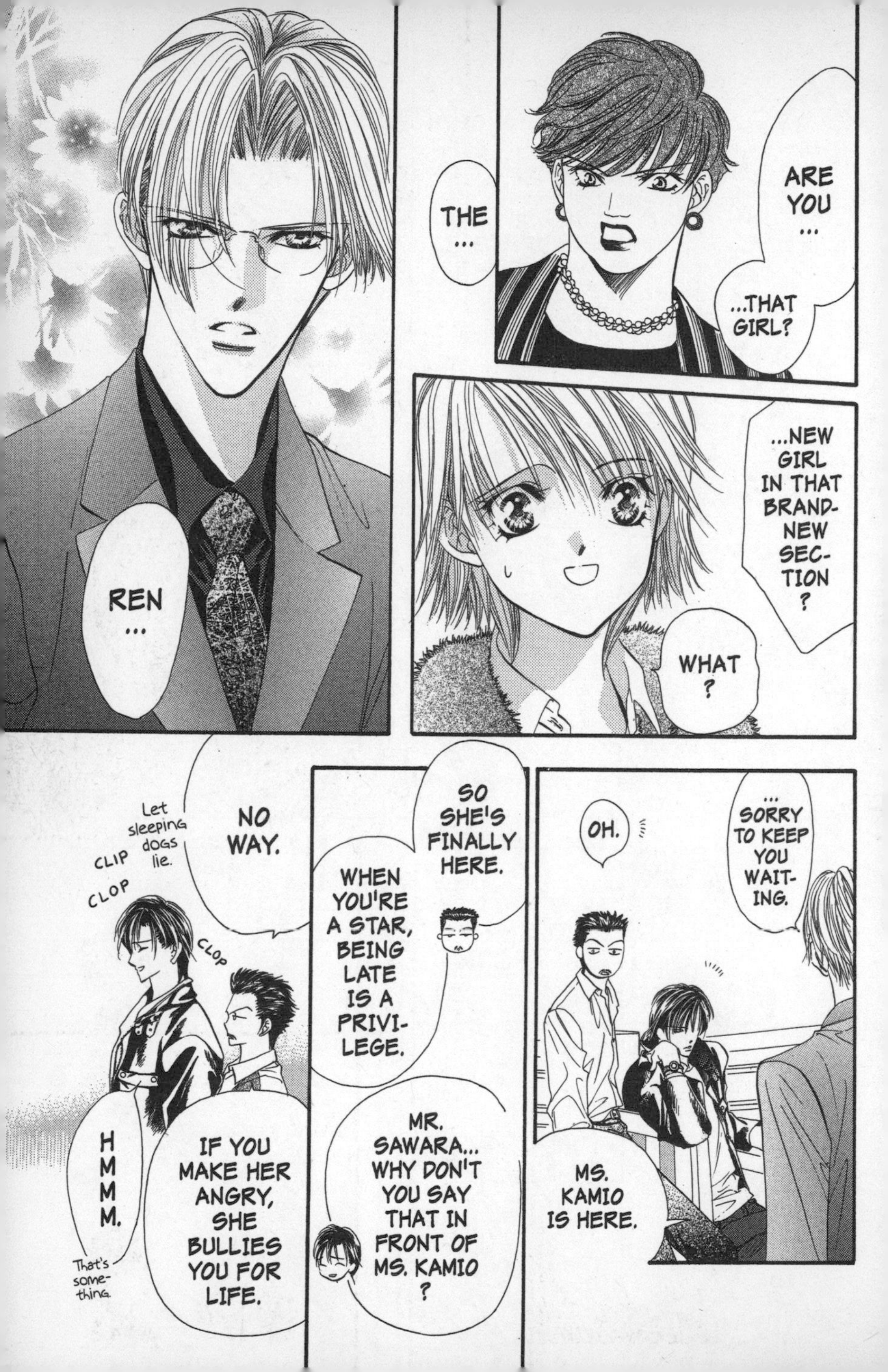
ARE YOU ...
THE ...
...THAT GIRL?
...NEW GIRL IN THAT BRAND-NEW SEC-TION?
WHAT?
REN ...
... SORRY TO KEEP YOU WAIT-ING.
OH.
MS. KAMIO IS HERE.
SO SHE'S FINALLY HERE.
WHEN YOU'RE A STAR, BEING LATE IS A PRIVI-LEGE.
MR. SAWARA... WHY DON'T YOU SAY THAT IN FRONT OF MS. KAMIO?
NO WAY.
Let sleeping dogs lie.
CLIP
CLOP
CLOP
IF YOU MAKE HER ANGRY, SHE BULLIES YOU FOR LIFE.
HMMM.
That's some-thing.

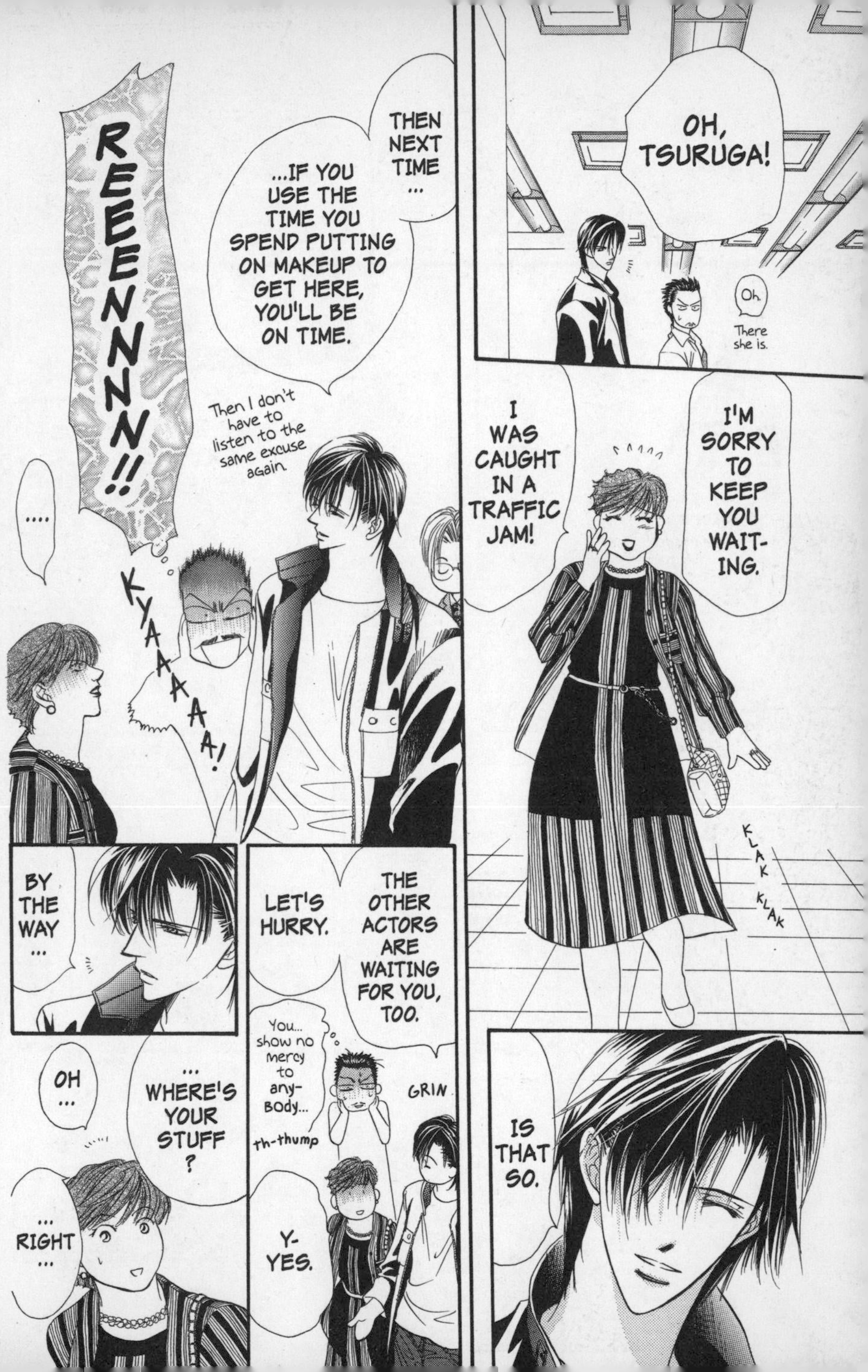
OH, TSURUGA!
Oh.
There she is.
I'M SORRY TO KEEP YOU WAIT-ING.
I WAS CAUGHT IN A TRAFFIC JAM!
KLAK KLAK
IS THAT SO.
THEN NEXT TIME ...
...IF YOU USE THE TIME YOU SPEND PUTTING ON MAKEUP TO GET HERE, YOU'LL BE ON TIME.
Then I don't have to listen to the same excuse again.
REEENNNN!!
KYAAAAAA!
....
THE OTHER ACTORS ARE WAITING FOR YOU, TOO.
LET'S HURRY.
GRIN
You... show no mercy to any-body...
th-thump
Y-YES.
BY THE WAY ...
... WHERE'S YOUR STUFF ?
OH ...
... RIGHT ...

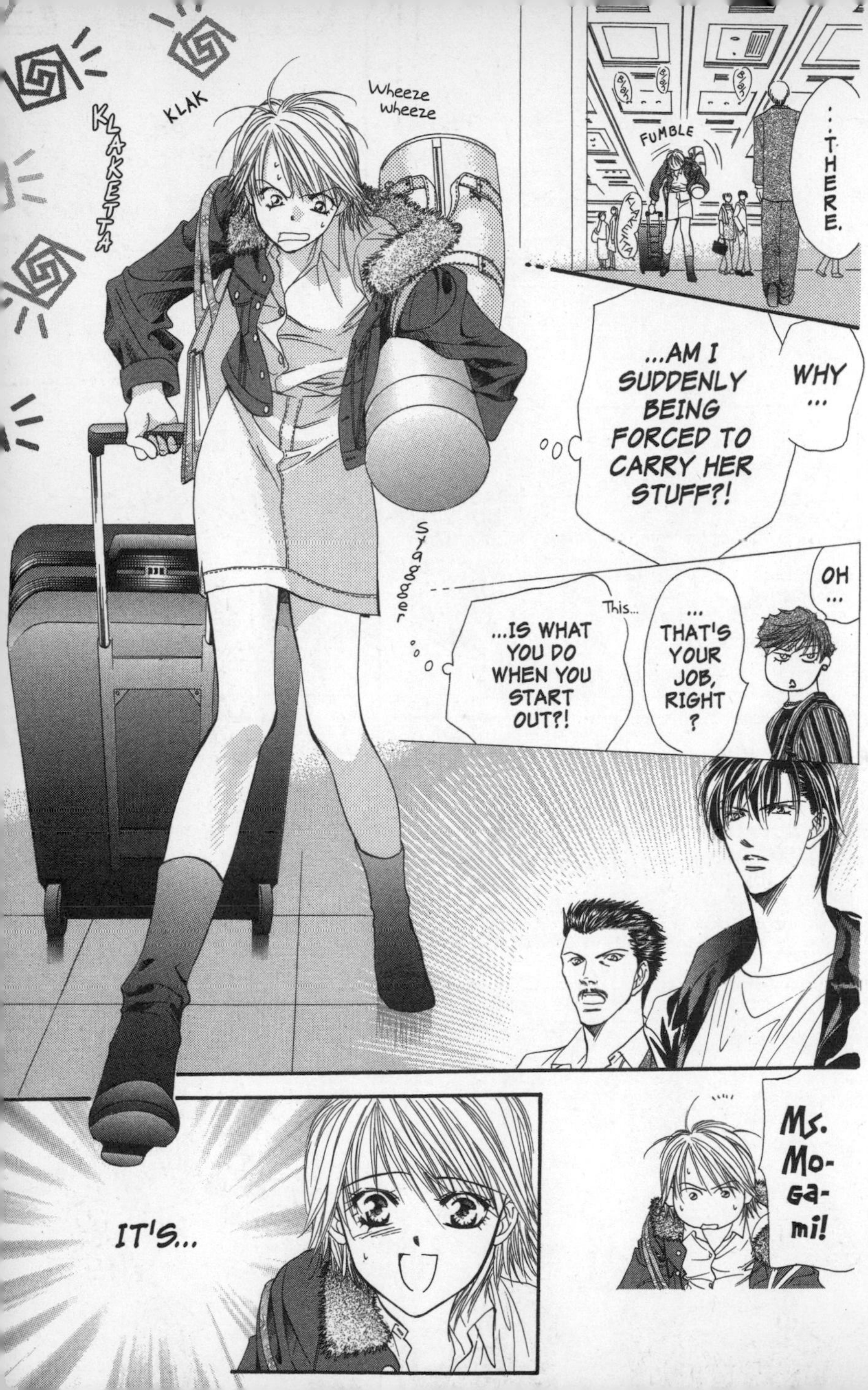
...THERE.
FUMBLE
KLAKETTA
WHY...
...AM I SUDDENLY BEING FORCED TO CARRY HER STUFF?!
OH...
...THAT'S YOUR JOB, RIGHT?
This...
...IS WHAT YOU DO WHEN YOU START OUT?!
KLAKETTA
KLAK
Wheeze wheeze
Stagger
Ms. Mo-ga-mi!
IT'S...

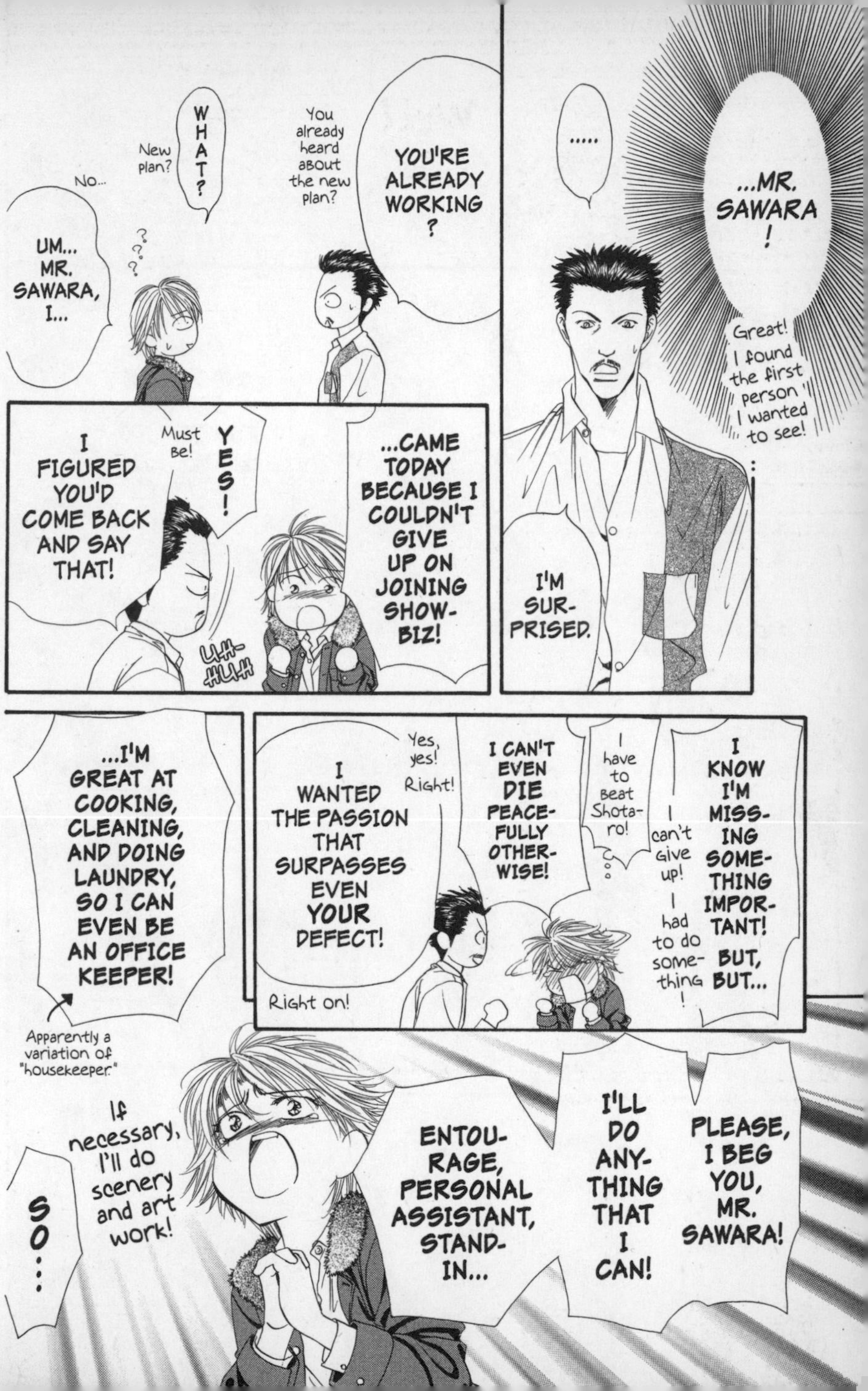

...MR. SAWARA!
Great! I found the first person I wanted to see!
.....
I'M SURPRISED.
YOU'RE ALREADY WORKING?
You already heard about the new plan?
WHAT?
New plan?
No...
UM... MR. SAWARA, I...
...CAME TODAY BECAUSE I COULDN'T GIVE UP ON JOINING SHOW-BIZ!
YES!
Must be!
I FIGURED YOU'D COME BACK AND SAY THAT!
UH-HUH
I KNOW I'M MISSING SOMETHING IMPORTANT! BUT, BUT...
I can't give up! I had to do something!
I have to beat Shotaro!
I CAN'T EVEN DIE PEACEFULLY OTHERWISE!
Yes, yes! Right!
I WANTED THE PASSION THAT SURPASSES EVEN YOUR DEFECT!
Right on!
...I'M GREAT AT COOKING, CLEANING, AND DOING LAUNDRY, SO I CAN EVEN BE AN OFFICE KEEPER!
Apparently a variation of "housekeeper."
PLEASE, I BEG YOU, MR. SAWARA!
I'LL DO ANYTHING THAT I CAN!
ENTOURAGE, PERSONAL ASSISTANT, STAND-IN...
If necessary, I'll do scenery and art work!
SO...

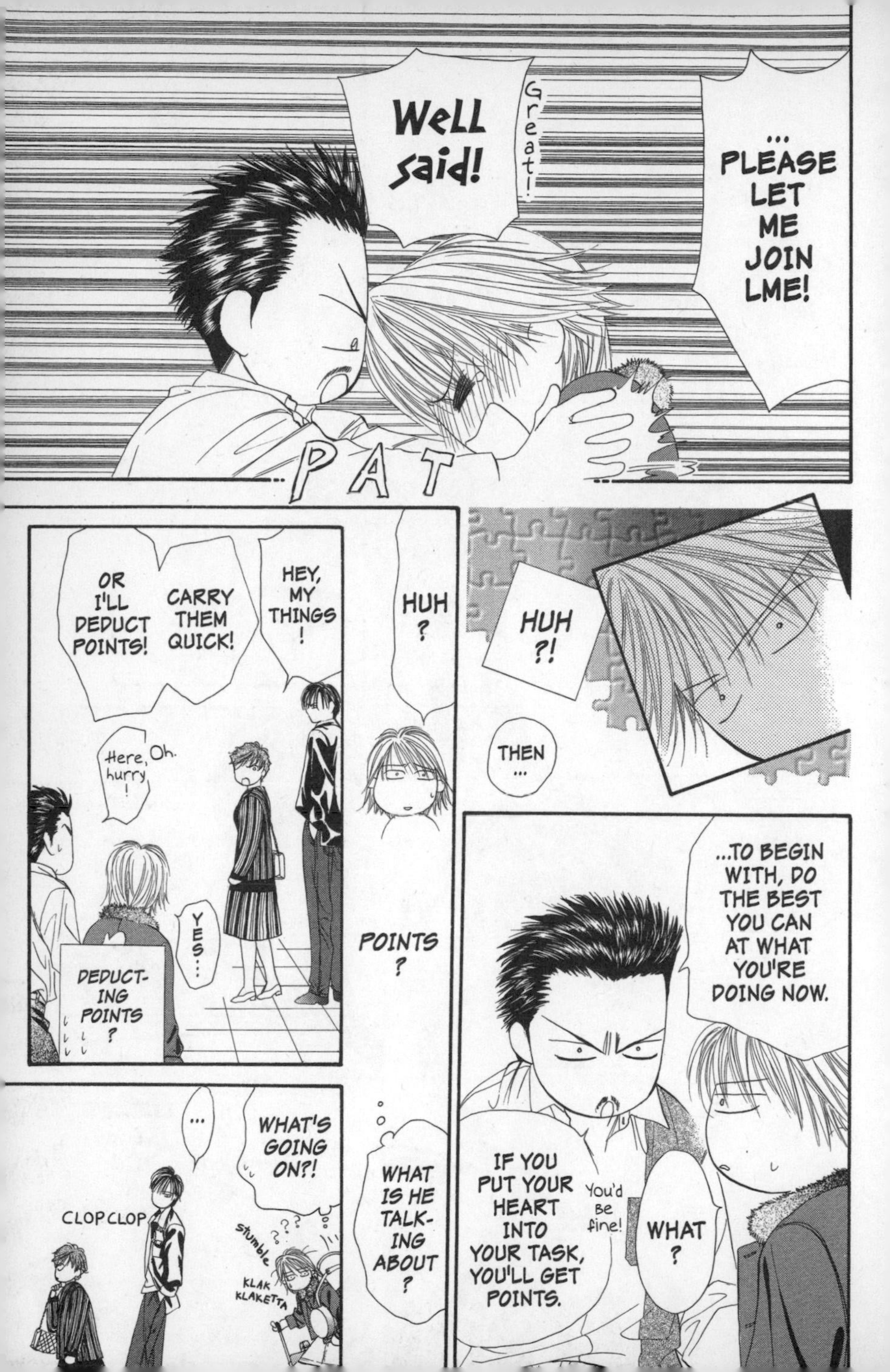
...PLEASE LET ME JOIN LME!
Well said!
Great!
PAT
HUH?!
THEN...
HUH?
HEY, MY THINGS!
CARRY THEM QUICK!
OR I'LL DEDUCT POINTS!
Oh.
Here, hurry!
YES...
DEDUCTING POINTS?
POINTS?
...TO BEGIN WITH, DO THE BEST YOU CAN AT WHAT YOU'RE DOING NOW.
WHAT?
You'd Be fine!
IF YOU PUT YOUR HEART INTO YOUR TASK, YOU'LL GET POINTS.
WHAT IS HE TALKING ABOUT?
WHAT'S GOING ON?!
...
CLOP CLOP
stumble
KLAK KLAKETTA

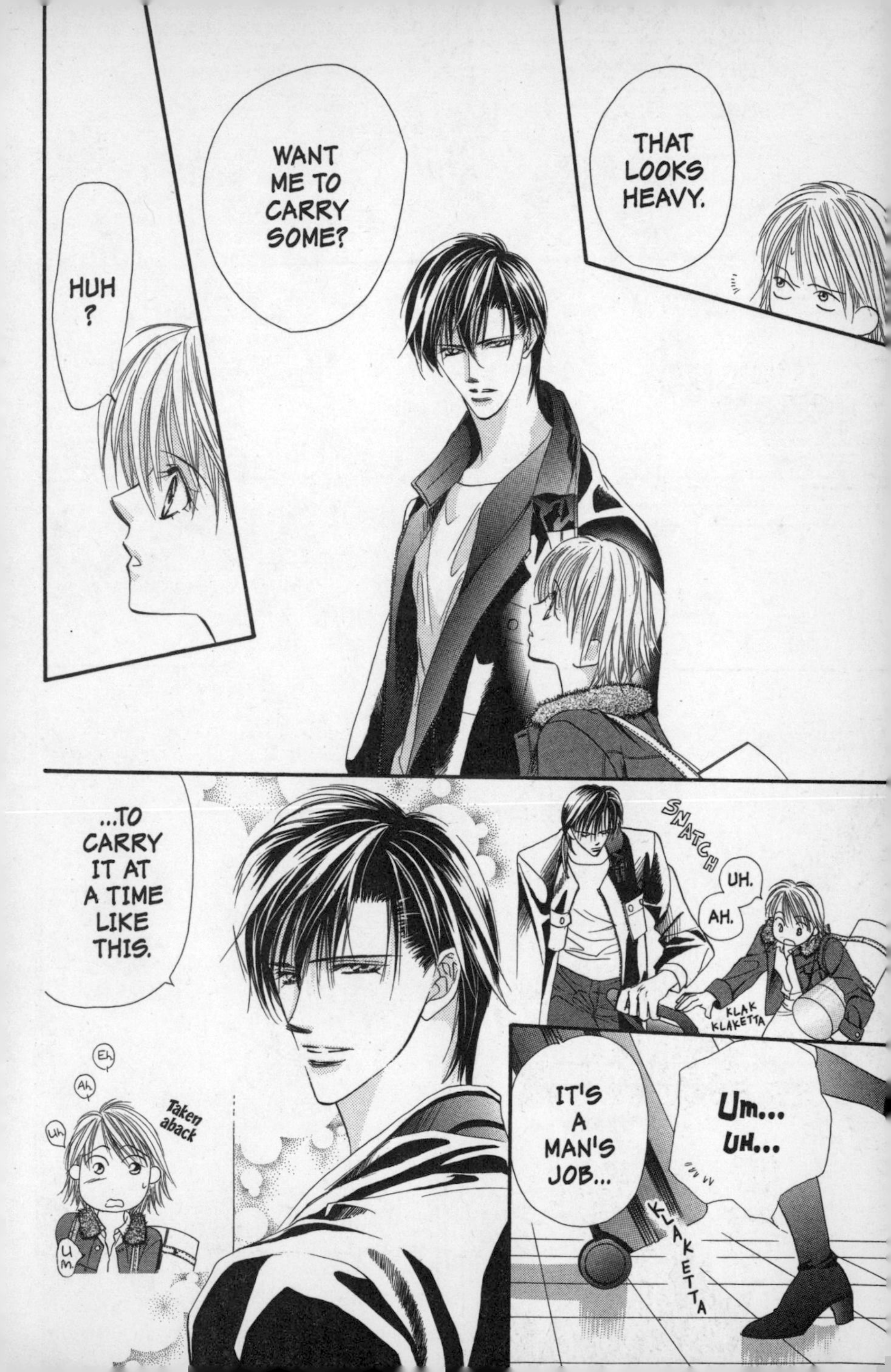
THAT LOOKS HEAVY.
WANT ME TO CARRY SOME?
HUH ?
SNATCH
UH.
AH.
KLAK KLAKETTA
Um... UH...
IT'S A MAN'S JOB...
KLAKETTA
...TO CARRY IT AT A TIME LIKE THIS.
Eh
Ah
Uh
Taken aback
Um.

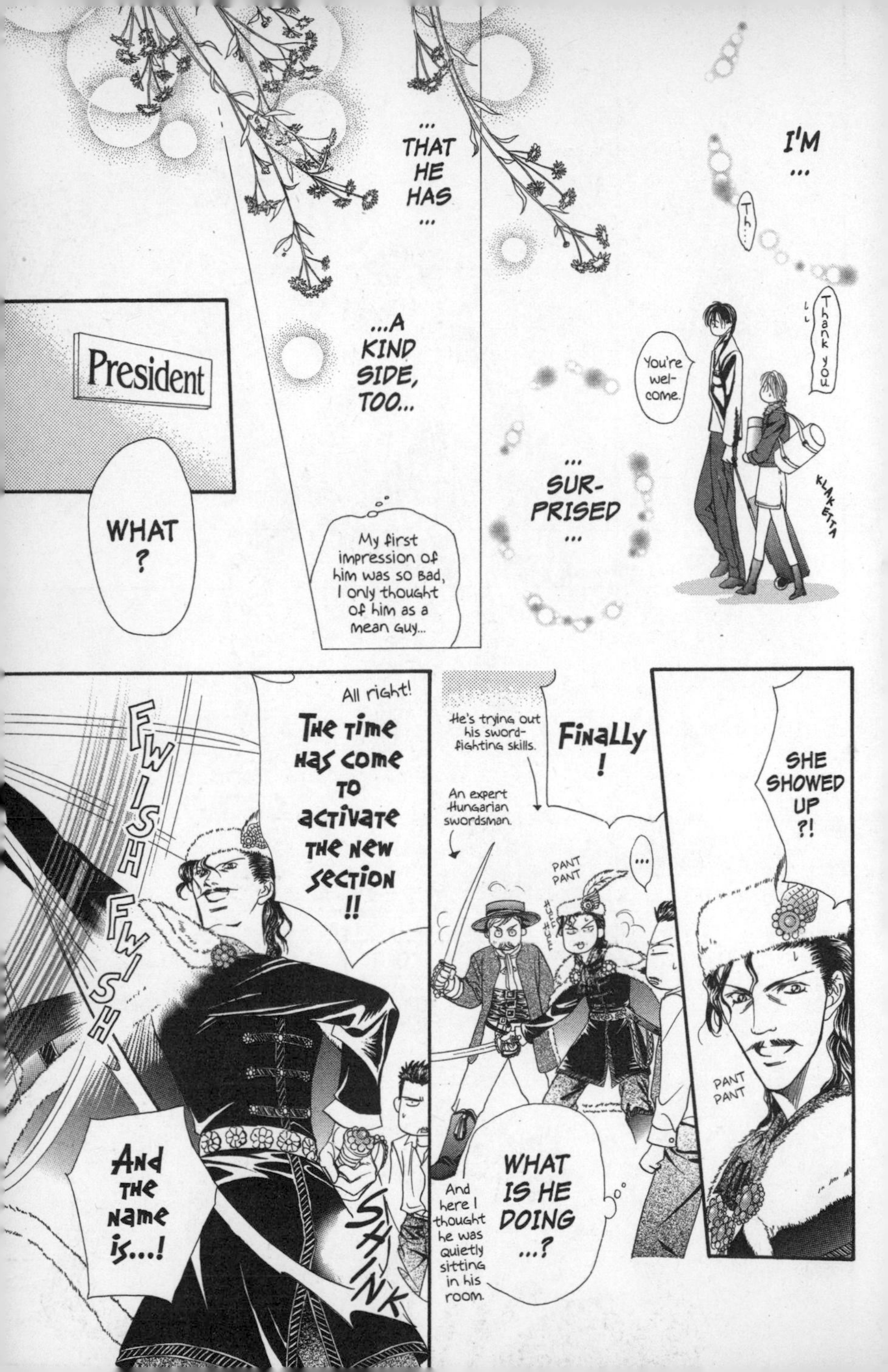
I'M ...
Th...
Thank you.
You're wel-come.
KLAKETTA
... SUR-PRISED ...
... THAT HE HAS ...
...A KIND SIDE, TOO...
My first impression of him was so bad, I only thought of him as a mean guy...
President
WHAT ?
SHE SHOWED UP ?!
PANT PANT
FINALLY !
He's trying out his sword-fighting skills.
An expert Hungarian swordsman.
PANT PANT
...
WHAT IS HE DOING ...?
And here I thought he was quietly sitting in his room.
All right!
The time has come to activate the new section !!
FWISH FWISH
SHINK
And the name is...!

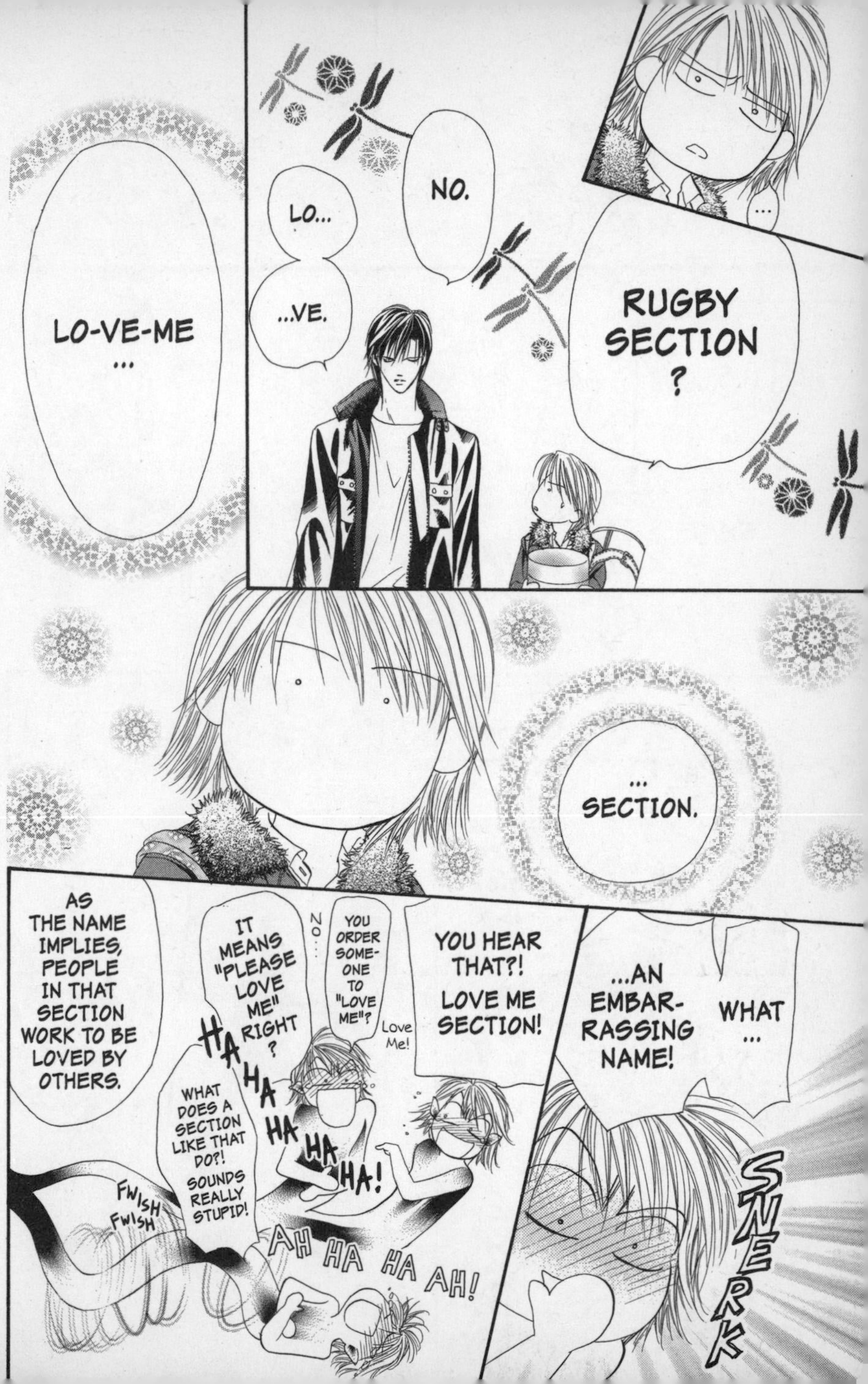
...
RUGBY SECTION?
NO.
LO...
...VE.
LO-VE-ME ...
... SECTION.
WHAT ...
...AN EMBARRASSING NAME!
SNERK
YOU HEAR THAT?! LOVE ME SECTION!
YOU ORDER SOMEONE TO "LOVE ME"?
NO...
IT MEANS "PLEASE LOVE ME" RIGHT?
Love Me!
HA HA HA HA HA!
AS THE NAME IMPLIES, PEOPLE IN THAT SECTION WORK TO BE LOVED BY OTHERS.
WHAT DOES A SECTION LIKE THAT DO?! SOUNDS REALLY STUPID!
FWISH FWISH
AH HA HA AH!

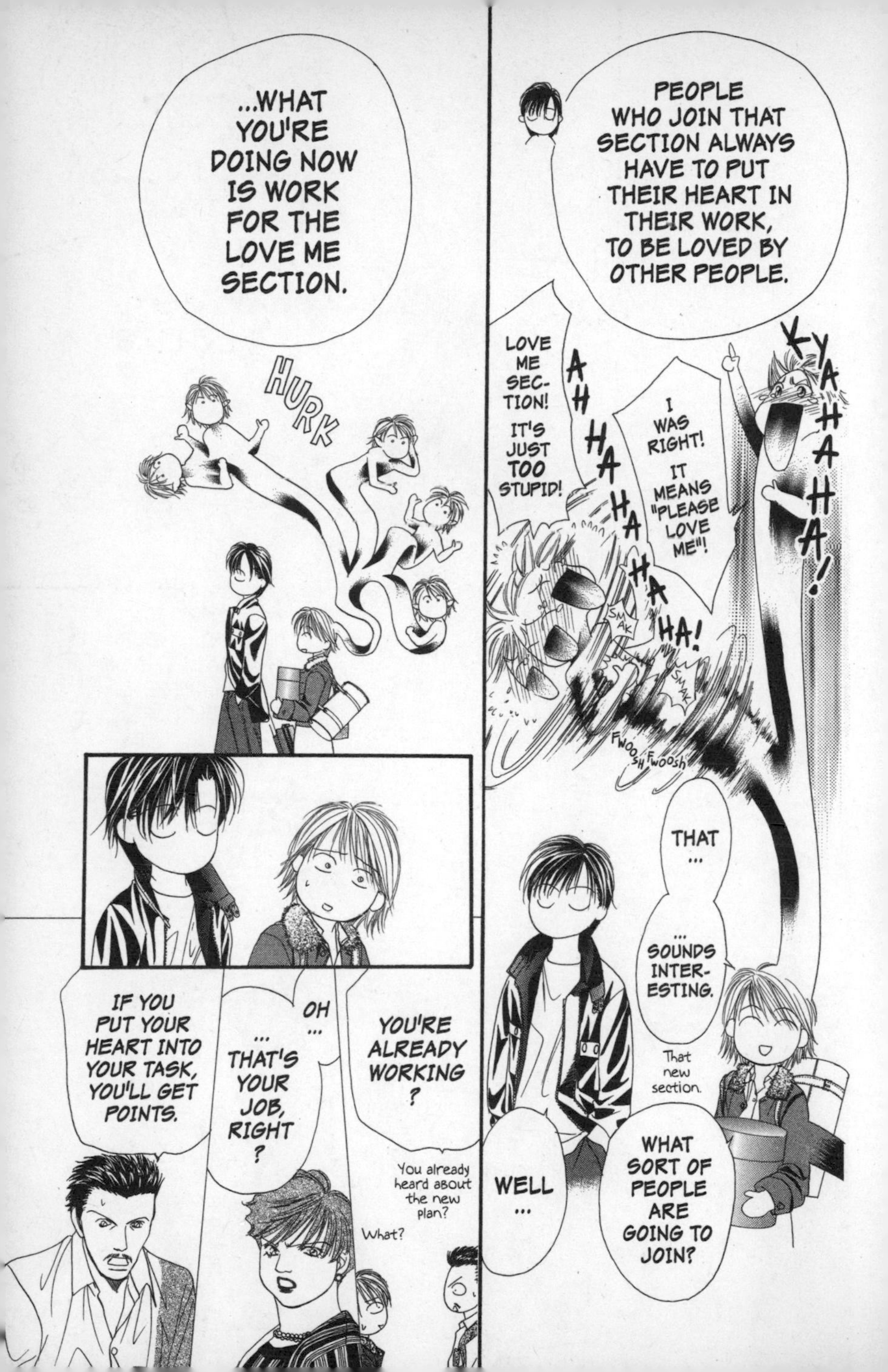
PEOPLE WHO JOIN THAT SECTION ALWAYS HAVE TO PUT THEIR HEART IN THEIR WORK, TO BE LOVED BY OTHER PEOPLE.
KYAHAHAHA!
I WAS RIGHT! IT MEANS "PLEASE LOVE ME"!
AHHAHAHAHAHA!
LOVE ME SECTION! IT'S JUST TOO STUPID!
SMAK
SMAK
FWOOSH FWOOSH
THAT ...
... SOUNDS INTERESTING.
That new section.
WHAT SORT OF PEOPLE ARE GOING TO JOIN?
WELL ...
...WHAT YOU'RE DOING NOW IS WORK FOR THE LOVE ME SECTION.
HURK
YOU'RE ALREADY WORKING?
You already heard about the new plan?
What?
OH ... ... THAT'S YOUR JOB, RIGHT?
IF YOU PUT YOUR HEART INTO YOUR TASK, YOU'LL GET POINTS.

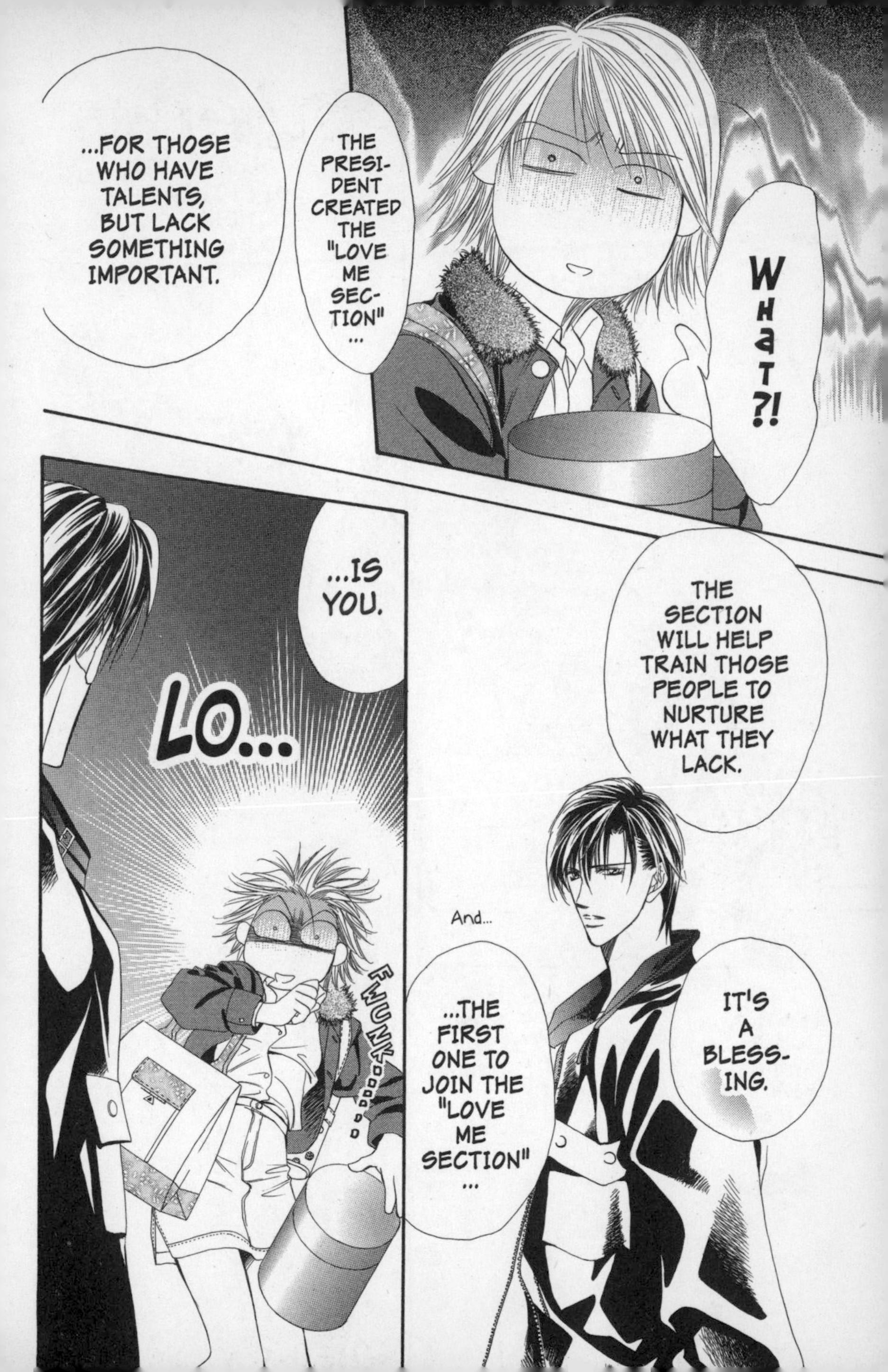
THE PRESIDENT CREATED THE "LOVE ME SECTION"...
...FOR THOSE WHO HAVE TALENTS, BUT LACK SOMETHING IMPORTANT.
WHAT?!
THE SECTION WILL HELP TRAIN THOSE PEOPLE TO NURTURE WHAT THEY LACK.
IT'S A BLESSING.
And...
...THE FIRST ONE TO JOIN THE "LOVE ME SECTION"...
...IS YOU.
LO...
FWUNK

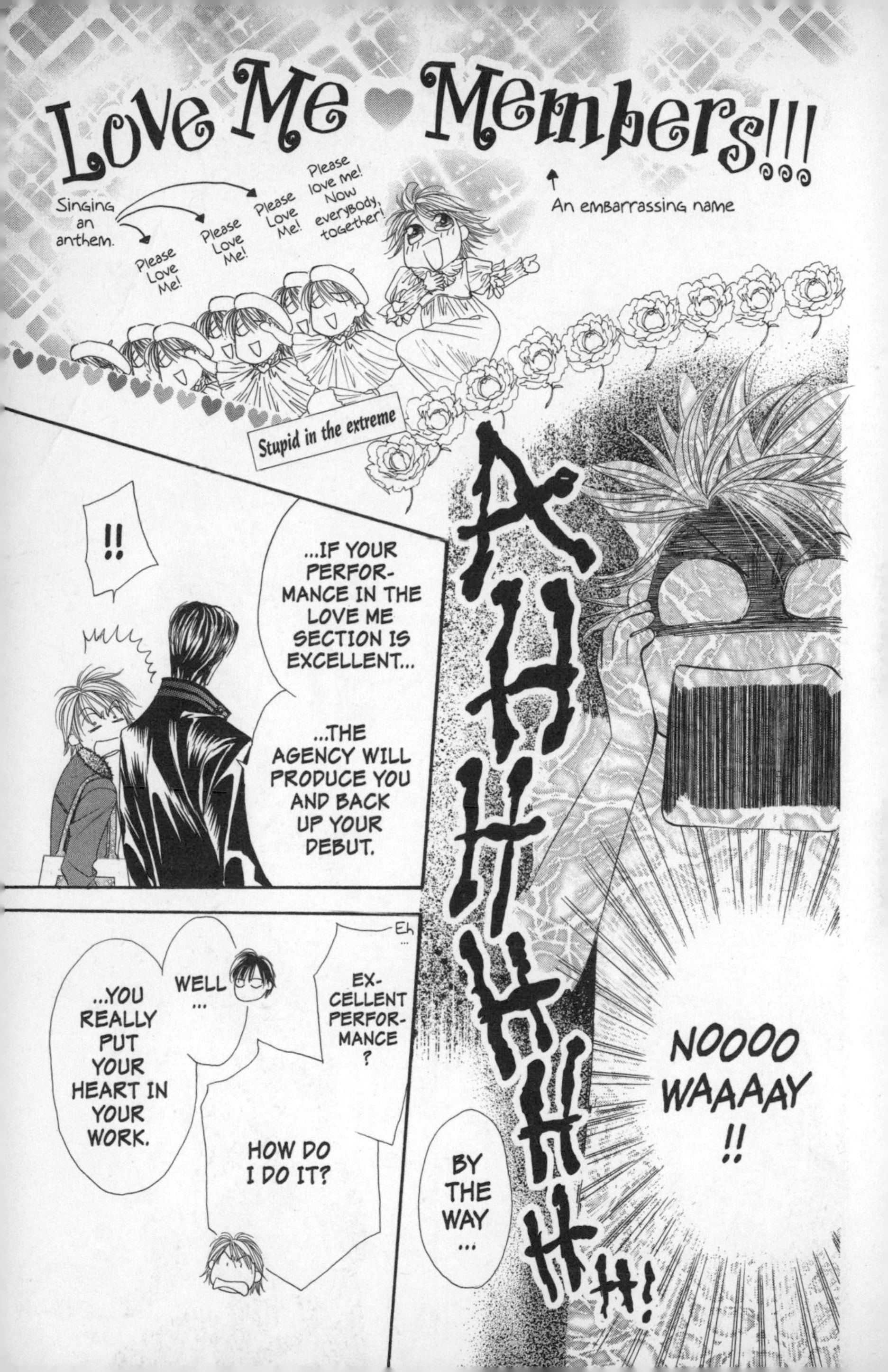
Love Me ♥ Members!!!
An embarrassing name
Please love me! Now everybody, together!
Please Love Me!
Please Love Me!
Please Love Me!
Singing an anthem.
Stupid in the extreme
AHHHHHHHH!
NOOOO WAAAAY !!
BY THE WAY ...
...IF YOUR PERFORMANCE IN THE LOVE ME SECTION IS EXCELLENT...
...THE AGENCY WILL PRODUCE YOU AND BACK UP YOUR DEBUT.
!!
Eh...
EXCELLENT PERFORMANCE?
WELL...
...YOU REALLY PUT YOUR HEART IN YOUR WORK.
HOW DO I DO IT?

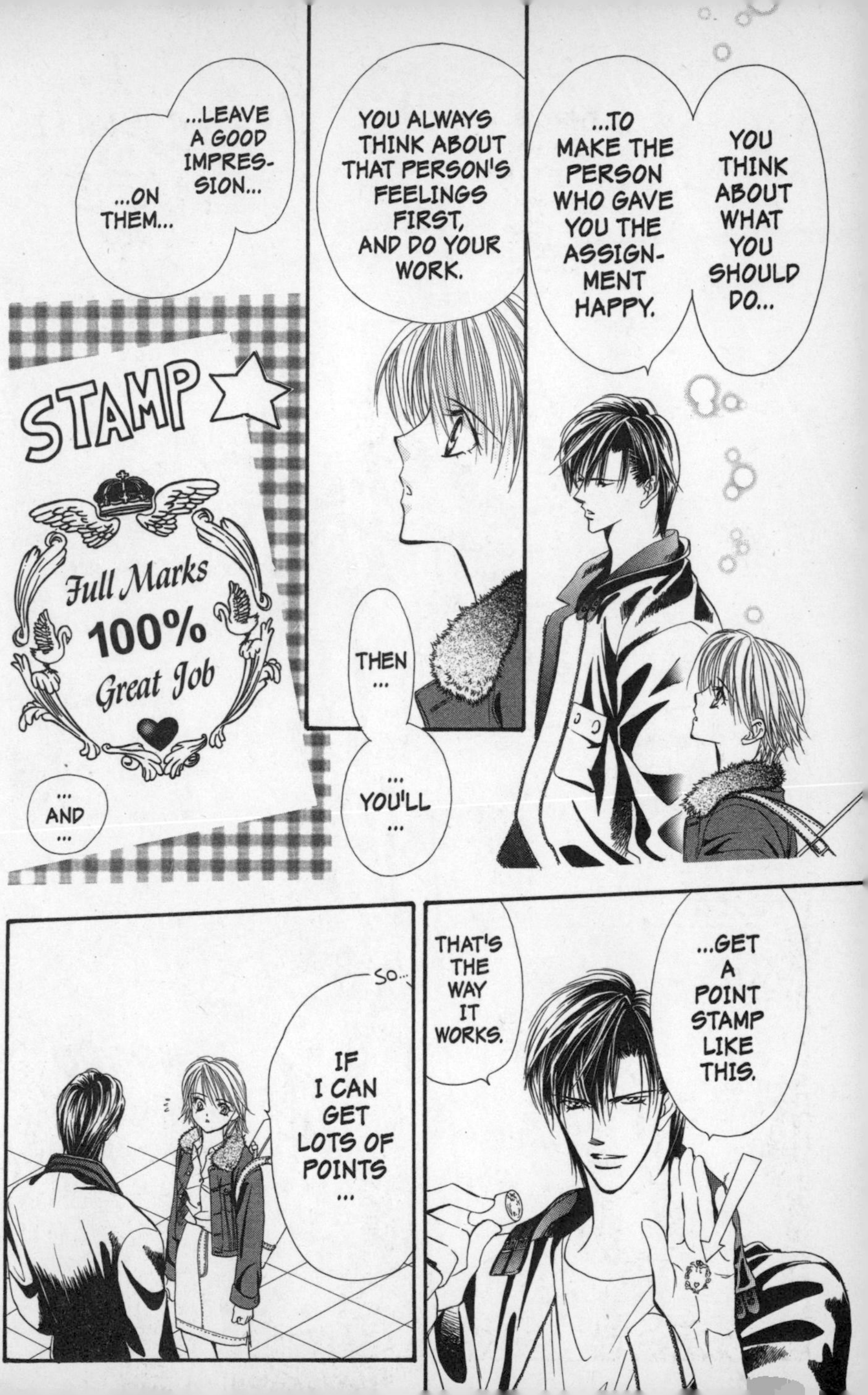

YOU THINK ABOUT WHAT YOU SHOULD DO...
...TO MAKE THE PERSON WHO GAVE YOU THE ASSIGNMENT HAPPY.
YOU ALWAYS THINK ABOUT THAT PERSON'S FEELINGS FIRST, AND DO YOUR WORK.
THEN...
...YOU'LL...
...LEAVE A GOOD IMPRESSION...
...ON THEM...
STAMP
Full Marks
100%
Great Job
...AND...
...GET A POINT STAMP LIKE THIS.
THAT'S THE WAY IT WORKS.
SO...
IF I CAN GET LOTS OF POINTS...

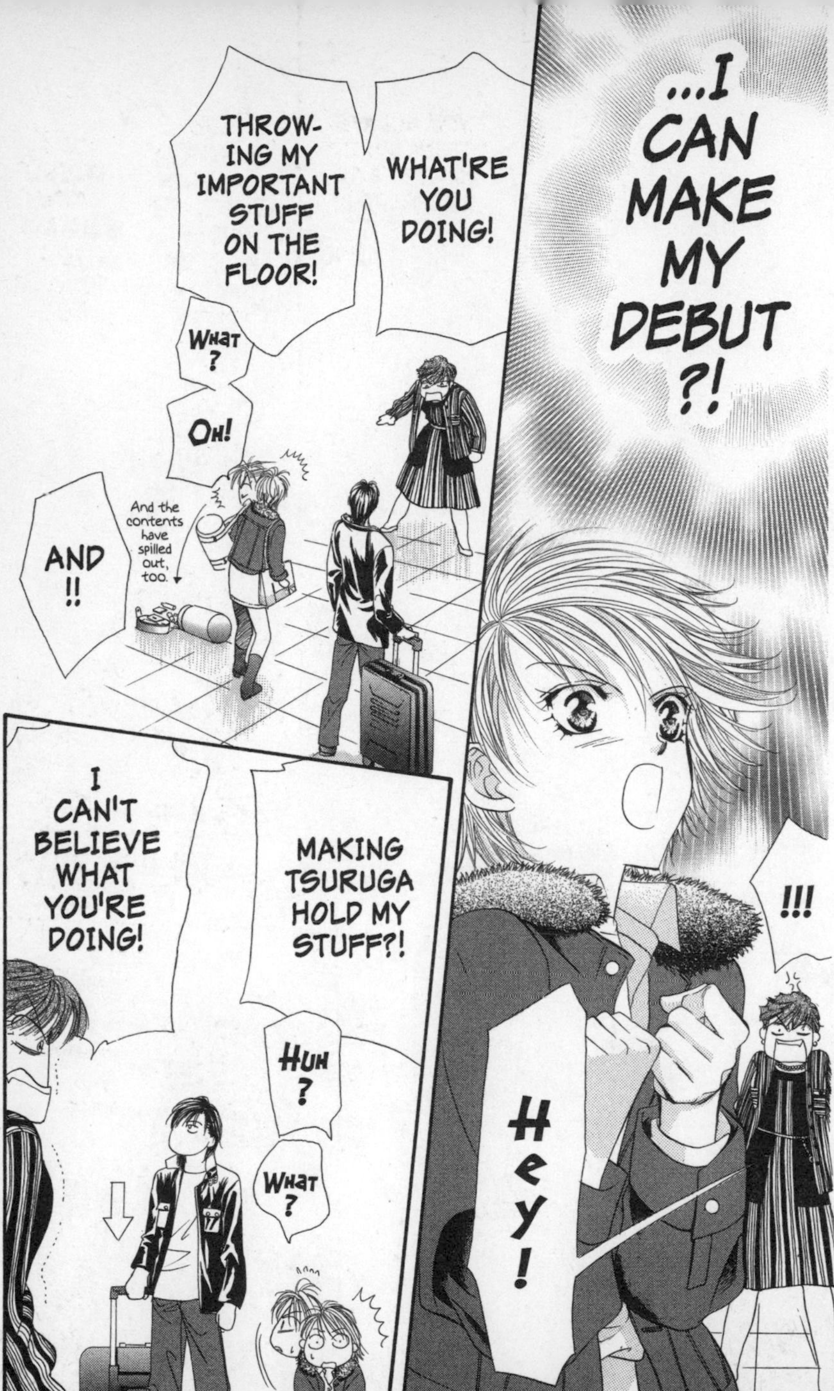
...I CAN MAKE MY DEBUT?!
!!!
Hey!
WHAT'RE YOU DOING!
THROWING MY IMPORTANT STUFF ON THE FLOOR!
WHAT?
OH!
And the contents have spilled out, too.
AND !!
MAKING TSURUGA HOLD MY STUFF?!
I CAN'T BELIEVE WHAT YOU'RE DOING!
HUH?
WHAT?

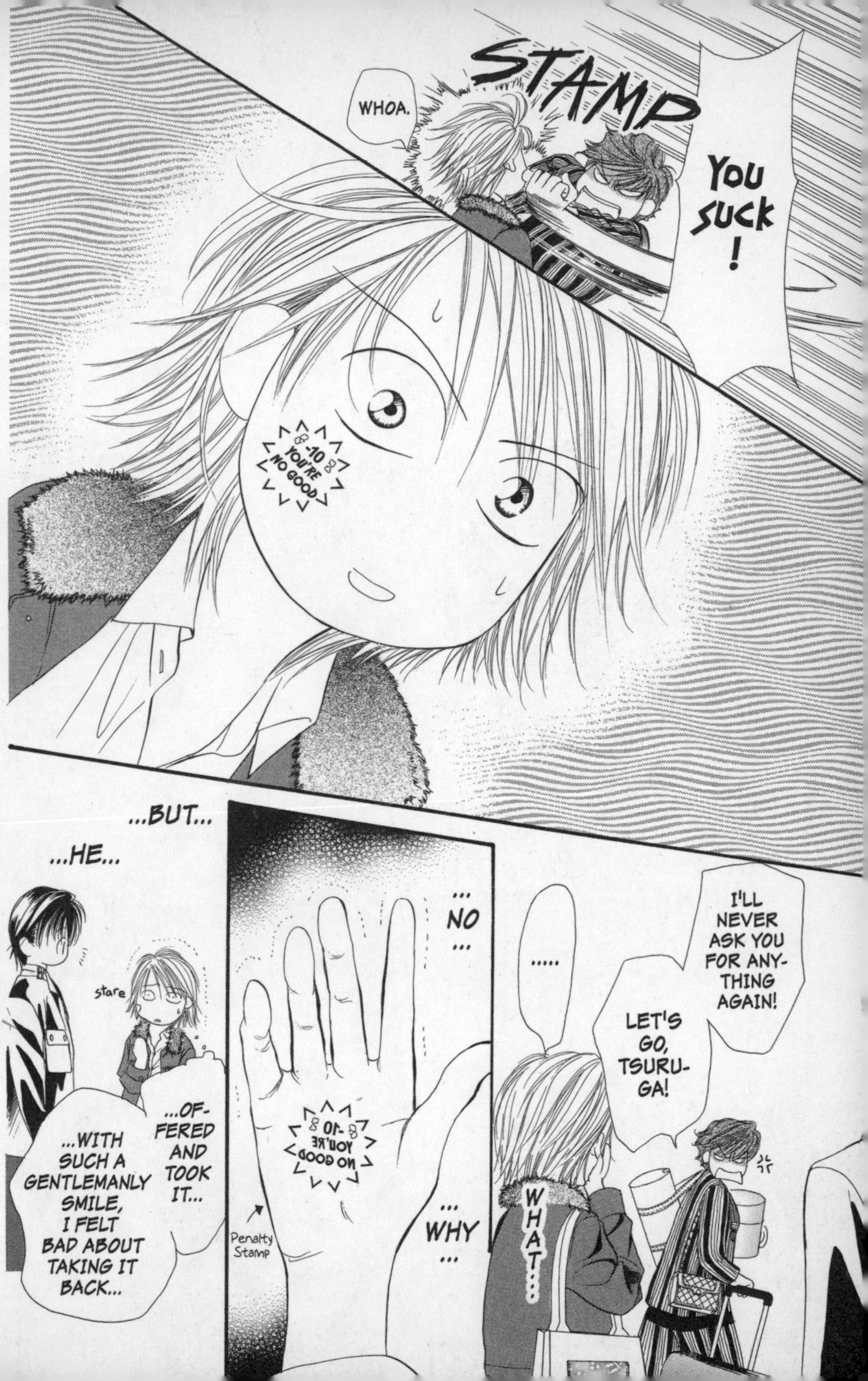
STAMP
YOU SUCK!
WHOA.
-10 YOU'RE NO GOOD
I'LL NEVER ASK YOU FOR ANYTHING AGAIN!
LET'S GO, TSURUGA!
.....
WHAT...
...NO...
...WHY...
-10 YOU'RE NO GOOD
Penalty Stamp
...BUT...
...HE...
stare
...OFFERED AND TOOK IT...
...WITH SUCH A GENTLEMANLY SMILE, I FELT BAD ABOUT TAKING IT BACK...

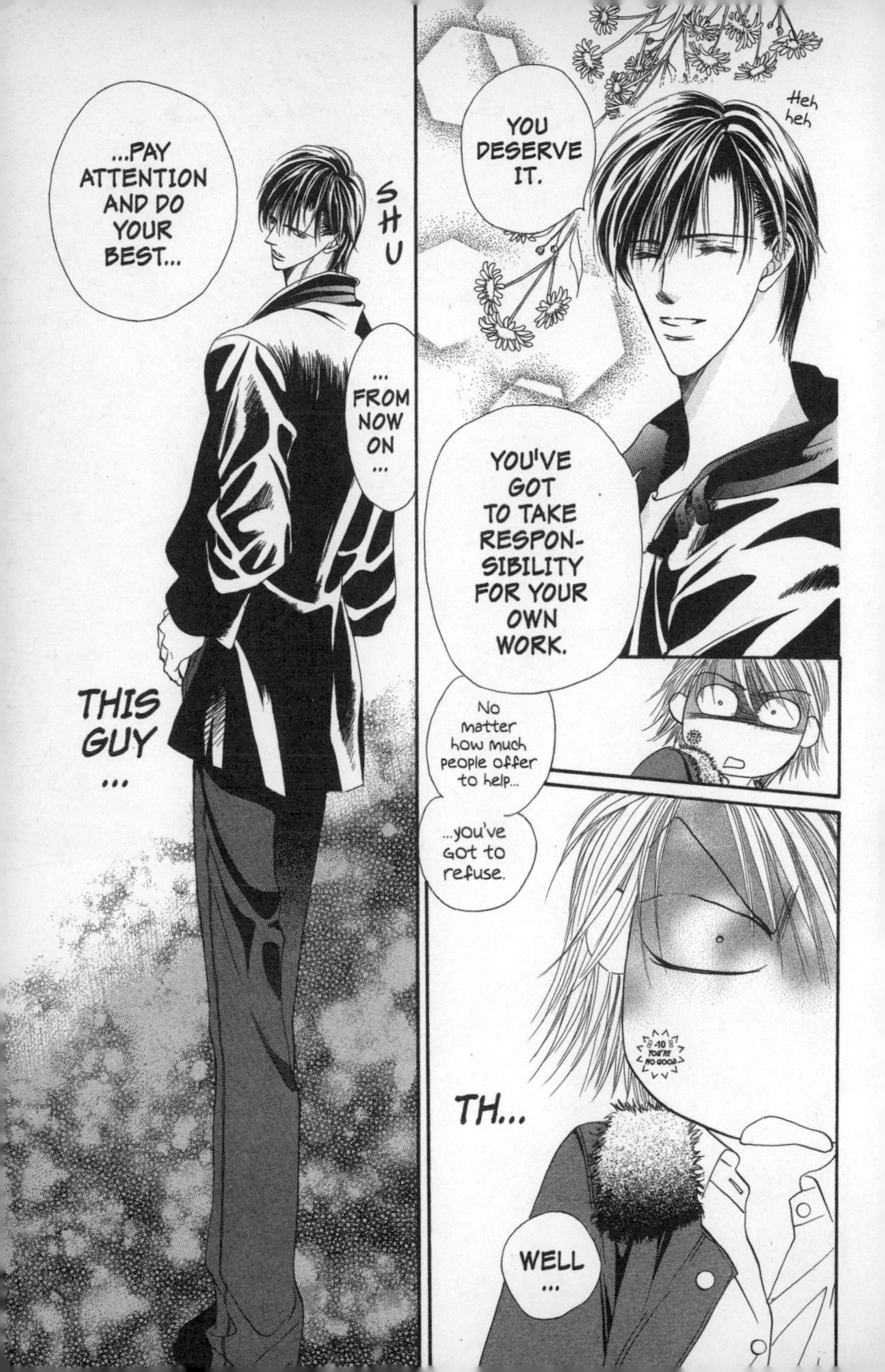

Heh heh
YOU DESERVE IT.
YOU'VE GOT TO TAKE RESPON-SIBILITY FOR YOUR OWN WORK.
No matter how much people offer to help...
...you've got to refuse.
-10 YOU'RE NO GOOD
TH...
WELL ...
... FROM NOW ON ...
SHU
...PAY ATTENTION AND DO YOUR BEST...
THIS GUY ...

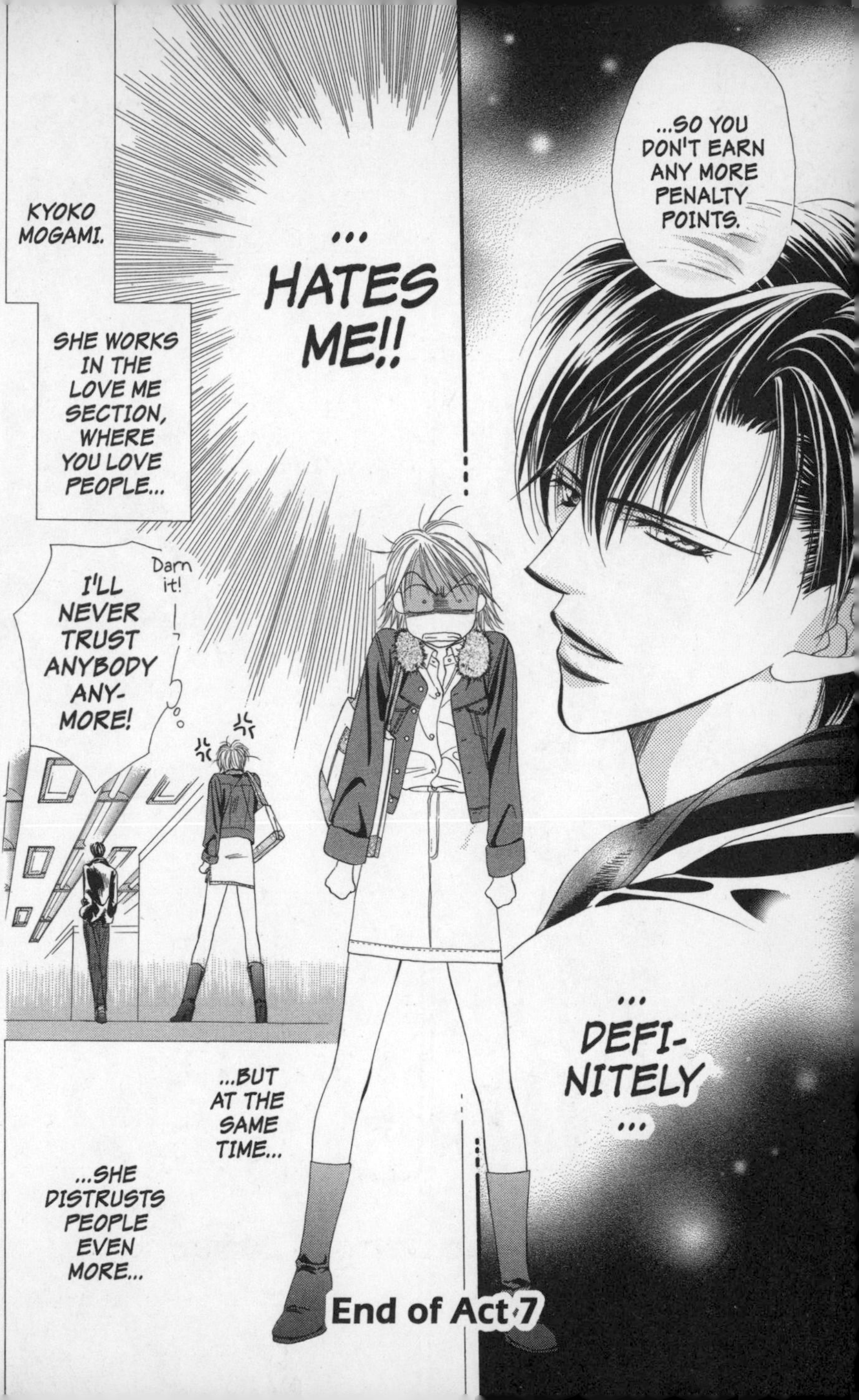
...SO YOU DON'T EARN ANY MORE PENALTY POINTS.
... DEFI- NITELY ...
KYOKO MOGAMI.
SHE WORKS IN THE LOVE ME SECTION, WHERE YOU LOVE PEOPLE...
... HATES ME!!
I'LL NEVER TRUST ANYBODY ANY- MORE!
Darn it!
...BUT AT THE SAME TIME...
...SHE DISTRUSTS PEOPLE EVEN MORE...
End of Act 7

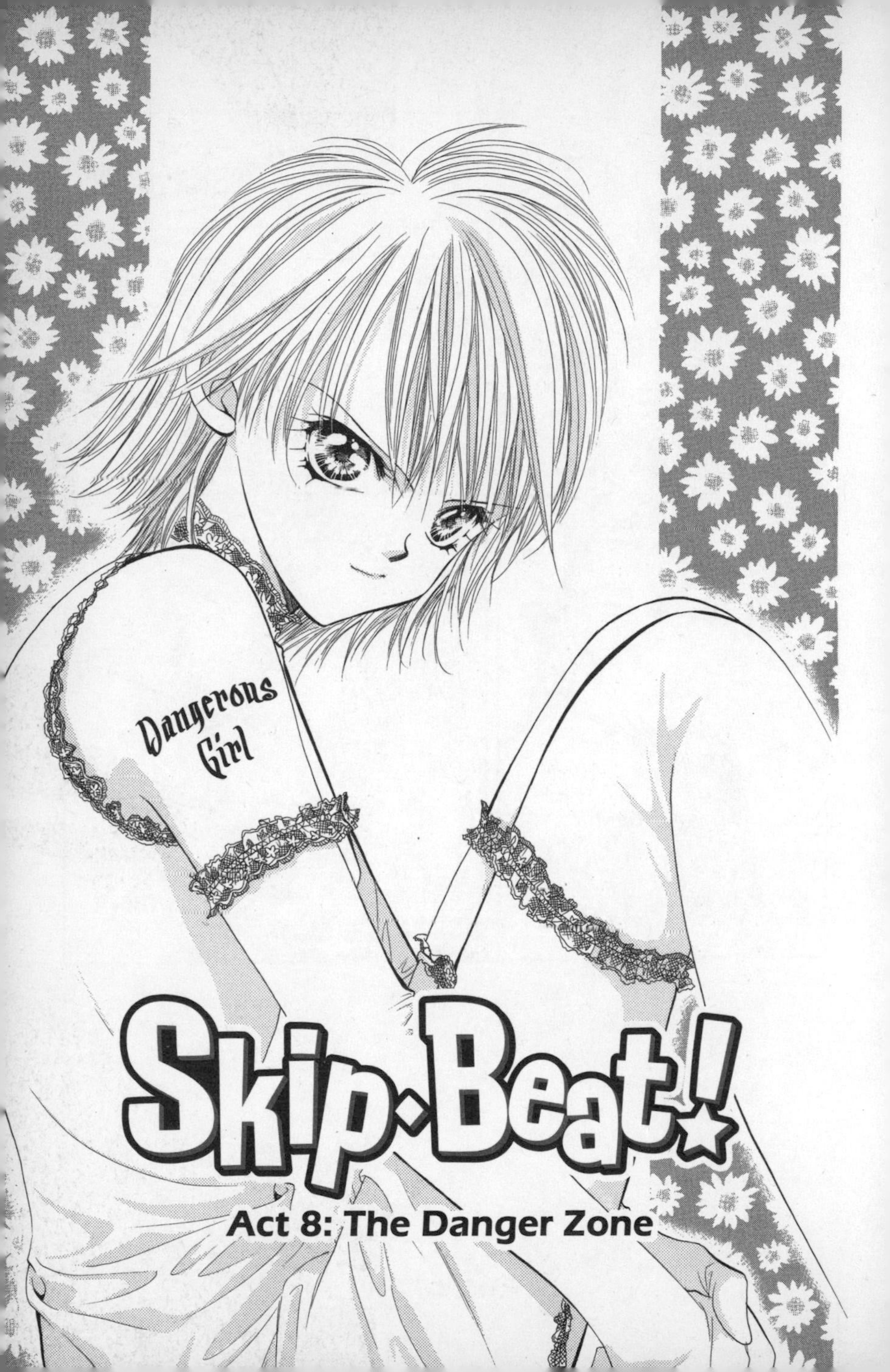
Dangerous Girl
Skip·Beat!
Act 8: The Danger Zone

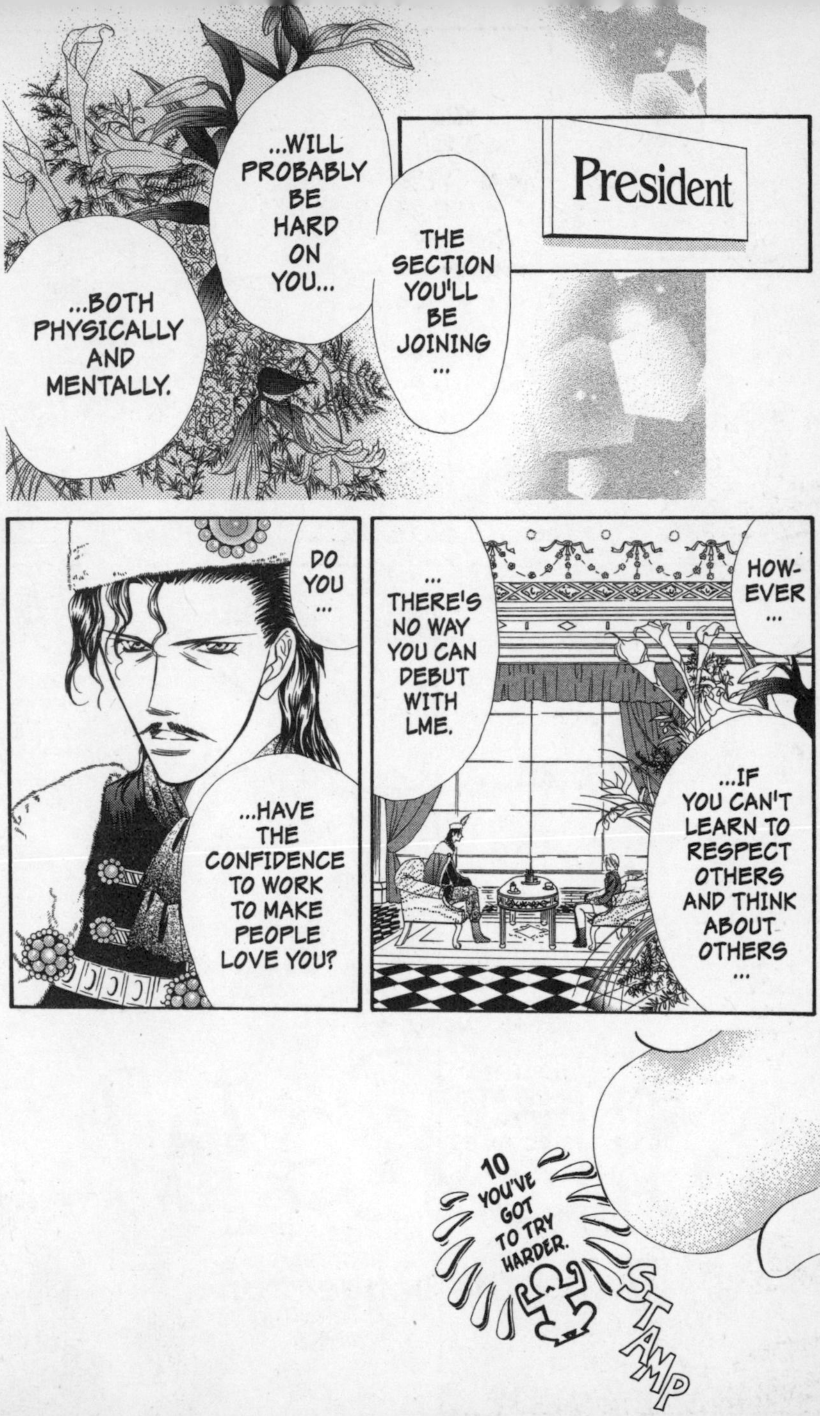
President
THE SECTION YOU'LL BE JOINING...
...WILL PROBABLY BE HARD ON YOU...
...BOTH PHYSICALLY AND MENTALLY.
HOW-EVER...
...IF YOU CAN'T LEARN TO RESPECT OTHERS AND THINK ABOUT OTHERS...
...THERE'S NO WAY YOU CAN DEBUT WITH LME.
DO YOU...
...HAVE THE CONFIDENCE TO WORK TO MAKE PEOPLE LOVE YOU?
10 YOU'VE GOT TO TRY HARDER.
STAMP

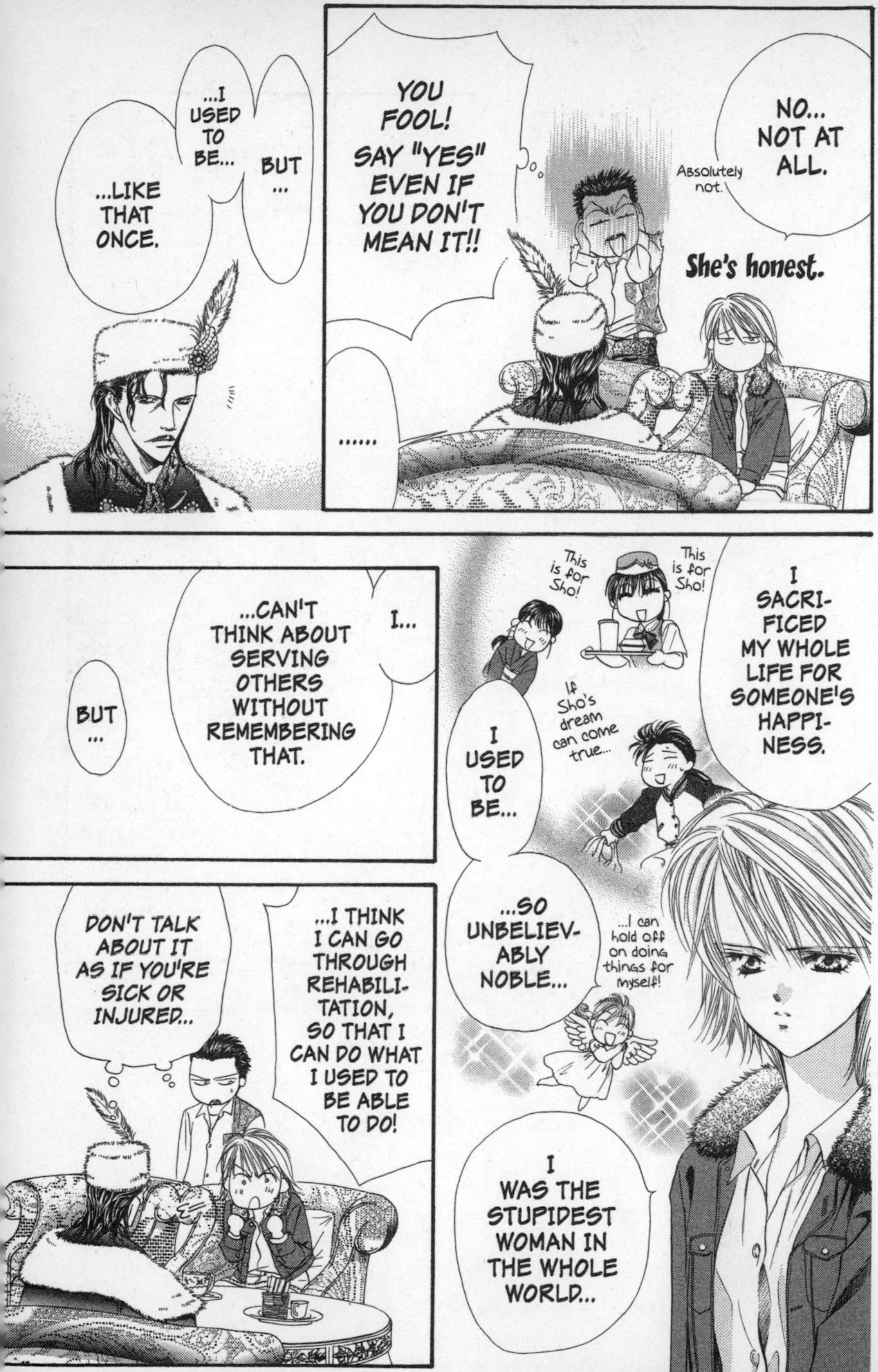
NO... NOT AT ALL.
Absolutely not.
She's honest.
YOU FOOL! SAY "YES" EVEN IF YOU DON'T MEAN IT!!
......
...I USED TO BE...
...LIKE THAT ONCE.
BUT ...
I SACRIFICED MY WHOLE LIFE FOR SOMEONE'S HAPPINESS.
This is for Sho!
This is for Sho!
If Sho's dream can come true...
I USED TO BE...
...SO UNBELIEVABLY NOBLE...
...I can hold off on doing things for myself!
I WAS THE STUPIDEST WOMAN IN THE WHOLE WORLD...
I...
...CAN'T THINK ABOUT SERVING OTHERS WITHOUT REMEMBERING THAT.
BUT ...
...I THINK I CAN GO THROUGH REHABILITATION, SO THAT I CAN DO WHAT I USED TO BE ABLE TO DO!
DON'T TALK ABOUT IT AS IF YOU'RE SICK OR INJURED...

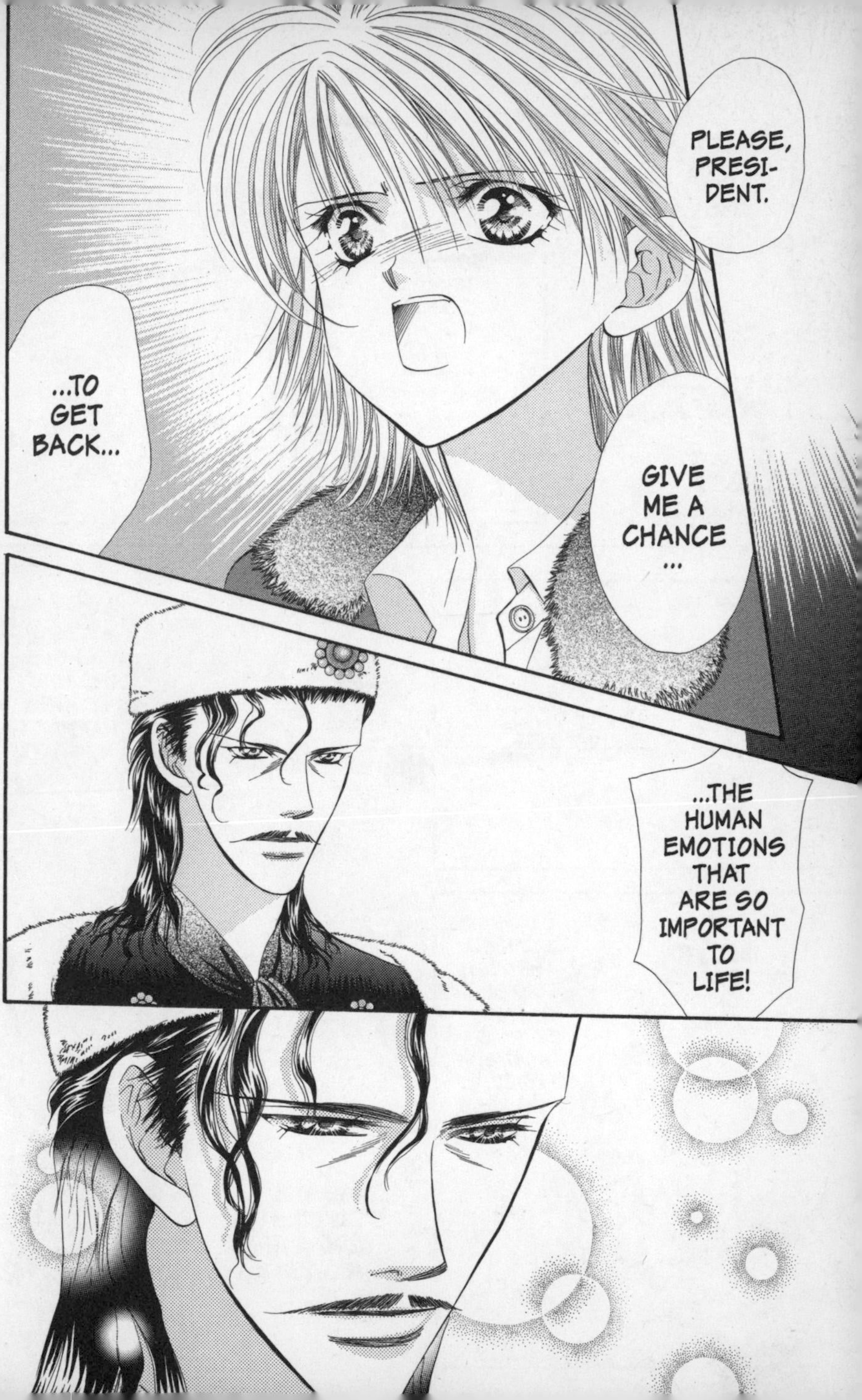
PLEASE, PRESIDENT.
GIVE ME A CHANCE ...
...TO GET BACK...
...THE HUMAN EMOTIONS THAT ARE SO IMPORTANT TO LIFE!

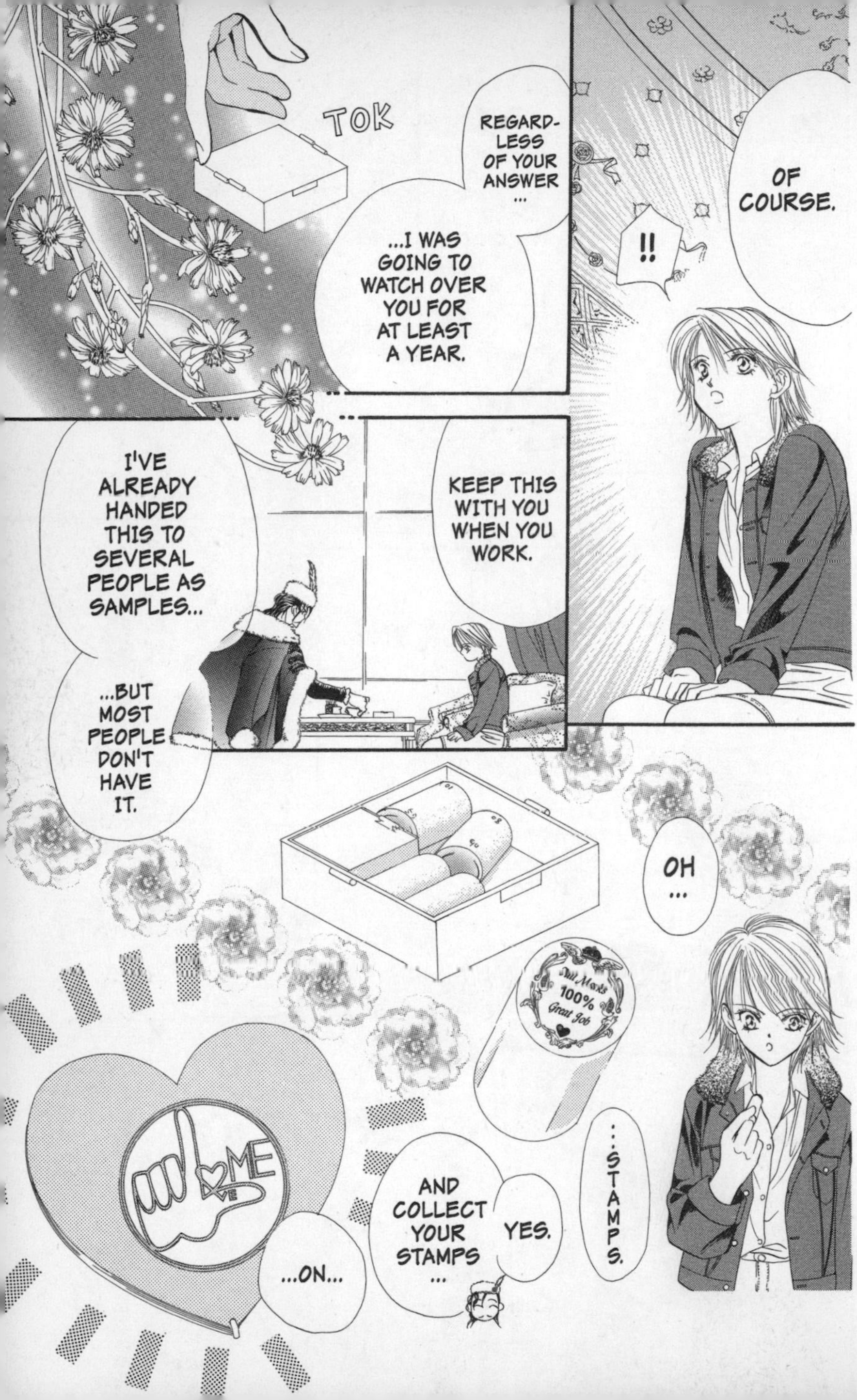
OF COURSE.
!!
TOK
REGARDLESS OF YOUR ANSWER...
...I WAS GOING TO WATCH OVER YOU FOR AT LEAST A YEAR.
KEEP THIS WITH YOU WHEN YOU WORK.
I'VE ALREADY HANDED THIS TO SEVERAL PEOPLE AS SAMPLES...
...BUT MOST PEOPLE DON'T HAVE IT.
OH...
100%
Great Job
...STAMPS.
YES.
AND COLLECT YOUR STAMPS...
...ON...
LOVE ME

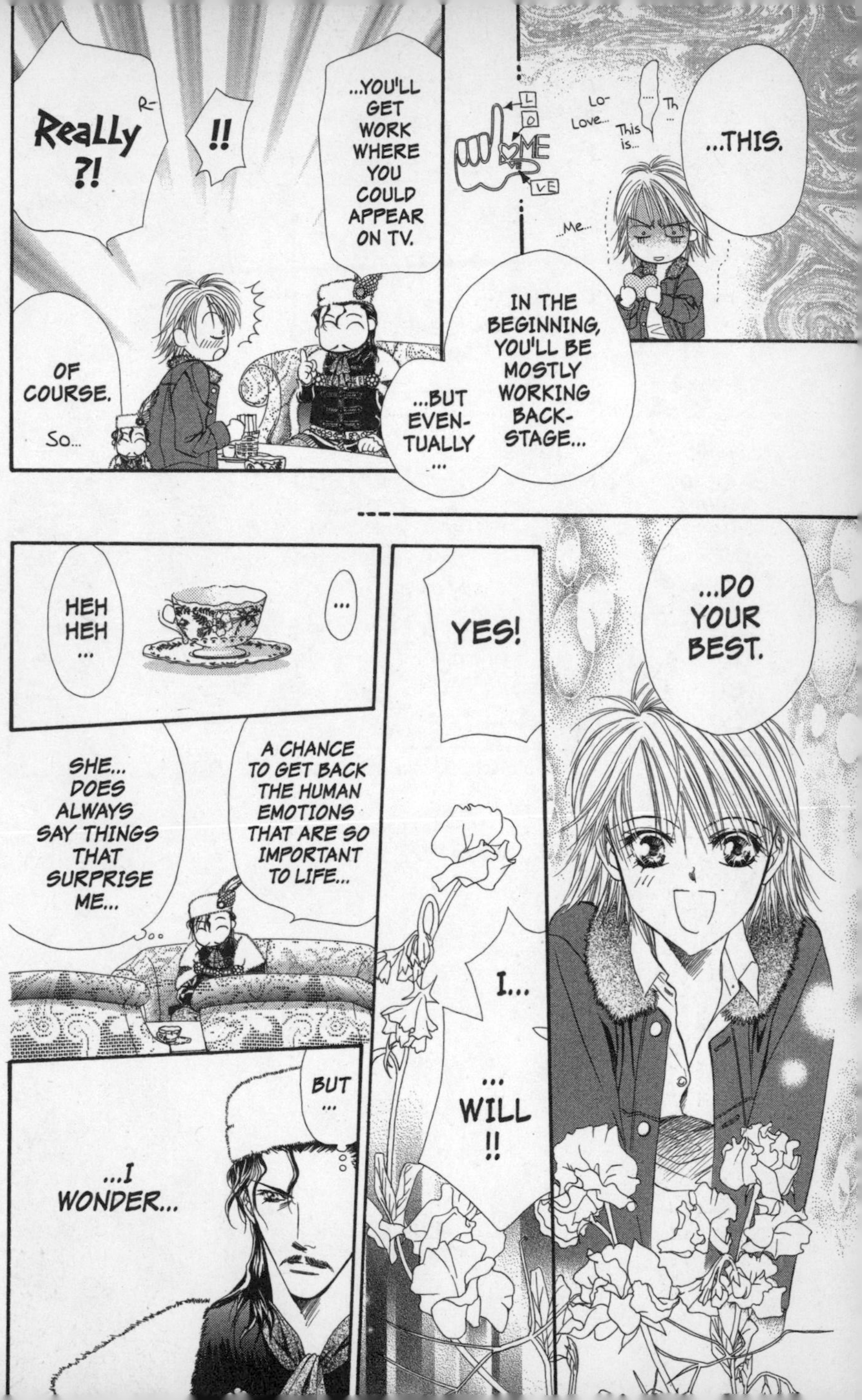
Lo-
Love...
This is...
Th ...
...THIS.
...Me...
IN THE BEGINNING, YOU'LL BE MOSTLY WORKING BACK-STAGE...
...BUT EVEN-TUALLY ...
...YOU'LL GET WORK WHERE YOU COULD APPEAR ON TV.
!!
R-
Really ?!
OF COURSE.
So...
...DO YOUR BEST.
YES!
I...
... WILL !!
...
HEH HEH ...
A CHANCE TO GET BACK THE HUMAN EMOTIONS THAT ARE SO IMPORTANT TO LIFE...
SHE... DOES ALWAYS SAY THINGS THAT SURPRISE ME...
BUT ...
...I WONDER...

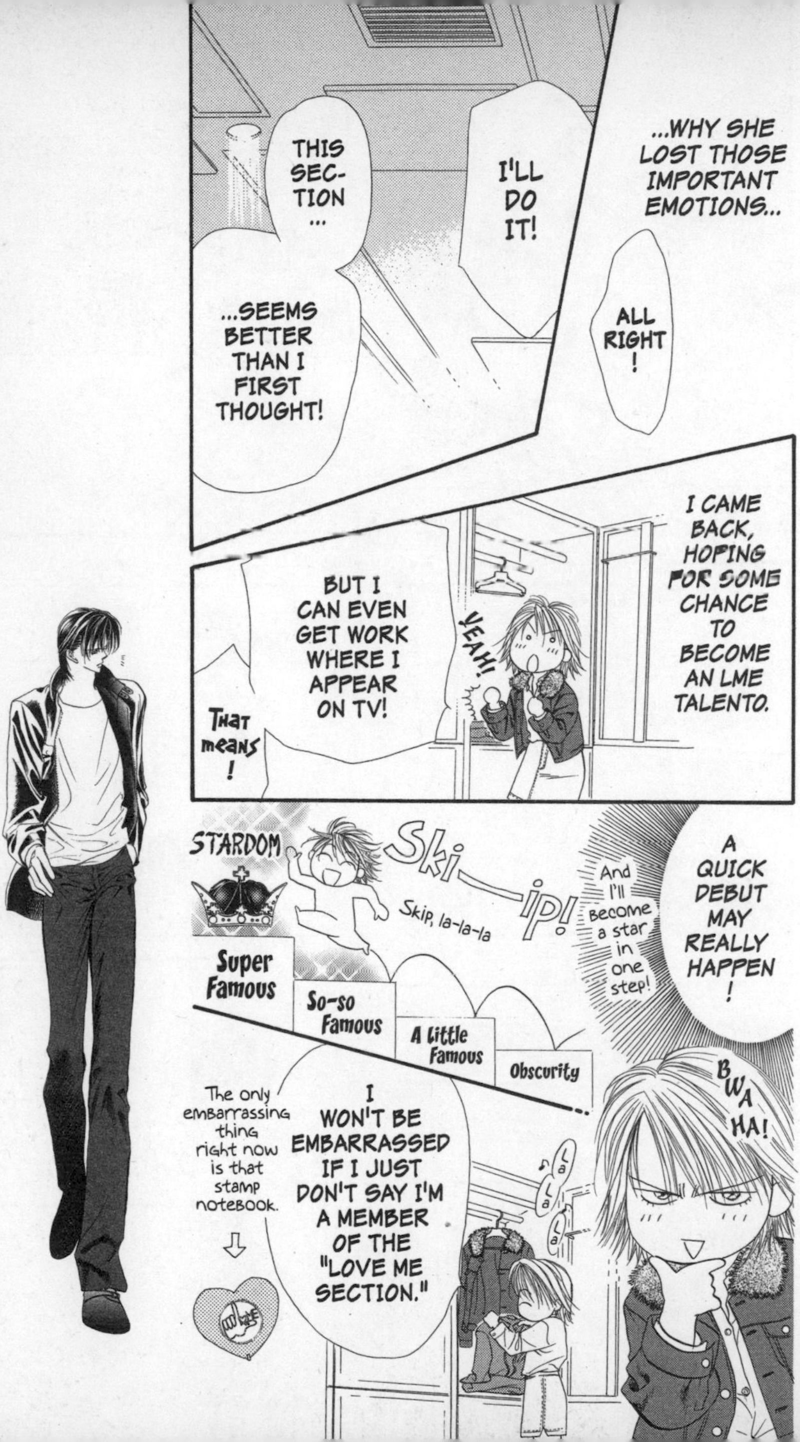
...WHY SHE LOST THOSE IMPORTANT EMOTIONS...
ALL RIGHT!
I'LL DO IT!
THIS SECTION...
...SEEMS BETTER THAN I FIRST THOUGHT!
I CAME BACK, HOPING FOR SOME CHANCE TO BECOME AN LME TALENTO.
YEAH!
BUT I CAN EVEN GET WORK WHERE I APPEAR ON TV!
That means!
A QUICK DEBUT MAY REALLY HAPPEN!
And I'll become a star in one step!
Ski—ip!
Skip, la-la-la
STARDOM
Super Famous
So-so Famous
A little Famous
Obscurity
BWAHA!
La La La
I WON'T BE EMBARRASSED IF I JUST DON'T SAY I'M A MEMBER OF THE "LOVE ME SECTION."
The only embarrassing thing right now is that stamp notebook.

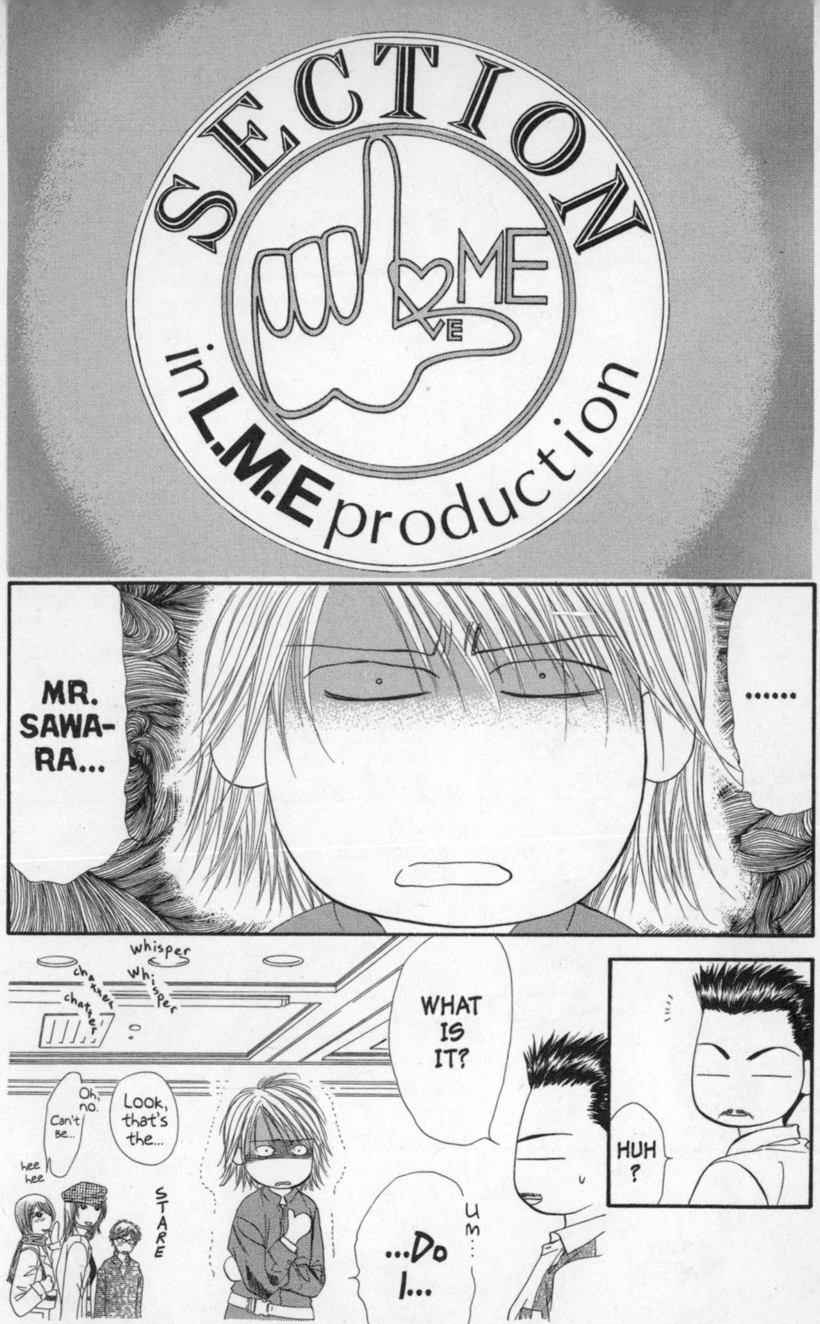
SECTION
ME
in L.M.E production
......
MR. SAWARA...
HUH?
WHAT IS IT?
Um...
...Do I...
whisper whisper
chatter chatter
STARE
Look, that's the...
Oh, no. Can't be...
hee hee

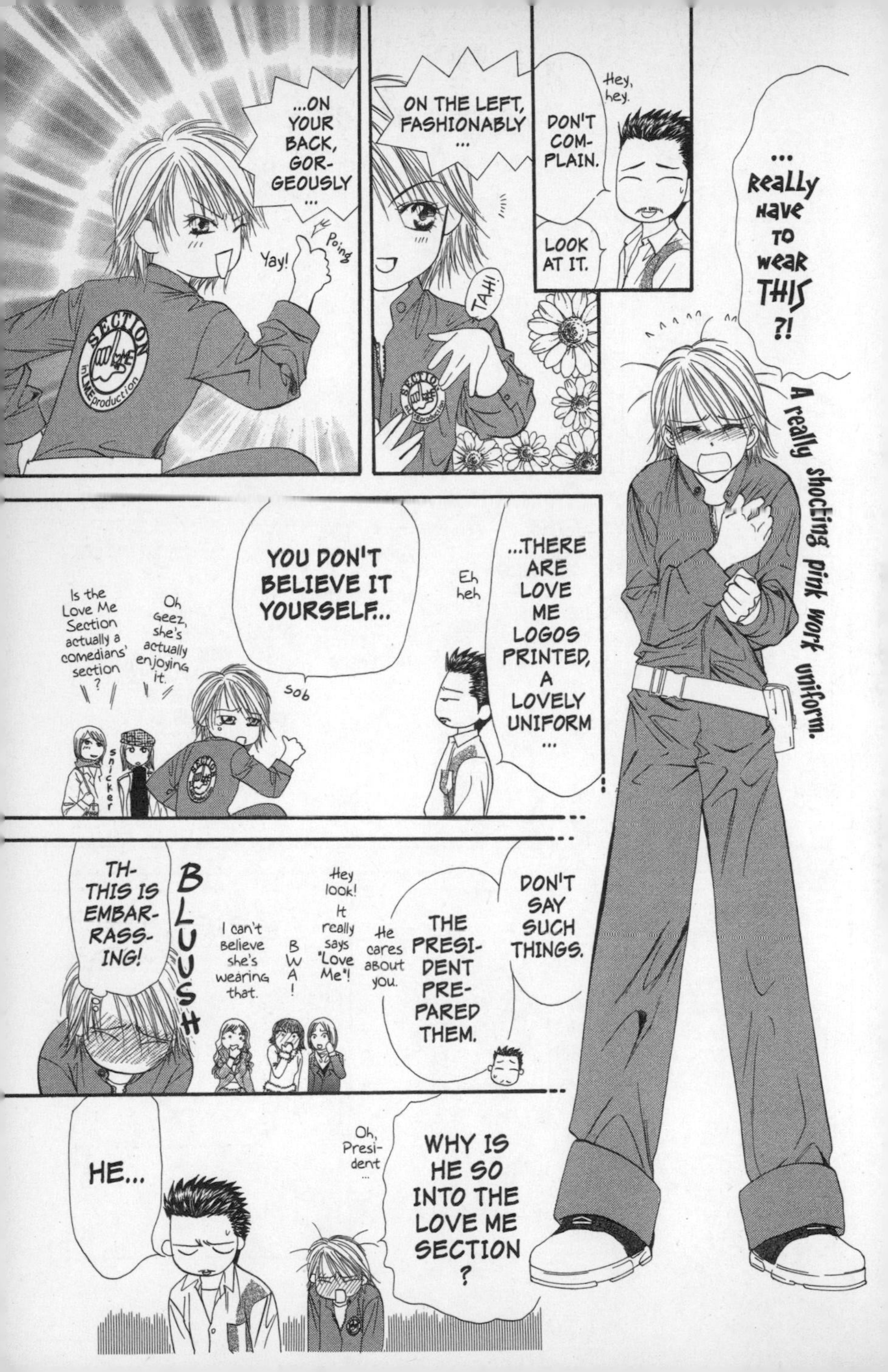

...REALLY HAVE TO WEAR THIS?!
A really shocking pink work uniform.
Hey, hey.
DON'T COMPLAIN.
LOOK AT IT.
ON THE LEFT, FASHIONABLY...
TAH!
...ON YOUR BACK, GORGEOUSLY...
Poing
Yay!
...THERE ARE LOVE ME LOGOS PRINTED, A LOVELY UNIFORM...
Eh heh
YOU DON'T BELIEVE IT YOURSELF...
sob
Oh Geez, she's actually enjoying it.
Is the Love Me Section actually a comedians' section?
snicker
DON'T SAY SUCH THINGS.
THE PRESIDENT PREPARED THEM.
He cares about you.
Hey look! It really says "Love Me"!
BWA!
I can't believe she's wearing that.
BLUUSH
TH-THIS IS EMBARRASSING!
WHY IS HE SO INTO THE LOVE ME SECTION?
Oh, President...
HE...

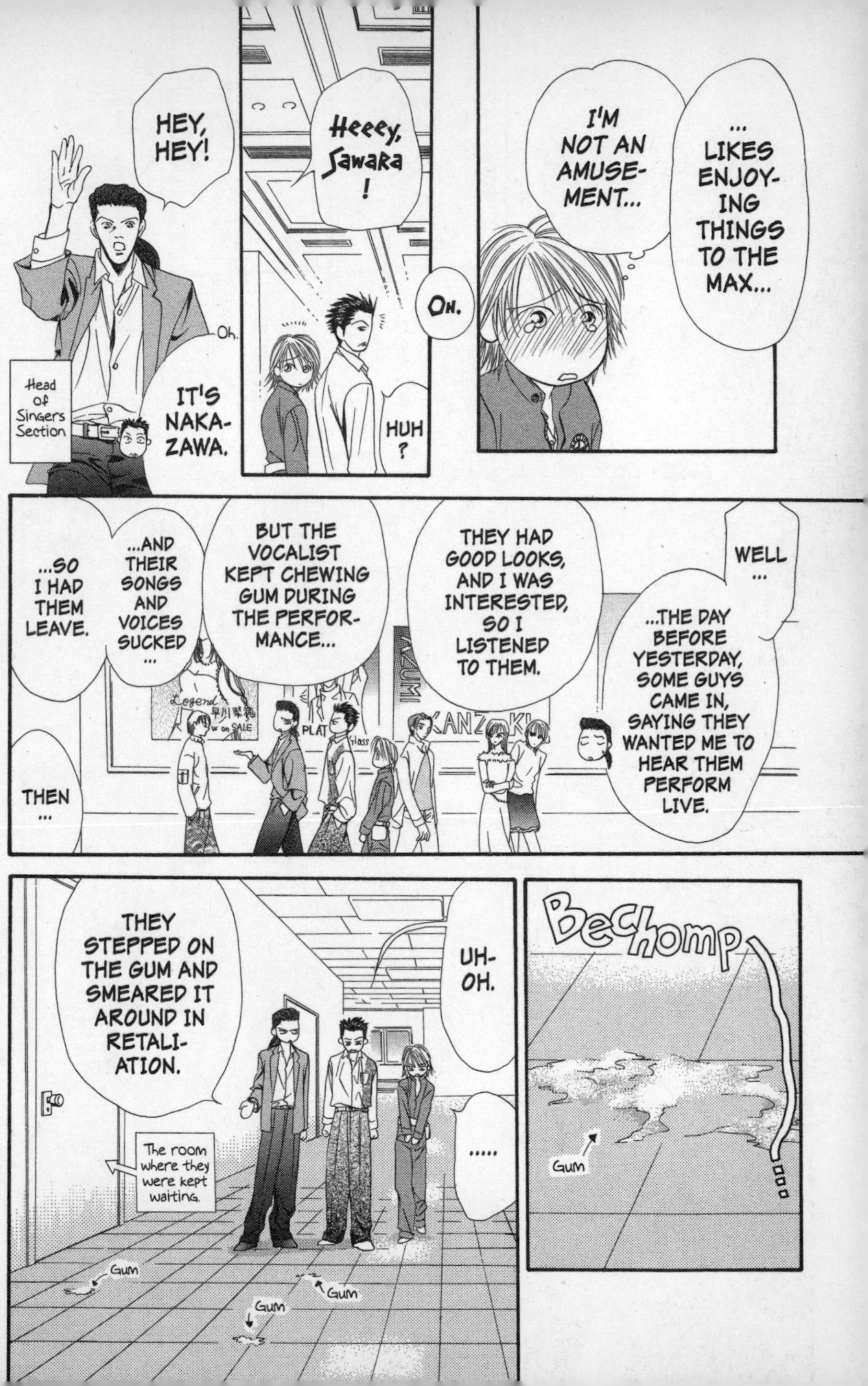
...LIKES ENJOYING THINGS TO THE MAX...
I'M NOT AN AMUSEMENT...
Heeey, Sawara!
OH.
HUH?
HEY, HEY!
Oh.
IT'S NAKAZAWA.
Head of Singers Section
WELL...
...THE DAY BEFORE YESTERDAY, SOME GUYS CAME IN, SAYING THEY WANTED ME TO HEAR THEM PERFORM LIVE.
THEY HAD GOOD LOOKS, AND I WAS INTERESTED, SO I LISTENED TO THEM.
BUT THE VOCALIST KEPT CHEWING GUM DURING THE PERFORMANCE...
...AND THEIR SONGS AND VOICES SUCKED...
...SO I HAD THEM LEAVE.
THEN...
Bechomp
Gum
UH-OH.
THEY STEPPED ON THE GUM AND SMEARED IT AROUND IN RETALIATION.
.....
The room where they were kept waiting.
Gum
Gum
Gum

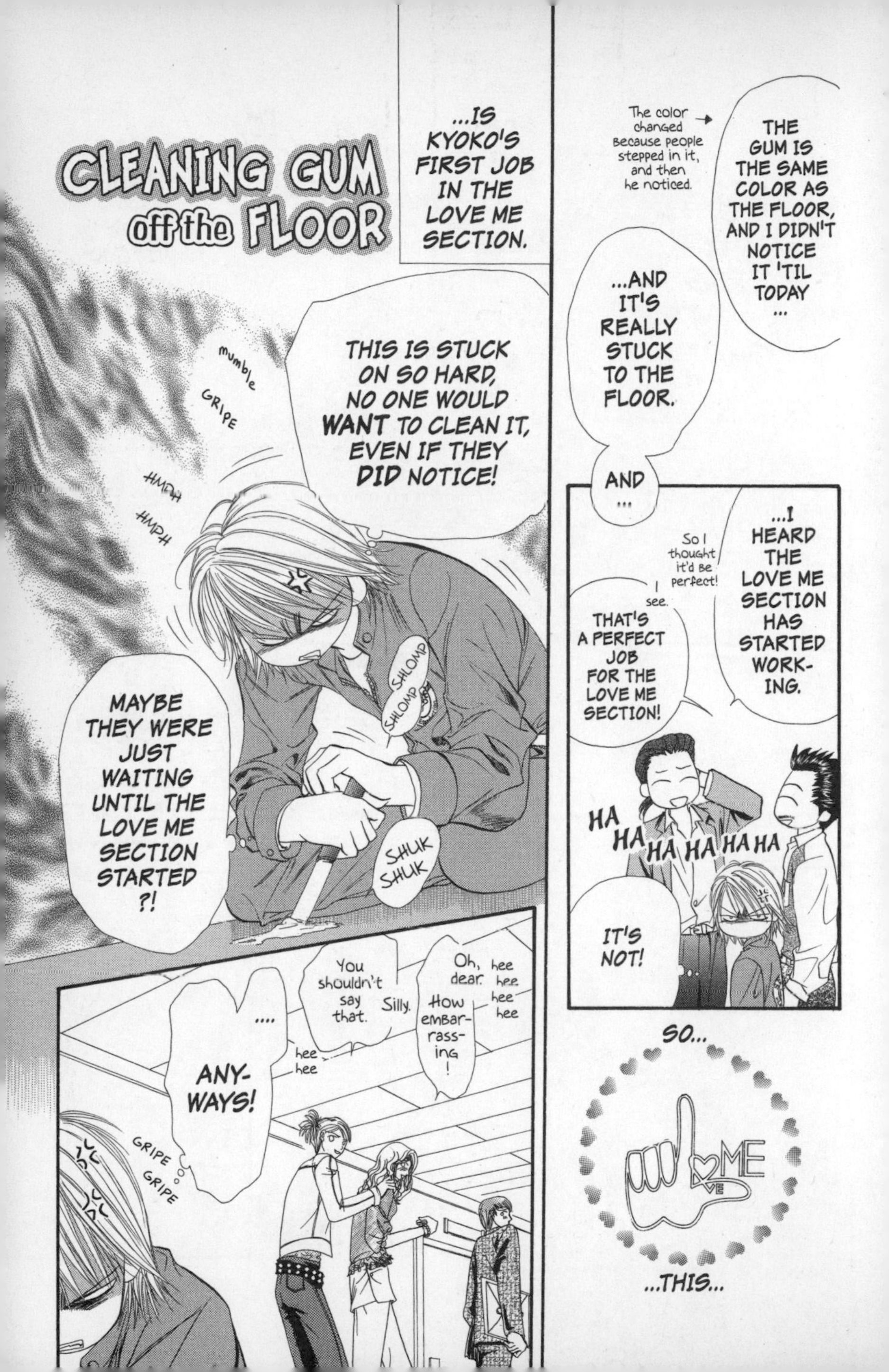
The color changed because people stepped in it, and then he noticed.
THE GUM IS THE SAME COLOR AS THE FLOOR, AND I DIDN'T NOTICE IT 'TIL TODAY...
...AND IT'S REALLY STUCK TO THE FLOOR.
AND...
...I HEARD THE LOVE ME SECTION HAS STARTED WORKING.
So I thought it'd be perfect!
I see.
THAT'S A PERFECT JOB FOR THE LOVE ME SECTION!
HA HA HA HA HA HA HA
IT'S NOT!
SO...
LOVE ME
...THIS...
...IS KYOKO'S FIRST JOB IN THE LOVE ME SECTION.
CLEANING GUM off the FLOOR
THIS IS STUCK ON SO HARD, NO ONE WOULD WANT TO CLEAN IT, EVEN IF THEY DID NOTICE!
mumble
GRIPE
HMPH
HMPH
SHLOMP
SHLOMP
SHUK
SHUK
MAYBE THEY WERE JUST WAITING UNTIL THE LOVE ME SECTION STARTED?!
Oh, dear. How embarrassing!
hee hee hee hee
You shouldn't say that.
Silly.
hee hee
....
ANY-WAYS!
GRIPE
GRIPE

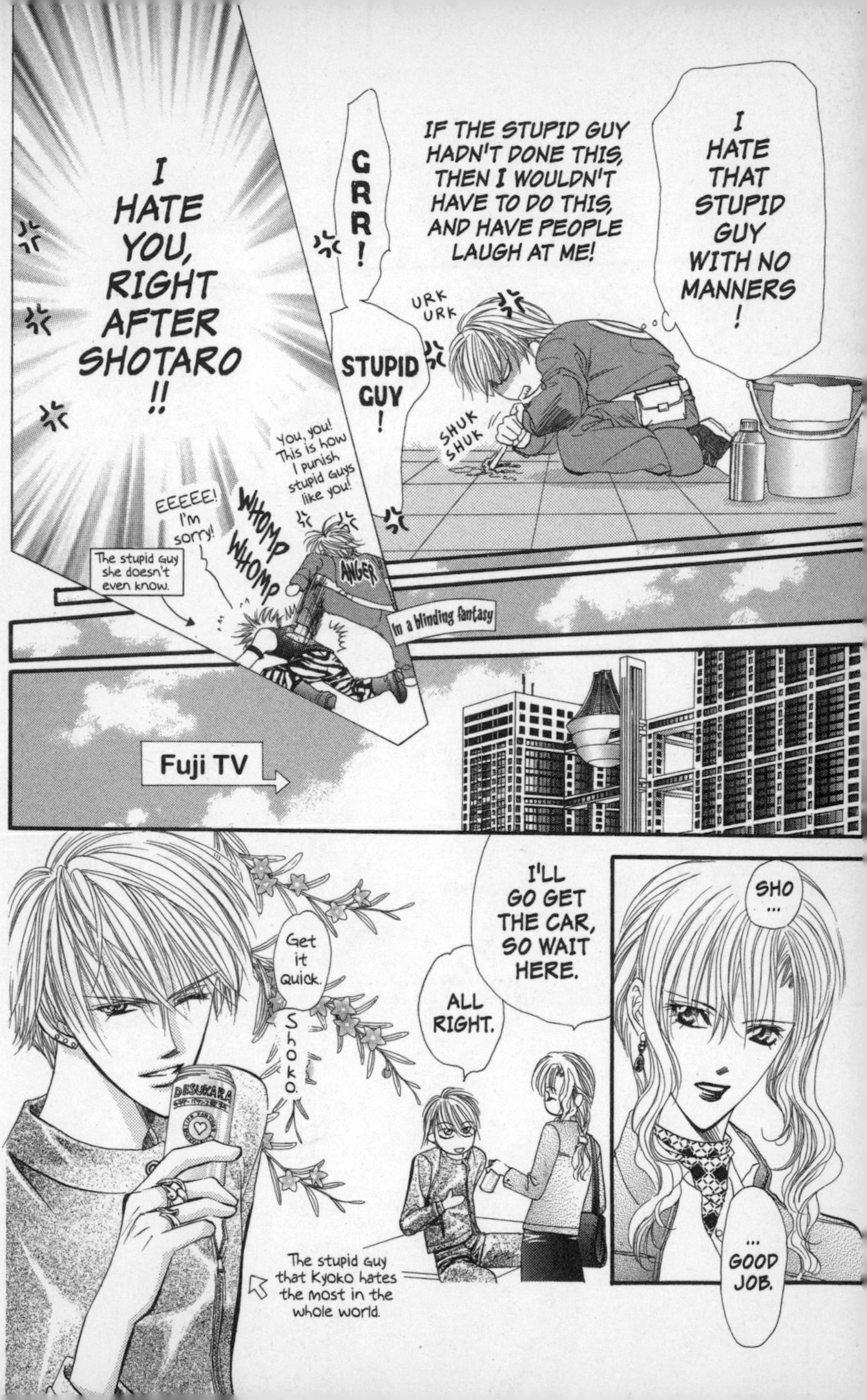
I HATE THAT STUPID GUY WITH NO MANNERS!
IF THE STUPID GUY HADN'T DONE THIS, THEN I WOULDN'T HAVE TO DO THIS, AND HAVE PEOPLE LAUGH AT ME!
GRR!
URK URK
STUPID GUY!
SHUK SHUK
I HATE YOU, RIGHT AFTER SHOTARO!!
You, you! This is how I punish stupid guys like you!
WHOMP WHOMP WHOMP
ANGER
EEEEE! I'm sorry!
The stupid guy she doesn't even know.
In a blinding fantasy
Fuji TV
SHO...
...GOOD JOB.
I'LL GO GET THE CAR, SO WAIT HERE.
ALL RIGHT.
Get it quick.
Shoko.
DESUKARA
The stupid guy that Kyoko hates the most in the whole world.

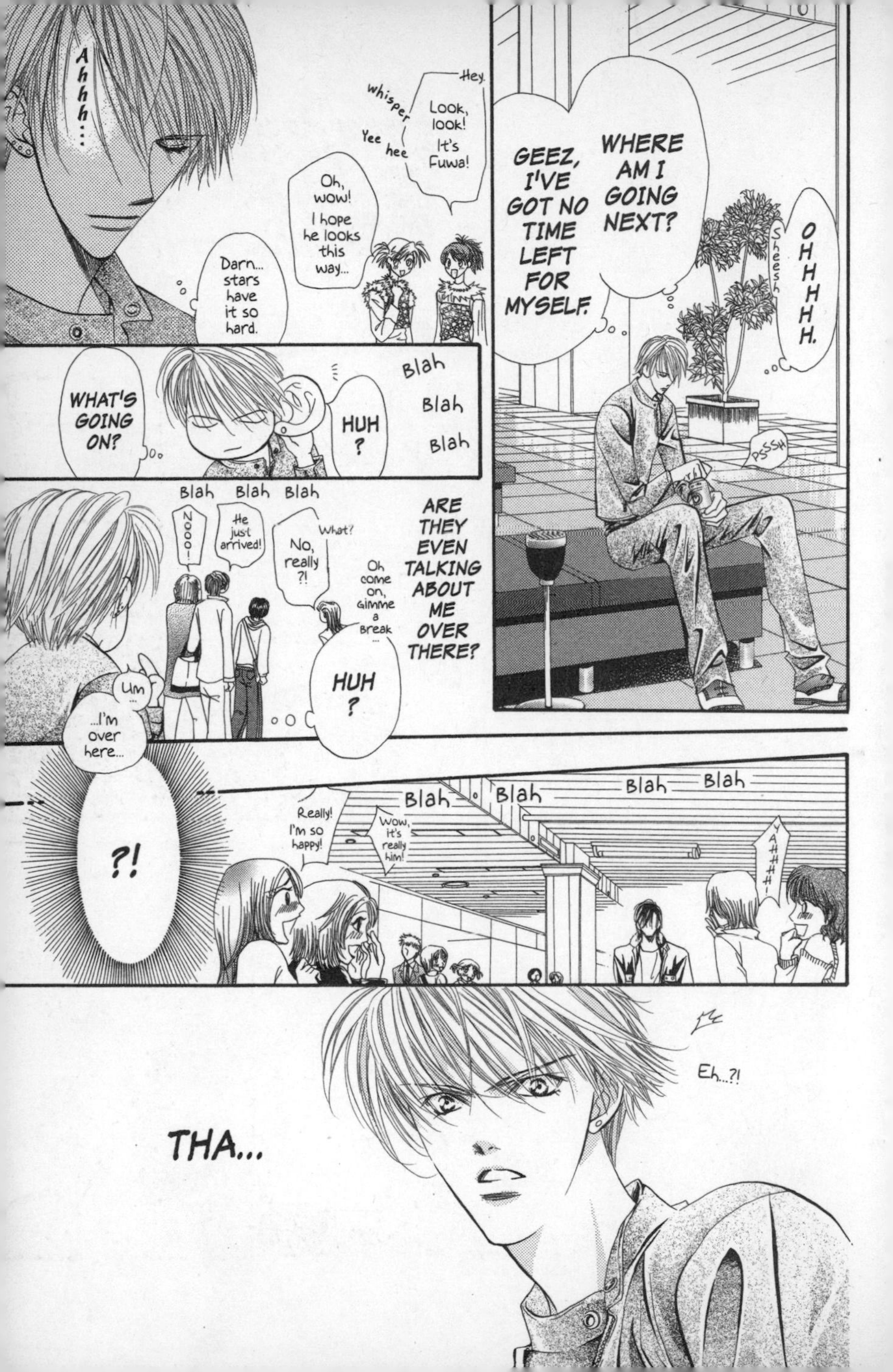
OHHHHH.
Sheesh
WHERE AM I GOING NEXT?
GEEZ, I'VE GOT NO TIME LEFT FOR MYSELF.
PSSSH
Hey.
Look, look! It's Fuwa!
whisper
Yee hee
Oh, wow! I hope he looks this way...
Darn... stars have it so hard.
Ahhh...
Blah
Blah
Blah
HUH ?
WHAT'S GOING ON?
ARE THEY EVEN TALKING ABOUT ME OVER THERE?
What?
No, really ?!
Oh come on, Gimme a Break ...
He just arrived!
Noooo!
Blah Blah Blah
HUH ?
Um ...
...I'm over here...
Blah Blah
Blah Blah
YAHHHH!
Wow, it's really him!
Really! I'm so happy!
?!
Eh...?!
THA...

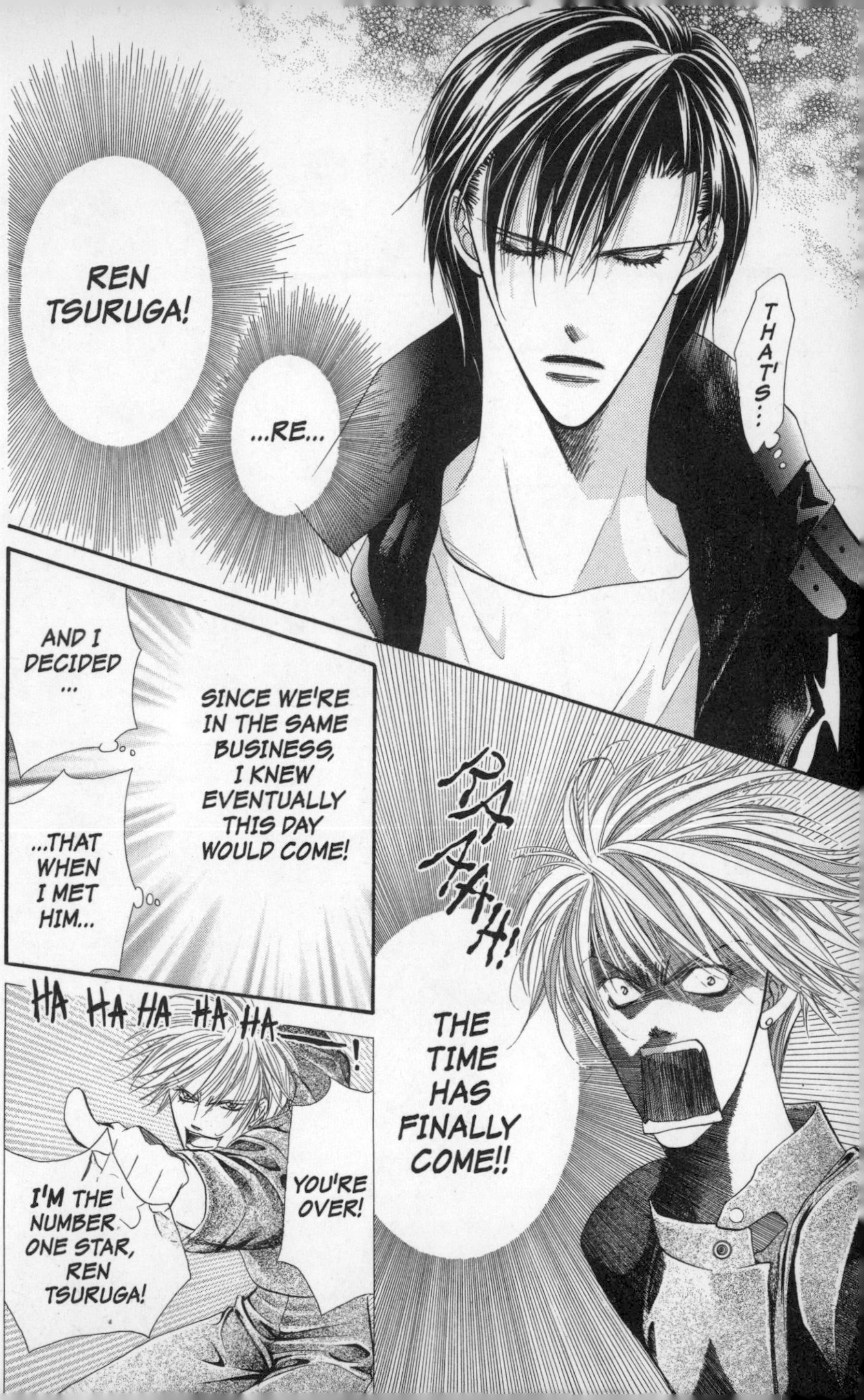

THAT'S...
...RE...
REN TSURUGA!
RAAAHH!
THE TIME HAS FINALLY COME!!
SINCE WE'RE IN THE SAME BUSINESS, I KNEW EVENTUALLY THIS DAY WOULD COME!
AND I DECIDED ...
...THAT WHEN I MET HIM...
HA HA HA HA HA—!
YOU'RE OVER!
I'M THE NUMBER ONE STAR, REN TSURUGA!

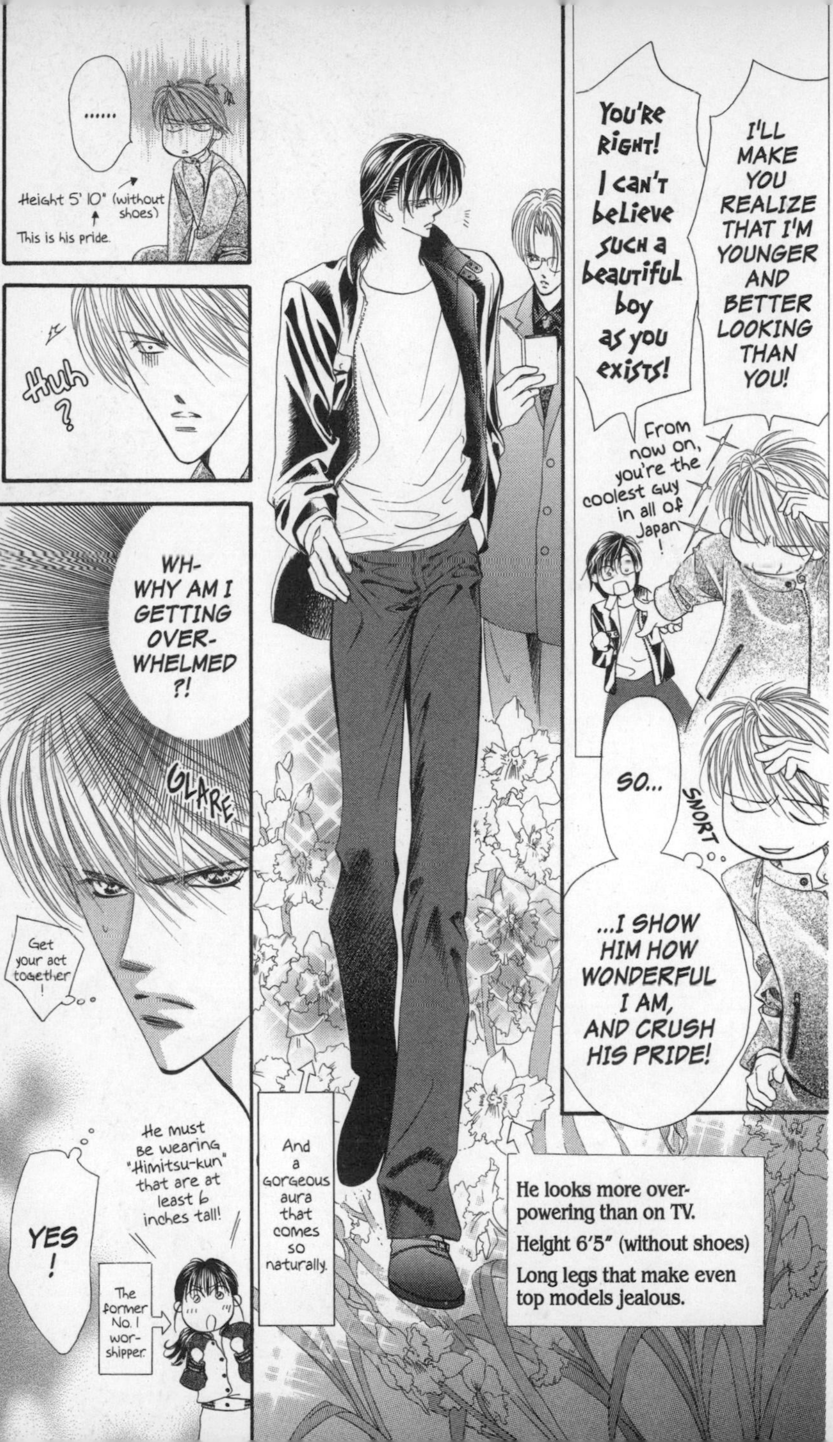

I'LL MAKE YOU REALIZE THAT I'M YOUNGER AND BETTER LOOKING THAN YOU!
YOU'RE RIGHT! I can't believe such a beautiful boy as you exists!
From now on, you're the coolest guy in all of Japan!
SO...
SNORT
...I SHOW HIM HOW WONDERFUL I AM, AND CRUSH HIS PRIDE!
He looks more over-powering than on TV.
Height 6'5" (without shoes)
Long legs that make even top models jealous.
And a gorgeous aura that comes so naturally.
......
Height 5' 10" (without shoes)
This is his pride.
Huh?
WH- WHY AM I GETTING OVER-WHELMED?!
GLARE
Get your act together!
He must be wearing "Himitsu-kun" that are at least 6 inches tall!
YES!
The former No. 1 wor-shipper.

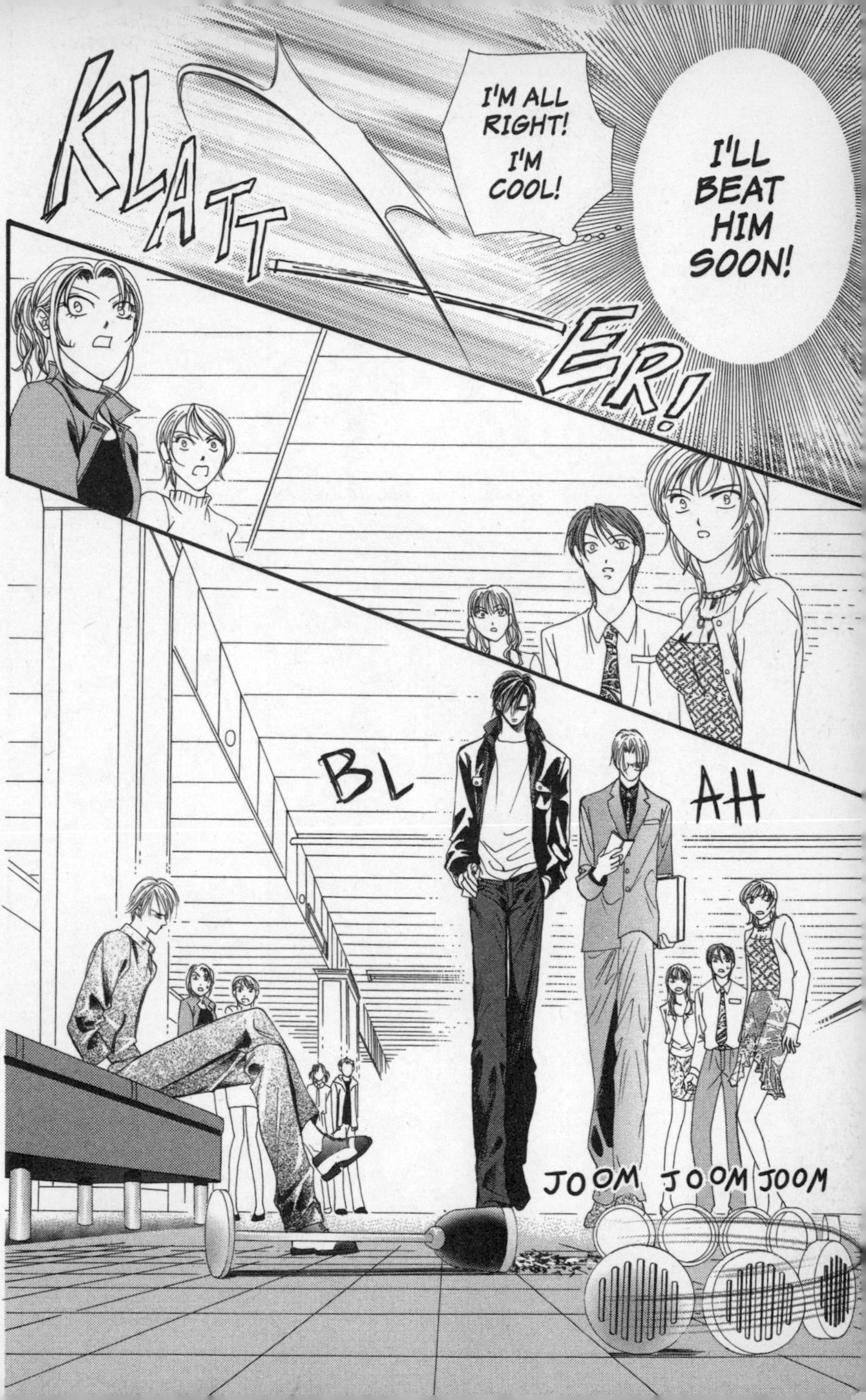
I'LL BEAT HIM SOON!
I'M ALL RIGHT! I'M COOL!
KLATT—ER!
BL AH
JOOM JOOM JOOM

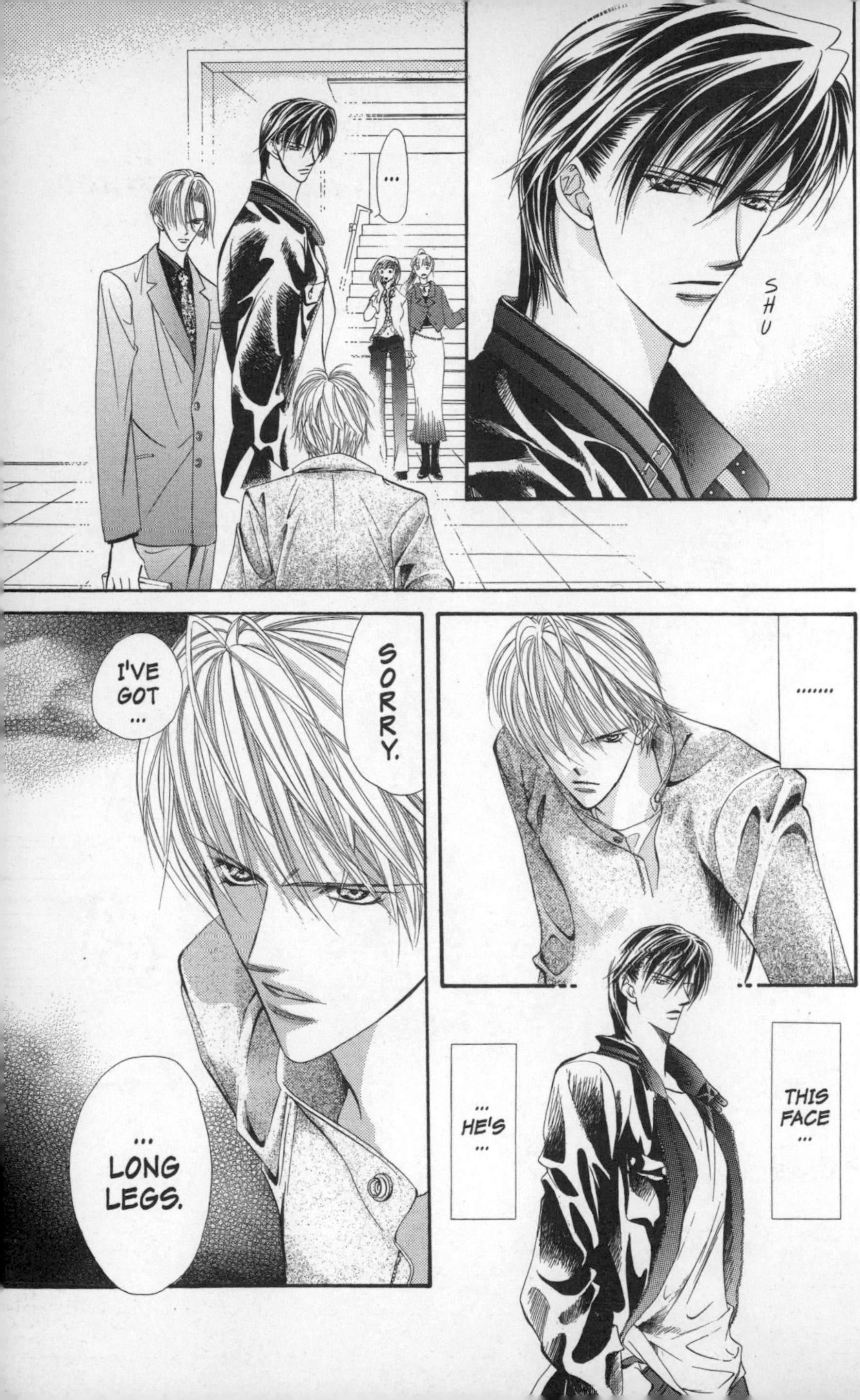
SHU
...
....
THIS FACE ...
... HE'S ...
SORRY.
I'VE GOT ...
... LONG LEGS.

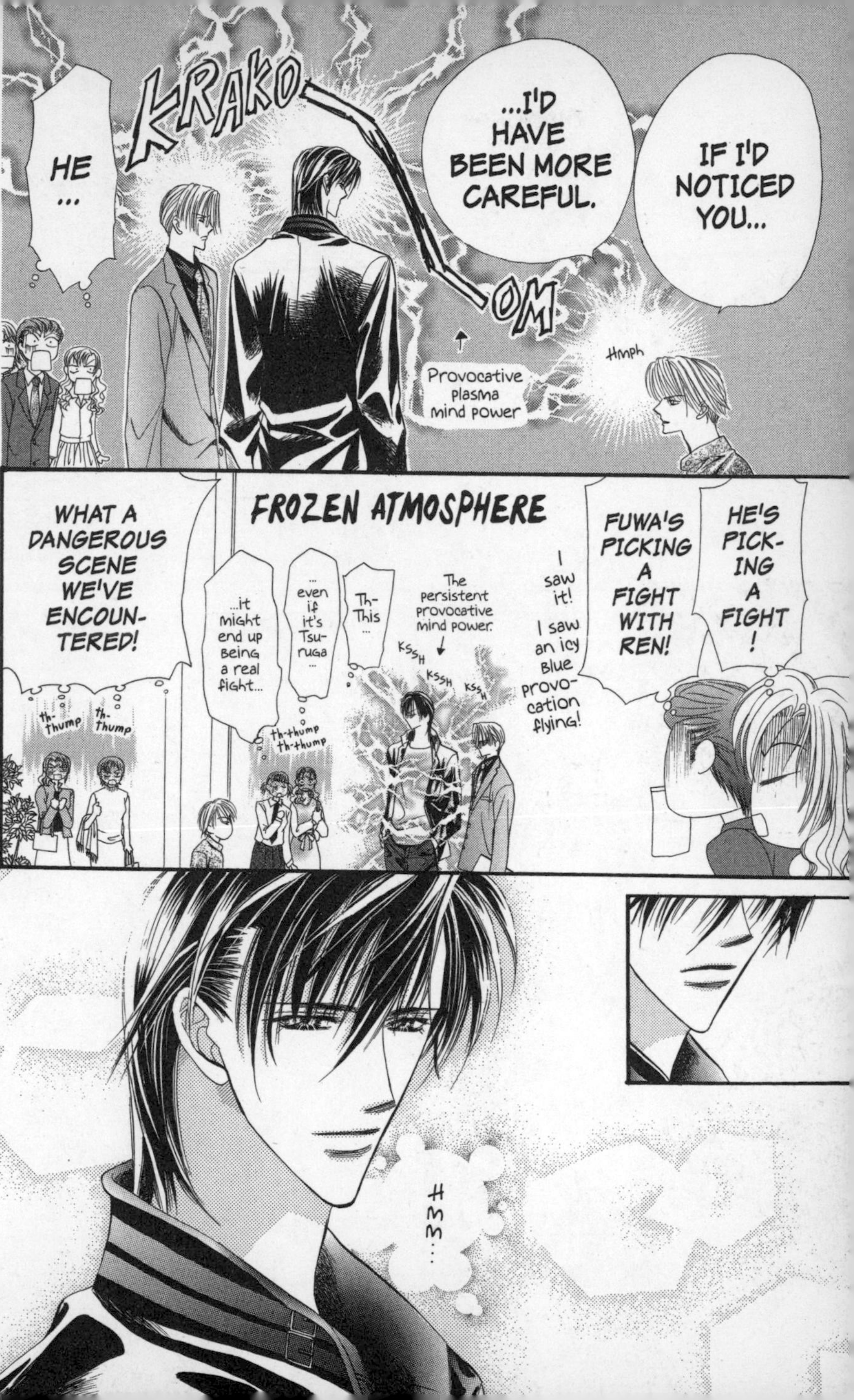
IF I'D NOTICED YOU...
...I'D HAVE BEEN MORE CAREFUL.
KRAKO-OM
Hmph
Provocative plasma mind power
HE ...
HE'S PICKING A FIGHT!
FUWA'S PICKING A FIGHT WITH REN!
I saw it! I saw an icy Blue provocation flying!
The persistent provocative mind power.
KSSH KSSH KSSH
FROZEN ATMOSPHERE
Th-This ...
... even if it's Tsuruga ...
...it might end up being a real fight...
th-thump th-thump
WHAT A DANGEROUS SCENE WE'VE ENCOUNTERED!
th-thump th-thump
HMM...

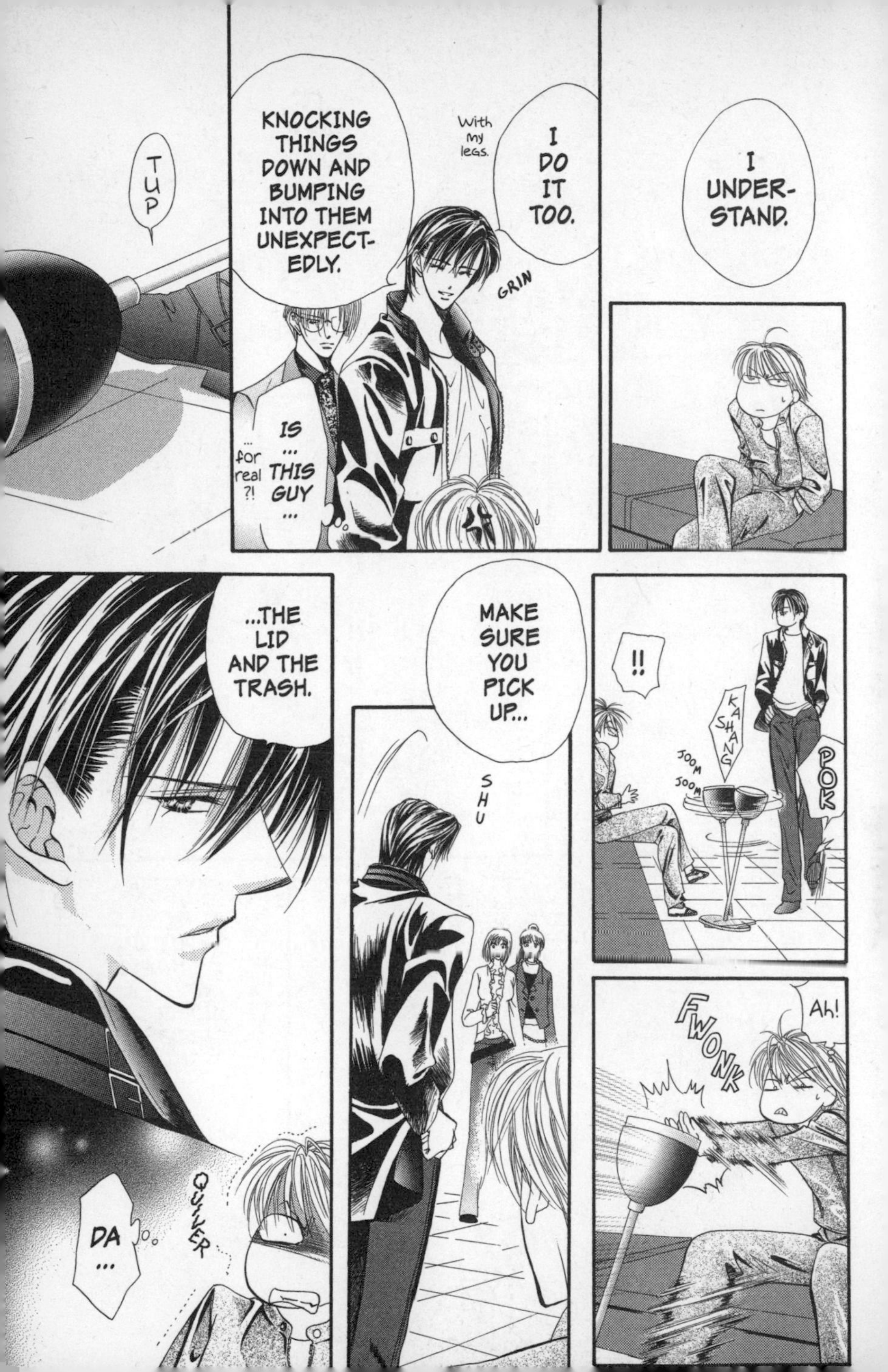
I UNDERSTAND.
KNOCKING THINGS DOWN AND BUMPING INTO THEM UNEXPECTEDLY.
I DO IT TOO.
With my legs.
GRIN
IS ... THIS GUY ...
... for real ?!
TUP
!!
KASHANG
JOOM JOOM
POK
FWONK
Ah!
MAKE SURE YOU PICK UP...
SHU
...THE LID AND THE TRASH.
QUIVER
DA ...

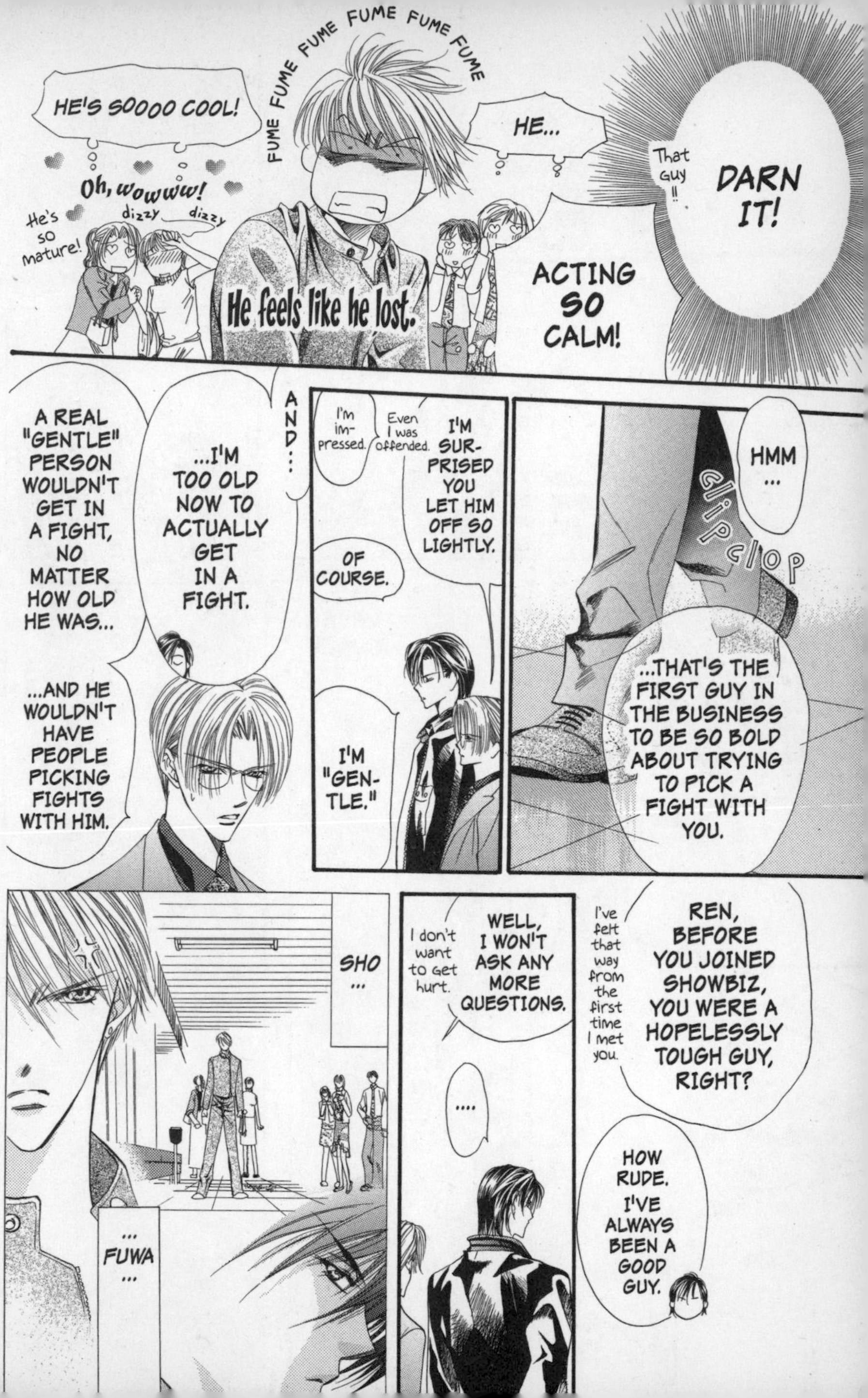

DARN IT!
That Guy !!
ACTING SO CALM!
HE...
FUME FUME FUME FUME FUME FUME
HE'S SOOOO COOL!
Oh, wowww!
He's so mature!
dizzy dizzy
He feels like he lost.
HMM ...
clip clop
...THAT'S THE FIRST GUY IN THE BUSINESS TO BE SO BOLD ABOUT TRYING TO PICK A FIGHT WITH YOU.
I'M SUR-PRISED YOU LET HIM OFF SO LIGHTLY.
Even I was offended.
I'm im-pressed.
OF COURSE.
I'M "GEN-TLE."
AND...
...I'M TOO OLD NOW TO ACTUALLY GET IN A FIGHT.
A REAL "GENTLE" PERSON WOULDN'T GET IN A FIGHT, NO MATTER HOW OLD HE WAS...
...AND HE WOULDN'T HAVE PEOPLE PICKING FIGHTS WITH HIM.
REN, BEFORE YOU JOINED SHOWBIZ, YOU WERE A HOPELESSLY TOUGH GUY, RIGHT?
I've felt that way from the first time I met you.
HOW RUDE. I'VE ALWAYS BEEN A GOOD GUY.
WELL, I WON'T ASK ANY MORE QUESTIONS.
I don't want to get hurt.
....
SHO ...
... FUWA ...

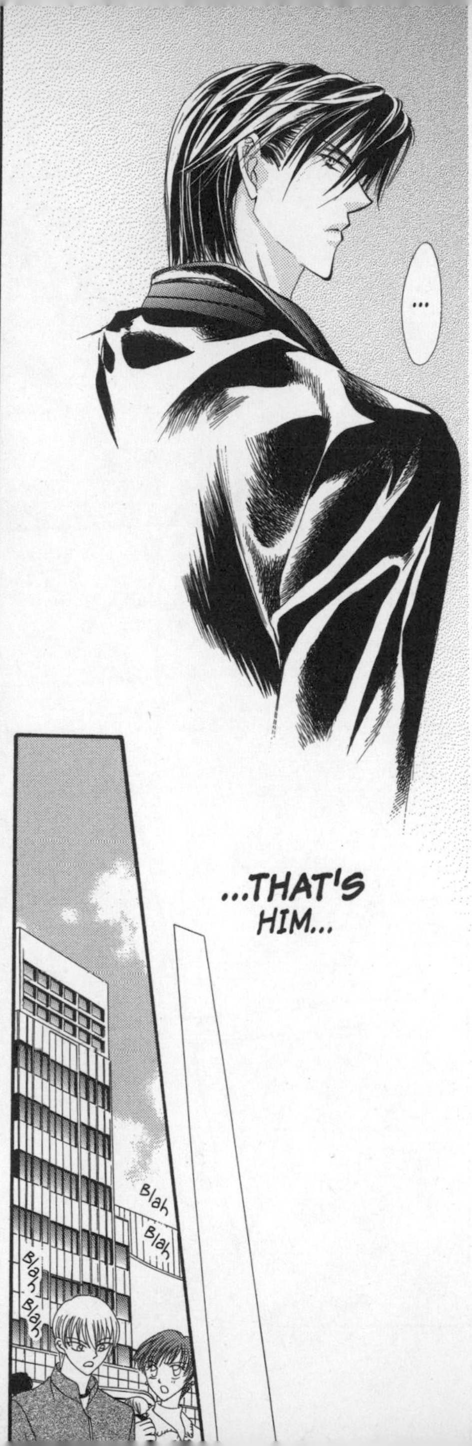
...
...THAT'S HIM...
Blah Blah
Blah Blah
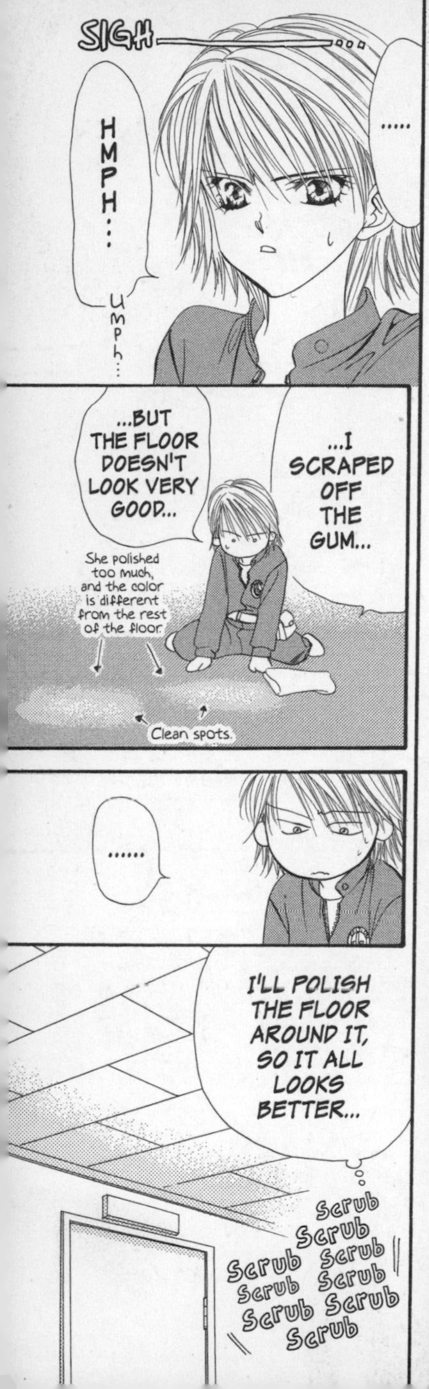
SIGH
.....
HMPH...
Umph...
...I SCRAPED OFF THE GUM...
...BUT THE FLOOR DOESN'T LOOK VERY GOOD...
She polished too much, and the color is different from the rest of the floor.
Clean spots.
......
I'LL POLISH THE FLOOR AROUND IT, SO IT ALL LOOKS BETTER...
Scrub Scrub Scrub Scrub Scrub Scrub Scrub Scrub Scrub

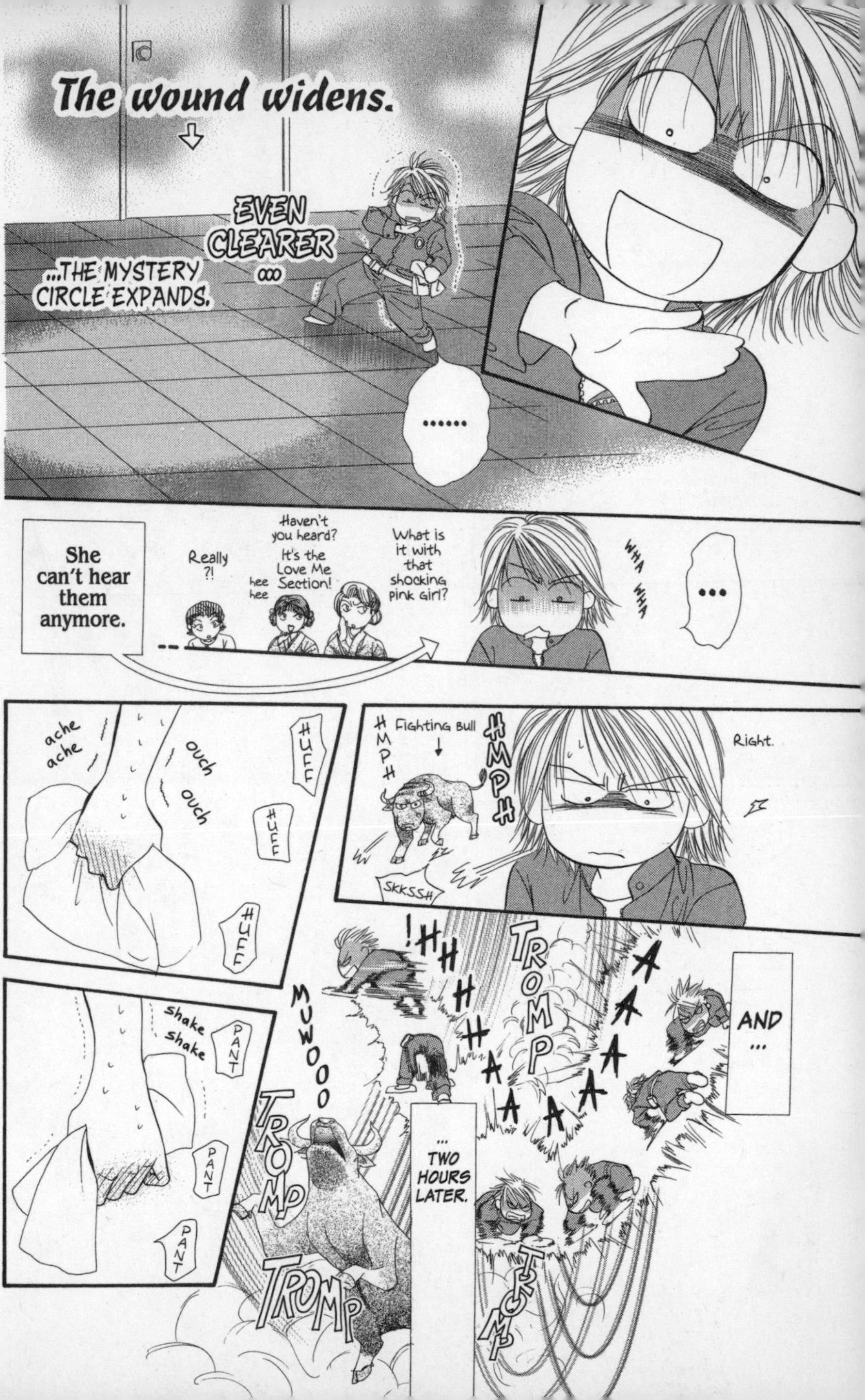

The wound widens.
EVEN CLEARER
ooo
...THE MYSTERY CIRCLE EXPANDS.
......
...
WHA WHA
What is it with that shocking pink girl?
Haven't you heard? It's the Love Me Section!
hee hee
Really ?!
She can't hear them anymore.
Right.
HMPH
Fighting Bull
HMPH
SKKSSH
HUFF
HUFF
HUFF
ouch ouch
ache ache
AND ...
AAAAAAA
TROMP
HHHHH!
... TWO HOURS LATER.
MUWOOOO
TROMP
TROMP
TROMP
shake shake
PANT
PANT
PANT

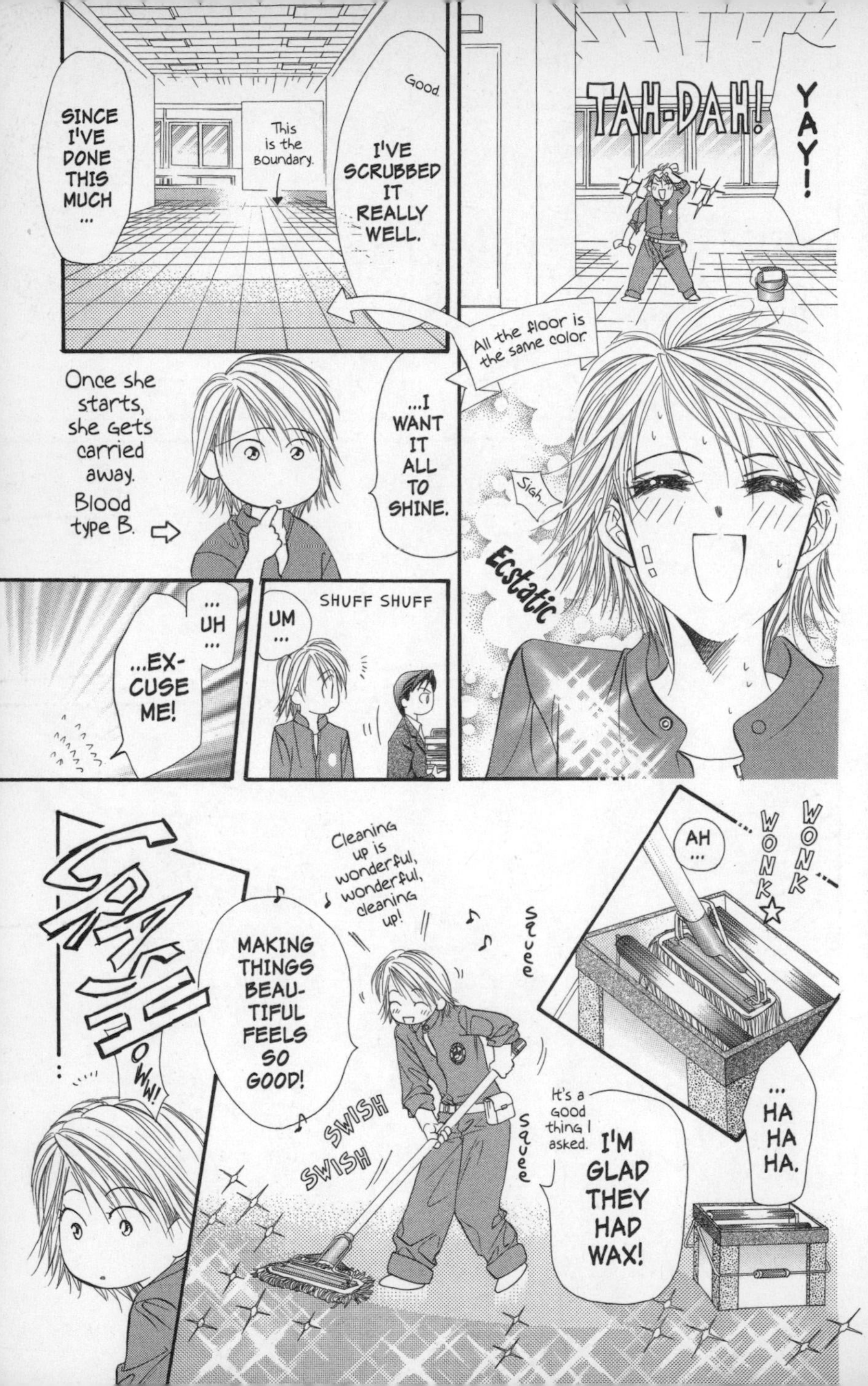
TAH-DAH!
YAY!
Good.
I'VE SCRUBBED IT REALLY WELL.
This is the boundary.
SINCE I'VE DONE THIS MUCH...
All the floor is the same color.
Sigh...
Ecstatic
...I WANT IT ALL TO SHINE.
Once she starts, she gets carried away. Blood type B.
SHUFF SHUFF
UM...
...UH...
...EX-CUSE ME!
WONK WONK☆
AH...
...HA HA HA.
It's a good thing I asked.
I'M GLAD THEY HAD WAX!
Squee
Squee
Cleaning up is wonderful, wonderful, cleaning up!
MAKING THINGS BEAU-TIFUL FEELS SO GOOD!
SWISH
SWISH
CRASH
OWW!

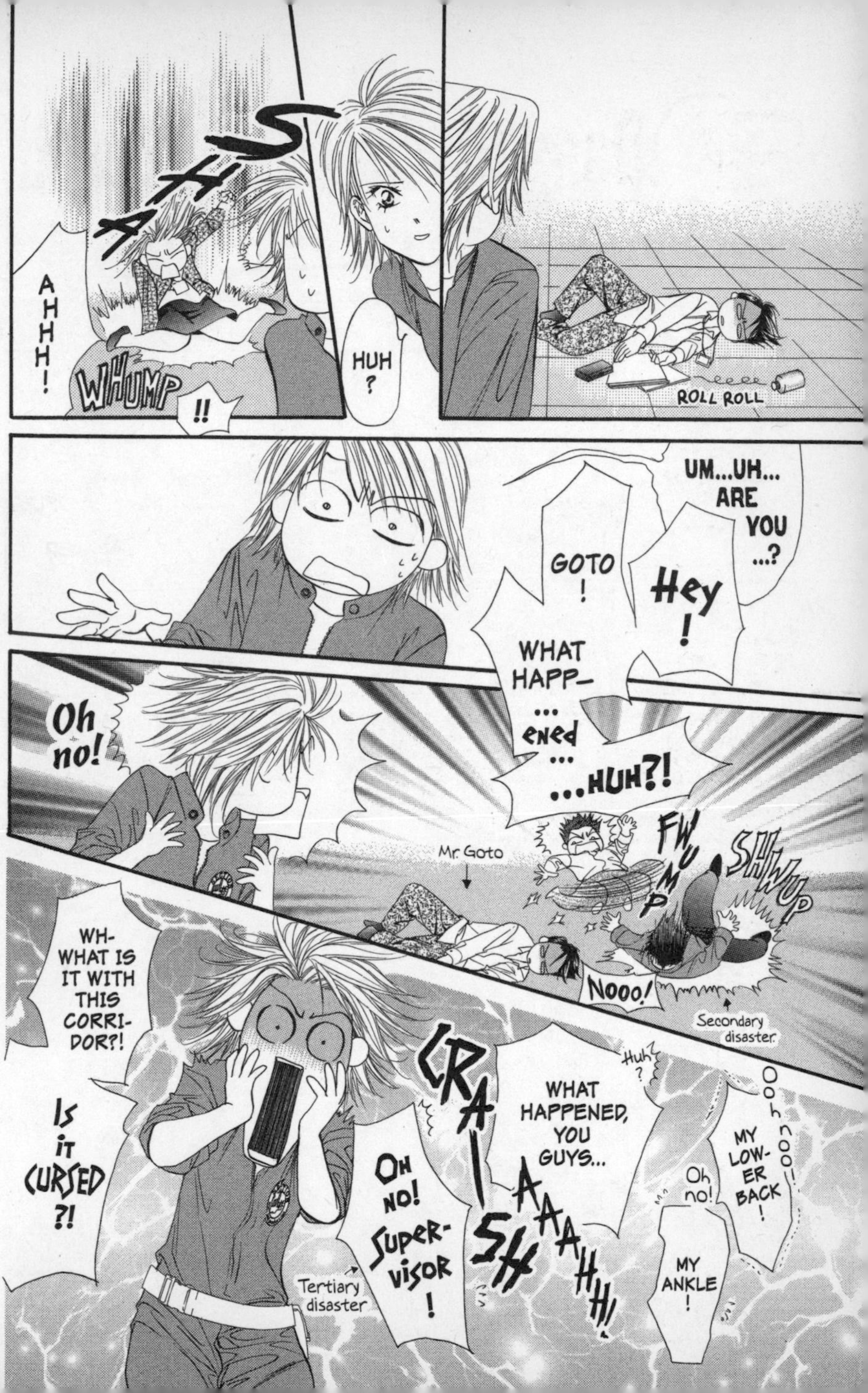
ROLL ROLL
HUH?
SHA
AHHH!
WHUMP
!!
UM...UH... ARE YOU ...?
Hey!
GOTO!
WHAT HAPP- ...ened...
...HUH?!
SHWUP
FWUMP
Oh no!
Mr. Goto
Nooo!
Secondary disaster.
Ooh nooo!
MY LOWER BACK!
Huh?
Oh no!
MY ANKLE!
WHAT HAPPENED, YOU GUYS...
CRAASH
AAAHH!
OH NO! SUPERVISOR!
Tertiary disaster
WH-WHAT IS IT WITH THIS CORRIDOR?!
Is it CURSED?!

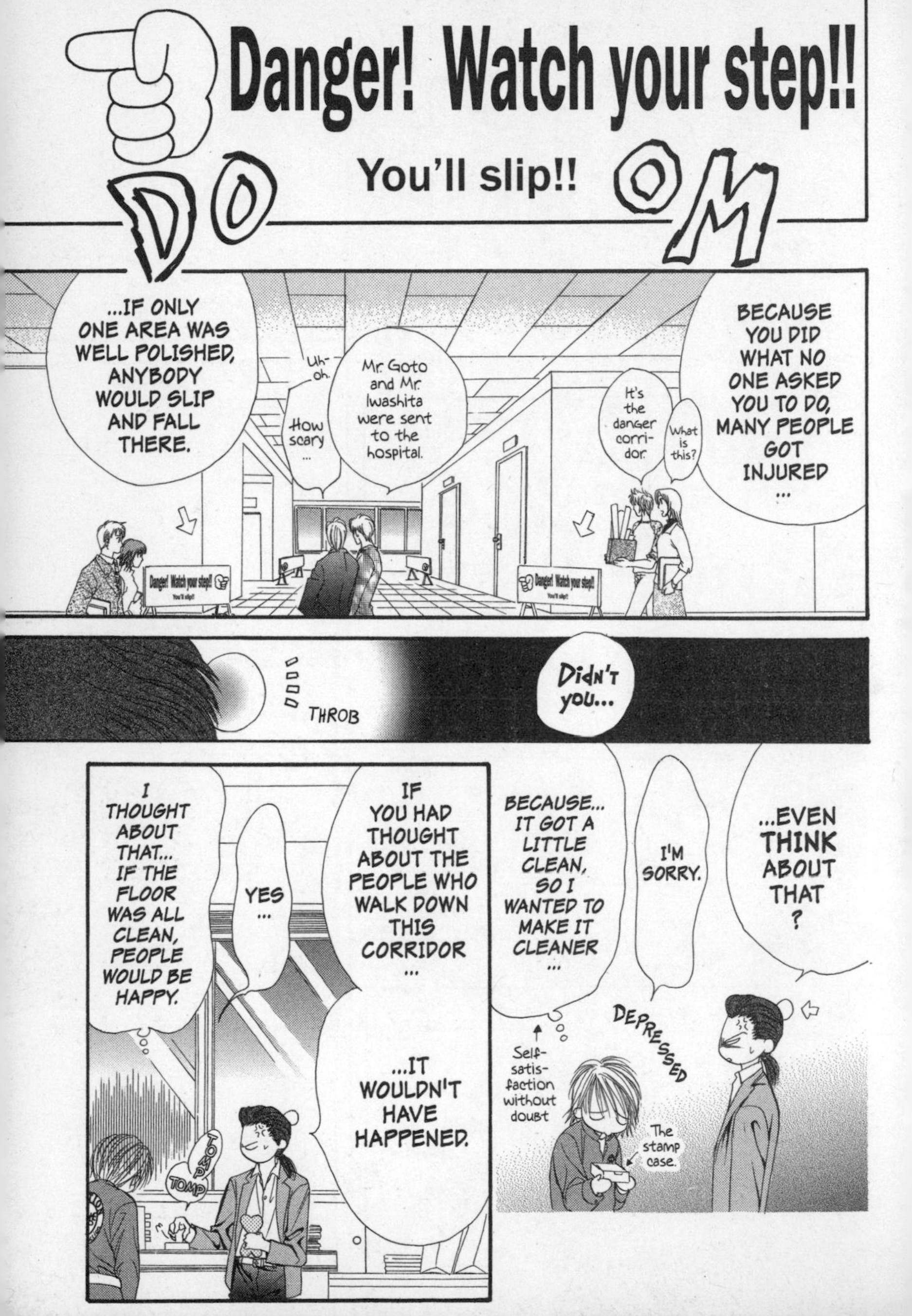
Danger! Watch your step!!
You'll slip!!
DOOM
BECAUSE YOU DID WHAT NO ONE ASKED YOU TO DO, MANY PEOPLE GOT INJURED ...
What is this?
It's the danger corridor.
Danger! Watch your step!! You'll slip!!
Mr. Goto and Mr. Iwashita were sent to the hospital.
Uh-oh.
How scary ...
...IF ONLY ONE AREA WAS WELL POLISHED, ANYBODY WOULD SLIP AND FALL THERE.
Danger! Watch your step!! You'll slip!!
Didn't you...
THROB
...EVEN THINK ABOUT THAT ?
I'M SORRY.
BECAUSE... IT GOT A LITTLE CLEAN, SO I WANTED TO MAKE IT CLEANER ...
DEPRESSED
Self-satisfaction without doubt
The stamp case.
IF YOU HAD THOUGHT ABOUT THE PEOPLE WHO WALK DOWN THIS CORRIDOR ...
YES ...
I THOUGHT ABOUT THAT... IF THE FLOOR WAS ALL CLEAN, PEOPLE WOULD BE HAPPY.
...IT WOULDN'T HAVE HAPPENED.
TOMP TOMP

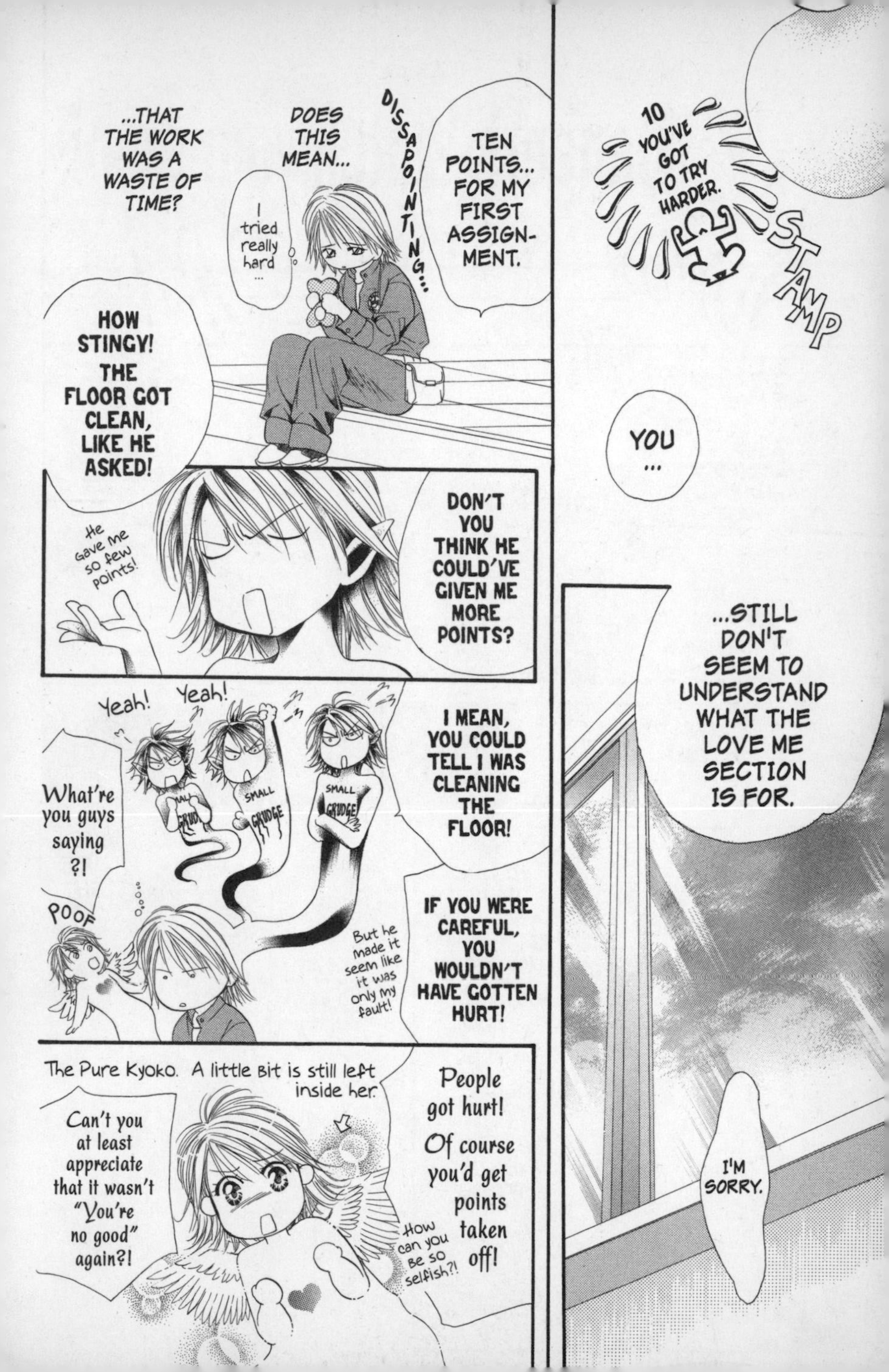
10 YOU'VE GOT TO TRY HARDER.
STAMP
YOU ...
...STILL DON'T SEEM TO UNDERSTAND WHAT THE LOVE ME SECTION IS FOR.
I'M SORRY.
TEN POINTS... FOR MY FIRST ASSIGNMENT.
DISSAPOINTING...
I tried really hard ...
DOES THIS MEAN...
...THAT THE WORK WAS A WASTE OF TIME?
HOW STINGY! THE FLOOR GOT CLEAN, LIKE HE ASKED!
DON'T YOU THINK HE COULD'VE GIVEN ME MORE POINTS?
He gave me so few points!
I MEAN, YOU COULD TELL I WAS CLEANING THE FLOOR!
Yeah!
Yeah!
SMALL GRUDGE
SMALL GRUDGE
What're you guys saying ?!
IF YOU WERE CAREFUL, YOU WOULDN'T HAVE GOTTEN HURT!
But he made it seem like it was only my fault!
POOF
People got hurt! Of course you'd get points taken off!
How can you be so selfish?!
The Pure Kyoko. A little bit is still left inside her.
Can't you at least appreciate that it wasn't "You're no good" again?!

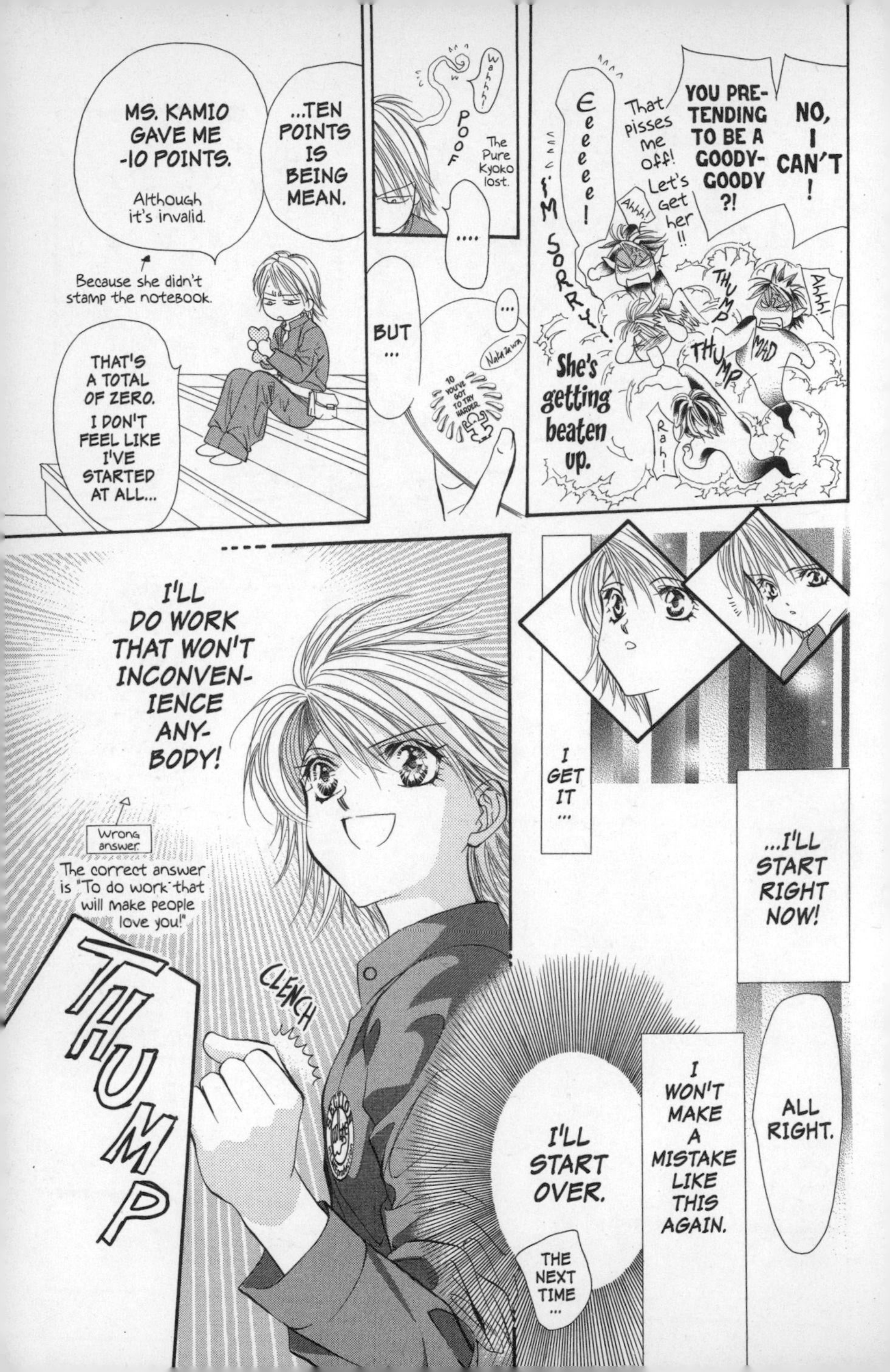
NO, I CAN'T!
YOU PRETENDING TO BE A GOODY-GOODY?!
That pisses me off! Let's get her!!
Eeeeee!
I'M SORRY!
Ahhh!
THUMP
Ahhh!
MAD
THUMP
Rah!
She's getting beaten up.
Wahhh!
POOF
The Pure Kyoko lost.
....
...
BUT ...
10 YOU'VE GOT TO TRY HARDER.
...TEN POINTS IS BEING MEAN.
MS. KAMIO GAVE ME -10 POINTS.
Although it's invalid.
Because she didn't stamp the notebook.
THAT'S A TOTAL OF ZERO.
I DON'T FEEL LIKE I'VE STARTED AT ALL...
I GET IT ...
...I'LL START RIGHT NOW!
ALL RIGHT.
I WON'T MAKE A MISTAKE LIKE THIS AGAIN.
I'LL START OVER.
THE NEXT TIME ...
I'LL DO WORK THAT WON'T INCONVENIENCE ANYBODY!
Wrong answer.
The correct answer is "To do work that will make people love you!"
CLENCH
THUMP

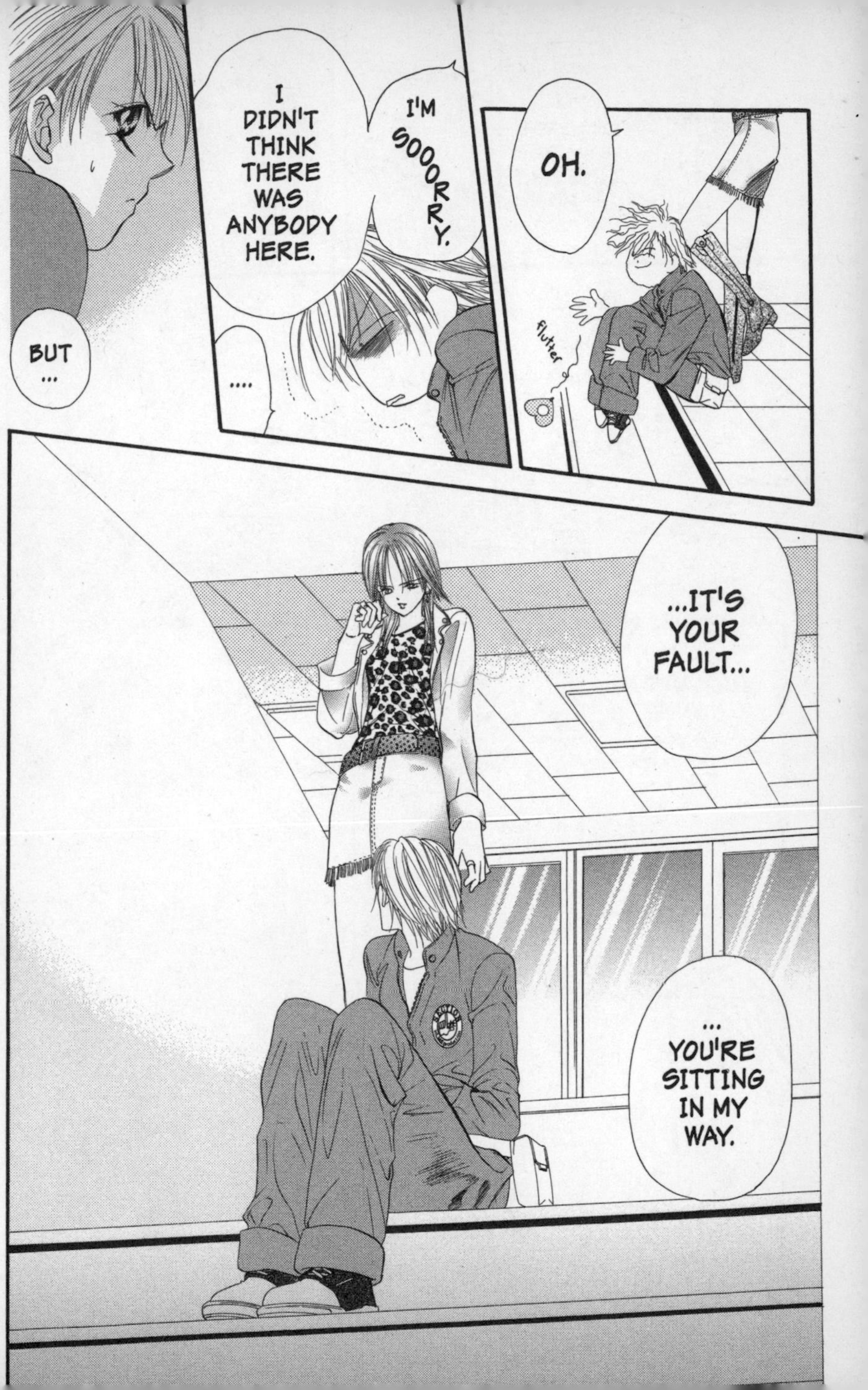
OH.
flutter
I'M SOOORRY.
I DIDN'T THINK THERE WAS ANYBODY HERE.
....
BUT ...
...IT'S YOUR FAULT...
... YOU'RE SITTING IN MY WAY.

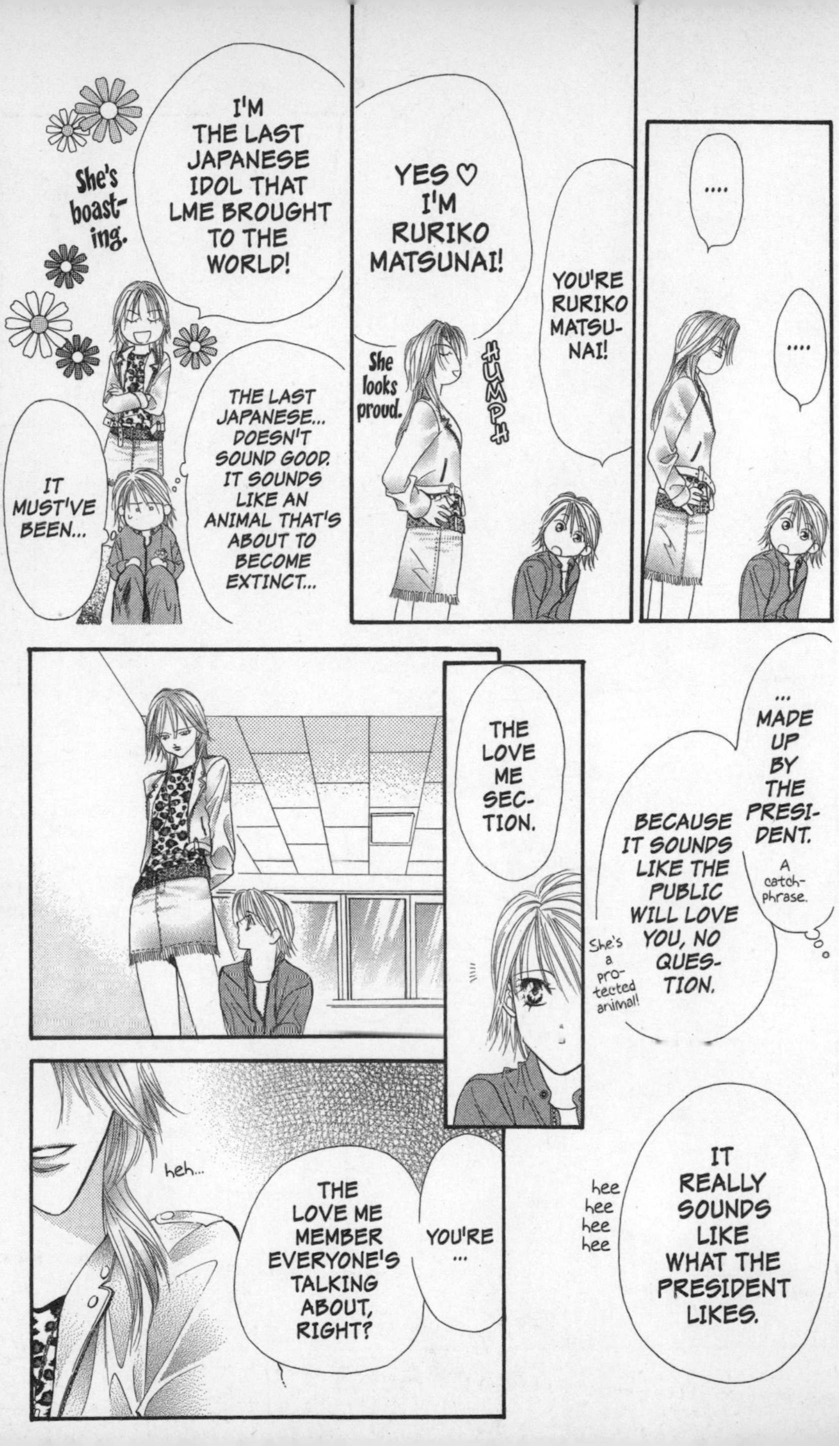
....
....
YOU'RE RURIKO MATSUNAI!
HUMPH
YES ♡ I'M RURIKO MATSUNAI!
She looks proud.
I'M THE LAST JAPANESE IDOL THAT LME BROUGHT TO THE WORLD!
She's boasting.
THE LAST JAPANESE... DOESN'T SOUND GOOD. IT SOUNDS LIKE AN ANIMAL THAT'S ABOUT TO BECOME EXTINCT...
IT MUST'VE BEEN...
... MADE UP BY THE PRESIDENT.
A catch-phrase.
BECAUSE IT SOUNDS LIKE THE PUBLIC WILL LOVE YOU, NO QUESTION.
She's a protected animal!
THE LOVE ME SECTION.
IT REALLY SOUNDS LIKE WHAT THE PRESIDENT LIKES.
hee hee hee hee
YOU'RE ...
THE LOVE ME MEMBER EVERYONE'S TALKING ABOUT, RIGHT?
heh...

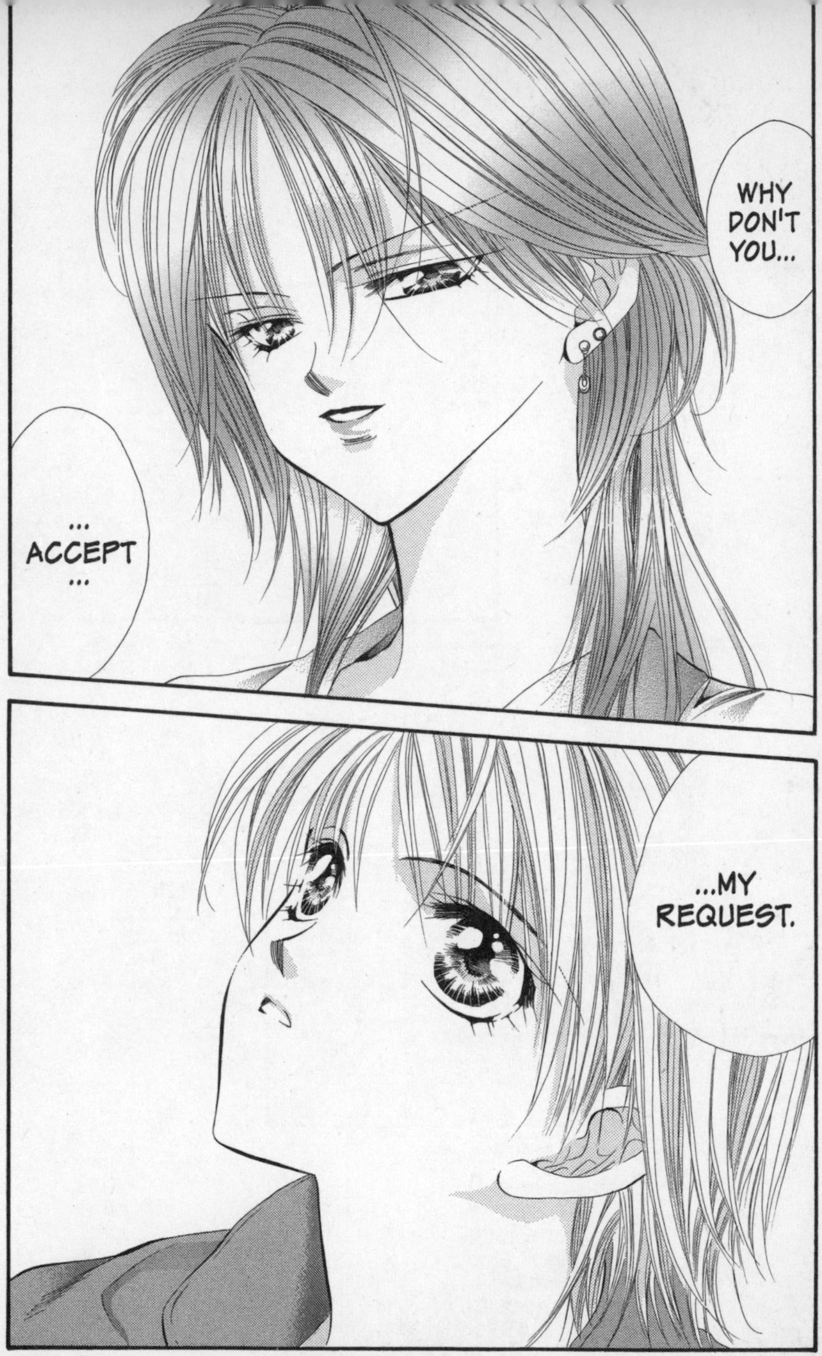
WHY DON'T YOU...
... ACCEPT ...
...MY REQUEST.

End of Act 8

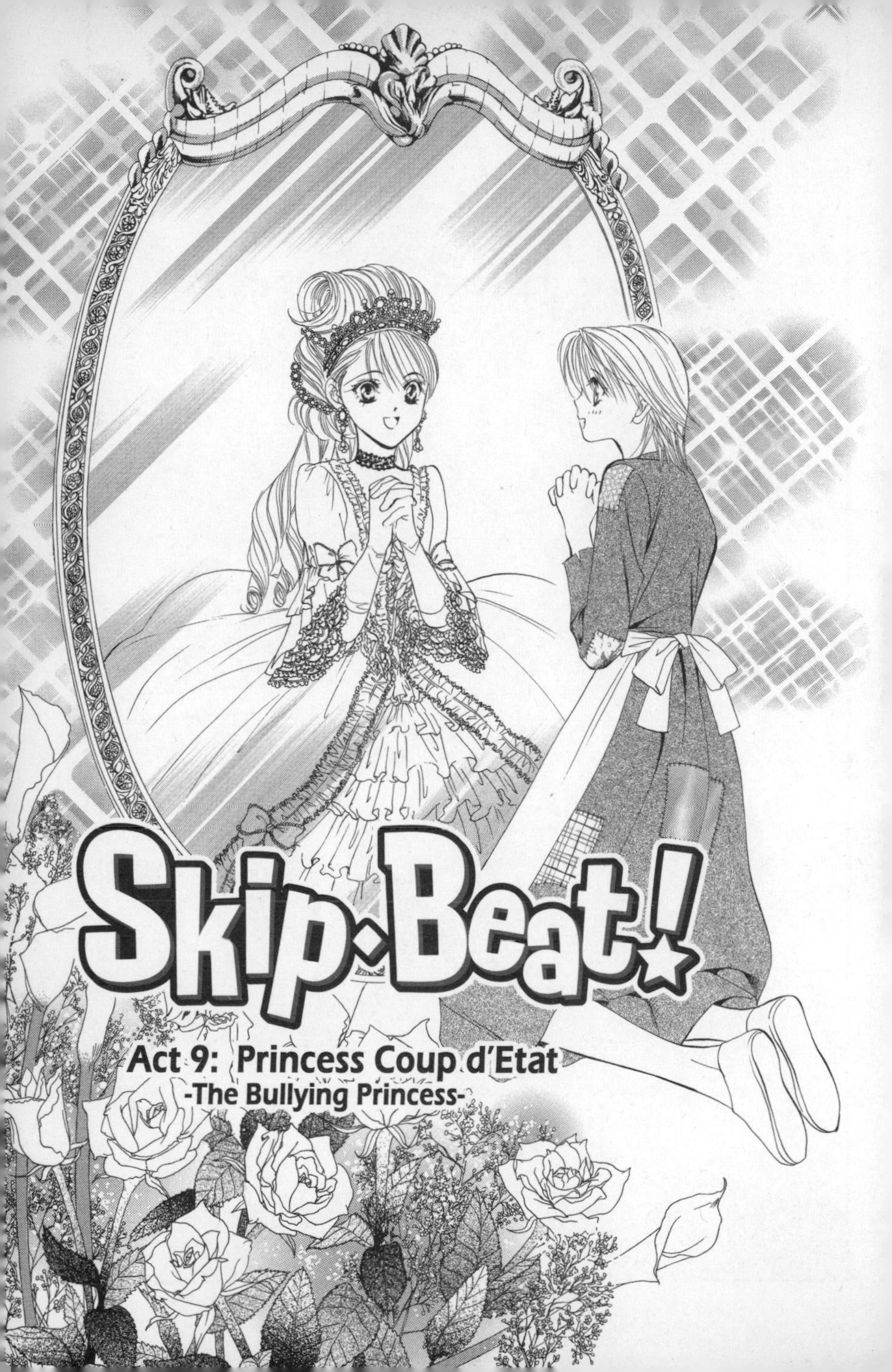
Skip·Beat!
Act 9: Princess Coup d'Etat
-The Bullying Princess-

Today's Target

Ruriko Matsunai (Idol Singer)

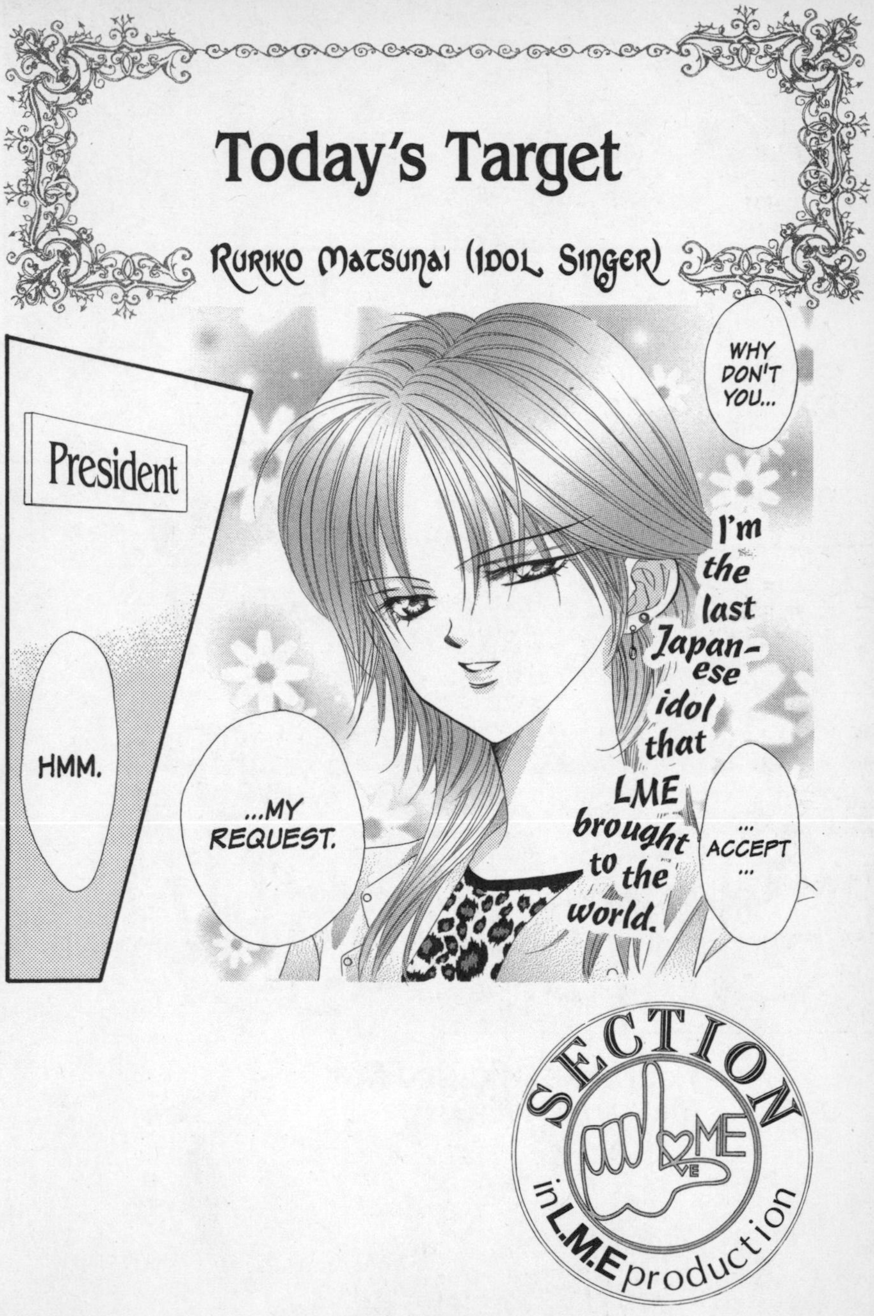
WHY DON'T YOU...
I'm the last Japanese idol that LME brought to the world.
... ACCEPT ...
...MY REQUEST.
President
HMM.

SECTION in L.M.E production

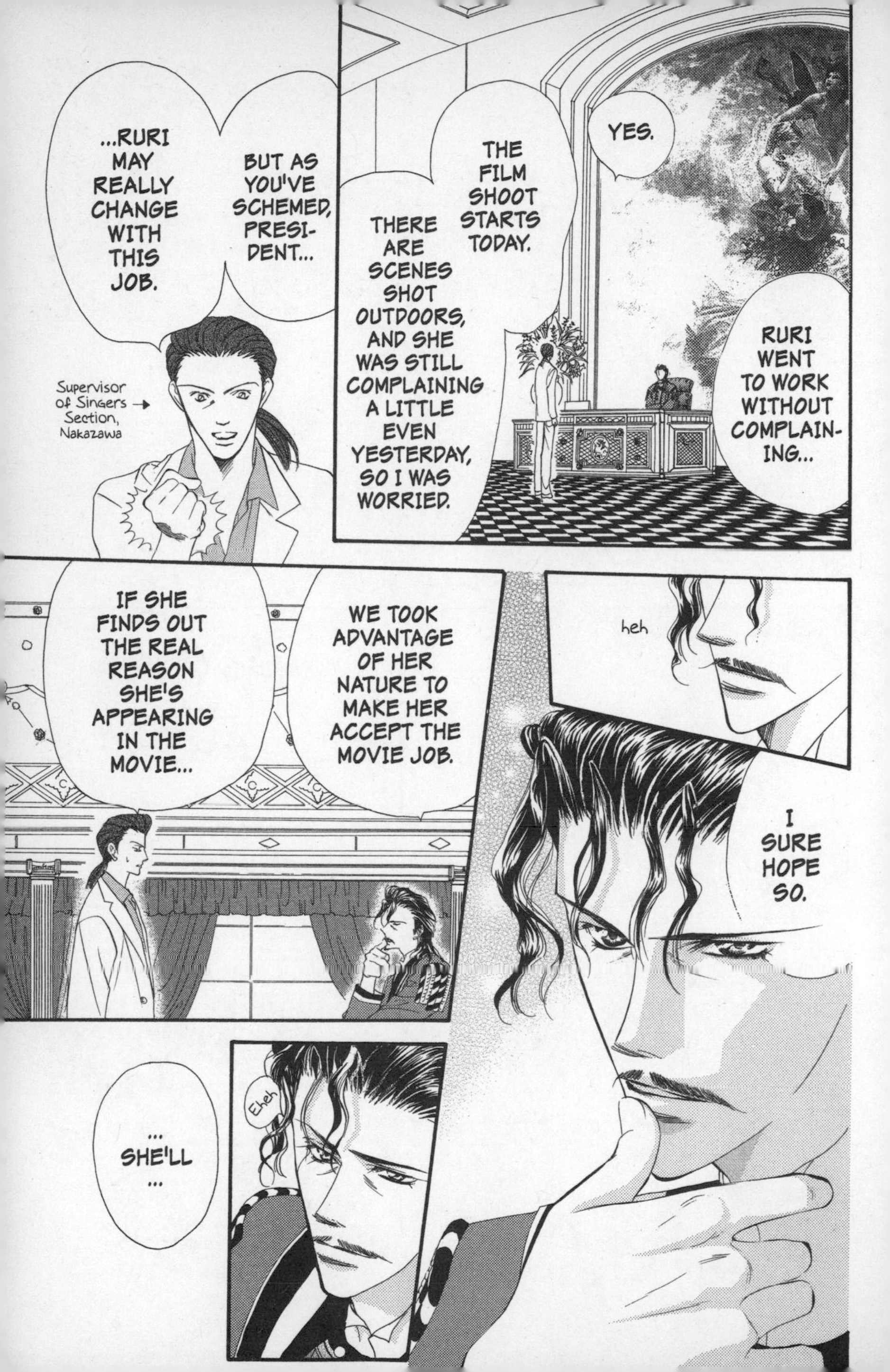
RURI WENT TO WORK WITHOUT COMPLAINING...
YES.
THE FILM SHOOT STARTS TODAY.
THERE ARE SCENES SHOT OUTDOORS, AND SHE WAS STILL COMPLAINING A LITTLE EVEN YESTERDAY, SO I WAS WORRIED.
BUT AS YOU'VE SCHEMED, PRESIDENT...
...RURI MAY REALLY CHANGE WITH THIS JOB.
Supervisor of Singers Section, Nakazawa
heh
I SURE HOPE SO.
WE TOOK ADVANTAGE OF HER NATURE TO MAKE HER ACCEPT THE MOVIE JOB.
IF SHE FINDS OUT THE REAL REASON SHE'S APPEARING IN THE MOVIE...
Eheh
...SHE'LL...

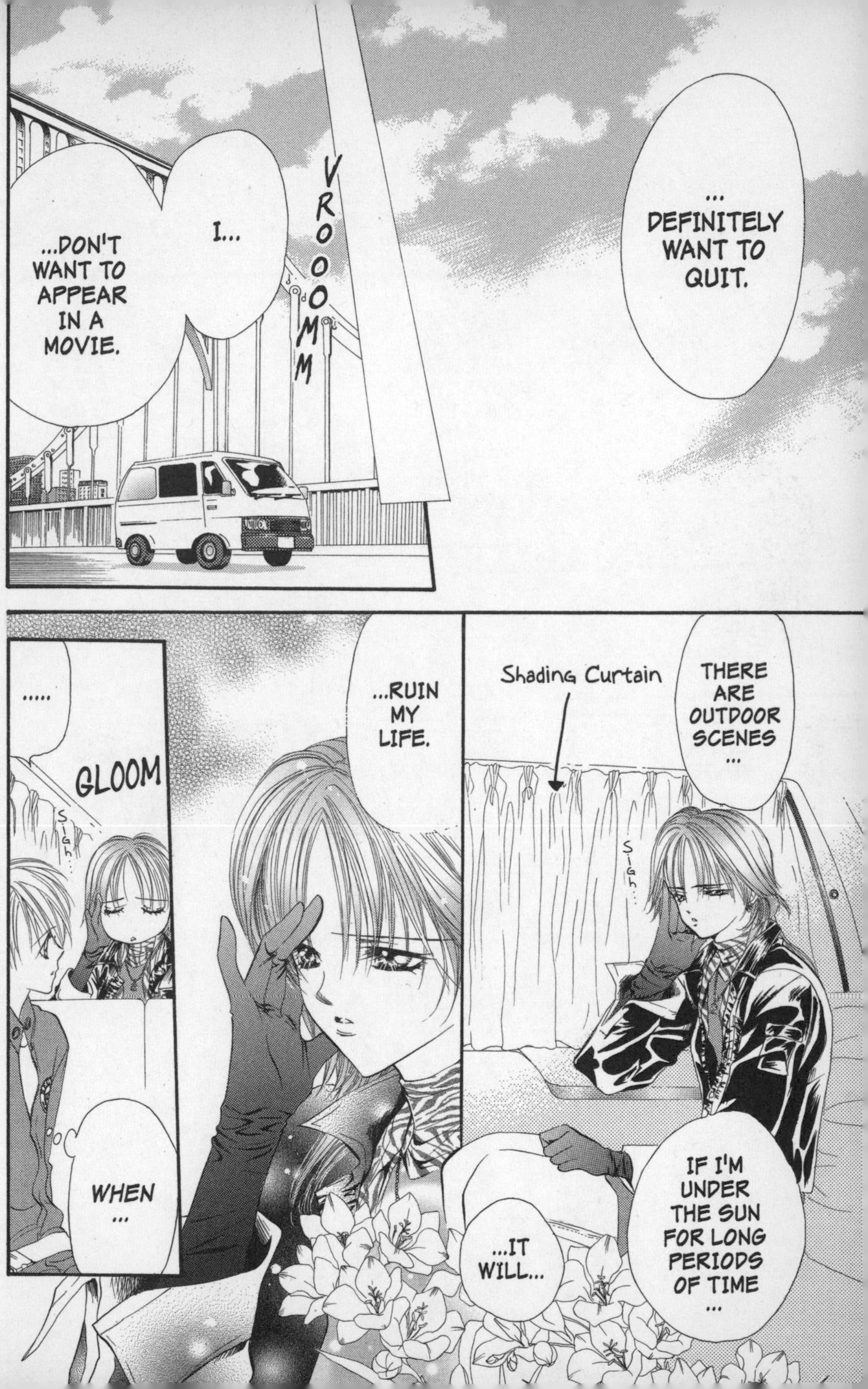
...DEFINITELY WANT TO QUIT.
VROOOMM
I...
...DON'T WANT TO APPEAR IN A MOVIE.
THERE ARE OUTDOOR SCENES...
Shading Curtain
Sigh...
IF I'M UNDER THE SUN FOR LONG PERIODS OF TIME...
...IT WILL...
...RUIN MY LIFE.
.....
GLOOM
Sigh...
WHEN...

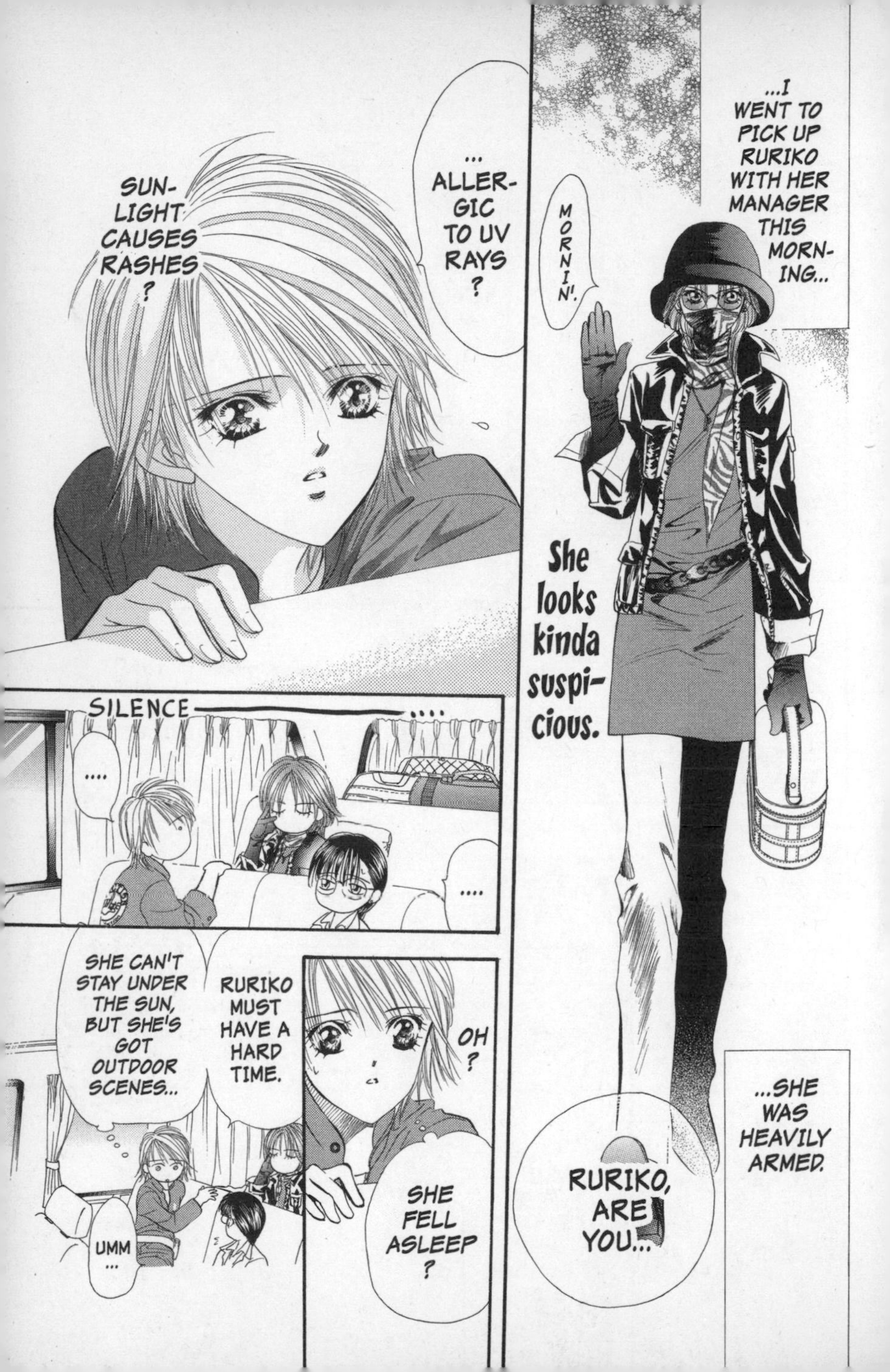
...I WENT TO PICK UP RURIKO WITH HER MANAGER THIS MORNING...
MORNIN'.
She looks kinda suspicious.
...SHE WAS HEAVILY ARMED.
RURIKO, ARE YOU...
...ALLERGIC TO UV RAYS?
SUNLIGHT CAUSES RASHES?
SILENCE....
....
....
OH?
SHE FELL ASLEEP?
RURIKO MUST HAVE A HARD TIME.
SHE CAN'T STAY UNDER THE SUN, BUT SHE'S GOT OUTDOOR SCENES...
UMM...

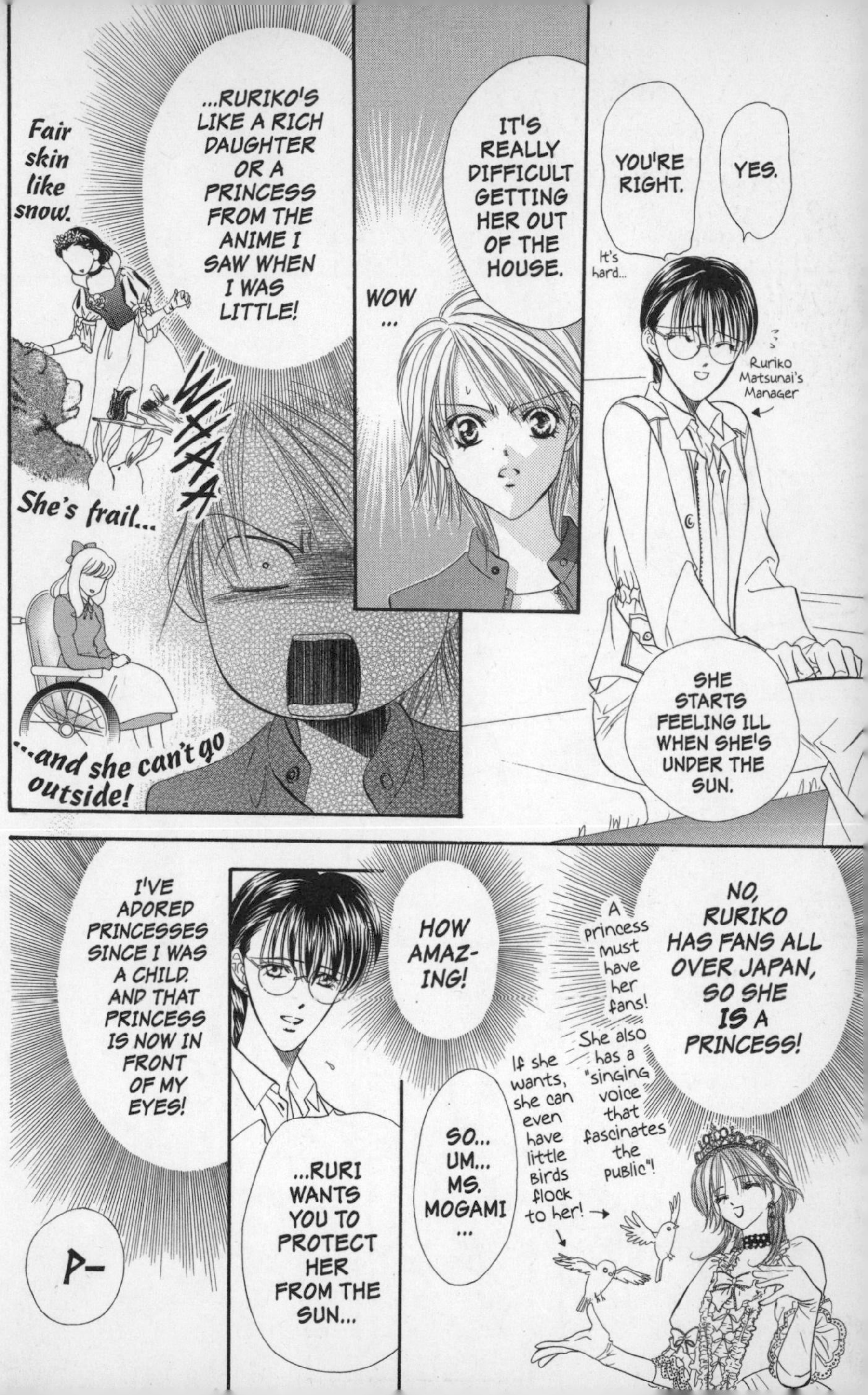
YES.
YOU'RE RIGHT.
It's hard...
Ruriko Matsunai's Manager
SHE STARTS FEELING ILL WHEN SHE'S UNDER THE SUN.
IT'S REALLY DIFFICULT GETTING HER OUT OF THE HOUSE.
WOW ...
...RURIKO'S LIKE A RICH DAUGHTER OR A PRINCESS FROM THE ANIME I SAW WHEN I WAS LITTLE!
Fair skin like snow.
WHAAA
She's frail...
...and she can't go outside!
NO, RURIKO HAS FANS ALL OVER JAPAN, SO SHE IS A PRINCESS!
A princess must have her fans!
She also has a "singing voice that fascinates the public"!
If she wants, she can even have little birds flock to her!
HOW AMAZ-ING!
SO... UM... MS. MOGAMI ...
...RURI WANTS YOU TO PROTECT HER FROM THE SUN...
I'VE ADORED PRINCESSES SINCE I WAS A CHILD. AND THAT PRINCESS IS NOW IN FRONT OF MY EYES!
P-

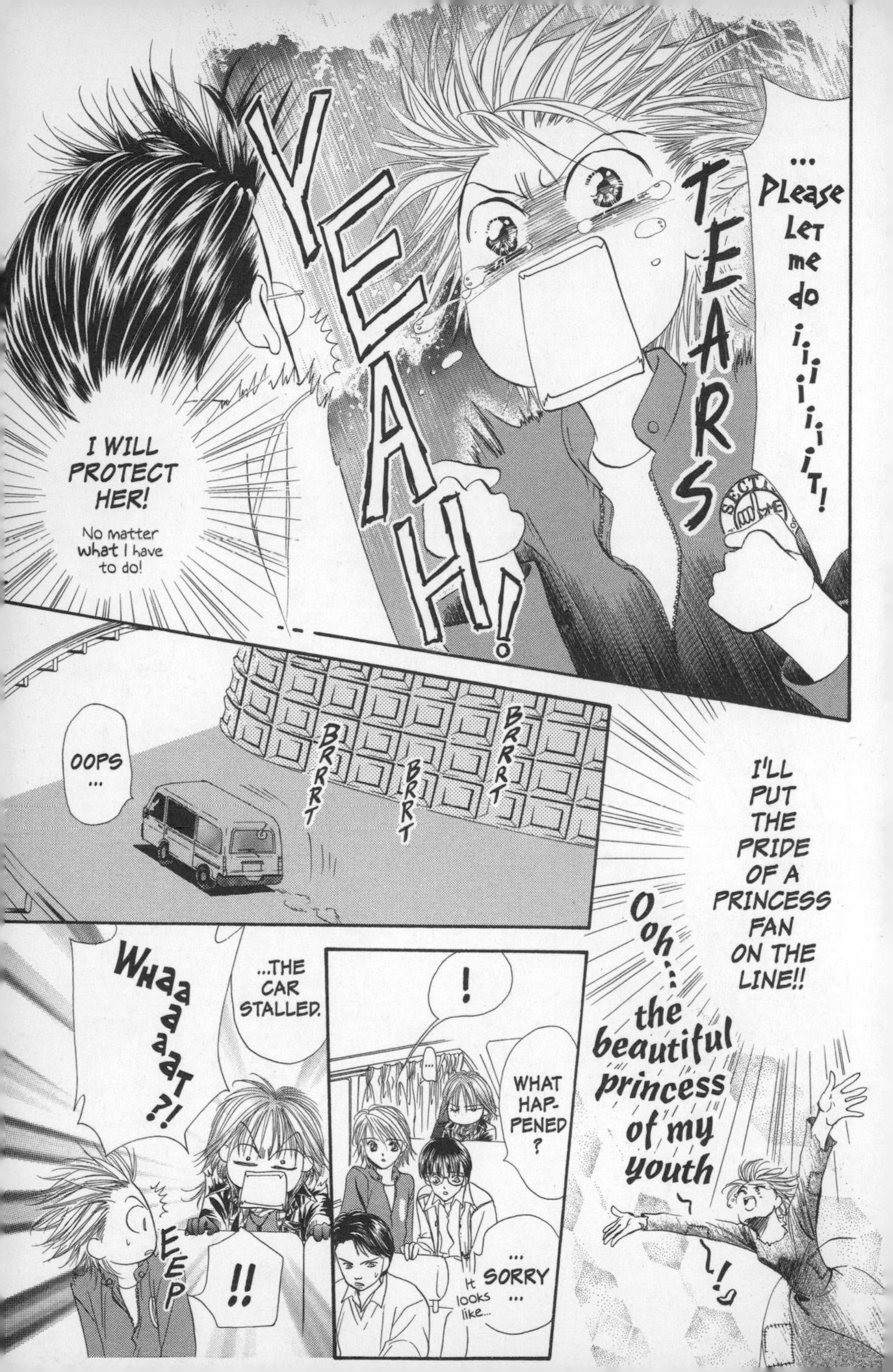
...Please let me do iiiiiiit!
TEARS
YEAH!
I WILL PROTECT HER!
No matter what I have to do!
I'LL PUT THE PRIDE OF A PRINCESS FAN ON THE LINE!!
BRRRT
BRRRT
BRRRT
OOPS ...
Ooh... the beautiful princess of my youth ~~!
!
...
WHAT HAP-PENED?
...SORRY...
It looks like...
...THE CAR STALLED.
Whaaaaaaat?!
EEP
!!

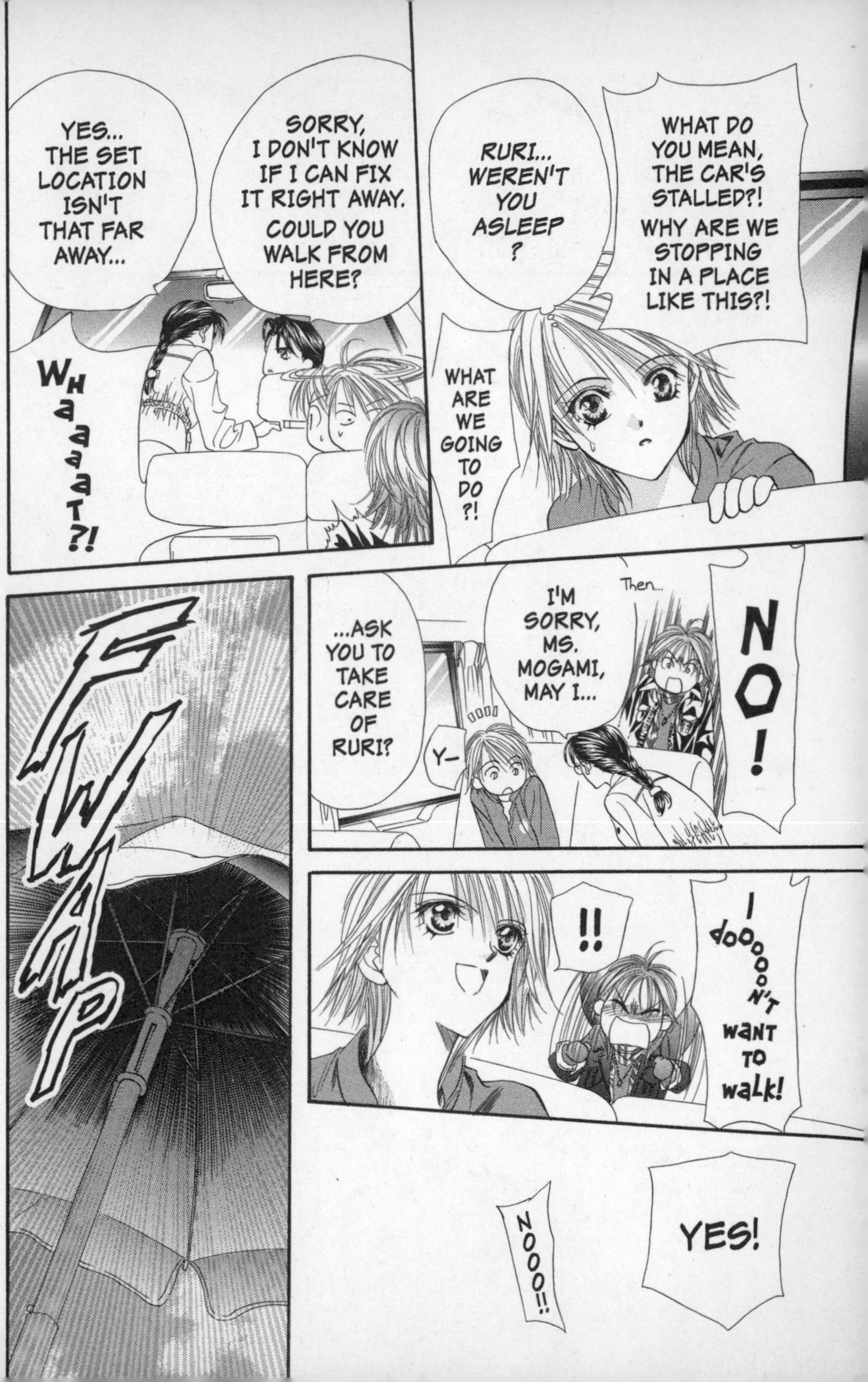

WHAT DO YOU MEAN, THE CAR'S STALLED?! WHY ARE WE STOPPING IN A PLACE LIKE THIS?!
RURI... WEREN'T YOU ASLEEP?
WHAT ARE WE GOING TO DO?!
SORRY, I DON'T KNOW IF I CAN FIX IT RIGHT AWAY.
COULD YOU WALK FROM HERE?
YES... THE SET LOCATION ISN'T THAT FAR AWAY...
WHaaaaT?!
NO!
Then...
I'M SORRY, MS. MOGAMI, MAY I...
...ASK YOU TO TAKE CARE OF RURI?
Y—
I doooooN'T want to walk!
!!
YES!
NOOOO!!
FWAP

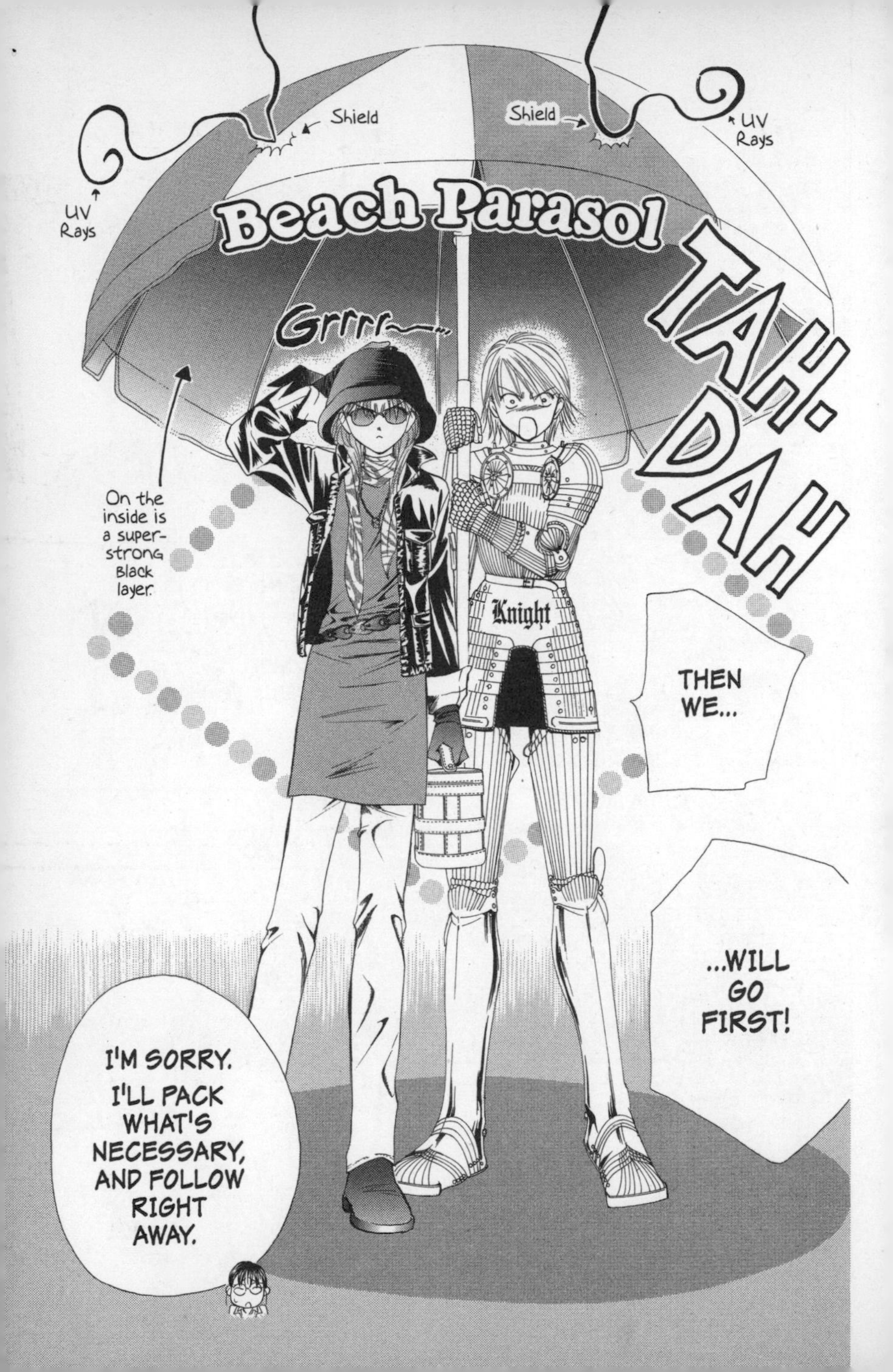
UV Rays
Shield
Shield
UV Rays
Beach Parasol
TAH-DAH
Grrrr~~...
On the inside is a super-strong black layer.
Knight
THEN WE...
...WILL GO FIRST!
I'M SORRY. I'LL PACK WHAT'S NECESSARY, AND FOLLOW RIGHT AWAY.

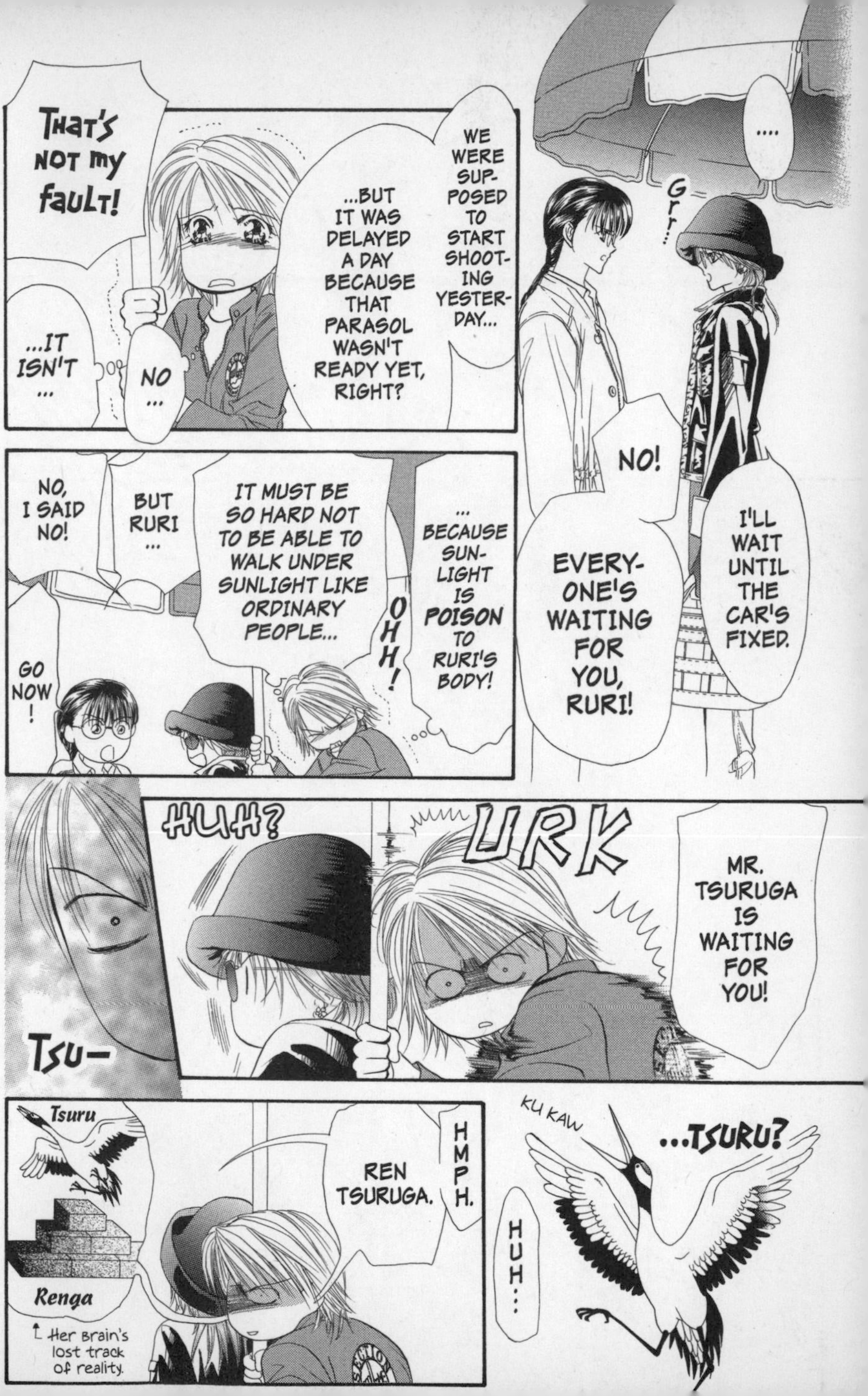

....
Grr...
NO!
I'LL WAIT UNTIL THE CAR'S FIXED.
EVERYONE'S WAITING FOR YOU, RURI!
WE WERE SUPPOSED TO START SHOOTING YESTERDAY...
...BUT IT WAS DELAYED A DAY BECAUSE THAT PARASOL WASN'T READY YET, RIGHT?
That's not my fault!
NO ...
...IT ISN'T ...
... BECAUSE SUNLIGHT IS POISON TO RURI'S BODY!
OHH!
IT MUST BE SO HARD NOT TO BE ABLE TO WALK UNDER SUNLIGHT LIKE ORDINARY PEOPLE...
BUT RURI ...
NO, I SAID NO!
GO NOW!
MR. TSURUGA IS WAITING FOR YOU!
URK
HUH?
TSU-
KU KAW
...TSURU?
HUH...
HMPH.
REN TSURUGA.
Tsuru
Renga
Her brain's lost track of reality.

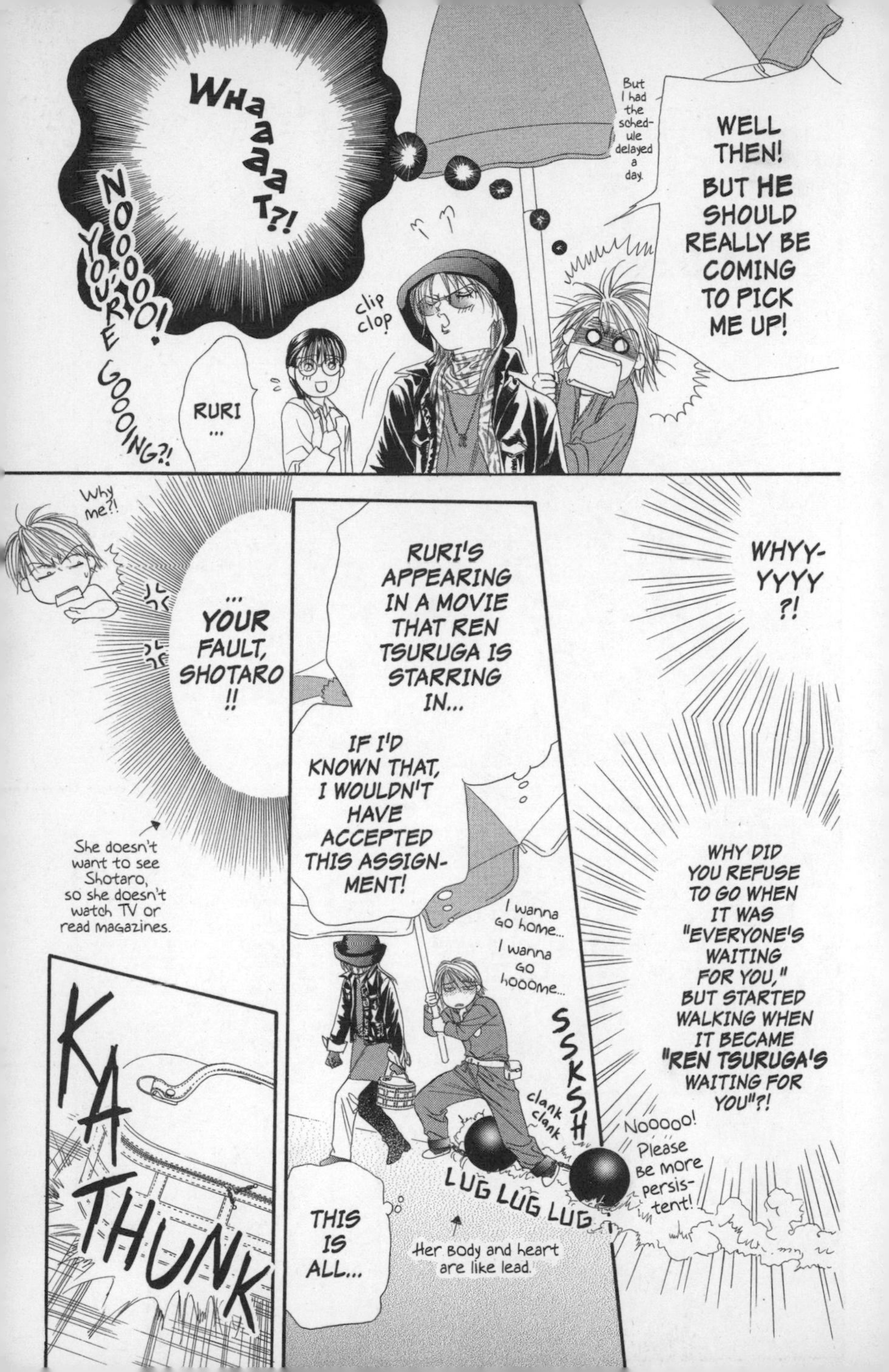
WELL THEN! BUT HE SHOULD REALLY BE COMING TO PICK ME UP!
But I had the sched-ule delayed a day.
WHAAAAAT?!
NOOOOOO! YOU'RE GOOOING?!
clip clop
RURI ...
WHYY-YYYY ?!
WHY DID YOU REFUSE TO GO WHEN IT WAS "EVERYONE'S WAITING FOR YOU," BUT STARTED WALKING WHEN IT BECAME "REN TSURUGA'S WAITING FOR YOU"?!
Nooooo! Please be more persis-tent!
RURI'S APPEARING IN A MOVIE THAT REN TSURUGA IS STARRING IN...
IF I'D KNOWN THAT, I WOULDN'T HAVE ACCEPTED THIS ASSIGN-MENT!
I wanna go home... I wanna go hooome...
SSKSH
clank clank
LUG LUG LUG
THIS IS ALL...
Her body and heart are like lead.
Why me?!
... YOUR FAULT, SHOTARO!!
She doesn't want to see Shotaro, so she doesn't watch TV or read magazines.
KA THUNK

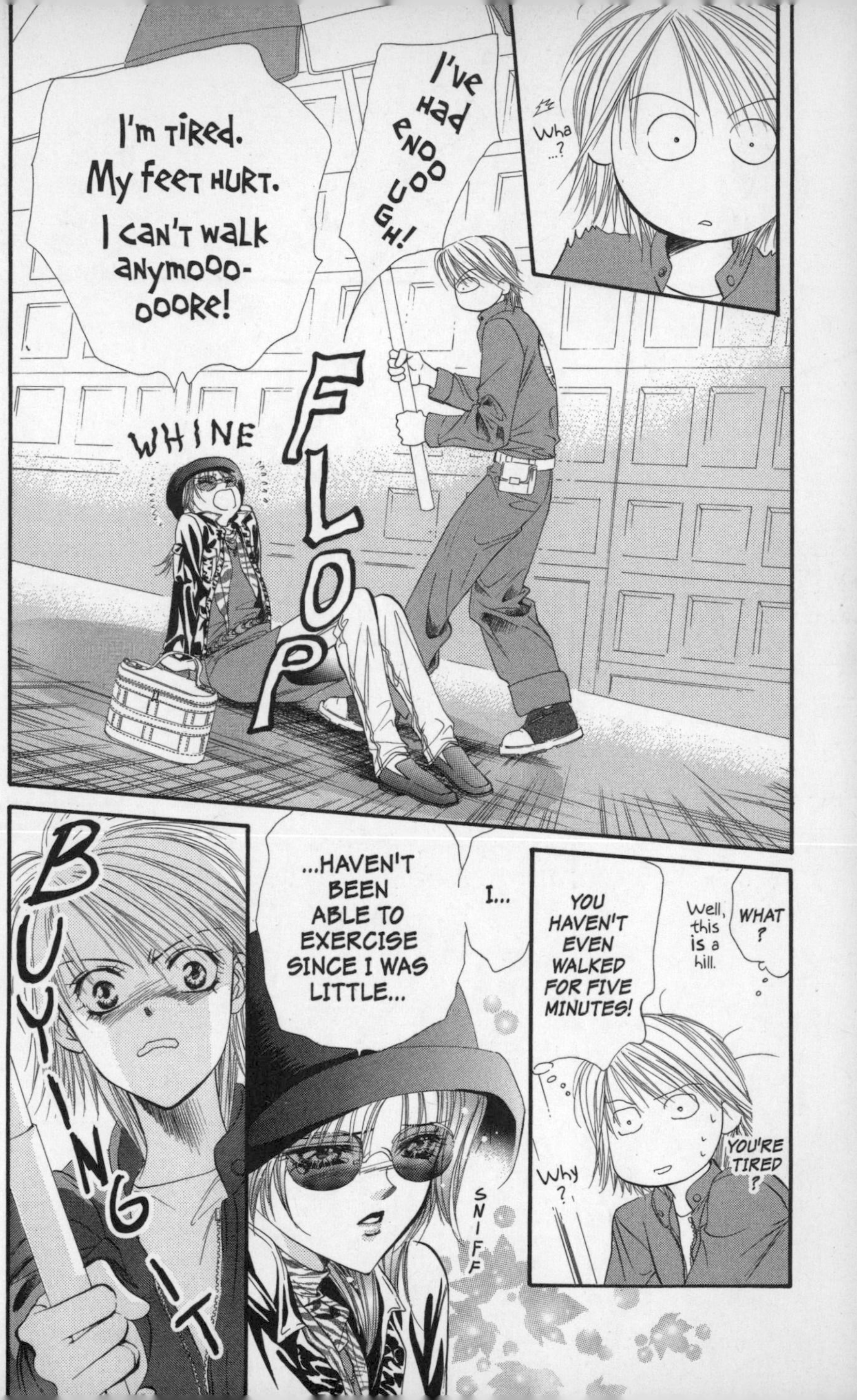
Wha ...?
I've had enoooough!
I'm tired. My feet hurt. I can't walk anymooo-ooore!
FLOP
WHINE
WHAT?
Well, this is a hill.
YOU HAVEN'T EVEN WALKED FOR FIVE MINUTES!
YOU'RE TIRED?
Why?
I...
...HAVEN'T BEEN ABLE TO EXERCISE SINCE I WAS LITTLE...
SNIFF
BUYING IT

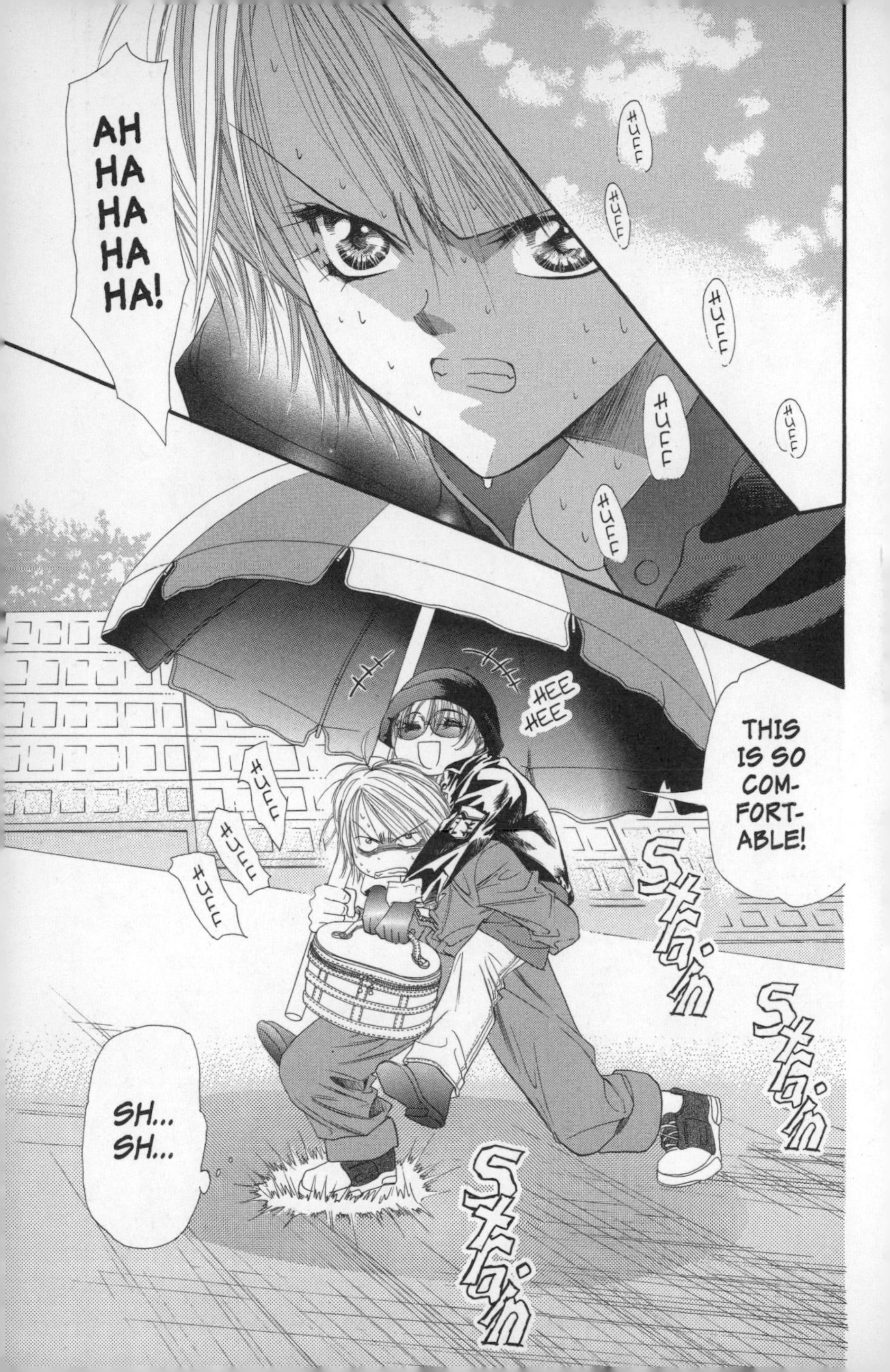

HUFF
HUFF
HUFF
HUFF
HUFF
HUFF
AH HA HA HA HA!
THIS IS SO COM-FORT-ABLE!
HEE HEE
Stan
Stan
HUFF
HUFF
HUFF
Stan
SH... SH...

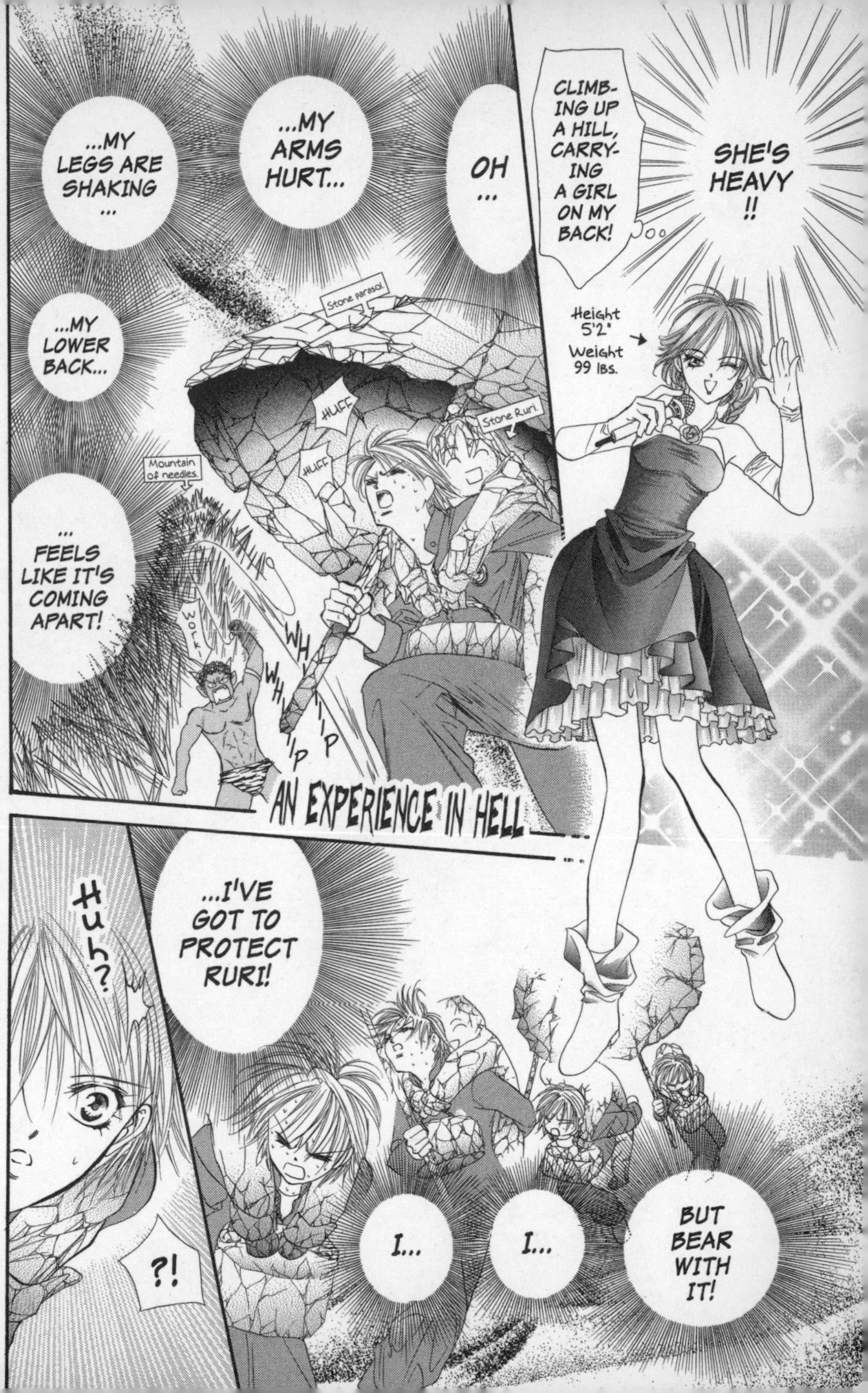
SHE'S HEAVY !!
CLIMBING UP A HILL, CARRYING A GIRL ON MY BACK!
Height 5'2" Weight 99 lbs.
OH ...
...MY ARMS HURT...
...MY LEGS ARE SHAKING ...
...MY LOWER BACK...
... FEELS LIKE IT'S COMING APART!
Stone parasol.
Stone Ruri.
HUFF
HUFF
Mountain of needles.
Work!
WHIP
WHIP
AN EXPERIENCE IN HELL
BUT BEAR WITH IT!
I...
I...
...I'VE GOT TO PROTECT RURI!
Huh?
?!

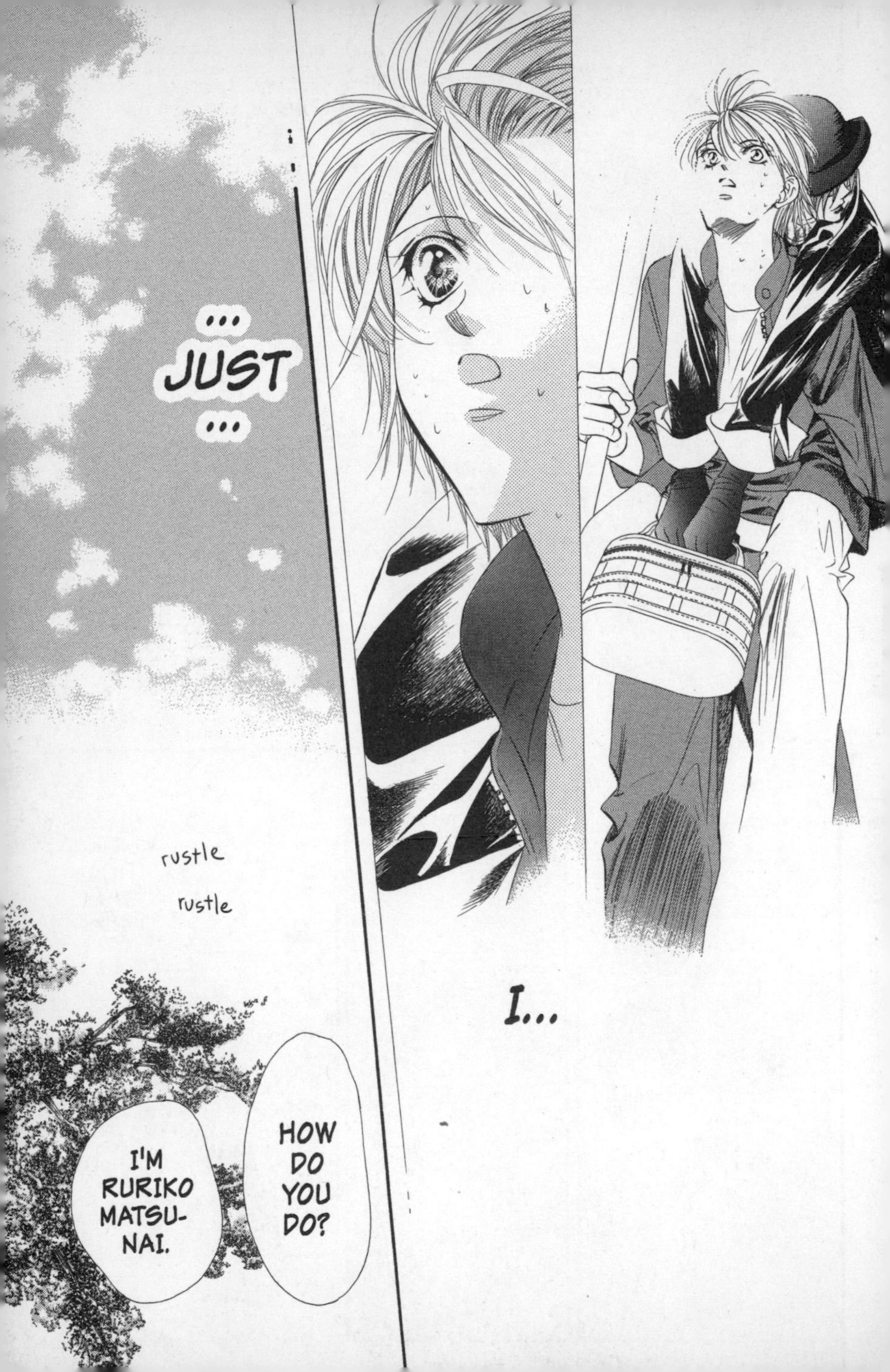
I...
...JUST...
rustle
rustle
HOW DO YOU DO?
I'M RURIKO MATSU-NAI.

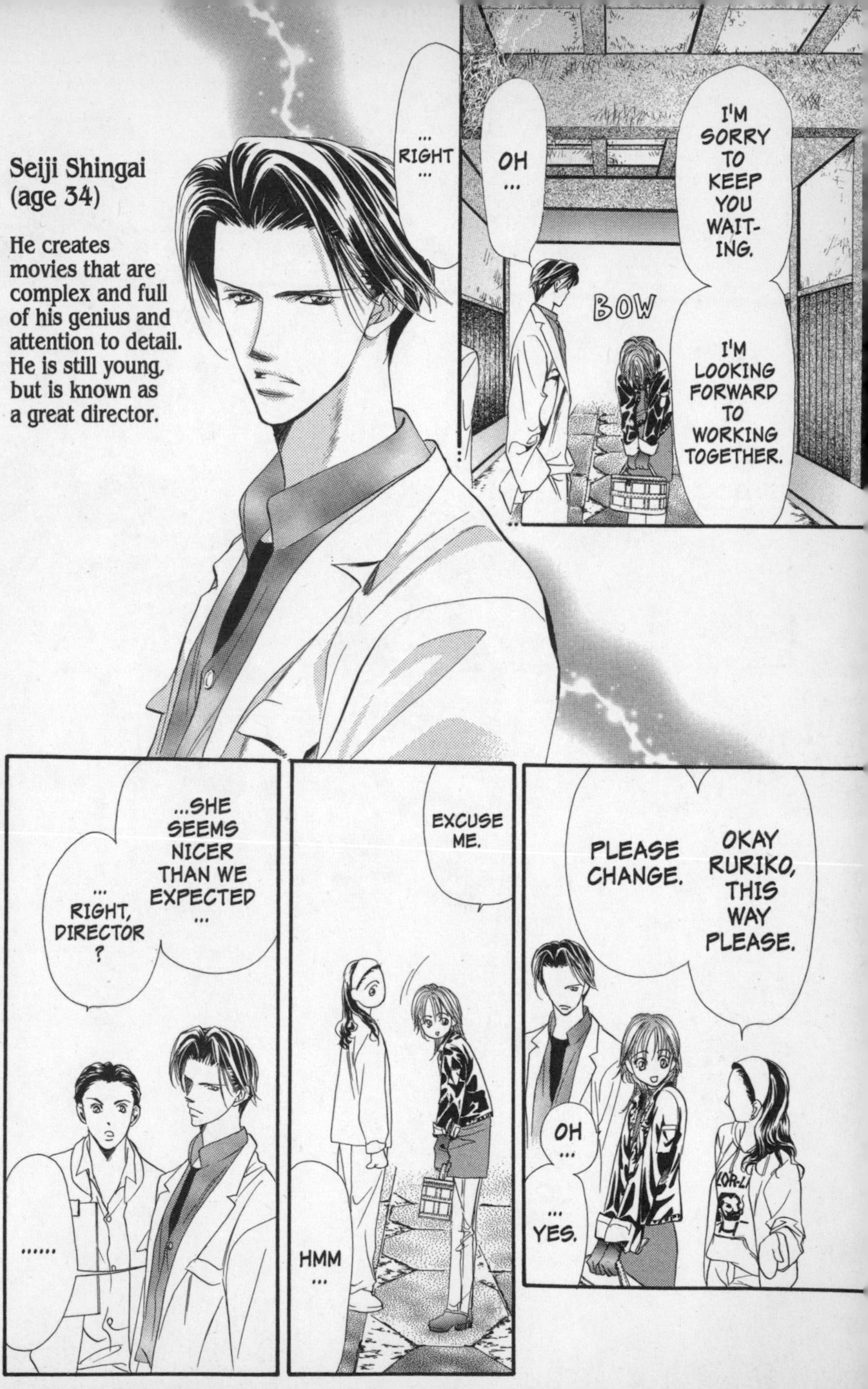
I'M SORRY TO KEEP YOU WAIT-ING.
BOW
I'M LOOKING FORWARD TO WORKING TOGETHER.
OH ...
... RIGHT ...
Seiji Shingai (age 34)
He creates movies that are complex and full of his genius and attention to detail. He is still young, but is known as a great director.
OKAY RURIKO, THIS WAY PLEASE.
PLEASE CHANGE.
OH ...
... YES.
EXCUSE ME.
HMM ...
...SHE SEEMS NICER THAN WE EXPECTED ...
... RIGHT, DIRECTOR ?
......

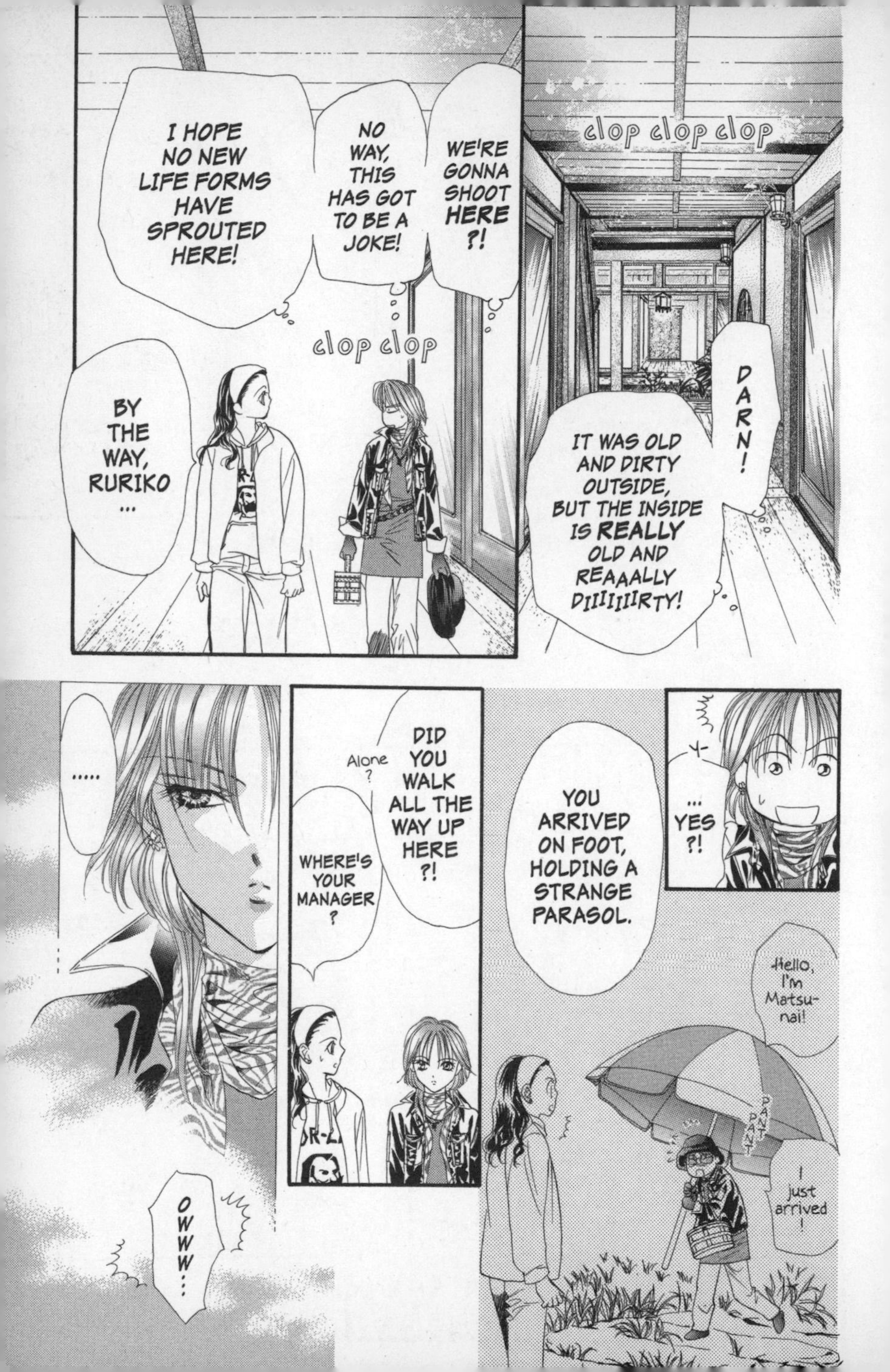

clop clop clop
IT WAS OLD AND DIRTY OUTSIDE, BUT THE INSIDE IS REALLY OLD AND REAAALLY DIIIIIIIRTY!
DARN!
WE'RE GONNA SHOOT HERE?!
NO WAY, THIS HAS GOT TO BE A JOKE!
I HOPE NO NEW LIFE FORMS HAVE SPROUTED HERE!
clop clop
BY THE WAY, RURIKO...
...YES?!
YOU ARRIVED ON FOOT, HOLDING A STRANGE PARASOL.
Hello, I'm Matsunai!
PANT PANT
I just arrived!
DID YOU WALK ALL THE WAY UP HERE?!
Alone?
WHERE'S YOUR MANAGER?
.....
OWWW...

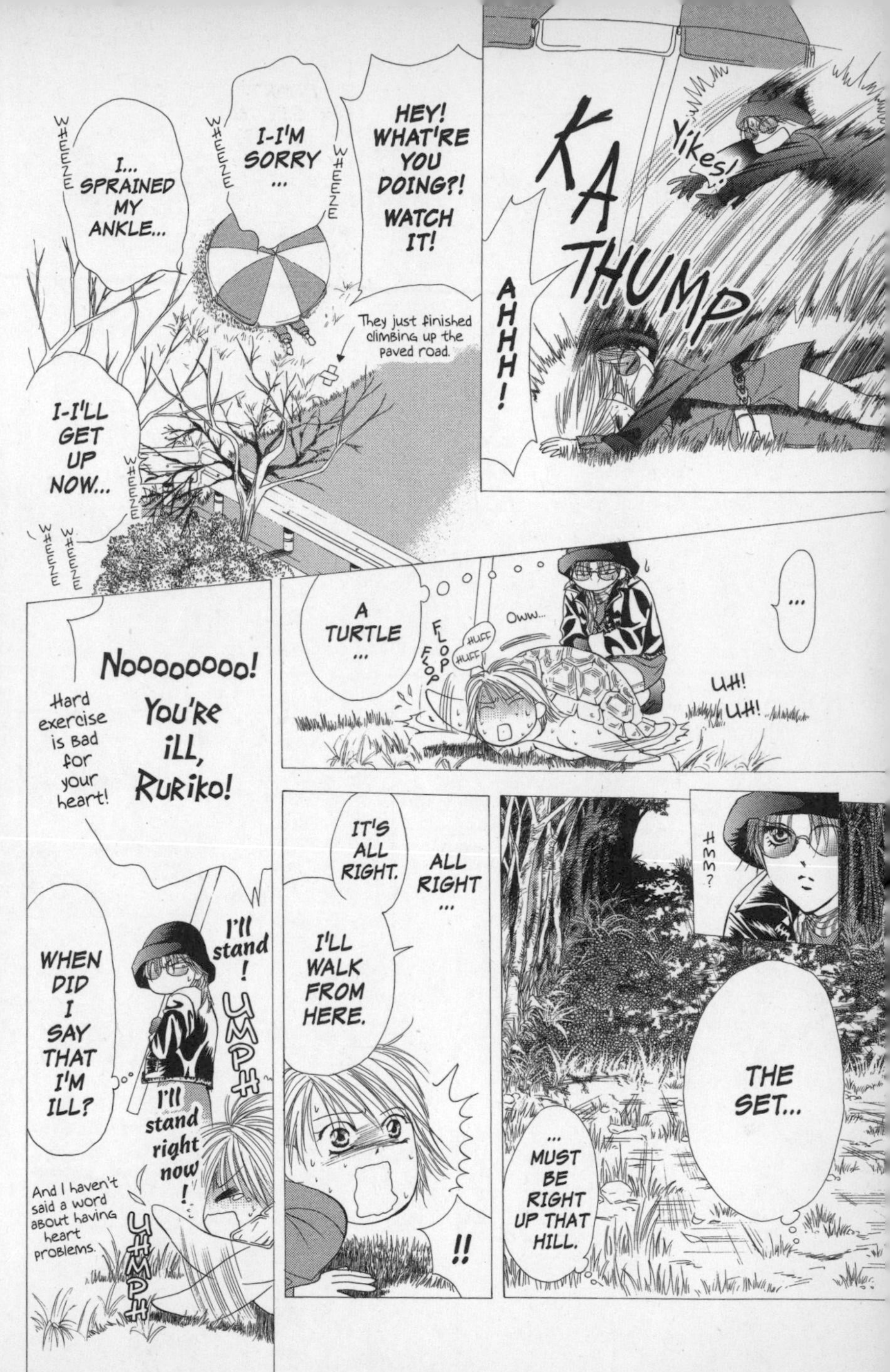
Yikes!
KA THUMP
AHHH!
HEY! WHAT'RE YOU DOING?! WATCH IT!
WHEEZE
I-I'M SORRY...
WHEEZE
WHEEZE
I... SPRAINED MY ANKLE...
They just finished climbing up the paved road.
I-I'LL GET UP NOW...
WHEEZE
WHEEZE WHEEZE
...
UH! UH!
Oww...
HUFF HUFF
FLOP FLOP
A TURTLE...
HMM?
THE SET...
...MUST BE RIGHT UP THAT HILL.
IT'S ALL RIGHT.
ALL RIGHT...
I'LL WALK FROM HERE.
!!
Noooooooo!
You're ill, Ruriko!
Hard exercise is bad for your heart!
WHEN DID I SAY THAT I'M ILL?
I'll stand!
UMPH
I'll stand right now!
UMPH
And I haven't said a word about having heart problems.

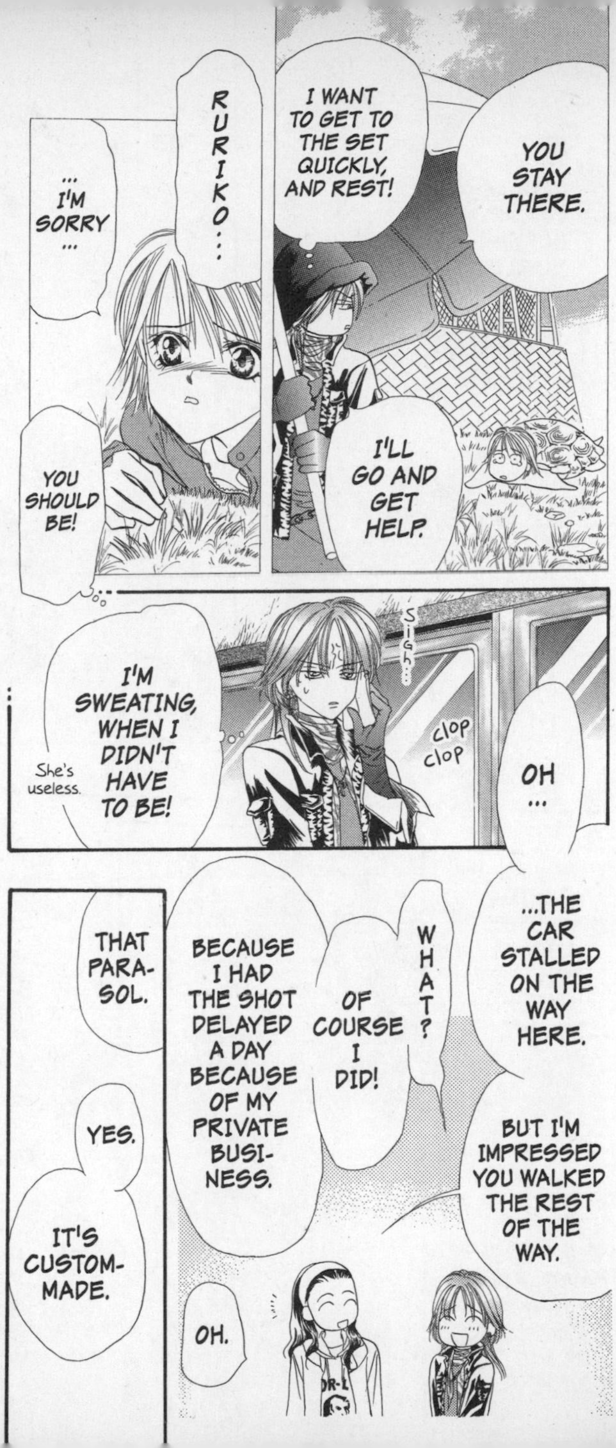
YOU STAY THERE.
I WANT TO GET TO THE SET QUICKLY, AND REST!
I'LL GO AND GET HELP.
RURIKO...
... I'M SORRY ...
YOU SHOULD BE!
Sigh...
I'M SWEATING, WHEN I DIDN'T HAVE TO BE!
She's useless.
clop clop
OH ...
...THE CAR STALLED ON THE WAY HERE.
BUT I'M IMPRESSED YOU WALKED THE REST OF THE WAY.
WHAT?
OF COURSE I DID!
BECAUSE I HAD THE SHOT DELAYED A DAY BECAUSE OF MY PRIVATE BUSI-NESS.
THAT PARA-SOL.
YES.
IT'S CUSTOM-MADE.
OH.
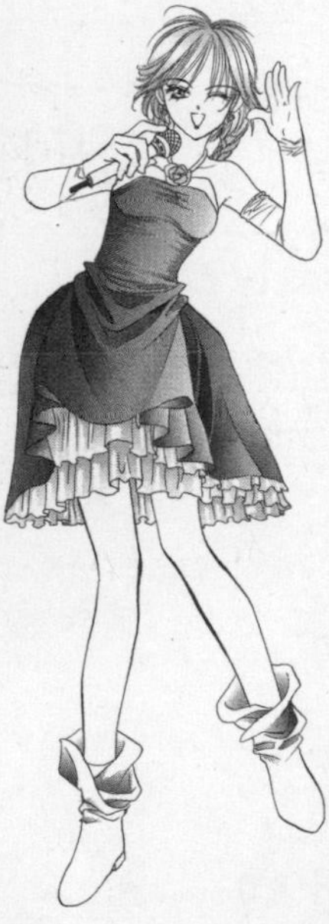

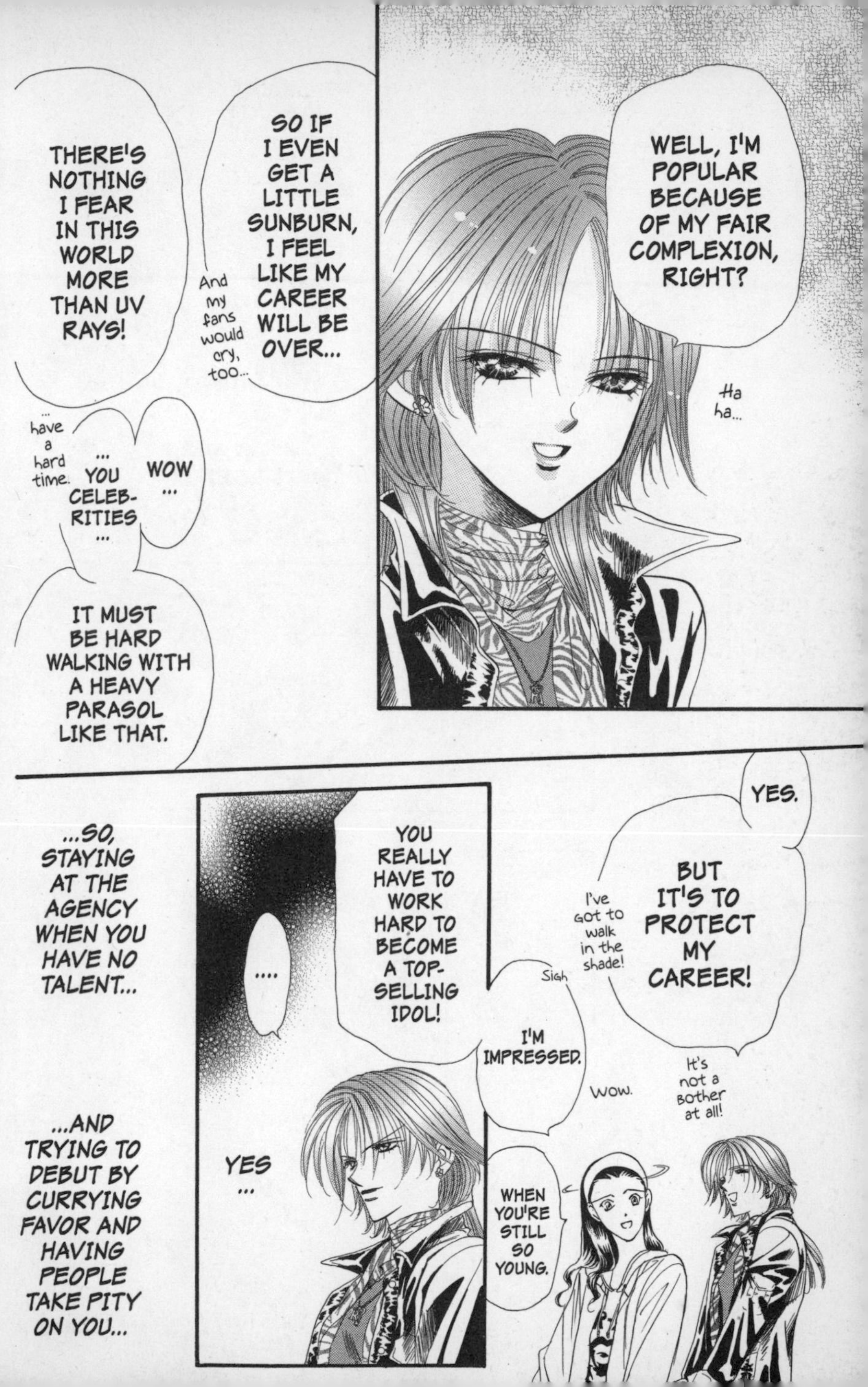
WELL, I'M POPULAR BECAUSE OF MY FAIR COMPLEXION, RIGHT?
Ha ha...
SO IF I EVEN GET A LITTLE SUNBURN, I FEEL LIKE MY CAREER WILL BE OVER...
And my fans would cry, too...
THERE'S NOTHING I FEAR IN THIS WORLD MORE THAN UV RAYS!
WOW...
...YOU CELEBRITIES...
...have a hard time.
IT MUST BE HARD WALKING WITH A HEAVY PARASOL LIKE THAT.
YES.
BUT IT'S TO PROTECT MY CAREER!
I've got to walk in the shade!
It's not a bother at all!
Sigh
I'M IMPRESSED.
Wow.
WHEN YOU'RE STILL SO YOUNG.
YOU REALLY HAVE TO WORK HARD TO BECOME A TOP-SELLING IDOL!
....
YES...
...SO, STAYING AT THE AGENCY WHEN YOU HAVE NO TALENT...
...AND TRYING TO DEBUT BY CURRYING FAVOR AND HAVING PEOPLE TAKE PITY ON YOU...

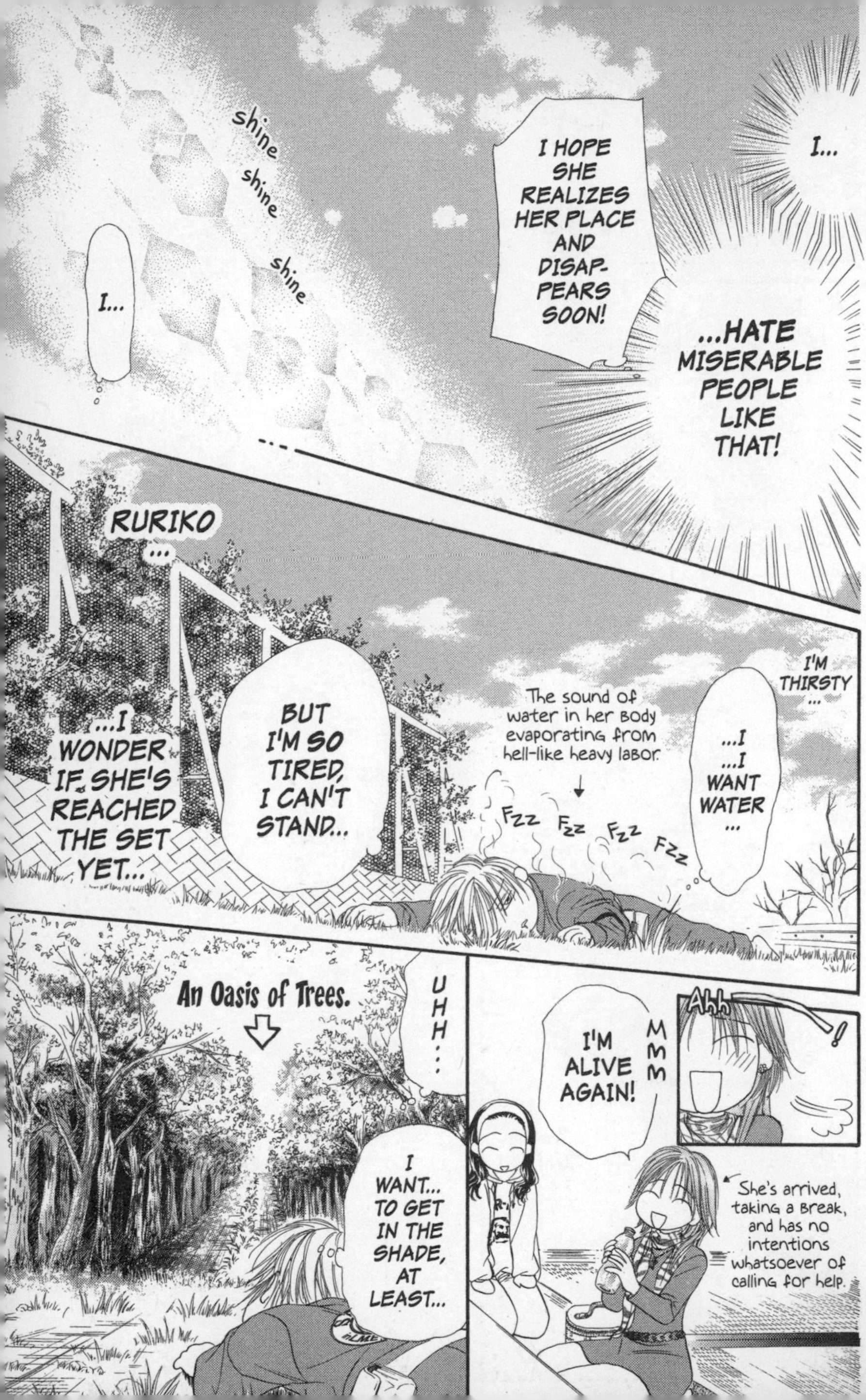
I...
...HATE MISERABLE PEOPLE LIKE THAT!
I HOPE SHE REALIZES HER PLACE AND DISAP-PEARS SOON!
shine shine shine
I...
...
I'M THIRSTY...
...I ...I WANT WATER...
The sound of water in her body evaporating from hell-like heavy labor.
Fzz Fzz Fzz Fzz
BUT I'M SO TIRED, I CAN'T STAND...
RURIKO...
...I WONDER IF SHE'S REACHED THE SET YET...
Ahh
!
MMM
I'M ALIVE AGAIN!
She's arrived, taking a break, and has no intentions whatsoever of calling for help.
UHH...
An Oasis of Trees.
I WANT... TO GET IN THE SHADE, AT LEAST...

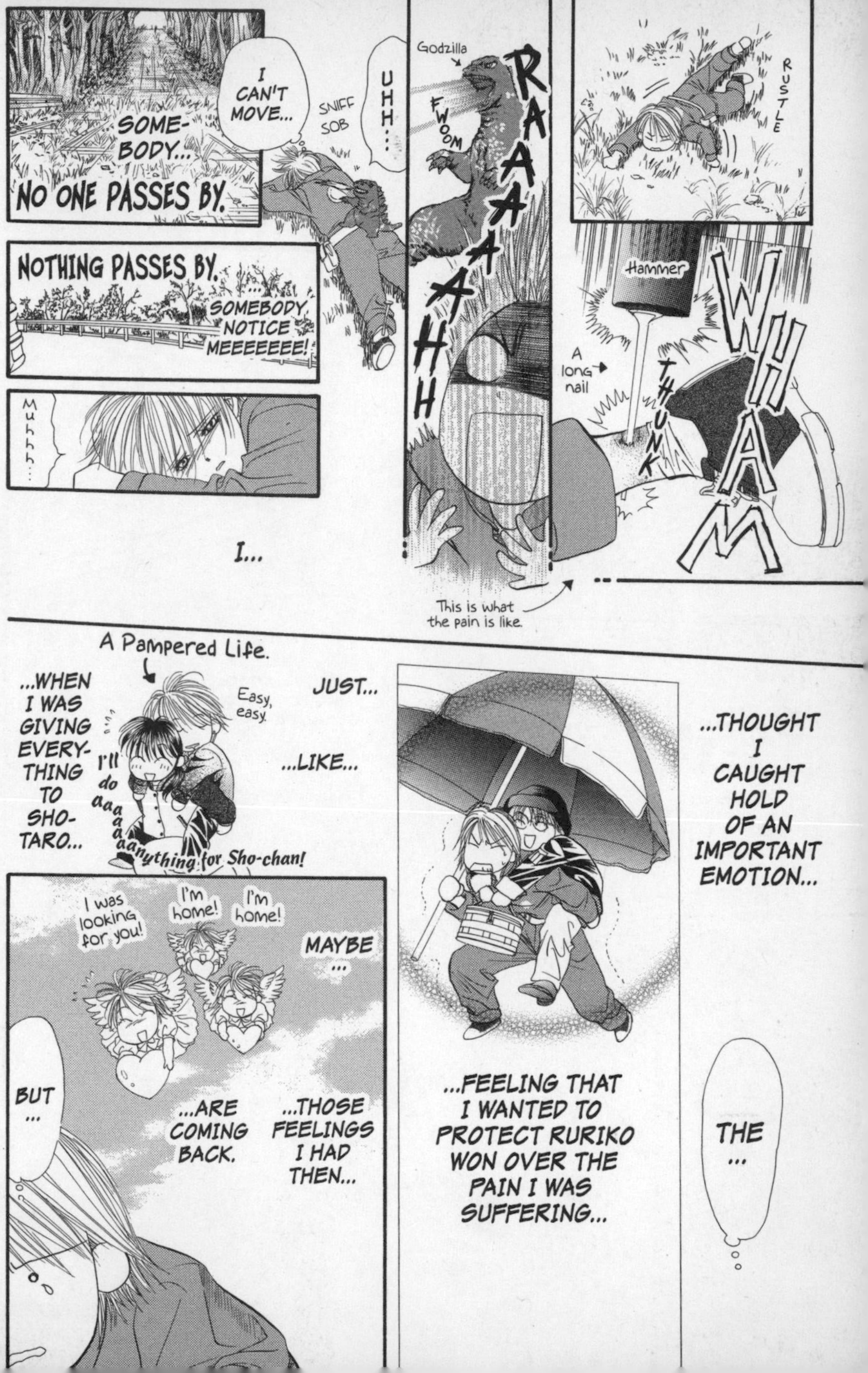

RUSTLE
Hammer
WHAM
THUNK
A long nail
RAAAAAAHH
Godzilla
FWOOM
This is what the pain is like.
UHH...
SNIFF SOB
I CAN'T MOVE...
...SOME-BODY...
NO ONE PASSES BY.
NOTHING PASSES BY.
...SOMEBODY NOTICE MEEEEEEE!
Muhhh...
I...
...THOUGHT I CAUGHT HOLD OF AN IMPORTANT EMOTION...
THE ...
...FEELING THAT I WANTED TO PROTECT RURIKO WON OVER THE PAIN I WAS SUFFERING...
JUST...
...LIKE...
A Pampered Life.
Easy, easy.
I'll do aaaaaaanything for Sho-chan!
...WHEN I WAS GIVING EVERY-THING TO SHO-TARO...
MAYBE ...
I'm home!
I'm home!
I was looking for you!
...THOSE FEELINGS I HAD THEN...
...ARE COMING BACK.
BUT ...

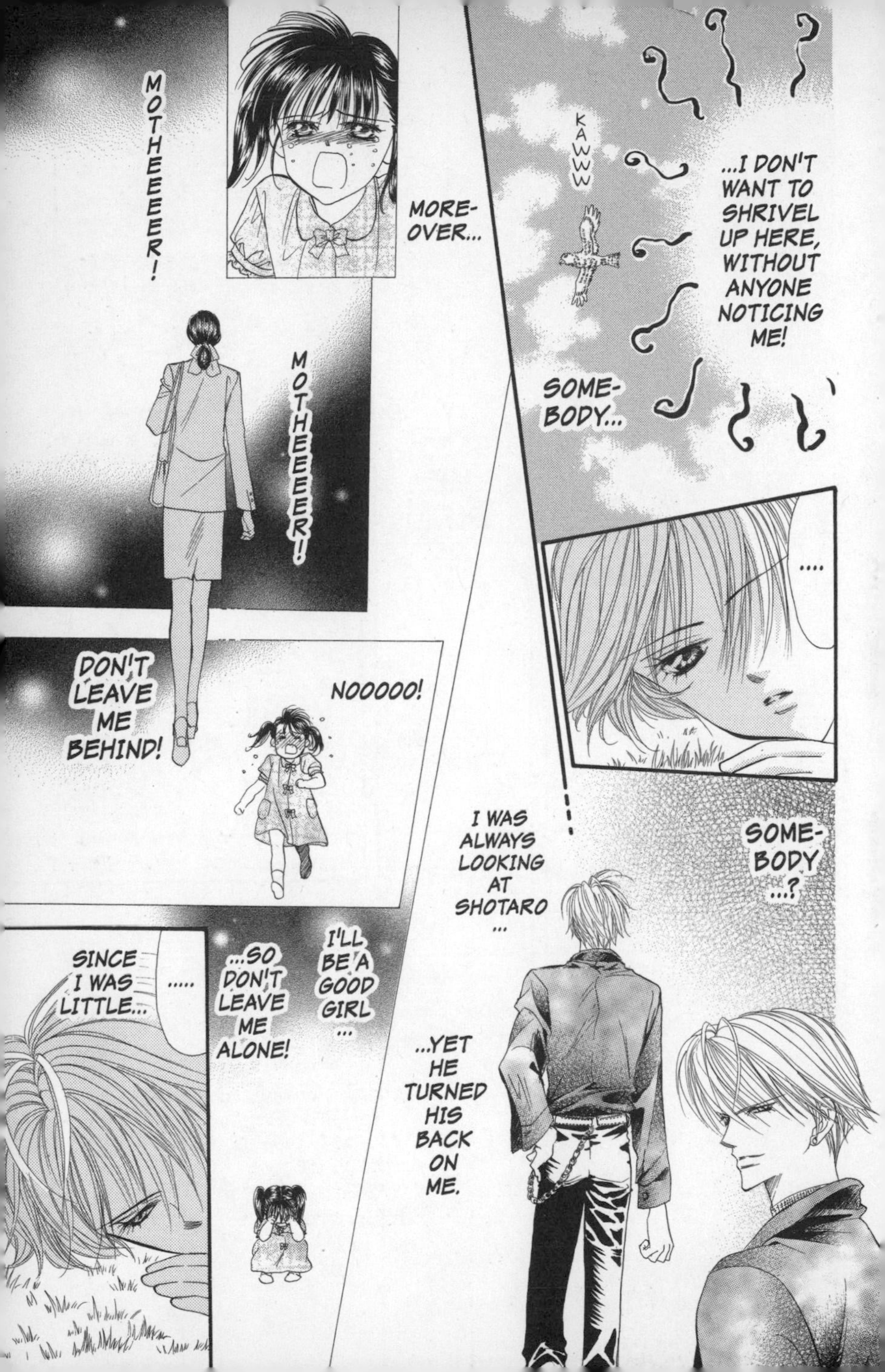
KAWWW
...I DON'T WANT TO SHRIVEL UP HERE, WITHOUT ANYONE NOTICING ME!
SOME-BODY...
....
SOME-BODY ...?
I WAS ALWAYS LOOKING AT SHOTARO ...
...YET HE TURNED HIS BACK ON ME.
MORE-OVER...
MOTHEEEER!
MOTHEEEEER!
NOOOOO!
DON'T LEAVE ME BEHIND!
I'LL BE A GOOD GIRL ...
...SO DON'T LEAVE ME ALONE!
.....
SINCE I WAS LITTLE...

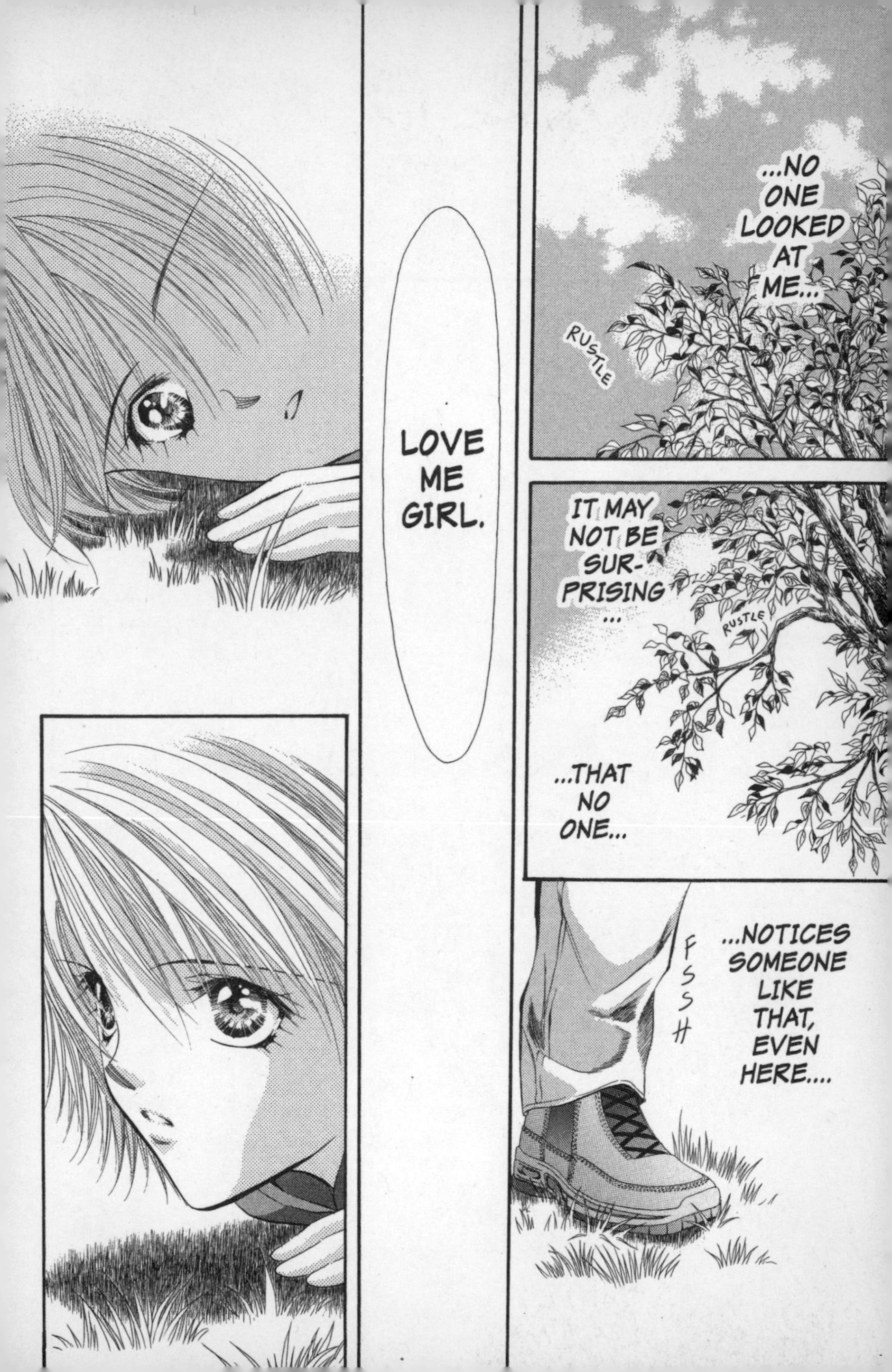
...NO ONE LOOKED AT ME...
RUSTLE
IT MAY NOT BE SUR-PRISING...
RUSTLE
...THAT NO ONE...
FSSH
...NOTICES SOMEONE LIKE THAT, EVEN HERE....
LOVE ME GIRL.

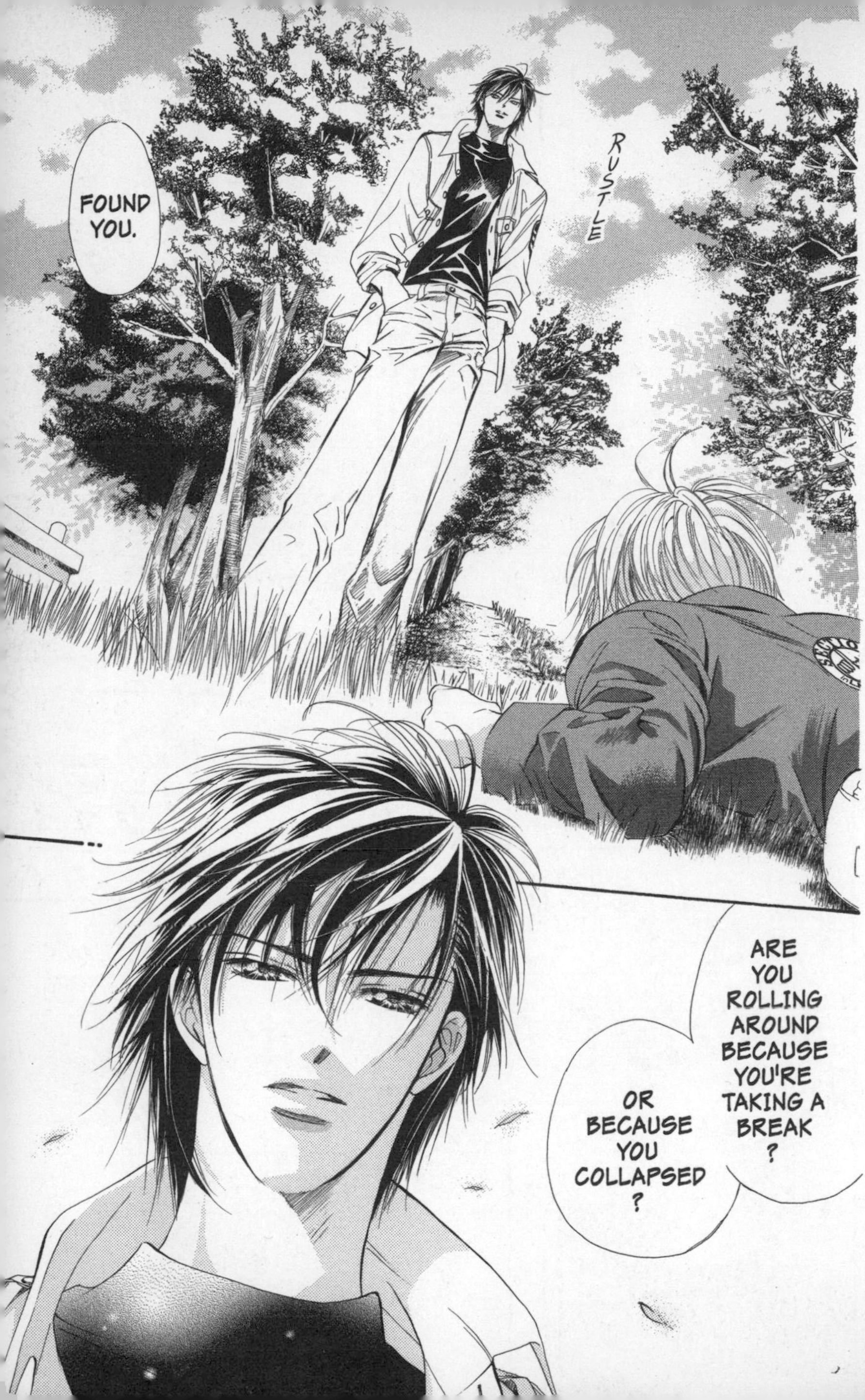
RUSTLE
FOUND YOU.
ARE YOU ROLLING AROUND BECAUSE YOU'RE TAKING A BREAK?
OR BECAUSE YOU COLLAPSED?

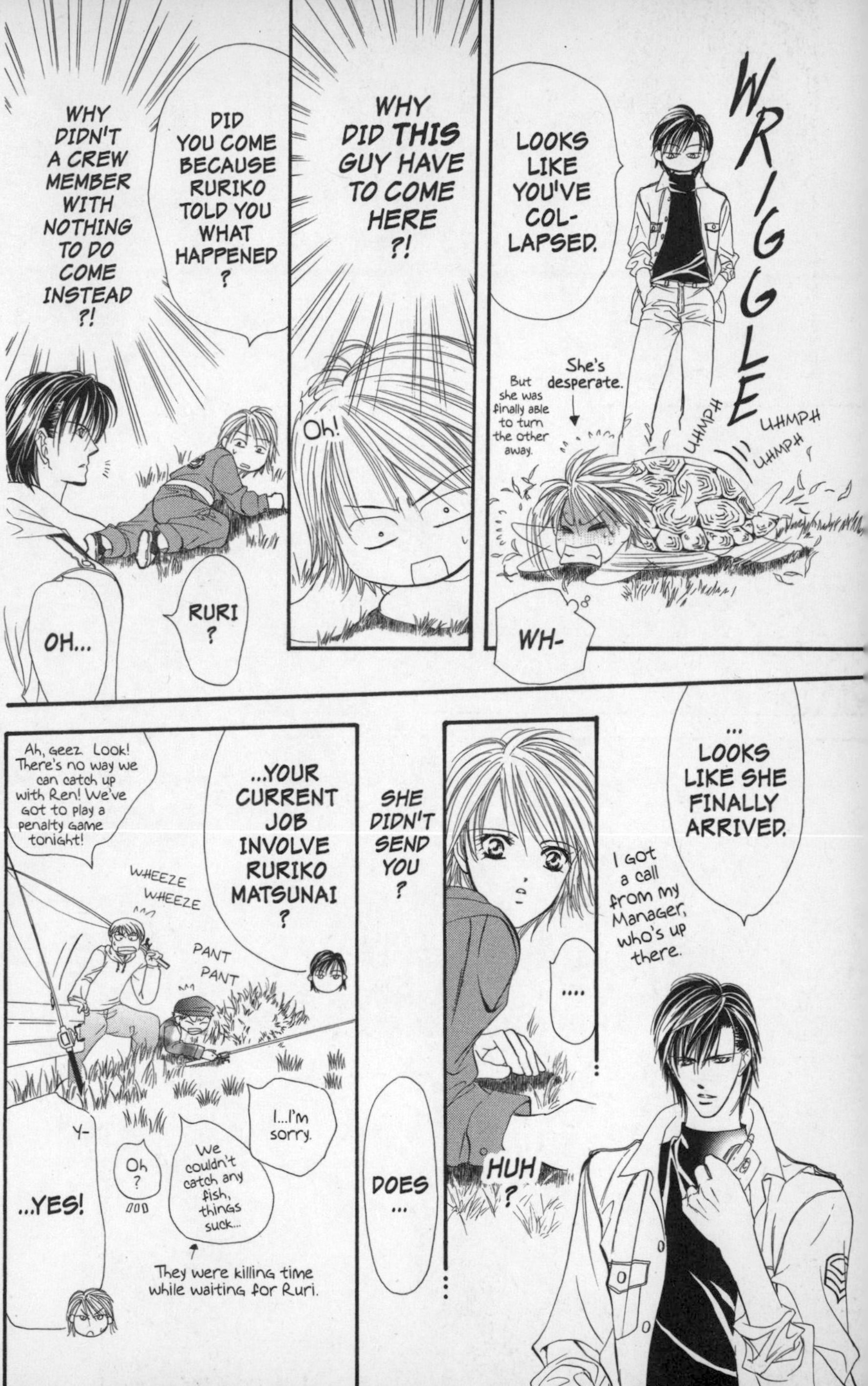
WRIGGLE
LOOKS LIKE YOU'VE COL-LAPSED.
She's desperate.
But she was finally able to turn the other away.
UHMPH
UHMPH
UHMPH
WH-
WHY DID THIS GUY HAVE TO COME HERE?!
Oh!
DID YOU COME BECAUSE RURIKO TOLD YOU WHAT HAPPENED?
WHY DIDN'T A CREW MEMBER WITH NOTHING TO DO COME INSTEAD?!
RURI?
OH...
...LOOKS LIKE SHE FINALLY ARRIVED.
I got a call from my Manager, who's up there.
....
HUH?
SHE DIDN'T SEND YOU?
DOES...
...YOUR CURRENT JOB INVOLVE RURIKO MATSUNAI?
Ah, geez. Look! There's no way we can catch up with Ren! We've got to play a penalty game tonight!
WHEEZE
WHEEZE
PANT
PANT
I...I'm sorry.
We couldn't catch any fish, things suck...
They were killing time while waiting for Ruri.
Oh?
Y-
...YES!

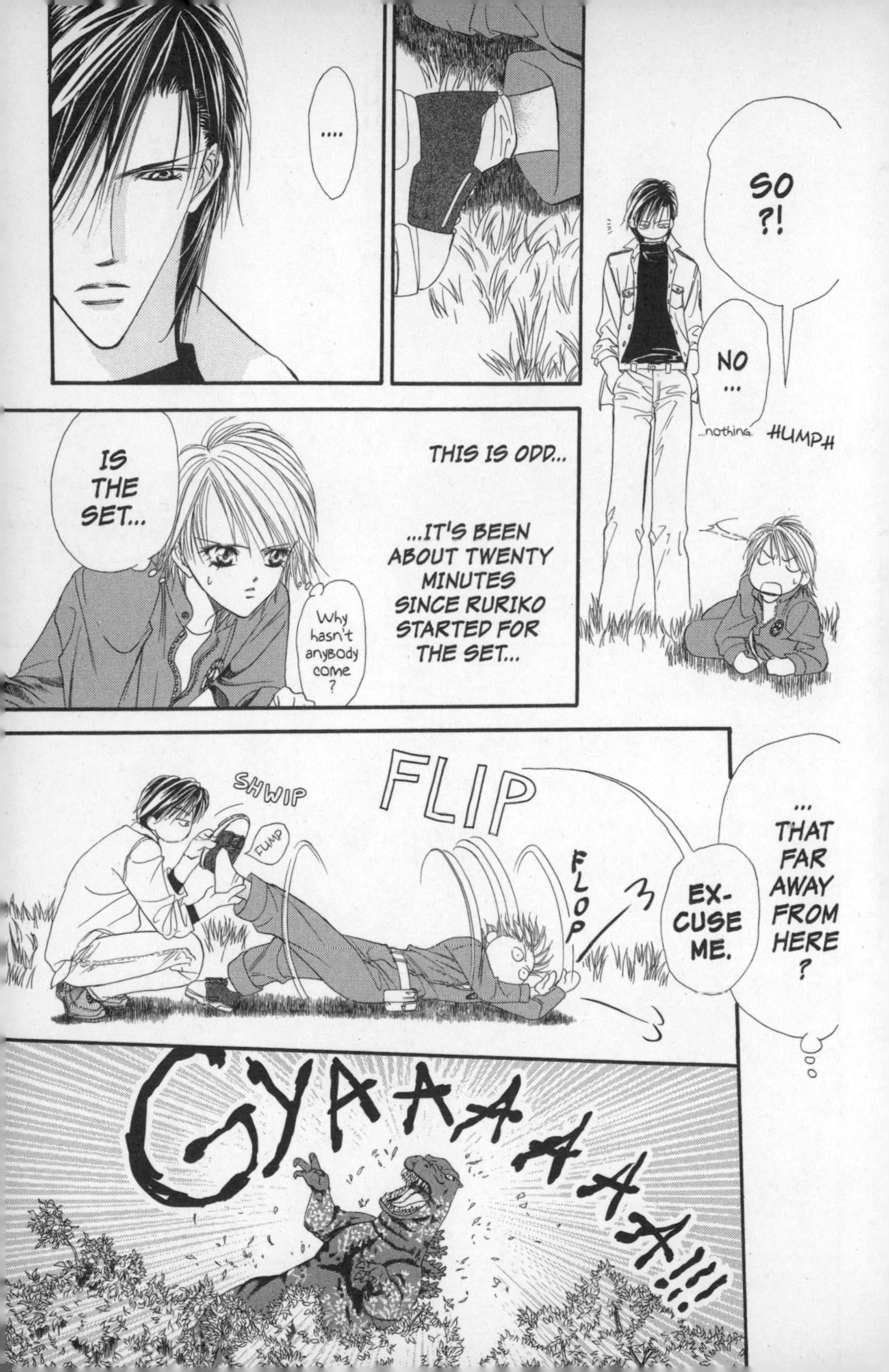
SO ?!
NO ...
...nothing.
HUMPH
....
THIS IS ODD...
...IT'S BEEN ABOUT TWENTY MINUTES SINCE RURIKO STARTED FOR THE SET...
IS THE SET...
Why hasn't anybody come ?
... THAT FAR AWAY FROM HERE ?
EX-CUSE ME.
FLOP
FLIP
SHWIP
FUMP
GYAAAAAA!!!

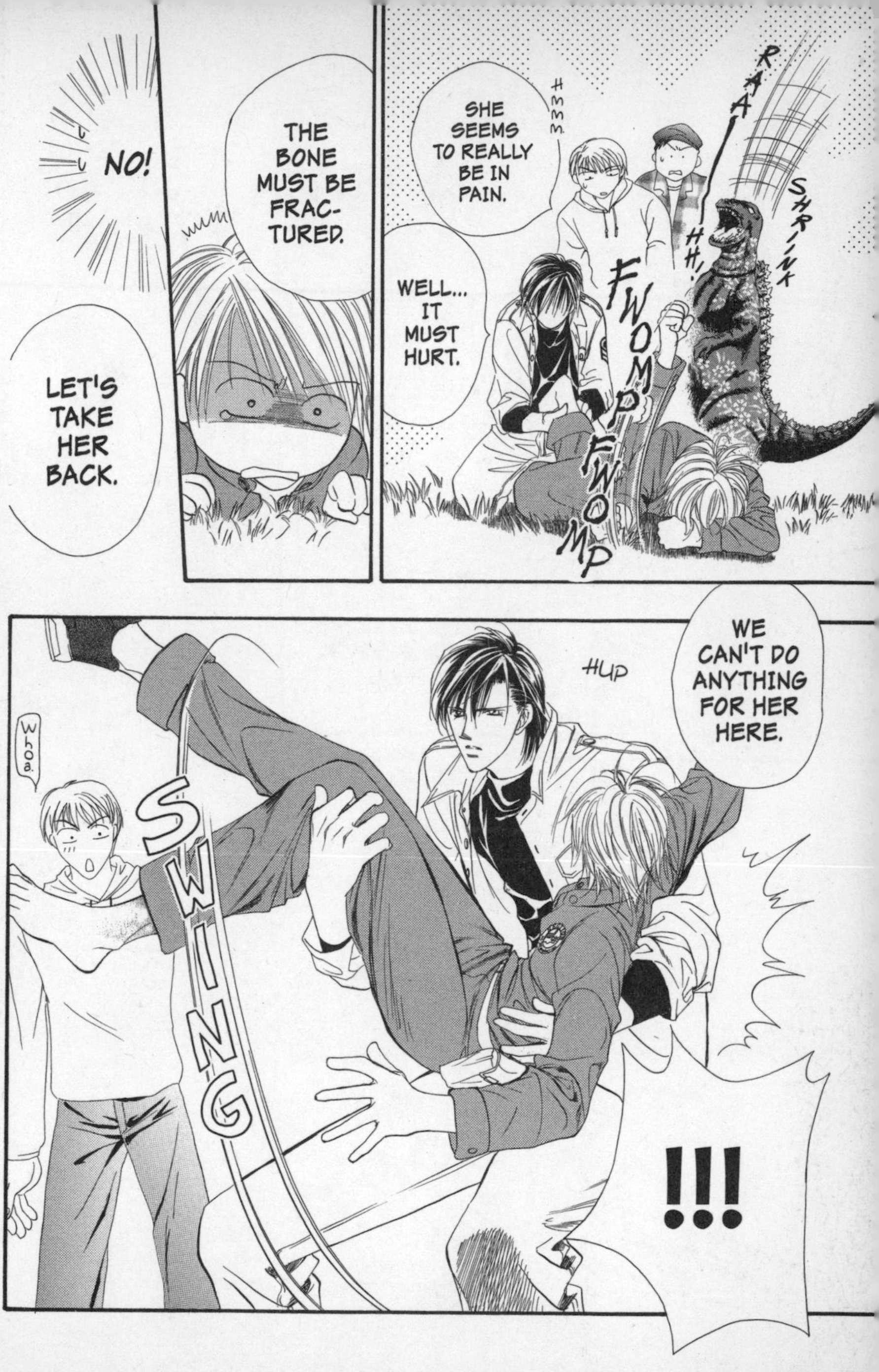
RAAAHH!
SHRIINK
HMMM.
SHE SEEMS TO REALLY BE IN PAIN.
WELL... IT MUST HURT.
FWOMP FWOMP FWOMP
THE BONE MUST BE FRAC-TURED.
NO!
LET'S TAKE HER BACK.
WE CAN'T DO ANYTHING FOR HER HERE.
HUP
Whoa.
SWING
!!!

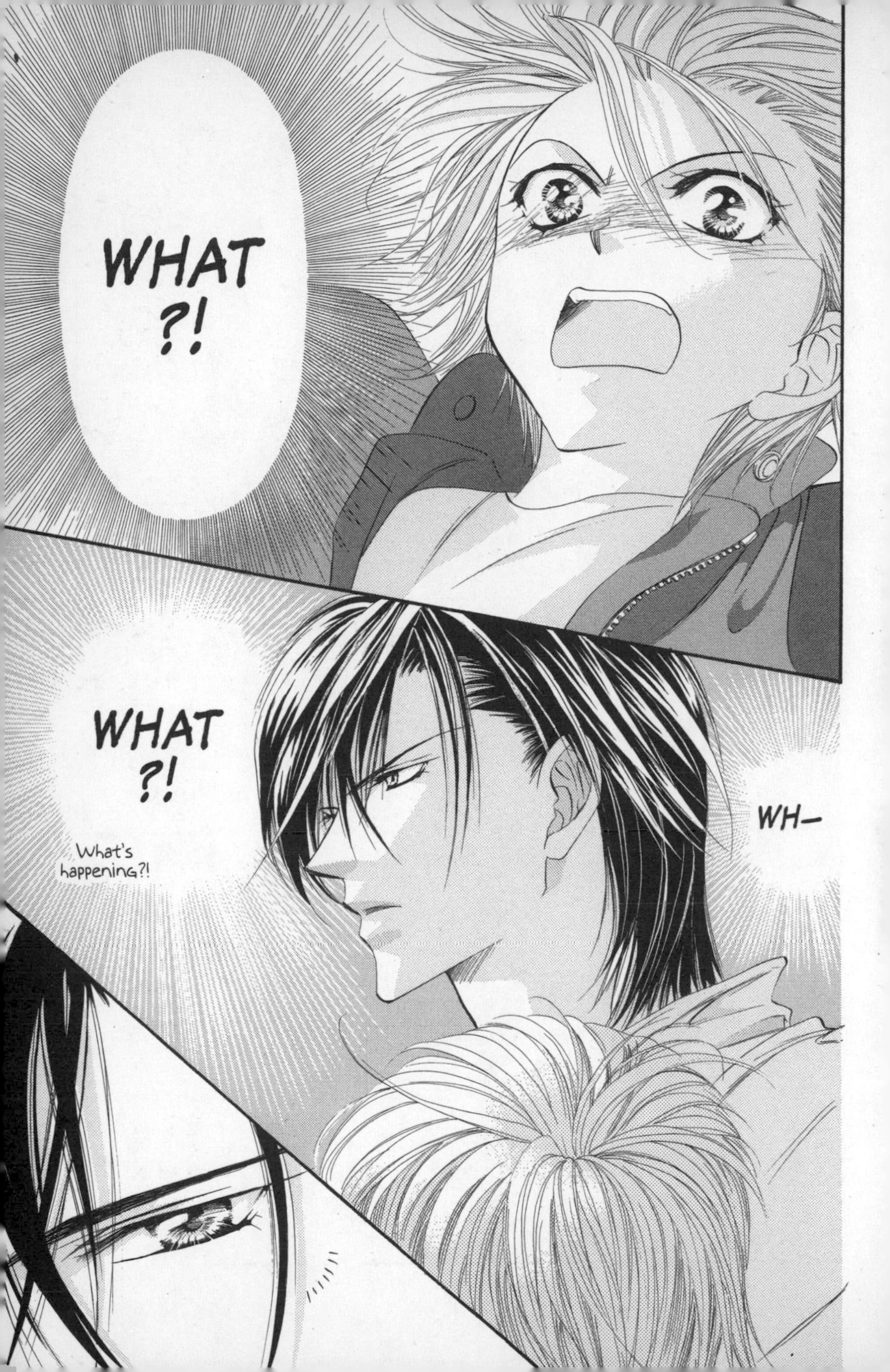
WHAT ?!
WH—
WHAT ?!
What's happening?!

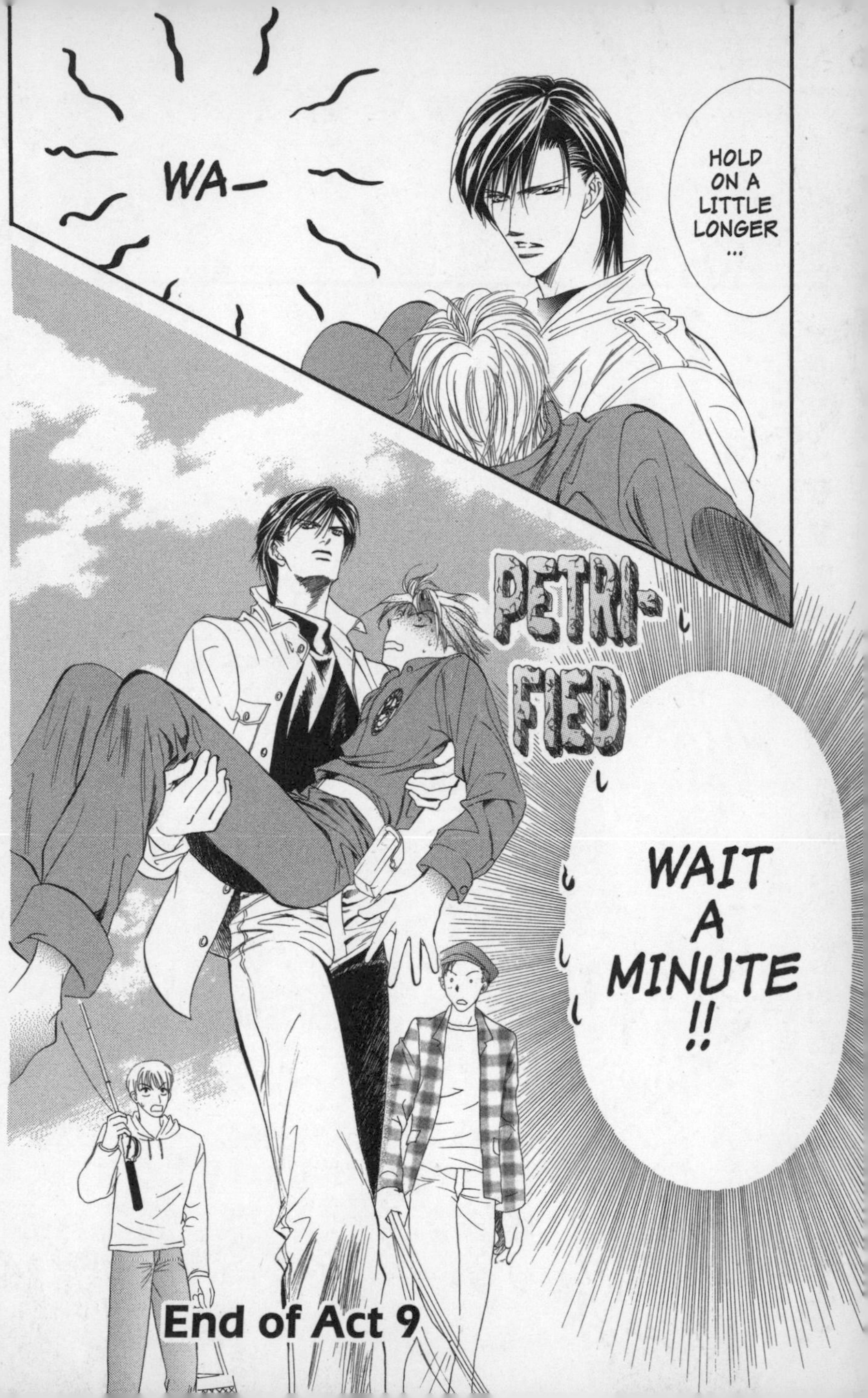
HOLD ON A LITTLE LONGER ...
WA—
PETRI-FIED
WAIT A MINUTE !!
End of Act 9

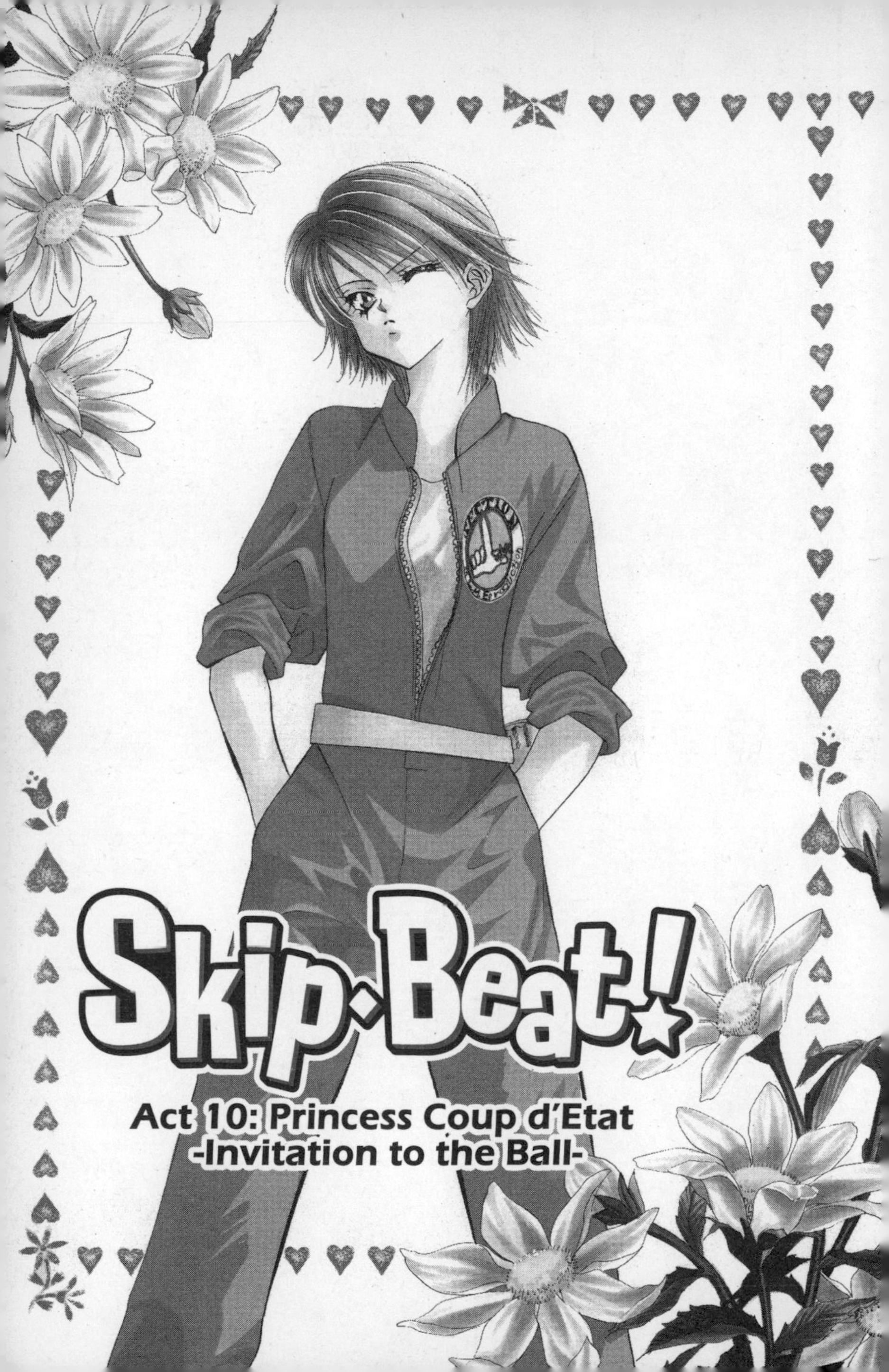
Skip·Beat!
Act 10: Princess Coup d'Etat
-Invitation to the Ball-

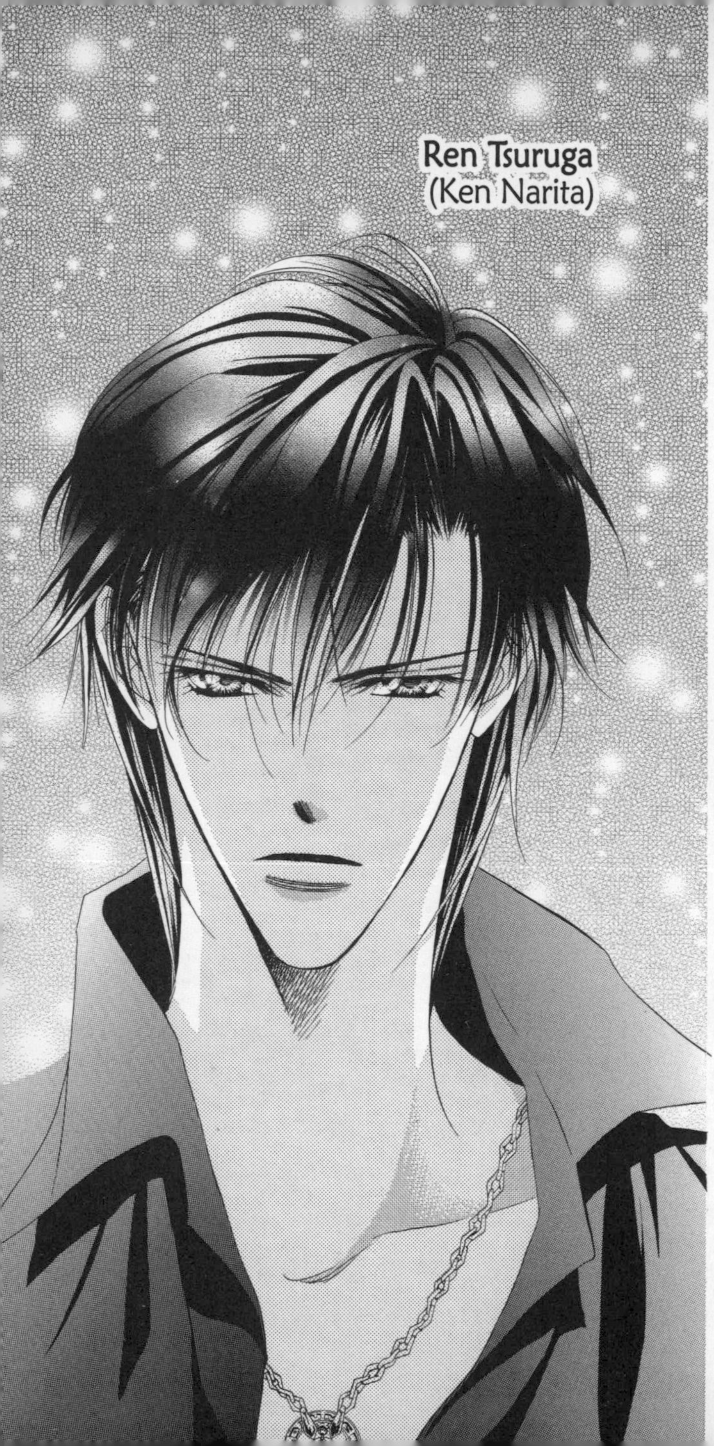
Ren Tsuruga
(Ken Narita)

So, when the last CD was made, I couldn't watch the post-recording, but I was able to watch it this time for *Skip Beat!*. The way everyone in the cast was acting, doing their best to get a feel for their characters, was really professional. There were many retakes, but they didn't make any faces. They did their work sincerely.

Especially when Miki Nagasawa-san, who played Kyoko, was acting, I was praying at her back and kept apologizing... ⁶⁶ ...Because...it was really really hard work...

Oh...

She played the ordinary Kyoko, the Pure Kyoko, and the Evil Kyoko all by herself. Besides, the first rehearsal she did to get a feel for the character was...

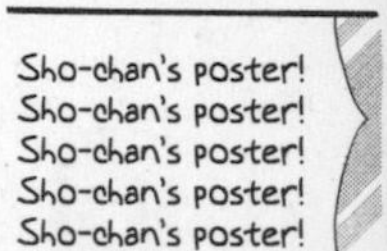
Sho-chan's poster!
Sho-chan's poster!
Sho-chan's poster!
Sho-chan's poster!
Sho-chan's poster!
Sho-chan's poster!
Sho-chan's poster!
Fast, in one breath.
YAAAAH!

Before she's even begun, she's out of breath... ⁶⁶

Uhh... I'm really sorry... Nagasawa-san... ⁶⁶

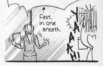

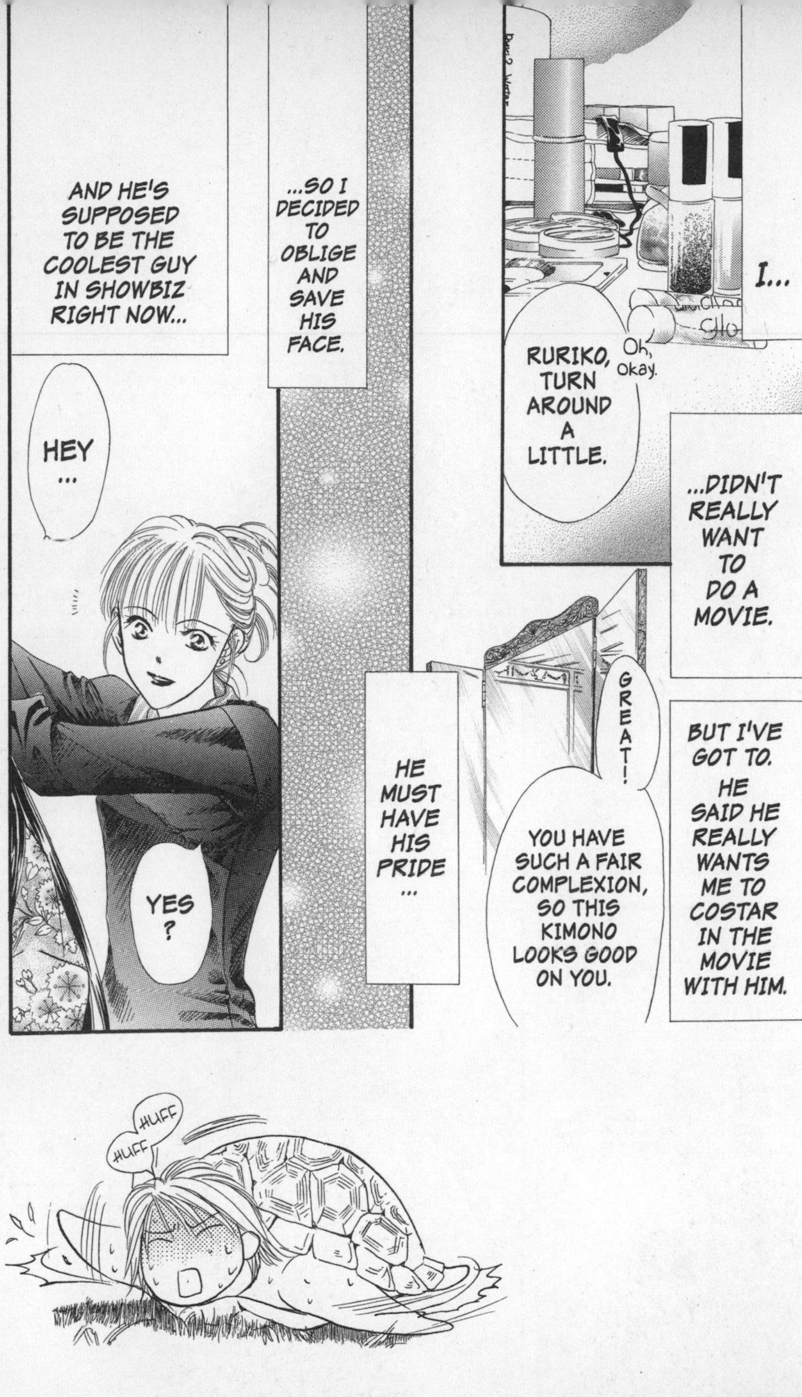
I...
RURIKO, TURN AROUND A LITTLE.
Oh, Okay.
...DIDN'T REALLY WANT TO DO A MOVIE.
BUT I'VE GOT TO. HE SAID HE REALLY WANTS ME TO COSTAR IN THE MOVIE WITH HIM.
GREAT!
YOU HAVE SUCH A FAIR COMPLEXION, SO THIS KIMONO LOOKS GOOD ON YOU.
HE MUST HAVE HIS PRIDE...
...SO I DECIDED TO OBLIGE AND SAVE HIS FACE.
AND HE'S SUPPOSED TO BE THE COOLEST GUY IN SHOWBIZ RIGHT NOW...
HEY...
YES?
HUFF
HUFF

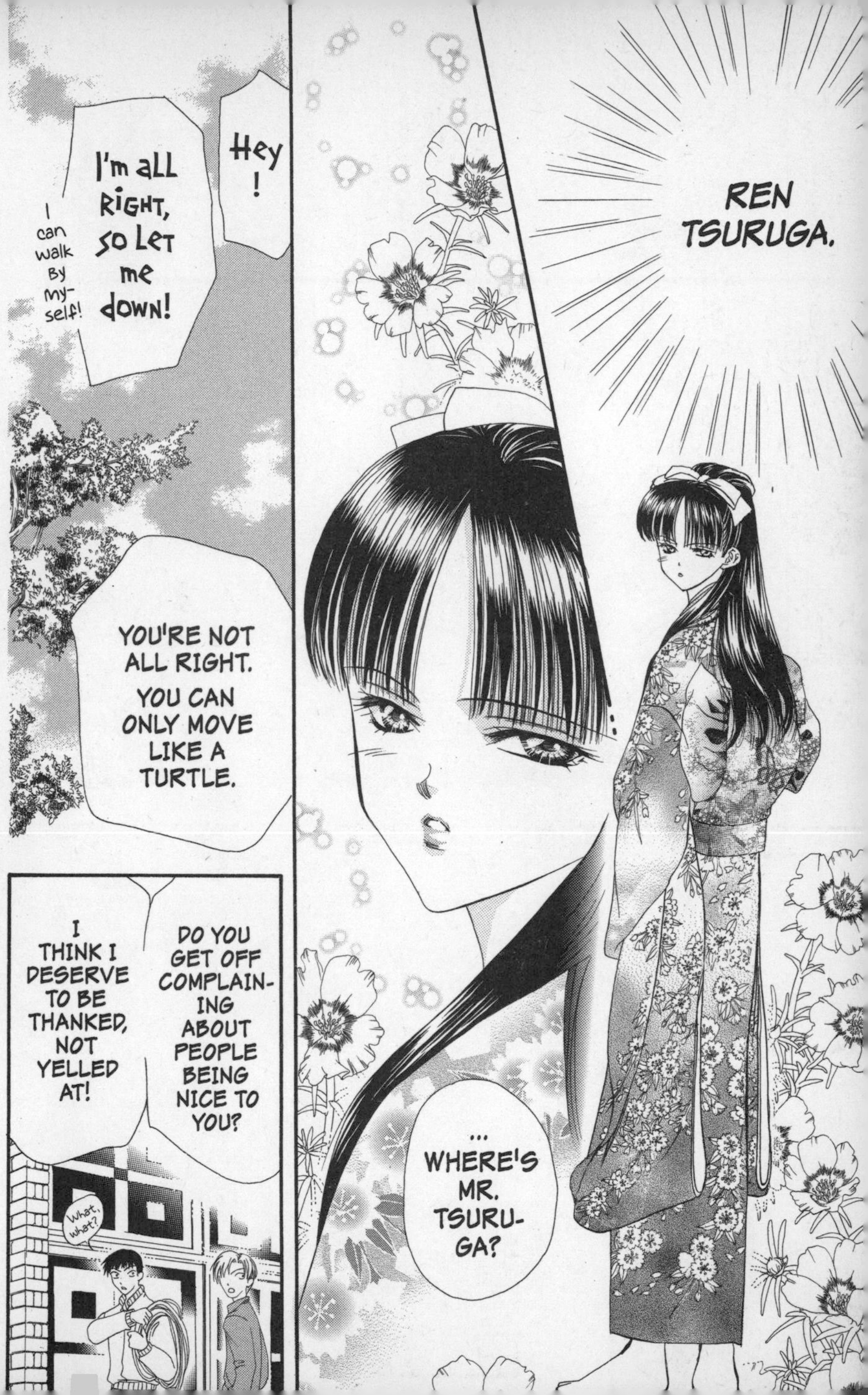
REN TSURUGA.
... WHERE'S MR. TSURU-GA?
Hey!
I'm all RIGHT, so Let me down!
I can walk By My-self!
YOU'RE NOT ALL RIGHT. YOU CAN ONLY MOVE LIKE A TURTLE.
DO YOU GET OFF COMPLAIN-ING ABOUT PEOPLE BEING NICE TO YOU?
I THINK I DESERVE TO BE THANKED, NOT YELLED AT!
What, what?

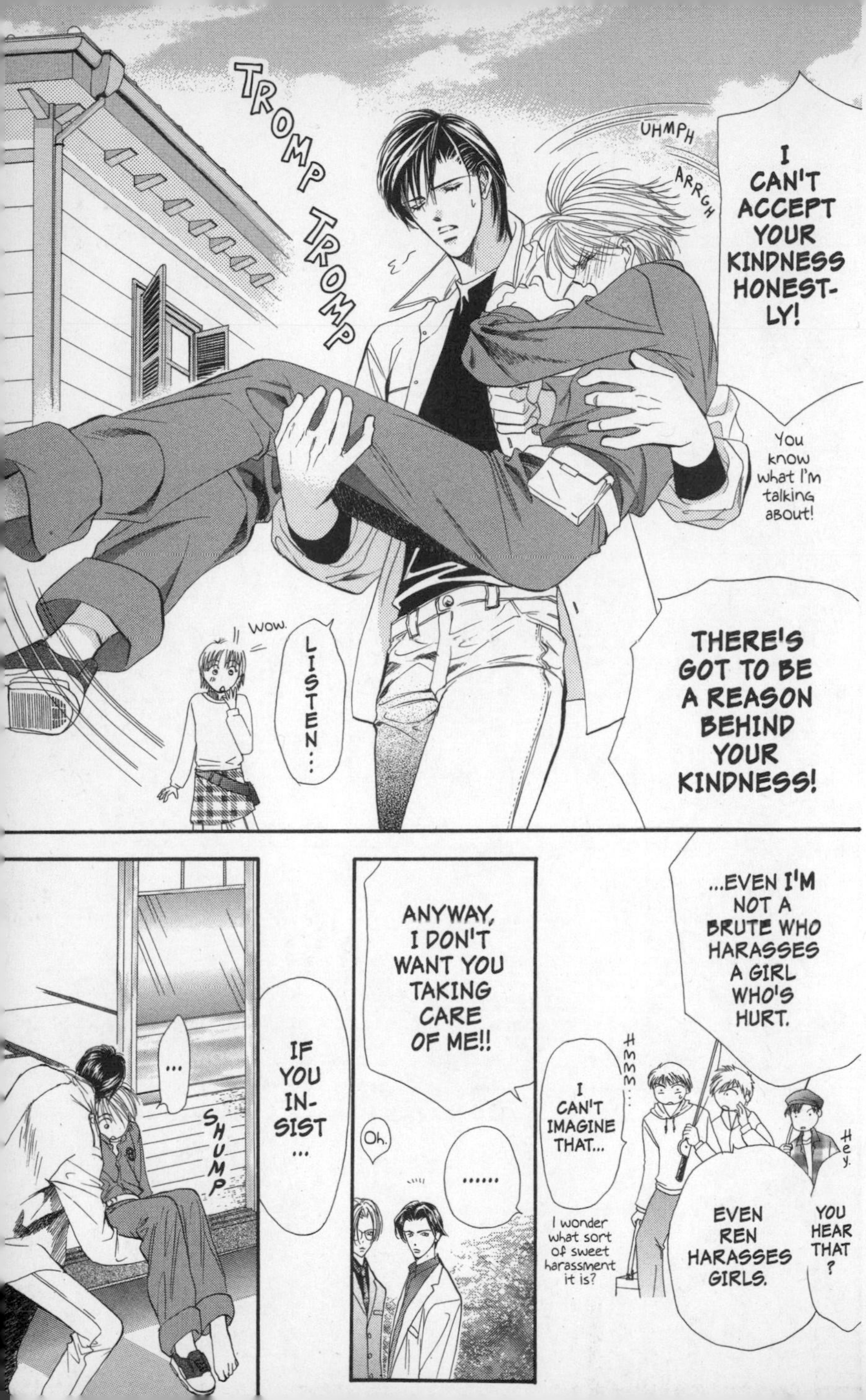

I CAN'T ACCEPT YOUR KINDNESS HONEST-LY!
UHMPH
ARRGH
You know what I'm talking about!
TROMP TROMP TROMP
THERE'S GOT TO BE A REASON BEHIND YOUR KINDNESS!
LISTEN...
WOW.
...EVEN I'M NOT A BRUTE WHO HARASSES A GIRL WHO'S HURT.
Hey.
YOU HEAR THAT?
EVEN REN HARASSES GIRLS.
HMMM...
I CAN'T IMAGINE THAT...
I wonder what sort of sweet harassment it is?
ANYWAY, I DON'T WANT YOU TAKING CARE OF ME!!
......
Oh.
IF YOU IN-SIST...
...
SHUMP

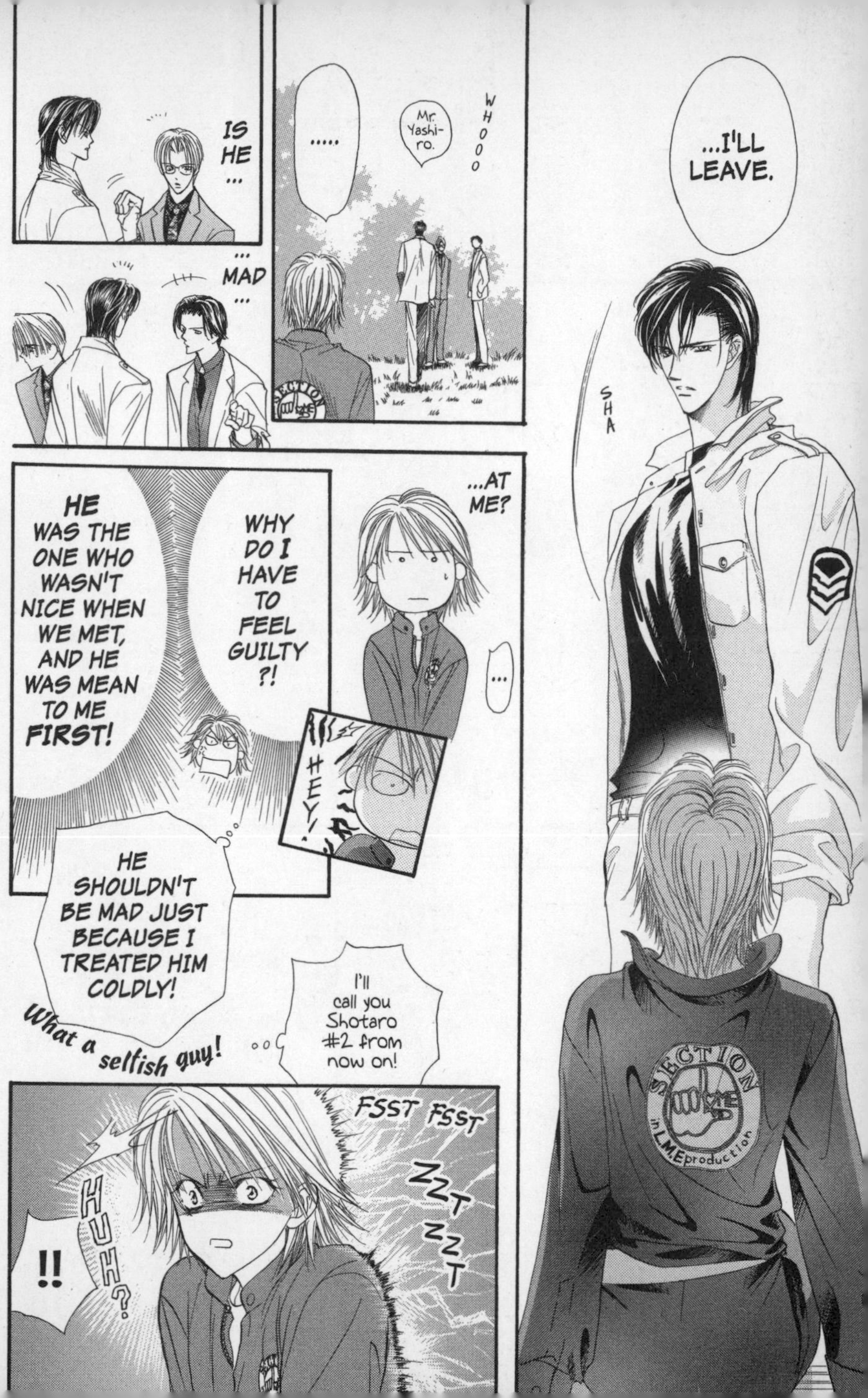
...I'LL LEAVE.
SHA
.....
Mr. Yashi-ro.
WHOOO
IS HE ...
... MAD ...
...AT ME?
WHY DO I HAVE TO FEEL GUILTY ?!
HE WAS THE ONE WHO WASN'T NICE WHEN WE MET, AND HE WAS MEAN TO ME FIRST!
...
HEY!
HE SHOULDN'T BE MAD JUST BECAUSE I TREATED HIM COLDLY!
I'll call you Shotaro #2 from now on!
What a selfish guy!
FSST FSST
ZZT ZZT
HUH?
!!

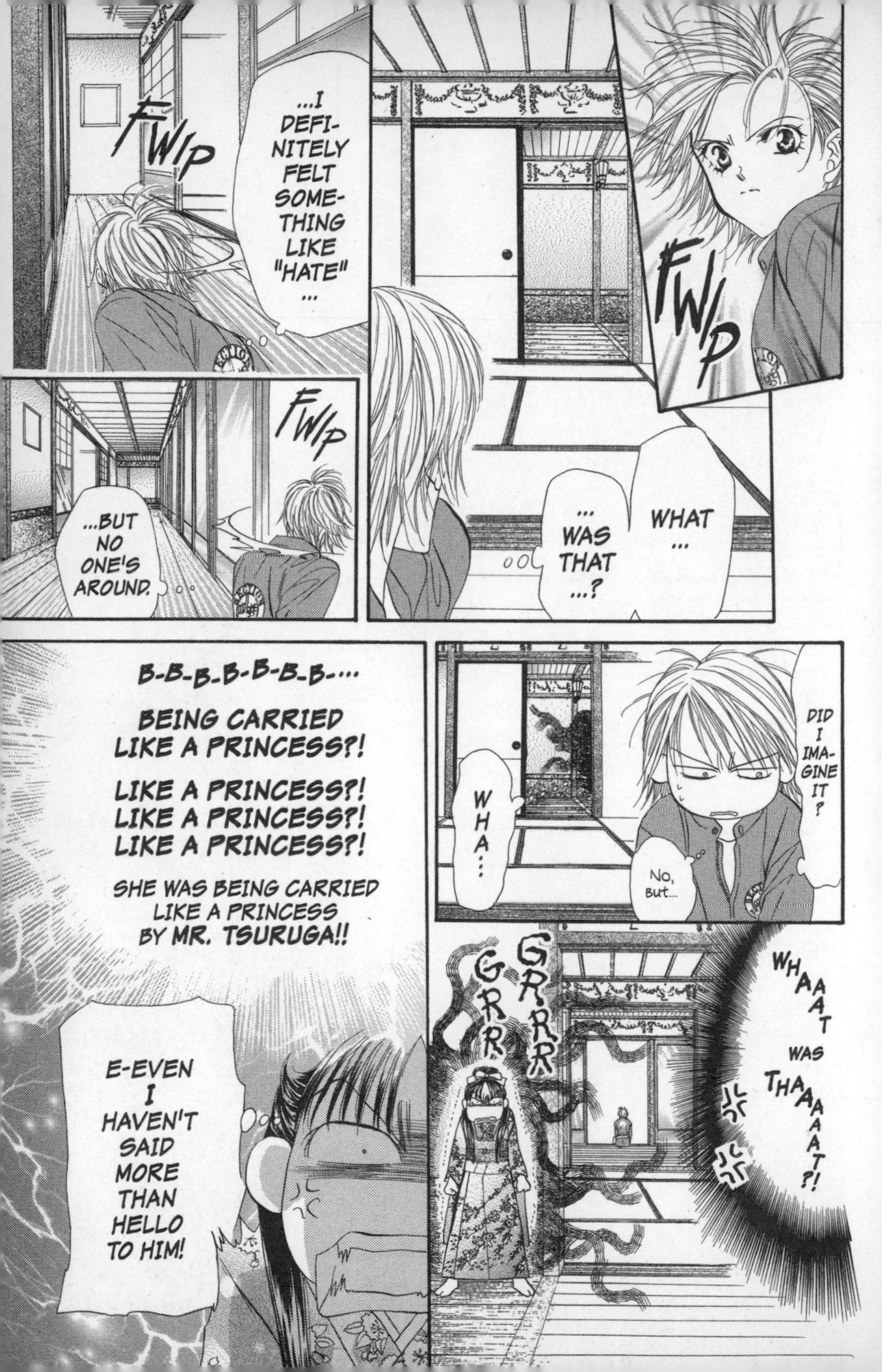
FWIP
WHAT...
...WAS THAT...?
FWIP
...I DEFINITELY FELT SOMETHING LIKE "HATE"...
FWIP
...BUT NO ONE'S AROUND.
DID I IMAGINE IT?
No, but...
WHA...
WHAAAAT WAS THAAAAAT?!
GRRR
GRRR
B-B-B-B-B-B-B-...
BEING CARRIED LIKE A PRINCESS?!
LIKE A PRINCESS?! LIKE A PRINCESS?! LIKE A PRINCESS?!
SHE WAS BEING CARRIED LIKE A PRINCESS BY MR. TSURUGA!!
E-EVEN I HAVEN'T SAID MORE THAN HELLO TO HIM!

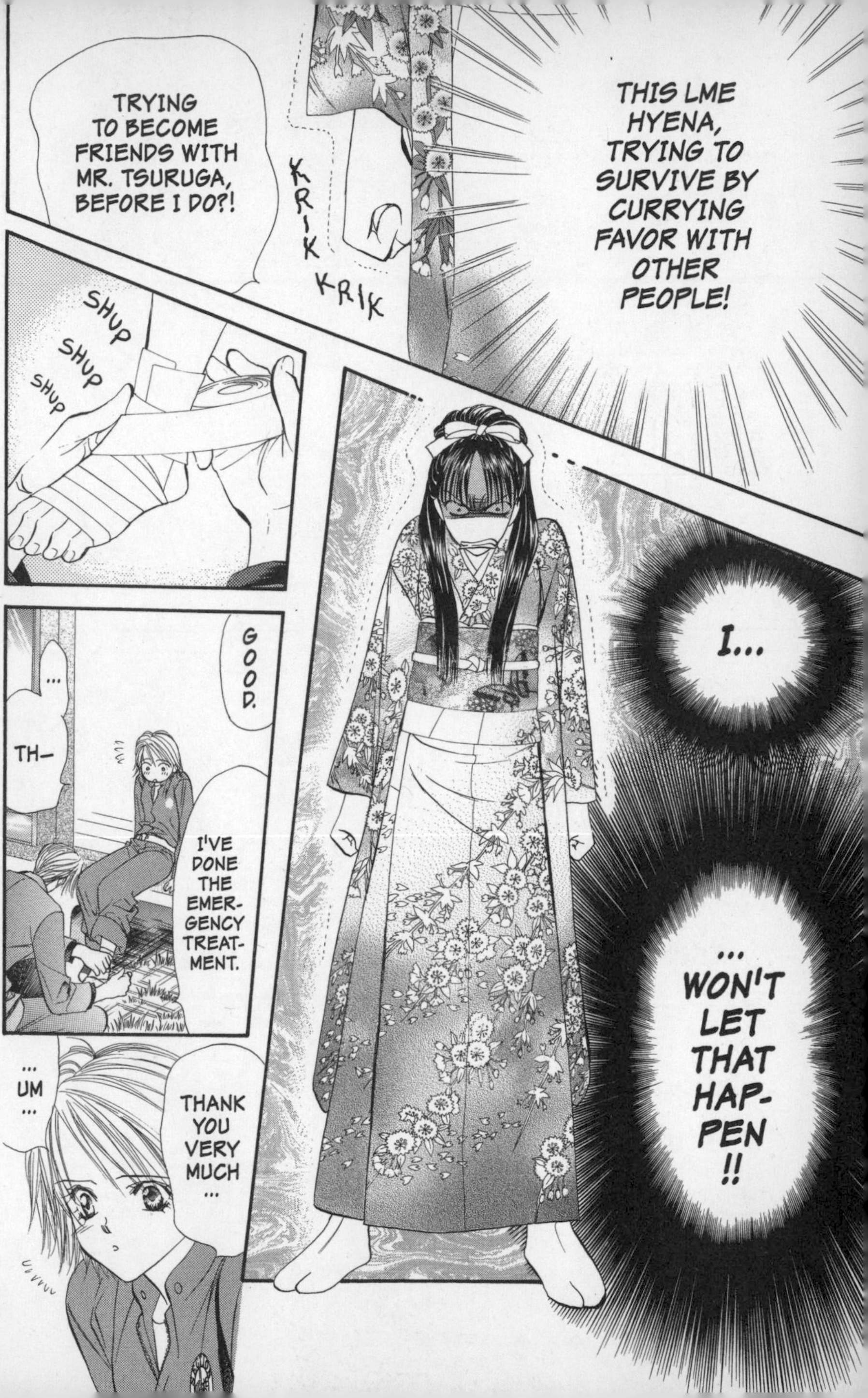
THIS LME HYENA, TRYING TO SURVIVE BY CURRYING FAVOR WITH OTHER PEOPLE!
KRIK KRIK
TRYING TO BECOME FRIENDS WITH MR. TSURUGA, BEFORE I DO?!
I...
...WON'T LET THAT HAP-PEN!!
SHUP SHUP SHUP
GOOD.
...
TH–
I'VE DONE THE EMERG-ENCY TREAT-MENT.
THANK YOU VERY MUCH...
...UM...

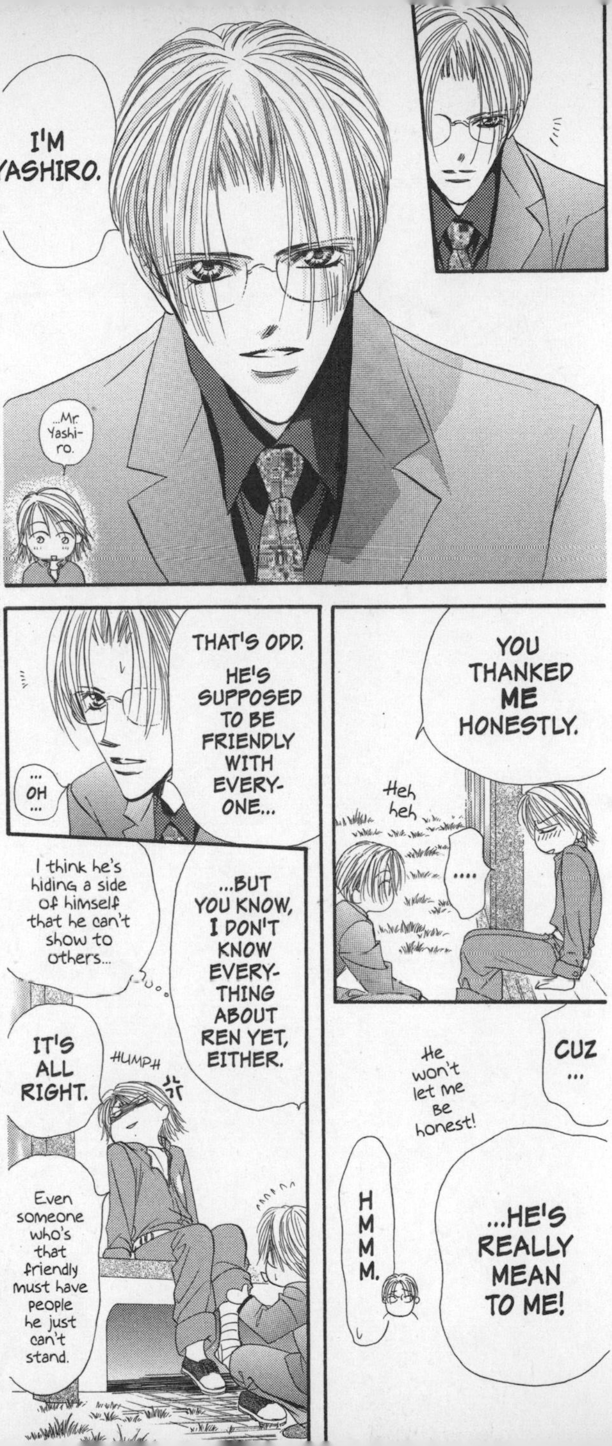
I'M YASHIRO.
...Mr. Yashiro.
YOU THANKED ME HONESTLY.
Heh heh
....
THAT'S ODD. HE'S SUPPOSED TO BE FRIENDLY WITH EVERYONE...
...OH...
...BUT YOU KNOW, I DON'T KNOW EVERYTHING ABOUT REN YET, EITHER.
I think he's hiding a side of himself that he can't show to others...
CUZ...
He won't let me be honest!
...HE'S REALLY MEAN TO ME!
HMMM.
IT'S ALL RIGHT.
HUMPH
Even someone who's that friendly must have people he just can't stand.

When I had my previous work Kurepara turned into a CD, I apparently made the voice actress who did the main character, Tsukasa, really tired...

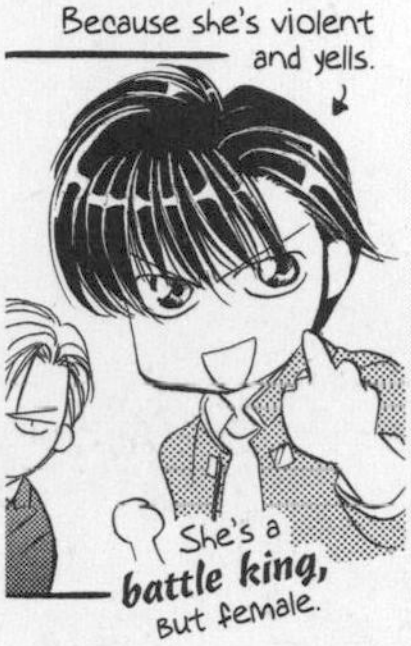
Because she's violent and yells.
She's a battle king, but female.

...and I felt really sorry then. Compared to Tsukasa, Kyoko is more girlish, and so it won't be as tiring as last time...that's what I was thinking, anyway. But it was a big mistake... It looks like the main characters I draw are all ones who are exahusting to portray...

But they're easy to draw...

However...!! The CD, which sucked the cast's blood and sweat and tears and souls, and stole (maybe) the staff's sleep and breaks, turned out wonderful, and my worries were kicked away.

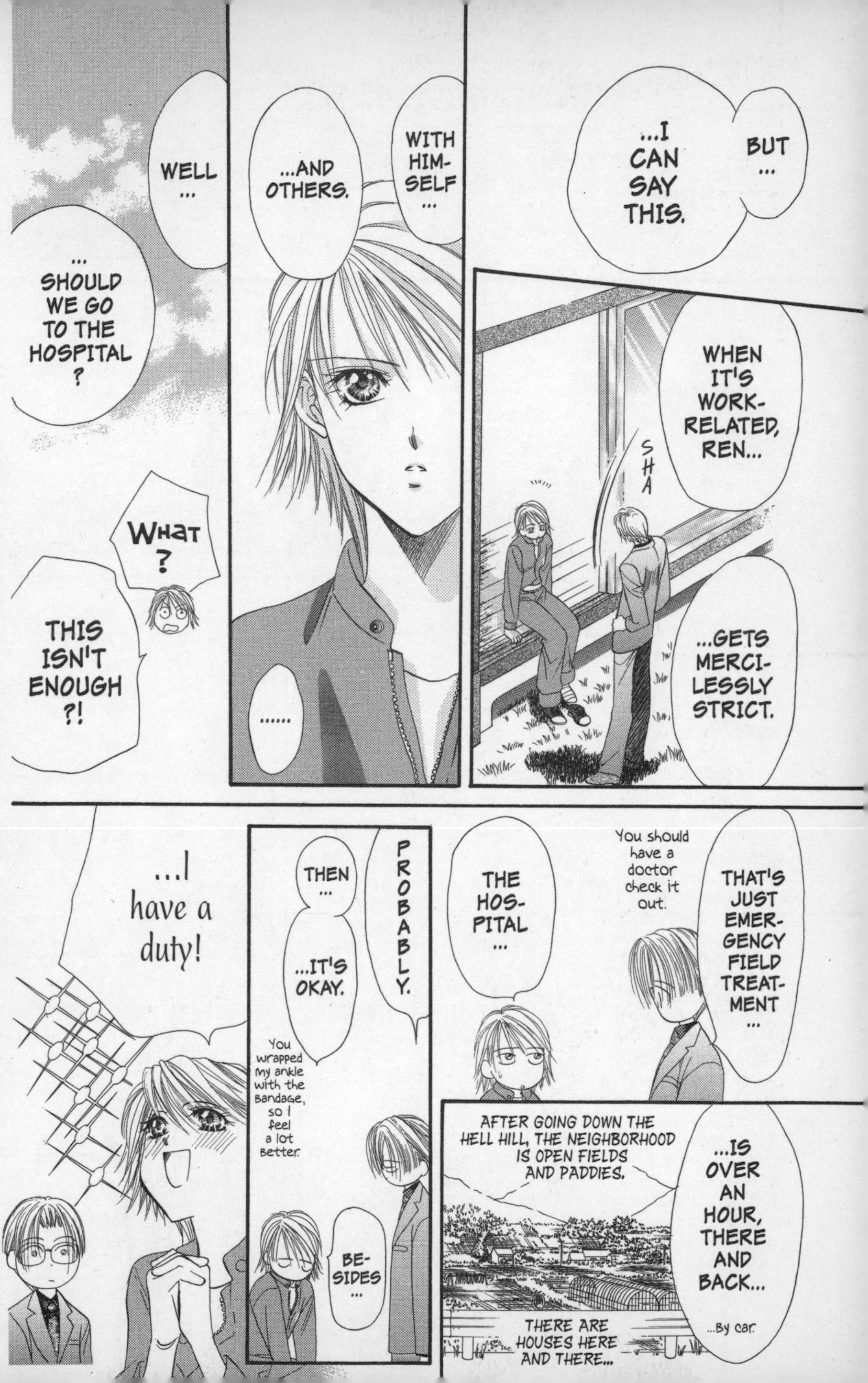
BUT ...
...I CAN SAY THIS.
WHEN IT'S WORK-RELATED, REN...
SHA
...GETS MERCILESSLY STRICT.
WITH HIMSELF ...
...AND OTHERS.
......
WELL ...
... SHOULD WE GO TO THE HOSPITAL?
WHAT?
THIS ISN'T ENOUGH?!
THAT'S JUST EMERGENCY FIELD TREATMENT ...
You should have a doctor check it out.
THE HOSPITAL ...
...IS OVER AN HOUR, THERE AND BACK...
...By car.
AFTER GOING DOWN THE HELL HILL, THE NEIGHBORHOOD IS OPEN FIELDS AND PADDIES.
THERE ARE HOUSES HERE AND THERE...
PROBABLY.
THEN ...
...IT'S OKAY.
You wrapped my ankle with the bandage, so I feel a lot better.
BESIDES ...
...I have a duty!

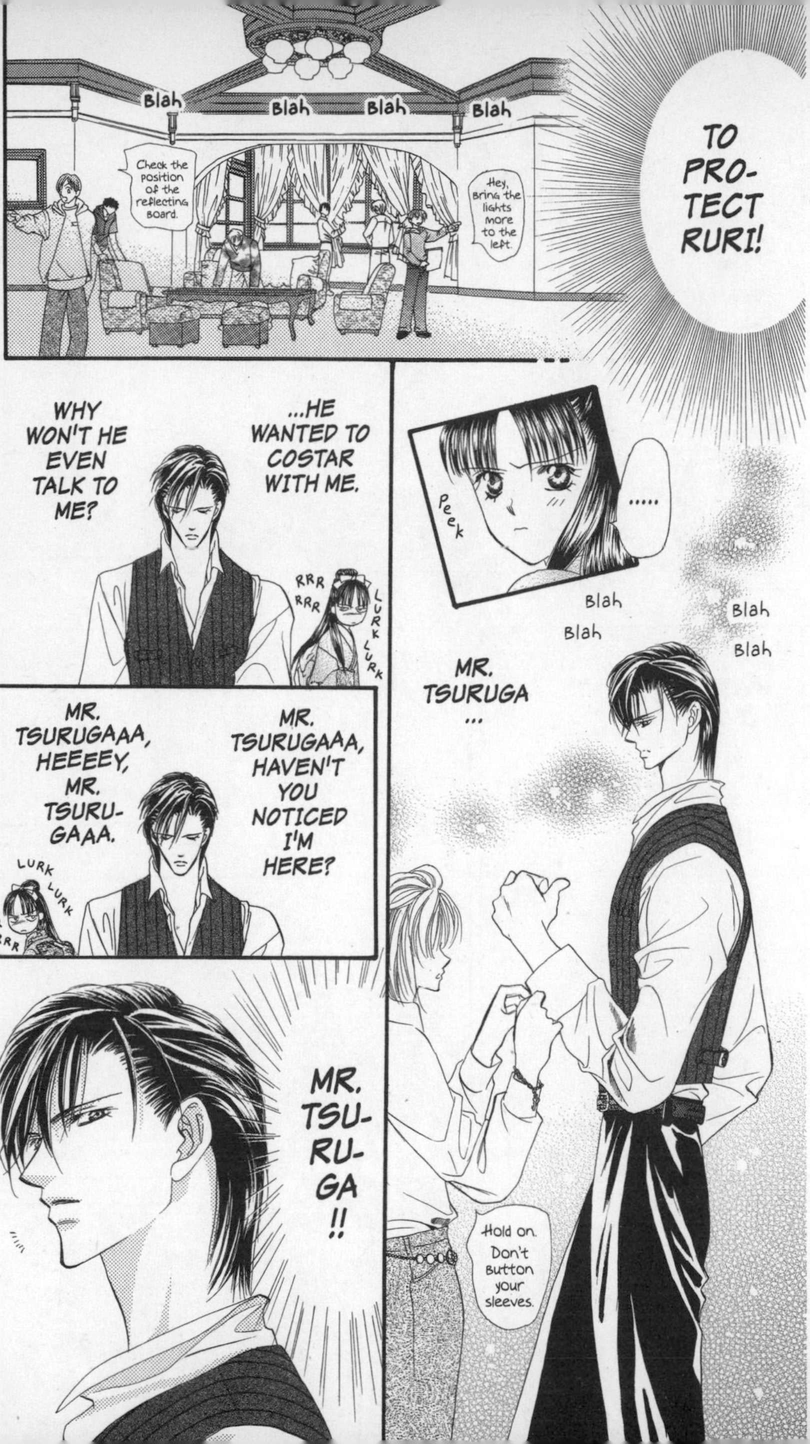
TO PROTECT RURI!
Blah
Blah
Blah
Blah
Hey, bring the lights more to the left.
Check the position of the reflecting board.
Peek
.....
Blah
Blah
Blah
Blah
MR. TSURUGA...
Hold on. Don't button your sleeves.
...HE WANTED TO COSTAR WITH ME.
WHY WON'T HE EVEN TALK TO ME?
RRR RRR
LURK LURK
MR. TSURUGAAA, HAVEN'T YOU NOTICED I'M HERE?
MR. TSURUGAAA, HEEEEY, MR. TSURUGAAA.
LURK LURK
RRR RRR
MR. TSURUGA!!

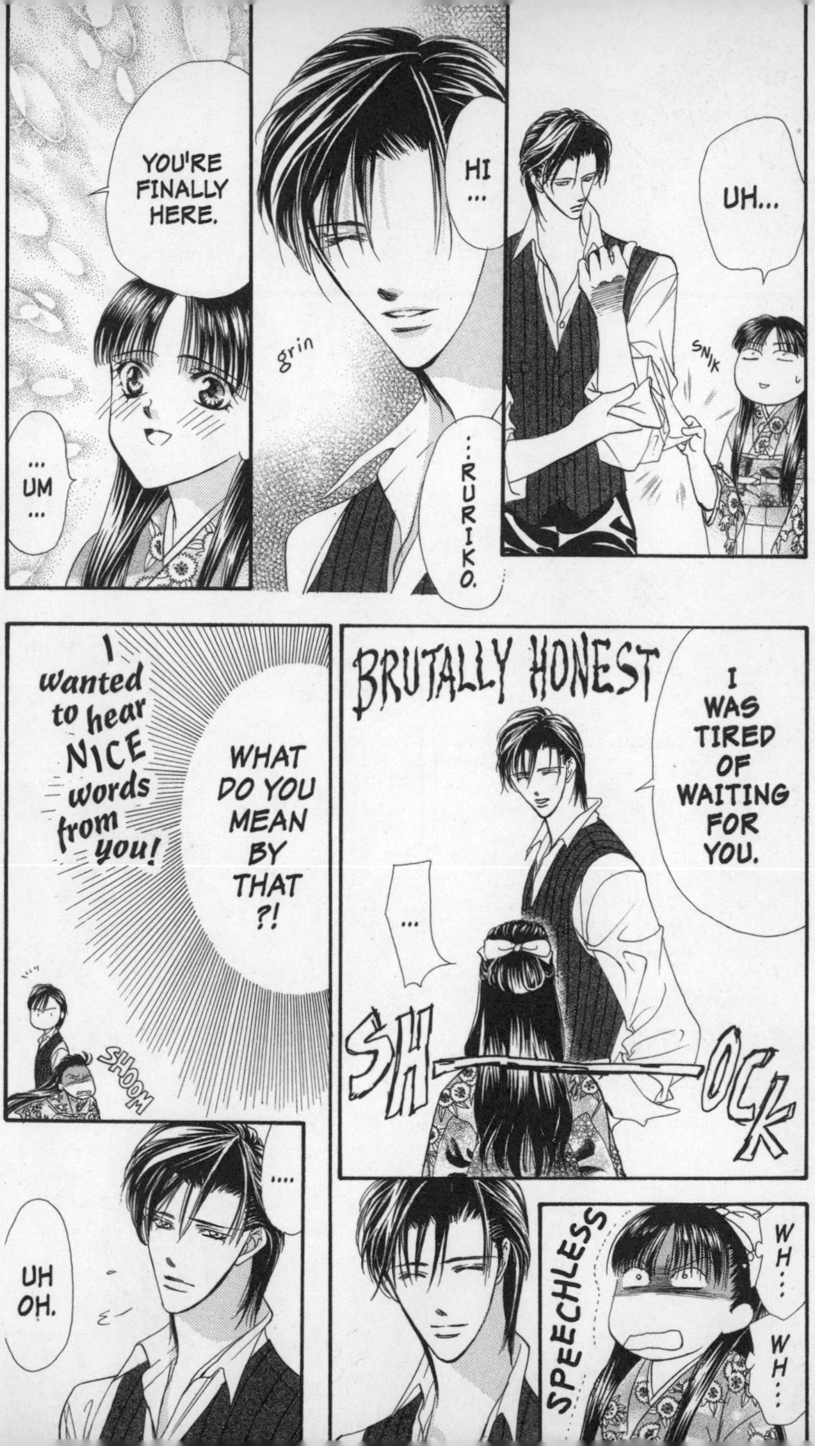
UH...
SNIK
HI ...
grin
...RURIKO.
YOU'RE FINALLY HERE.
... UM ...
BRUTALLY HONEST
I WAS TIRED OF WAITING FOR YOU.
...
SH-OCK
WHAT DO YOU MEAN BY THAT?!
I wanted to hear NICE words from you!
SHOOM
SPEECHLESS
WH...
WH...
....
UH OH.

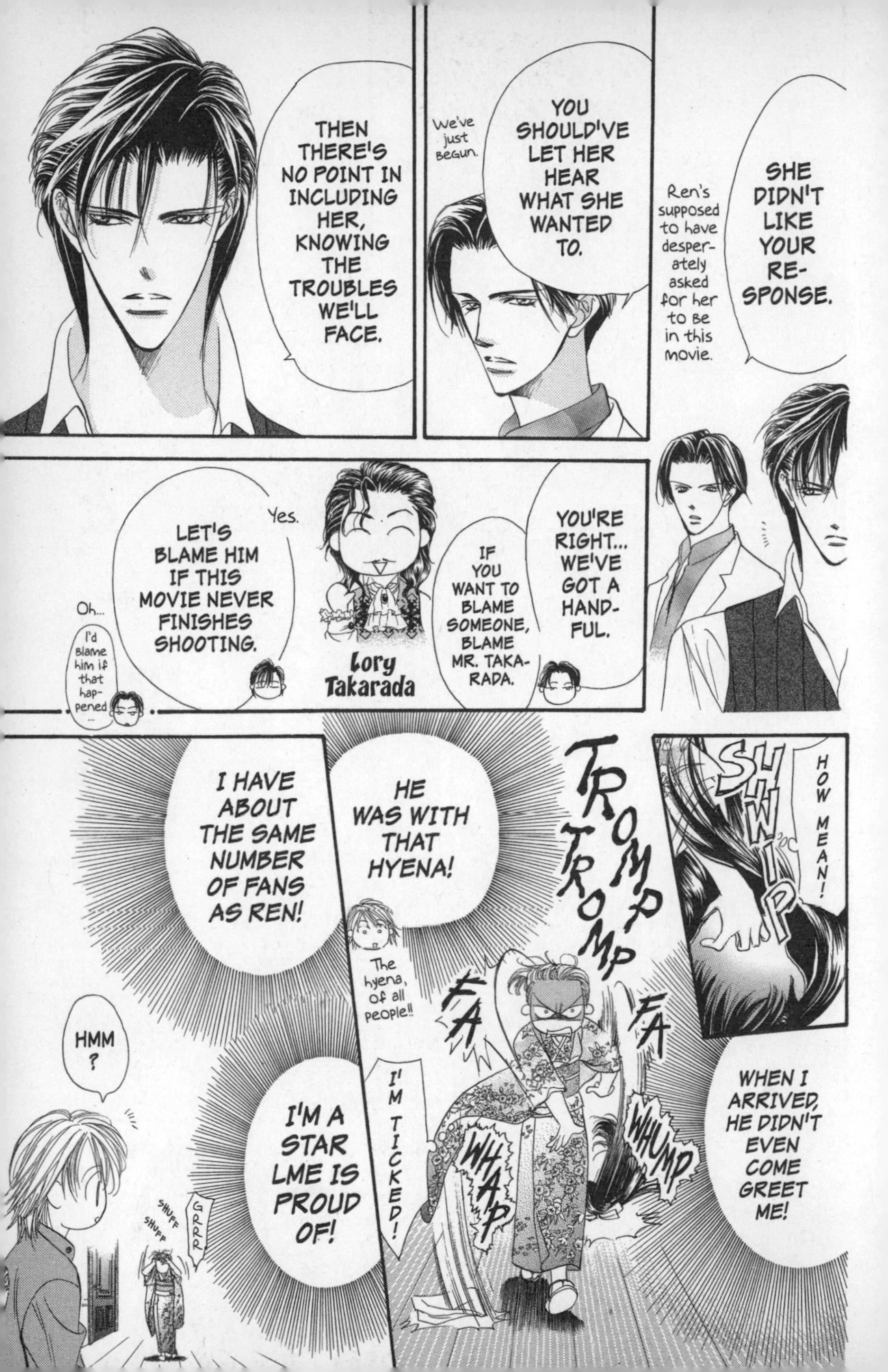

SHE DIDN'T LIKE YOUR RE-SPONSE.
Ren's supposed to have desper-ately asked for her to be in this movie.
YOU SHOULD'VE LET HER HEAR WHAT SHE WANTED TO.
We've just begun.
THEN THERE'S NO POINT IN INCLUDING HER, KNOWING THE TROUBLES WE'LL FACE.
YOU'RE RIGHT... WE'VE GOT A HAND-FUL.
IF YOU WANT TO BLAME SOMEONE, BLAME MR. TAKA-RADA.
Lory Takarada
Yes.
LET'S BLAME HIM IF THIS MOVIE NEVER FINISHES SHOOTING.
Oh...
I'd blame him if that hap-pened...
SHWIP
HOW MEAN!
TROMP TROMP TROMP
WHEN I ARRIVED, HE DIDN'T EVEN COME GREET ME!
HE WAS WITH THAT HYENA!
The hyena, of all people!!
I HAVE ABOUT THE SAME NUMBER OF FANS AS REN!
FA
FA
WHUMP
WHAP
I'M TICKED!
I'M A STAR LME IS PROUD OF!
HMM?
SHUFF SHUFF
GRRR

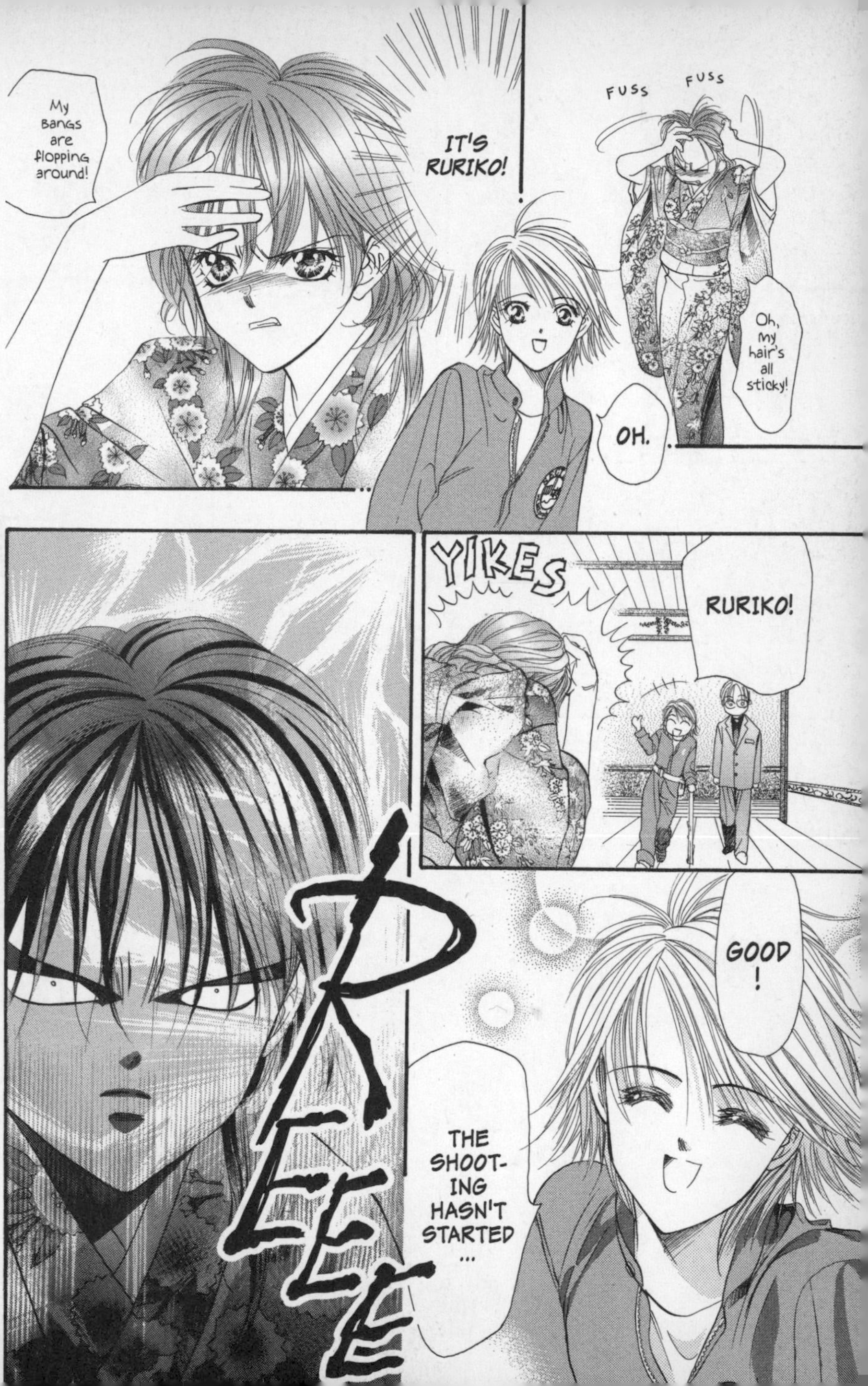
FUSS FUSS
Oh, my hair's all sticky!
OH.
IT'S RURIKO!
My bangs are flopping around!
YIKES
RURIKO!
GOOD!
THE SHOOTING HASN'T STARTED ...
REEEE

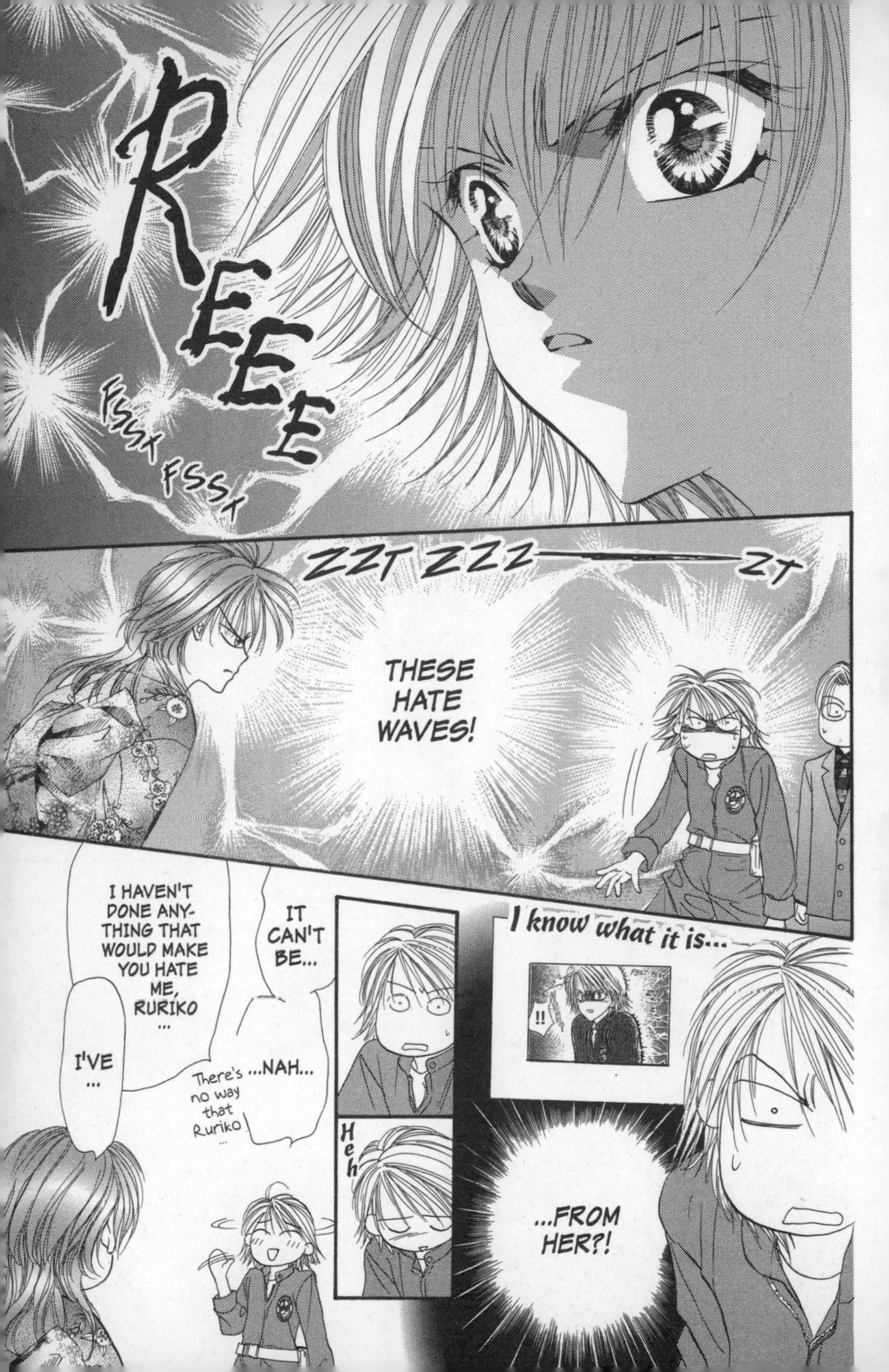

REEE
FSSX FSSX
ZZT ZZZ——ZT
THESE HATE WAVES!
I know what it is...
!!
...FROM HER?!
IT CAN'T BE...
...NAH...
Heh
I HAVEN'T DONE ANYTHING THAT WOULD MAKE YOU HATE ME, RURIKO ...
I'VE ...
There's no way that Ruriko ...

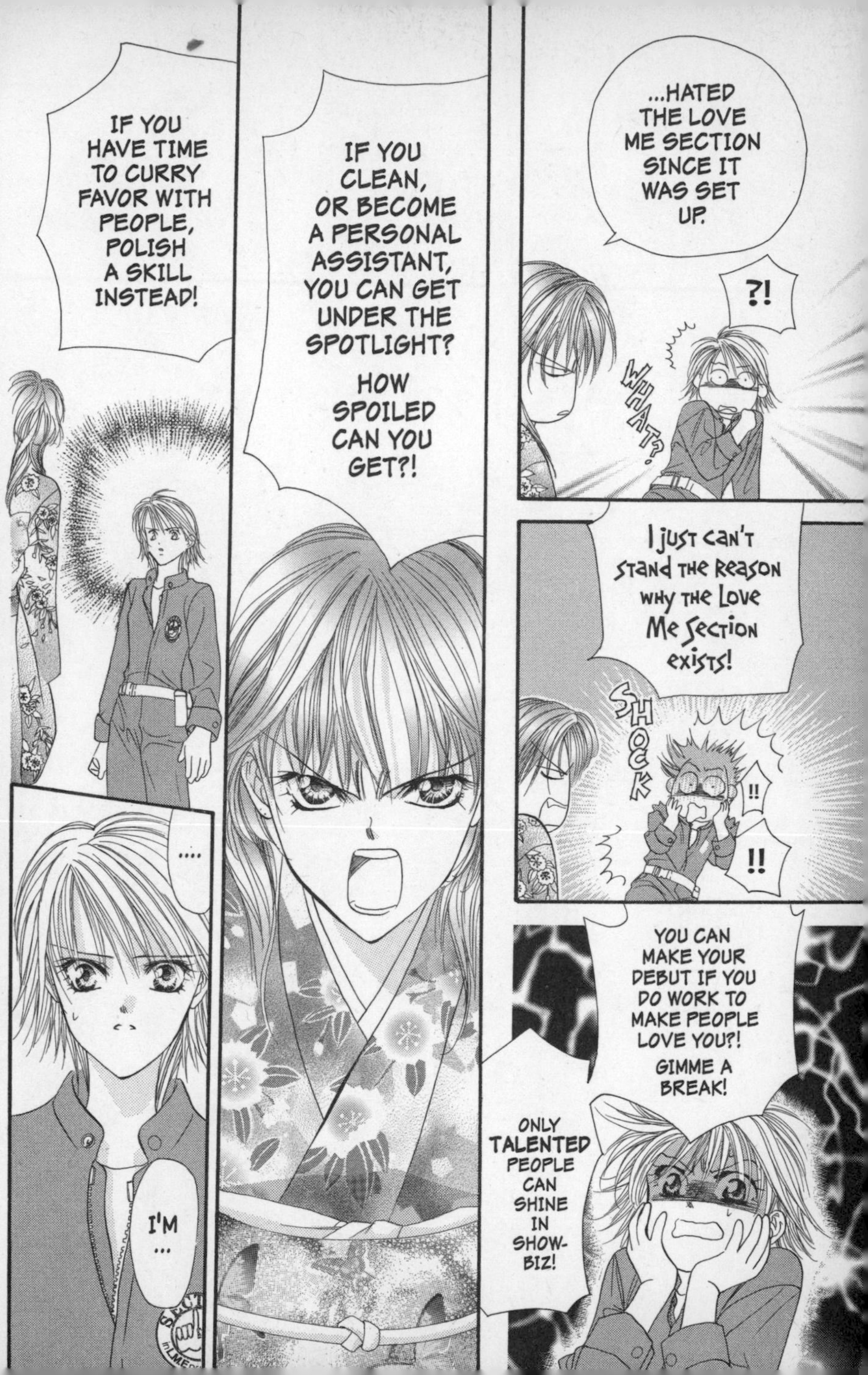

...HATED THE LOVE ME SECTION SINCE IT WAS SET UP.
?!
WHAT?
I just can't stand the reason why the Love Me Section exists!
SHOCK
!!
!!
YOU CAN MAKE YOUR DEBUT IF YOU DO WORK TO MAKE PEOPLE LOVE YOU?! GIMME A BREAK!
ONLY TALENTED PEOPLE CAN SHINE IN SHOW-BIZ!
IF YOU CLEAN, OR BECOME A PERSONAL ASSISTANT, YOU CAN GET UNDER THE SPOTLIGHT?
HOW SPOILED CAN YOU GET?!
IF YOU HAVE TIME TO CURRY FAVOR WITH PEOPLE, POLISH A SKILL INSTEAD!
....
I'M ...

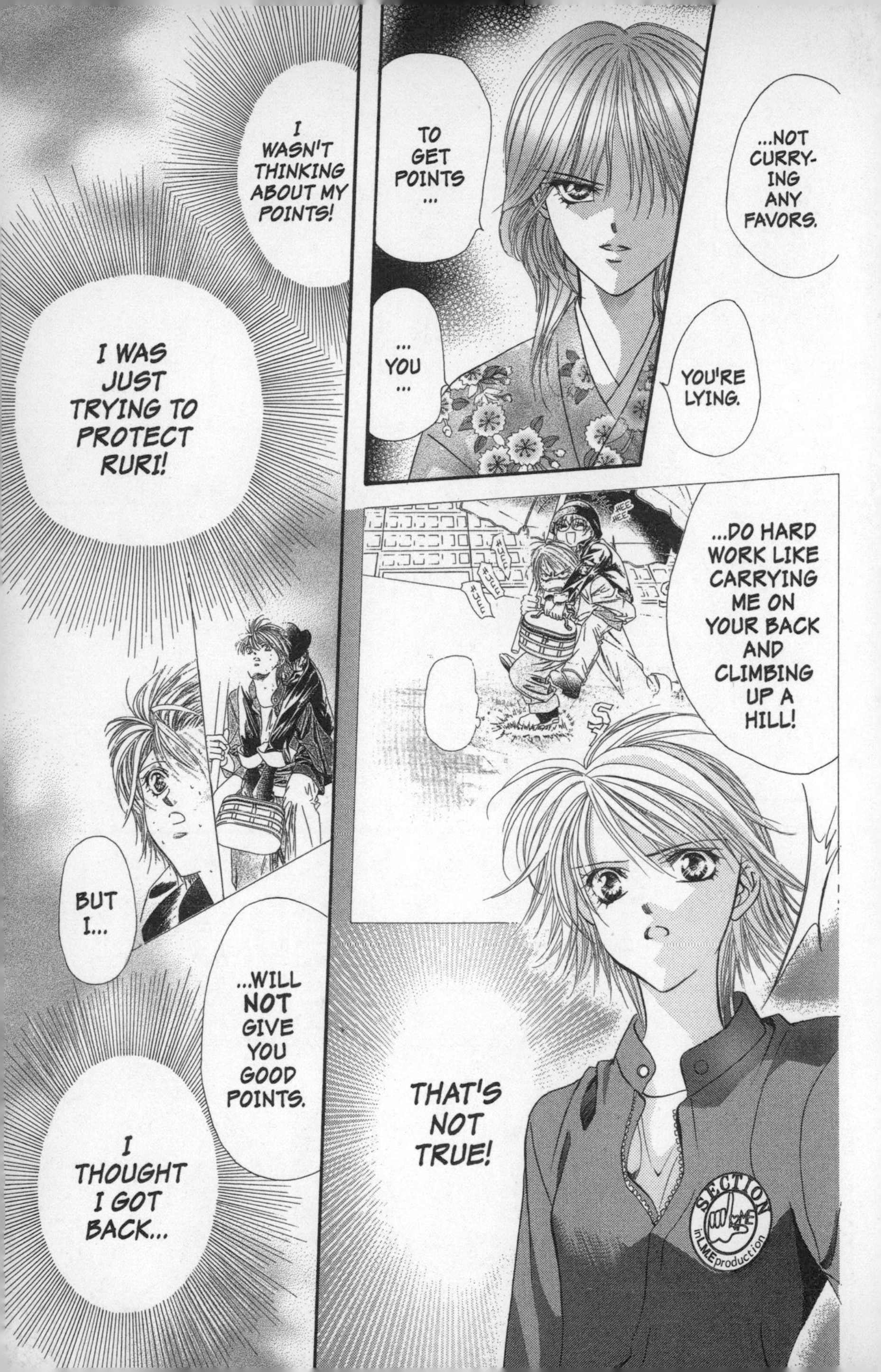
...NOT CURRYING ANY FAVORS.
TO GET POINTS ...
YOU'RE LYING.
... YOU ...
I WASN'T THINKING ABOUT MY POINTS!
I WAS JUST TRYING TO PROTECT RURI!
...DO HARD WORK LIKE CARRYING ME ON YOUR BACK AND CLIMBING UP A HILL!
BUT I...
...WILL NOT GIVE YOU GOOD POINTS.
THAT'S NOT TRUE!
I THOUGHT I GOT BACK...
SECTION
inLMEproduction

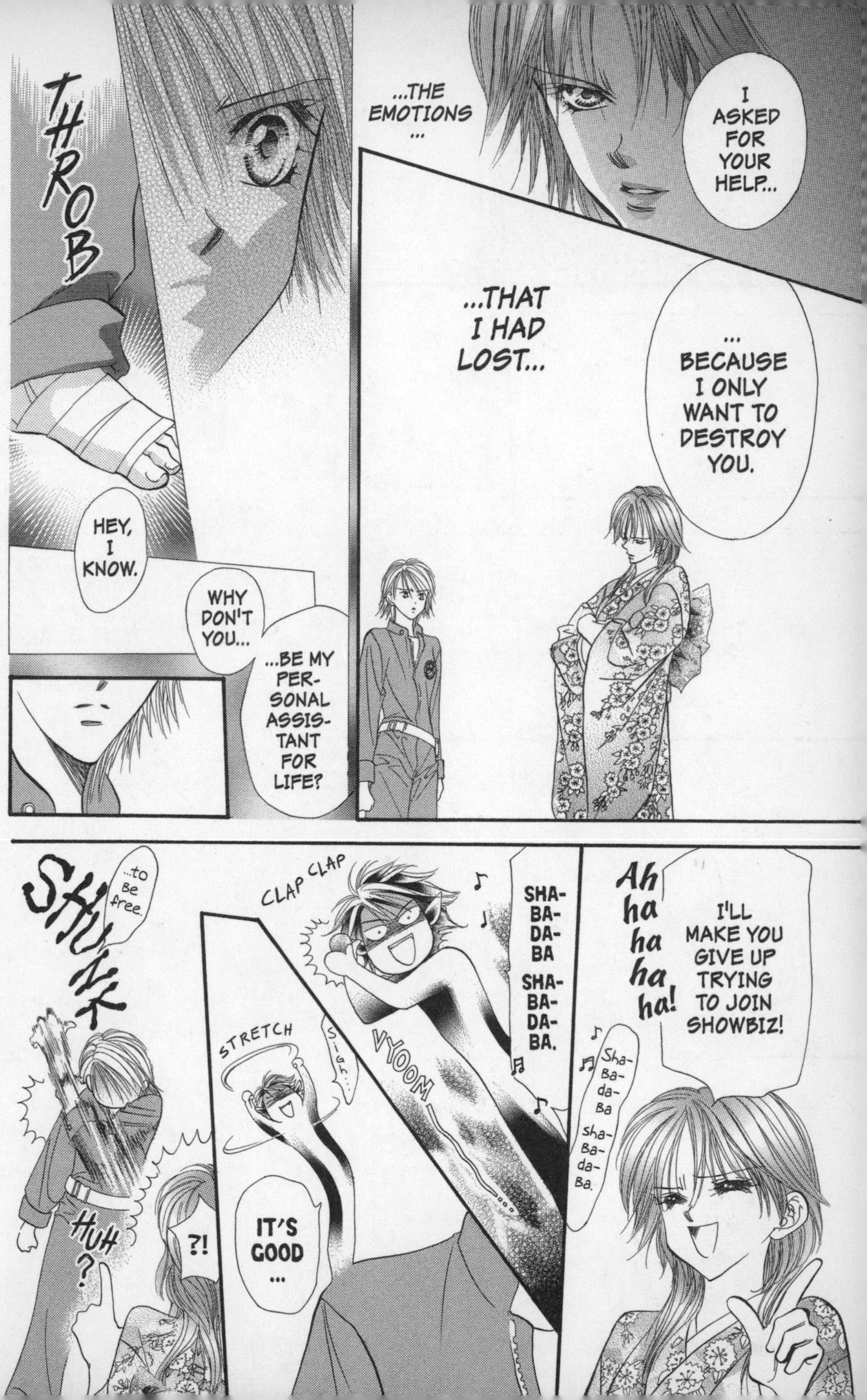
I ASKED FOR YOUR HELP...
...THE EMOTIONS ...
... BECAUSE I ONLY WANT TO DESTROY YOU.
...THAT I HAD LOST...
THROB
HEY, I KNOW.
WHY DON'T YOU...
...BE MY PERSONAL ASSISTANT FOR LIFE?
Ah ha ha ha ha!
I'LL MAKE YOU GIVE UP TRYING TO JOIN SHOWBIZ!
Sha-Ba-da-Ba sha-Ba-da-Ba.
CLAP CLAP
SHA-BA-DA-BA SHA-BA-DA-BA.
VYOOM
STRETCH
Sigh...
IT'S GOOD ...
...to be free.
SHUNK
HUH?
?!

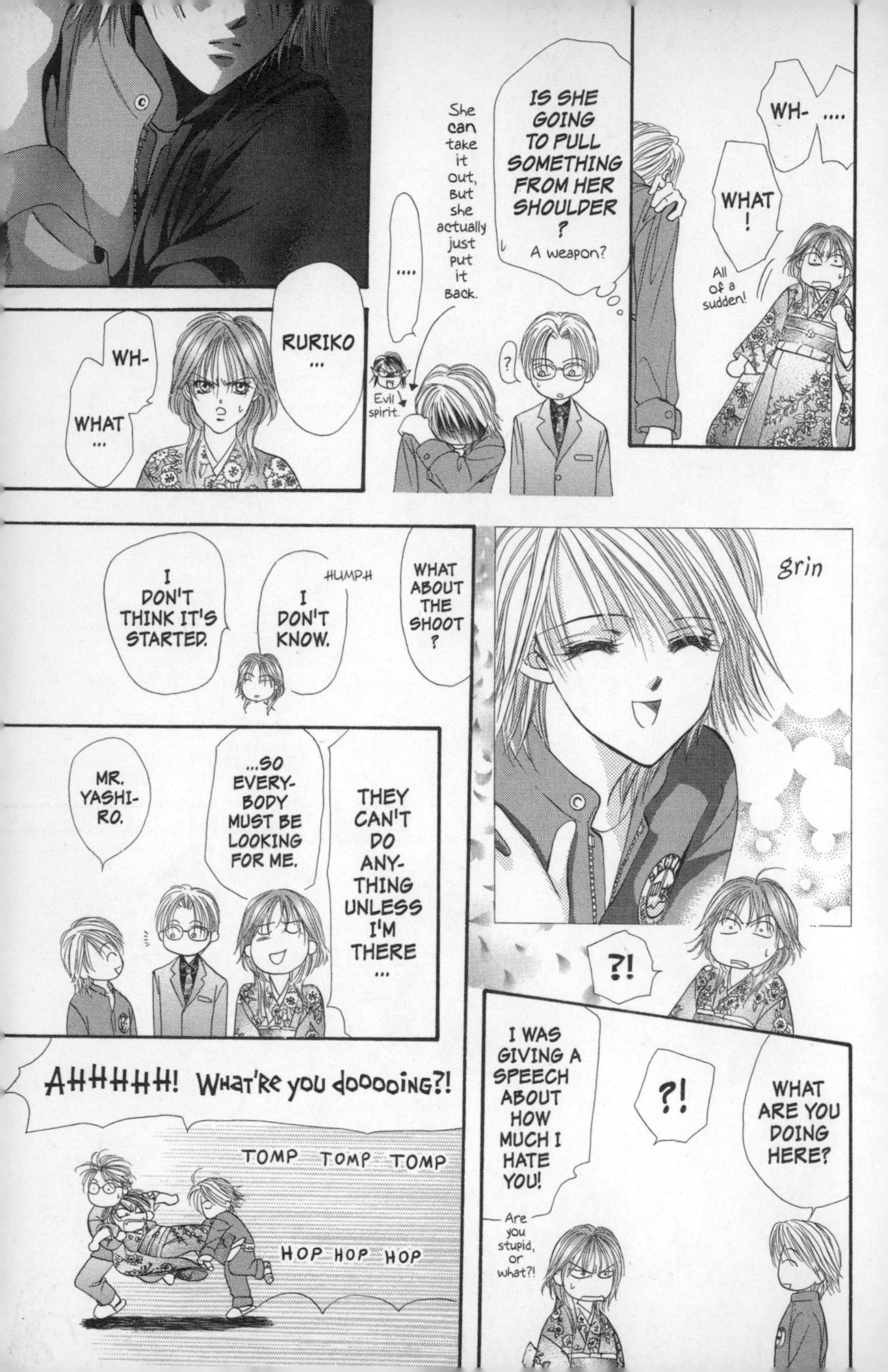
WH- ....
WHAT!
All of a sudden!
IS SHE GOING TO PULL SOMETHING FROM HER SHOULDER?
A weapon?
She can take it out, But she actually just put it Back.
....
?
Evil spirit.
RURIKO...
WH- WHAT...
grin
WHAT ABOUT THE SHOOT?
HUMPH
I DON'T KNOW.
I DON'T THINK IT'S STARTED.
?!
THEY CAN'T DO ANYTHING UNLESS I'M THERE...
...SO EVERYBODY MUST BE LOOKING FOR ME.
MR. YASHIRO.
WHAT ARE YOU DOING HERE?
?!
I WAS GIVING A SPEECH ABOUT HOW MUCH I HATE YOU!
Are you stupid, or what?!
AHHHHH! What're you doooooing?!
TOMP TOMP TOMP
HOP HOP HOP

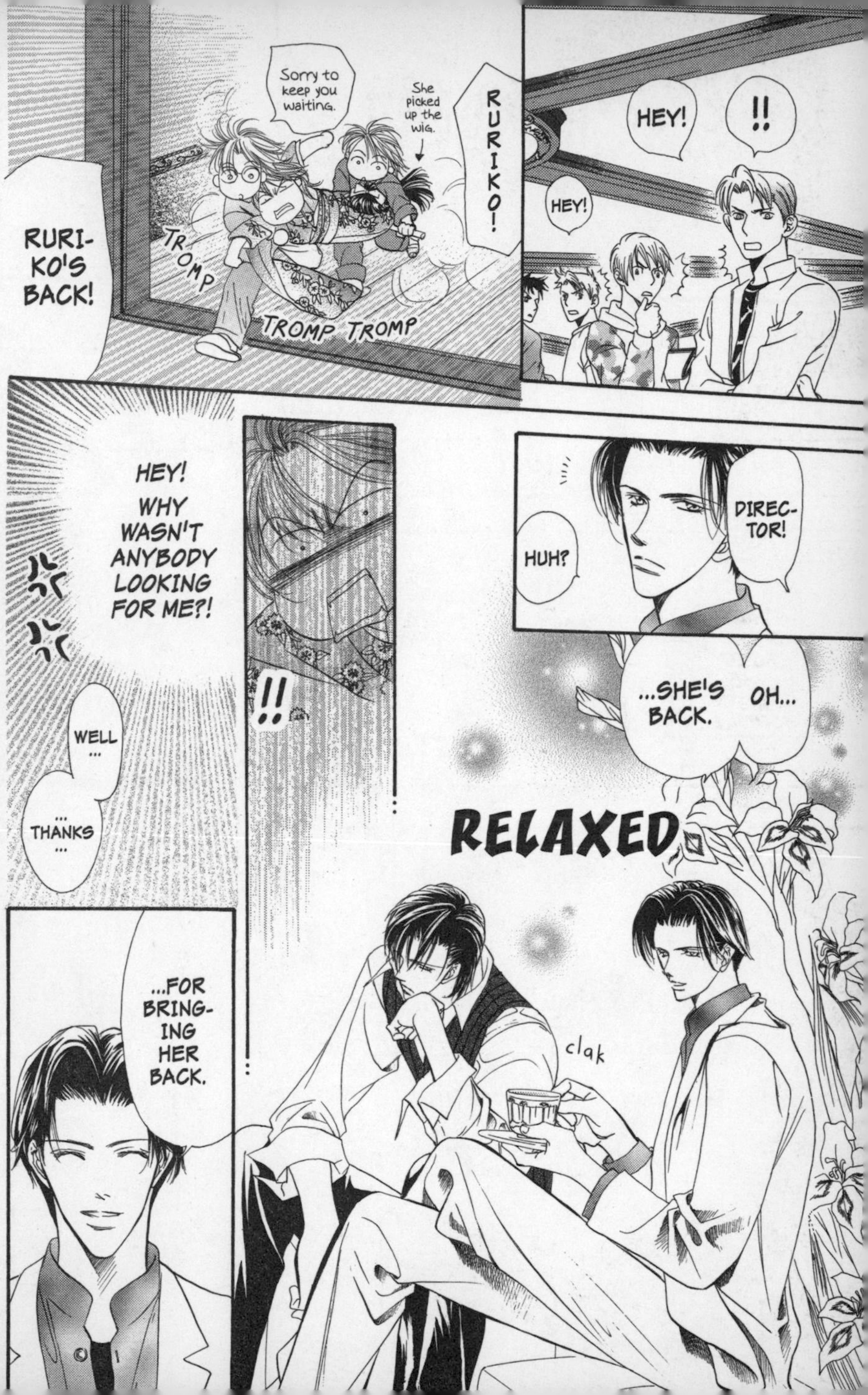
!!
HEY!
HEY!
RURIKO!
She picked up the wig.
Sorry to keep you waiting.
TROMP
TROMP TROMP
RURI-KO'S BACK!
DIRECTOR!
HUH?
OH...
...SHE'S BACK.
RELAXED
clak
!!
HEY! WHY WASN'T ANYBODY LOOKING FOR ME?!
WELL...
...THANKS...
...FOR BRINGING HER BACK.

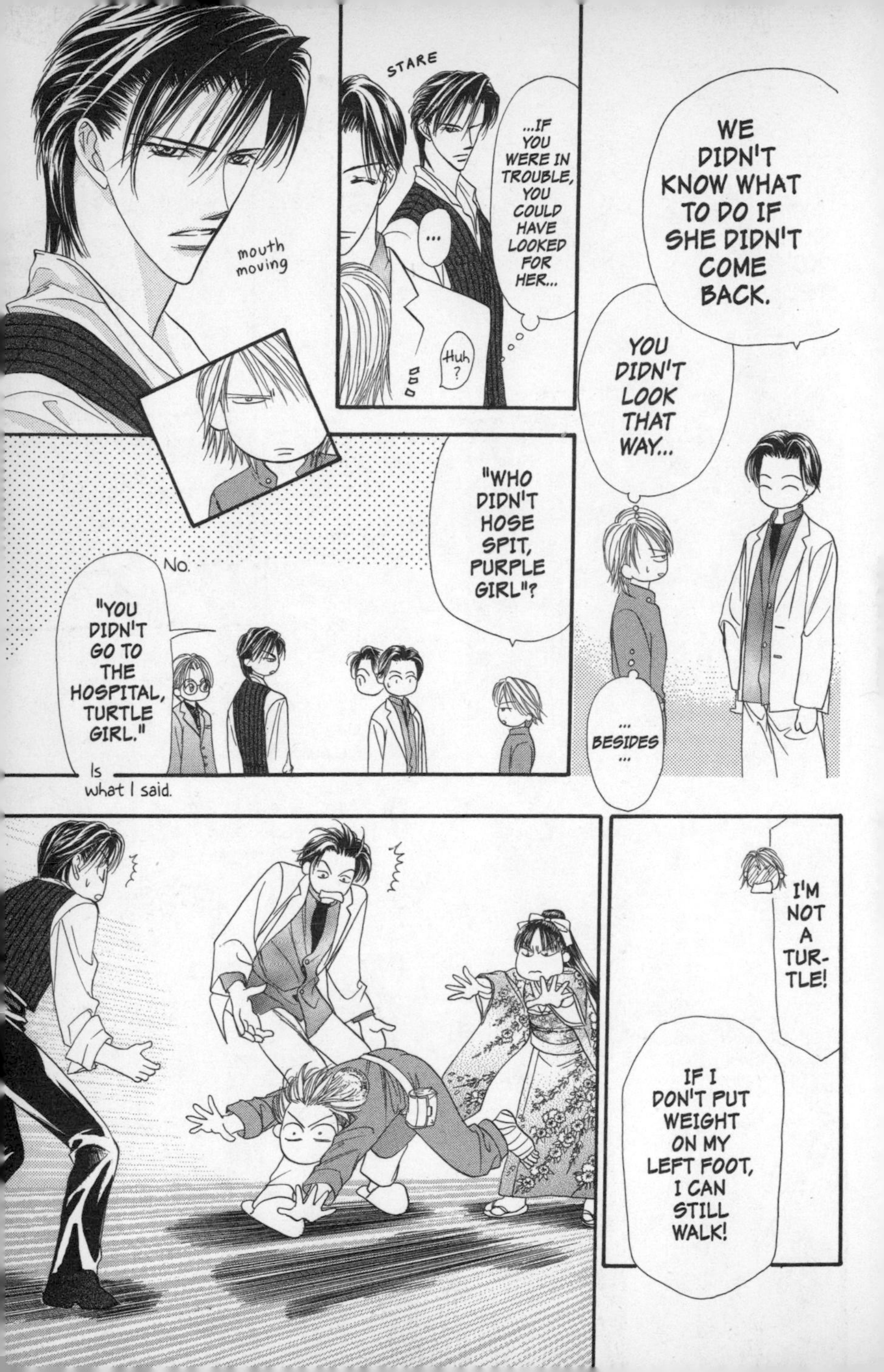
WE DIDN'T KNOW WHAT TO DO IF SHE DIDN'T COME BACK.
YOU DIDN'T LOOK THAT WAY...
...BESIDES...
STARE
...IF YOU WERE IN TROUBLE, YOU COULD HAVE LOOKED FOR HER...
...
Huh?
mouth moving
"WHO DIDN'T HOSE SPIT, PURPLE GIRL"?
No.
"YOU DIDN'T GO TO THE HOSPITAL, TURTLE GIRL."
Is what I said.
I'M NOT A TURTLE!
IF I DON'T PUT WEIGHT ON MY LEFT FOOT, I CAN STILL WALK!

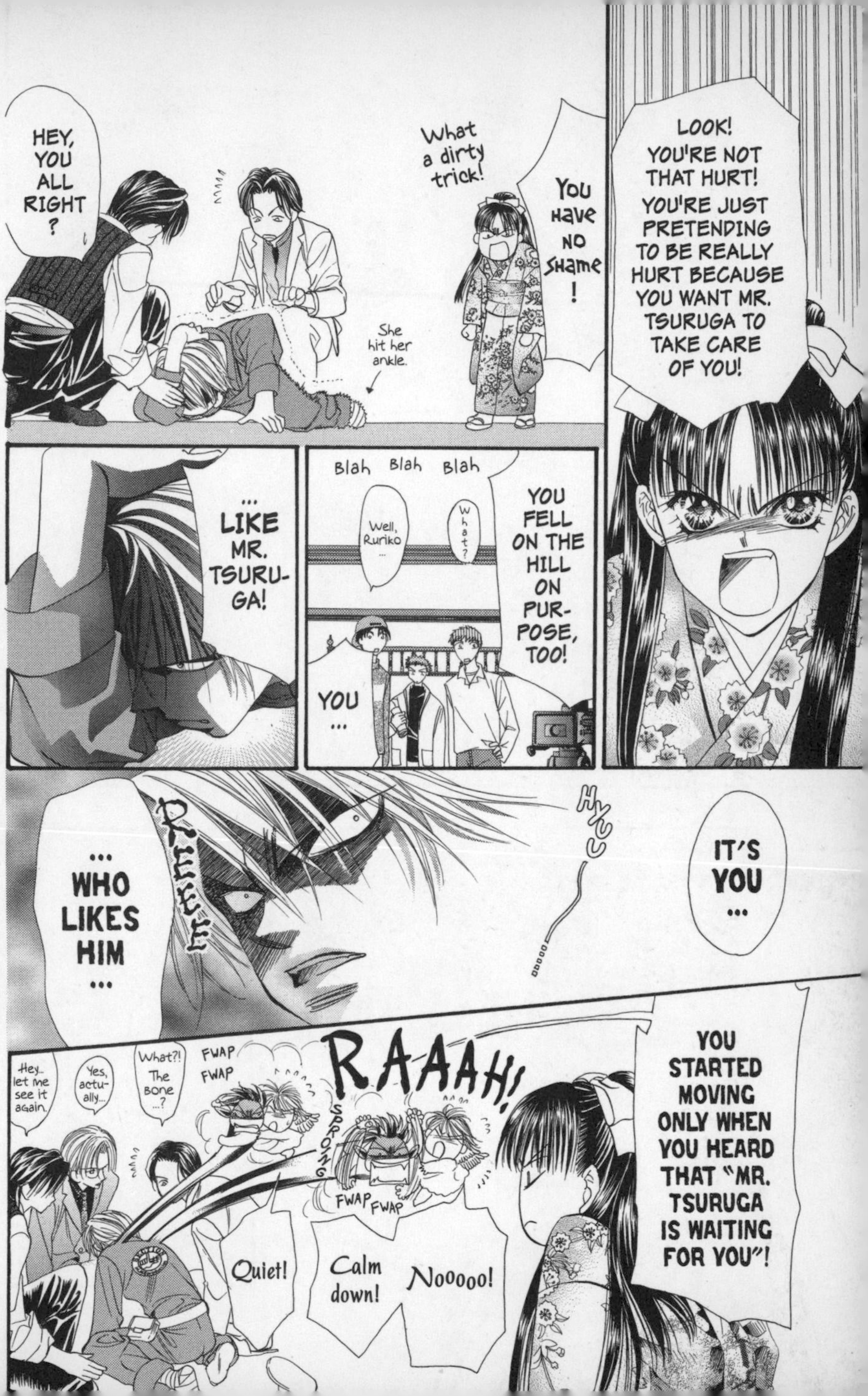
LOOK! YOU'RE NOT THAT HURT! YOU'RE JUST PRETENDING TO BE REALLY HURT BECAUSE YOU WANT MR. TSURUGA TO TAKE CARE OF YOU!
You have no shame!
What a dirty trick!
She hit her ankle.
HEY, YOU ALL RIGHT?
YOU FELL ON THE HILL ON PURPOSE, TOO!
Blah Blah Blah
What?
Well, Ruriko...
YOU...
... LIKE MR. TSURUGA!
IT'S YOU...
HYUU
REEEE
... WHO LIKES HIM...
YOU STARTED MOVING ONLY WHEN YOU HEARD THAT "MR. TSURUGA IS WAITING FOR YOU"!
RAAAH!
SPRONG
Nooooo!
Calm down!
Quiet!
FWAP FWAP
FWAP FWAP
What?! The Bone...?
Yes, actually...
Hey... let me see it again.

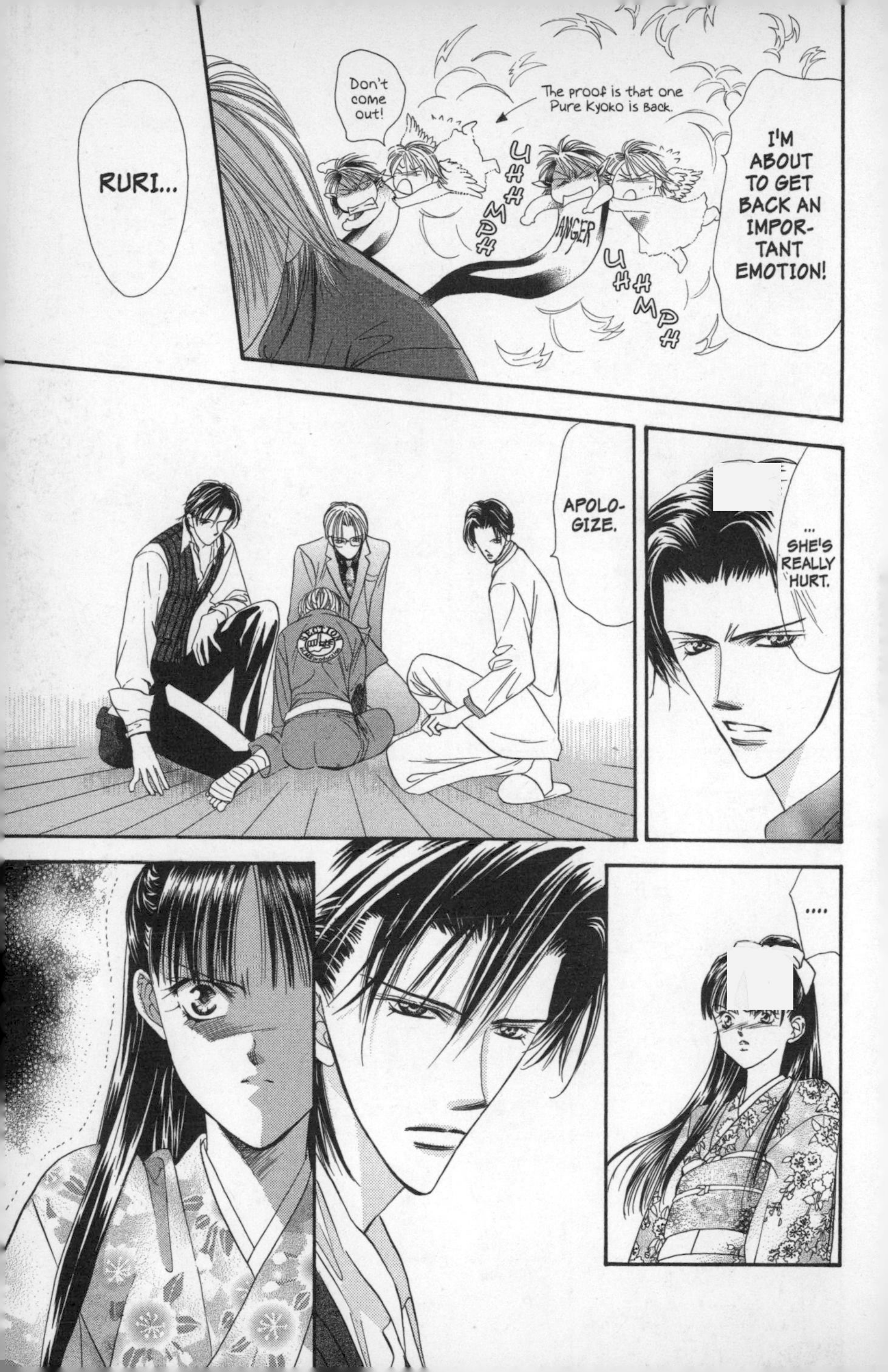
I'M ABOUT TO GET BACK AN IMPORTANT EMOTION!
The proof is that one Pure Kyoko is Back.
UHHMPH
ANGER
UHHMPH
Don't come out!
RURI...
... SHE'S REALLY HURT.
APOLOGIZE.
....

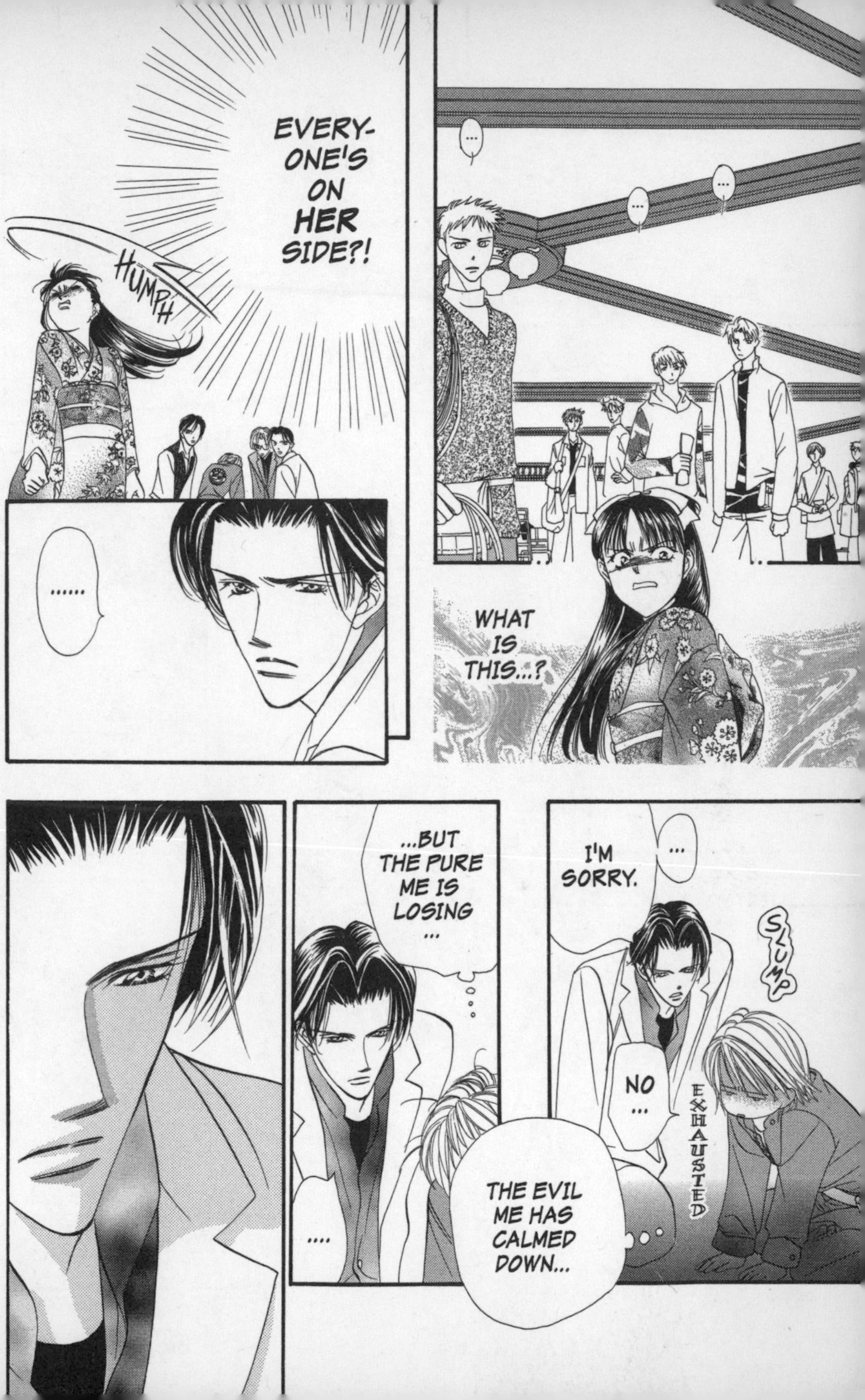
...
...
...
HUMPH
EVERY-ONE'S ON HER SIDE?!
WHAT IS THIS...?
......
...
I'M SORRY.
SLUMP
NO...
EXHAUSTED
THE EVIL ME HAS CALMED DOWN...
...BUT THE PURE ME IS LOSING...
....

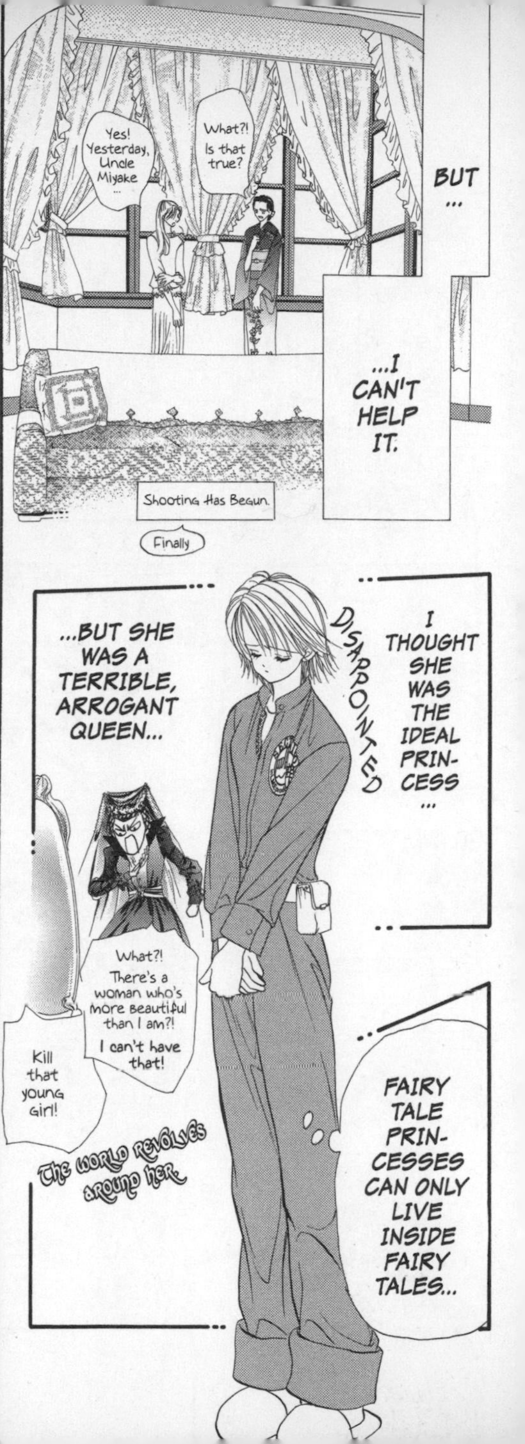
BUT ...
...I CAN'T HELP IT.
What?! Is that true?
Yes! Yesterday, Uncle Miyake ...
Finally
Shooting Has Begun.
I THOUGHT SHE WAS THE IDEAL PRIN-CESS ...
DISAPPOINTED
...BUT SHE WAS A TERRIBLE, ARROGANT QUEEN...
What?! There's a woman who's more beautiful than I am?! I can't have that!
Kill that young Girl!
THE WORLD REVOLVES AROUND HER
FAIRY TALE PRIN-CESSES CAN ONLY LIVE INSIDE FAIRY TALES...

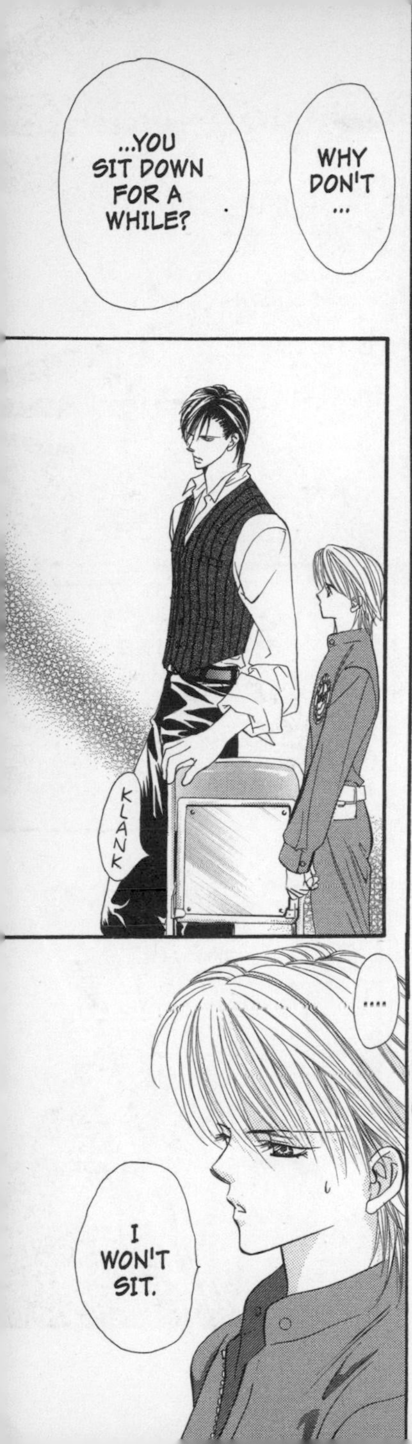
WHY DON'T ...
...YOU SIT DOWN FOR A WHILE?
KLANK
....
I WON'T SIT.

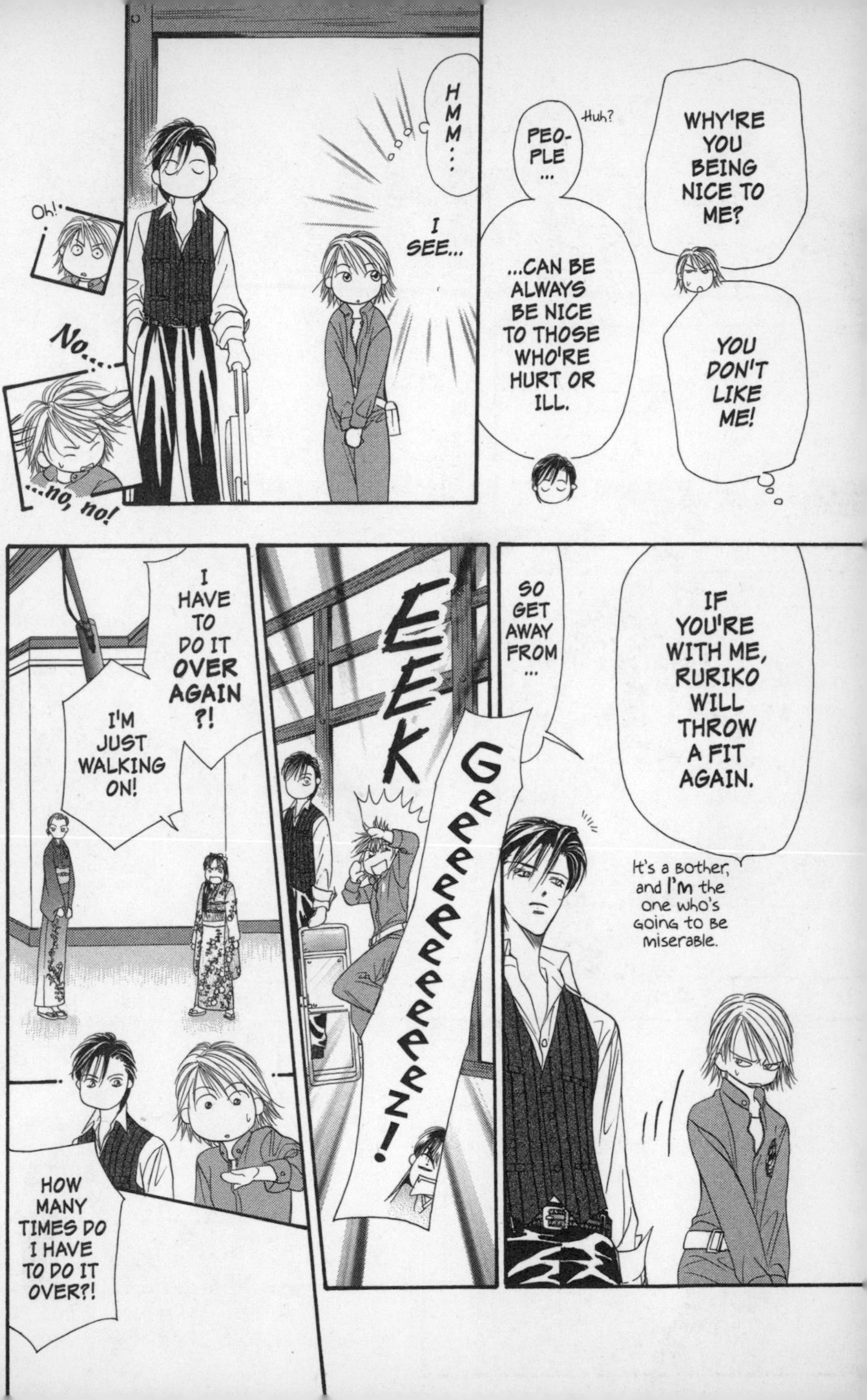

WHY'RE YOU BEING NICE TO ME?
YOU DON'T LIKE ME!
Huh?
PEO-PLE ...
...CAN BE ALWAYS BE NICE TO THOSE WHO'RE HURT OR ILL.
HMM...
I SEE...
Oh!
No...
...no, no!
IF YOU'RE WITH ME, RURIKO WILL THROW A FIT AGAIN.
It's a bother, and I'm the one who's going to be miserable.
SO GET AWAY FROM ...
EEK
Geeeeeeeeez!
I HAVE TO DO IT OVER AGAIN?!
I'M JUST WALKING ON!
HOW MANY TIMES DO I HAVE TO DO IT OVER?!

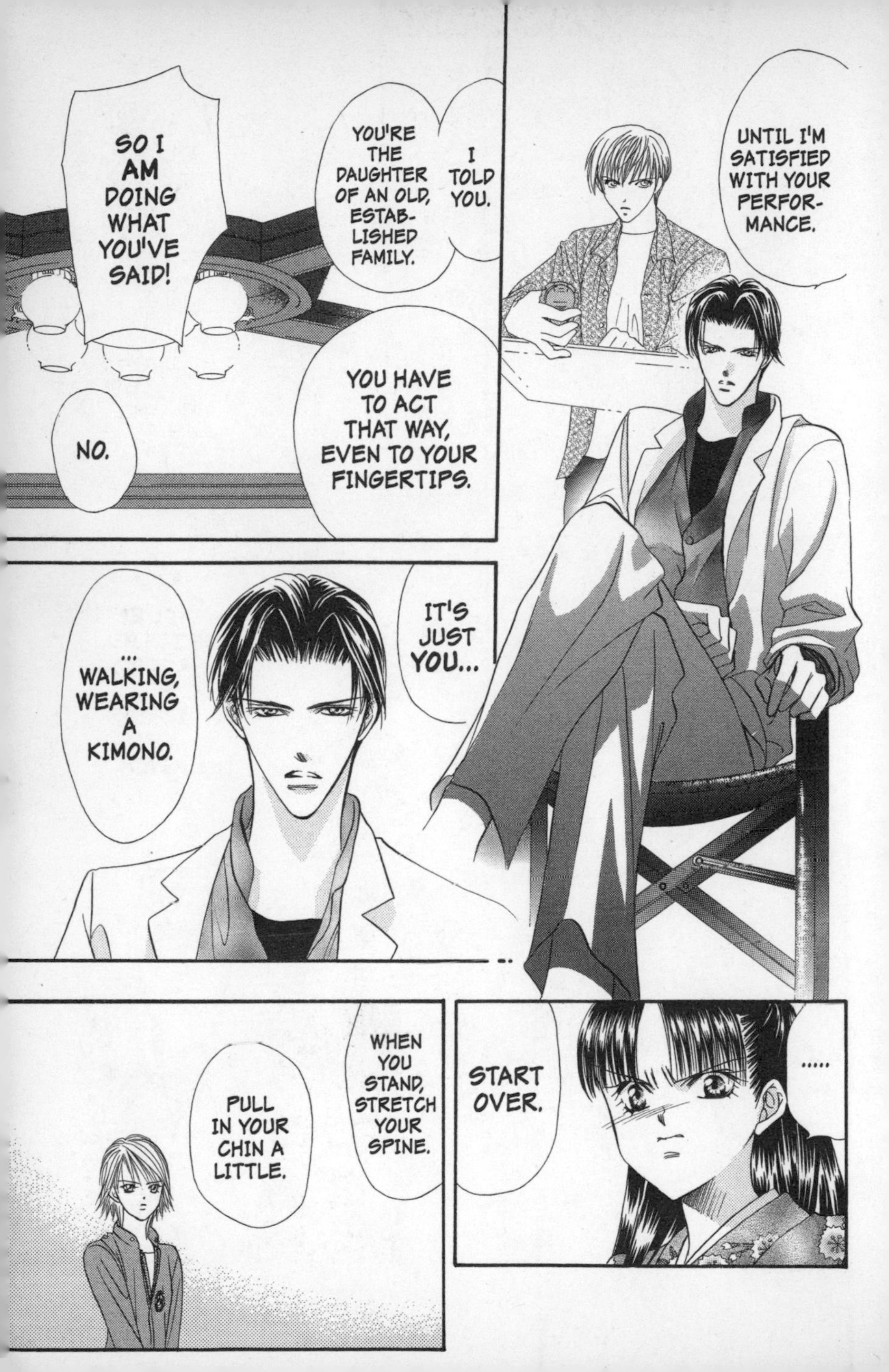
UNTIL I'M SATISFIED WITH YOUR PERFORMANCE.
I TOLD YOU.
YOU'RE THE DAUGHTER OF AN OLD, ESTABLISHED FAMILY.
YOU HAVE TO ACT THAT WAY, EVEN TO YOUR FINGERTIPS.
SO I AM DOING WHAT YOU'VE SAID!
NO.
IT'S JUST YOU...
...WALKING, WEARING A KIMONO.
.....
START OVER.
WHEN YOU STAND, STRETCH YOUR SPINE.
PULL IN YOUR CHIN A LITTLE.

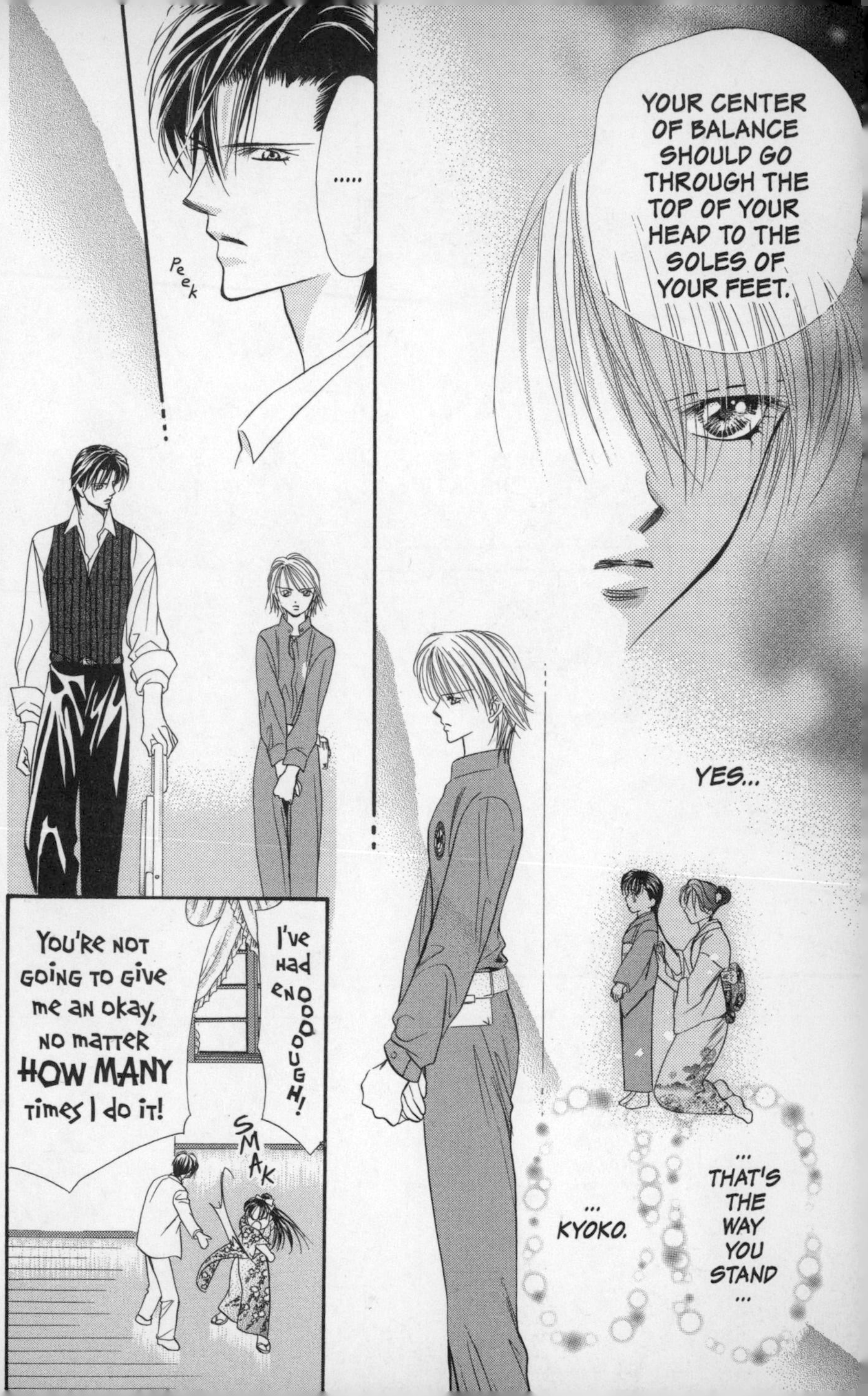
YOUR CENTER OF BALANCE SHOULD GO THROUGH THE TOP OF YOUR HEAD TO THE SOLES OF YOUR FEET.
YES...
... THAT'S THE WAY YOU STAND ...
... KYOKO.
.....
Peek
I've had ENOOOOOUGH!
You're not going to give me an okay, no matter HOW MANY times I do it!
SMAK

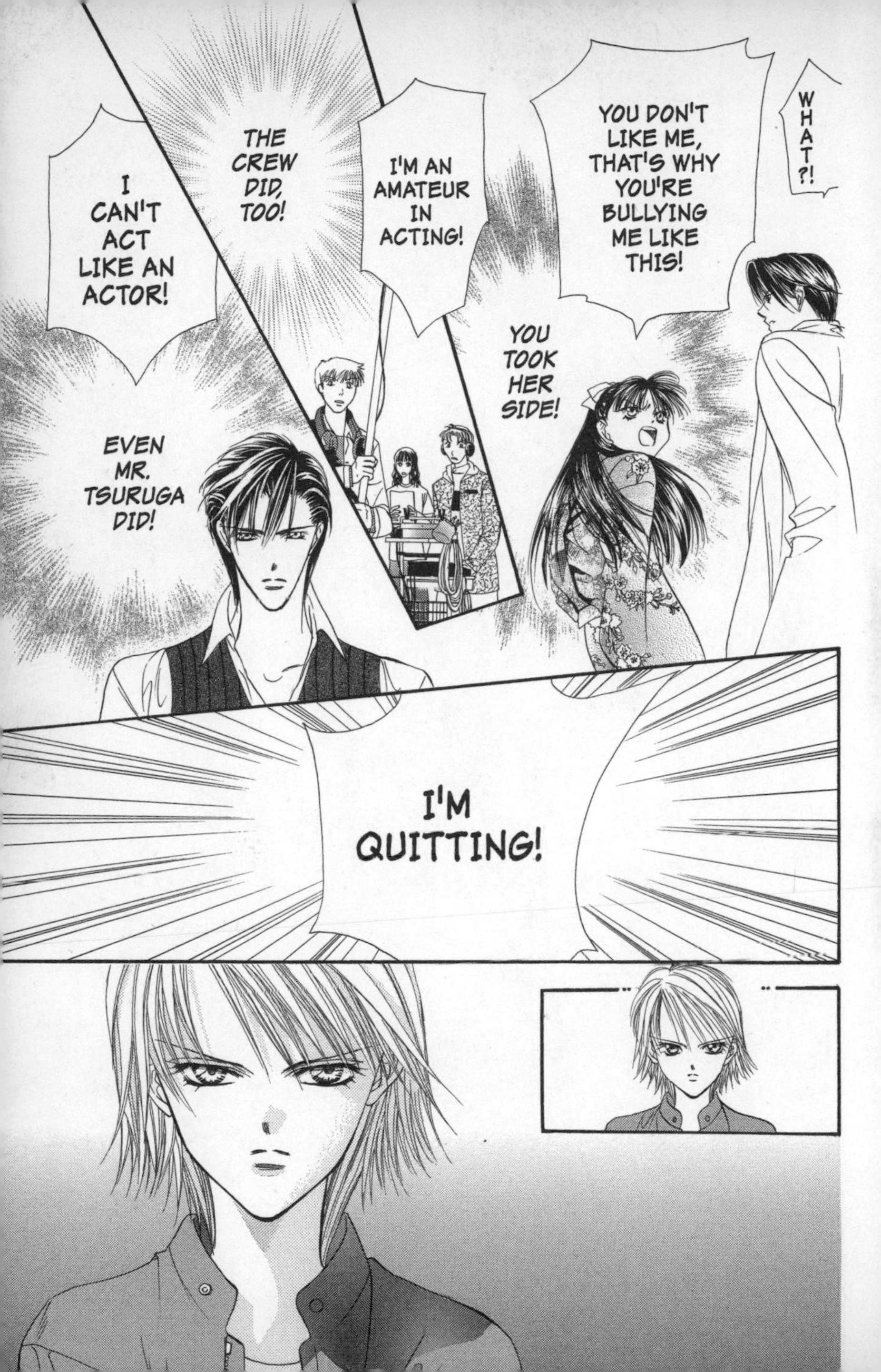
WHAT?!
YOU DON'T LIKE ME, THAT'S WHY YOU'RE BULLYING ME LIKE THIS!
YOU TOOK HER SIDE!
EVEN MR. TSURUGA DID!
THE CREW DID, TOO!
I'M AN AMATEUR IN ACTING!
I CAN'T ACT LIKE AN ACTOR!
I'M QUITTING!

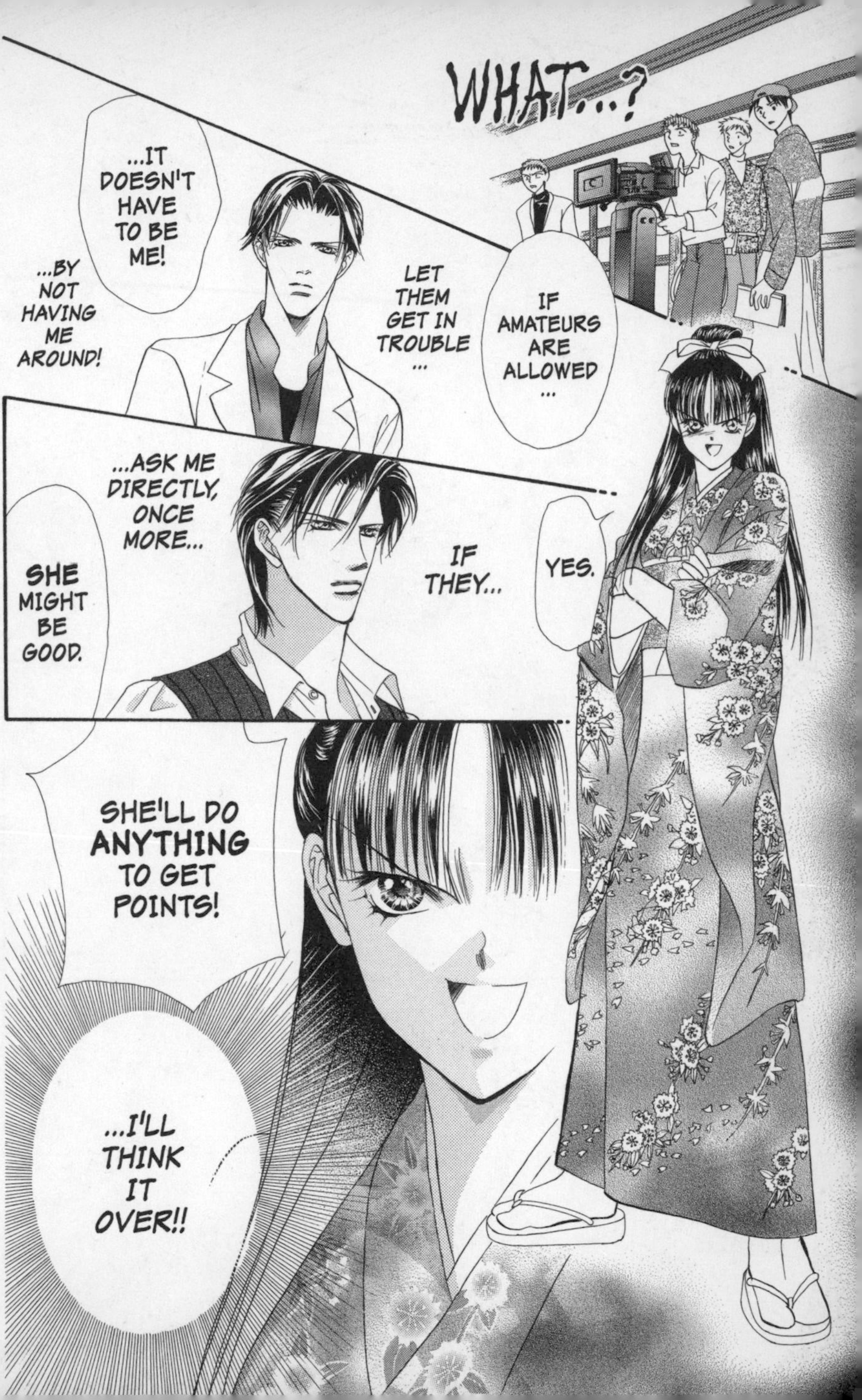
WHAT...?
IF AMATEURS ARE ALLOWED...
LET THEM GET IN TROUBLE...
...IT DOESN'T HAVE TO BE ME!
...BY NOT HAVING ME AROUND!
YES.
IF THEY...
...ASK ME DIRECTLY, ONCE MORE...
SHE MIGHT BE GOOD.
SHE'LL DO ANYTHING TO GET POINTS!
...I'LL THINK IT OVER!!

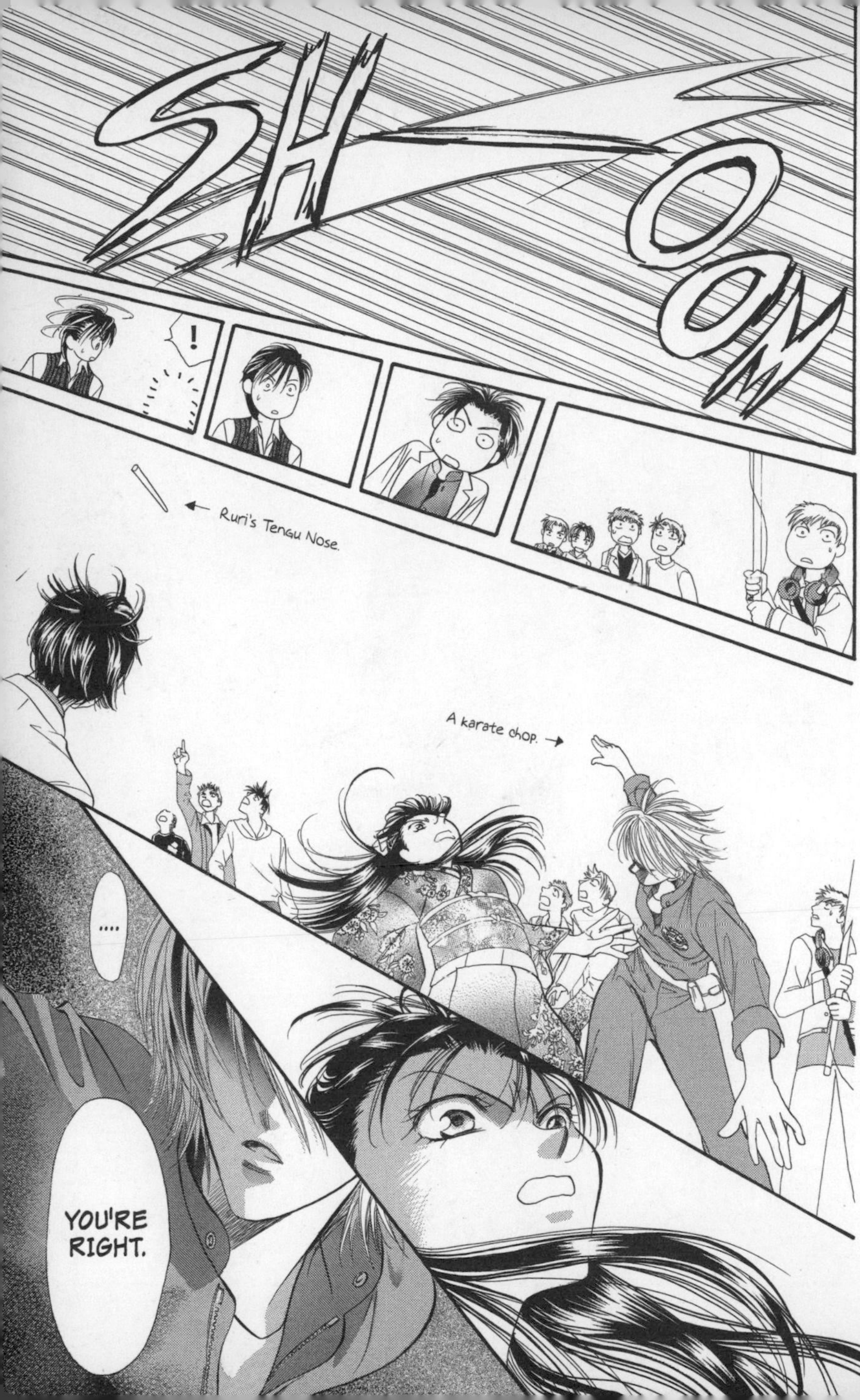
SH—OOM
!
Ruri's Tengu Nose.
A karate chop.
....
YOU'RE RIGHT.

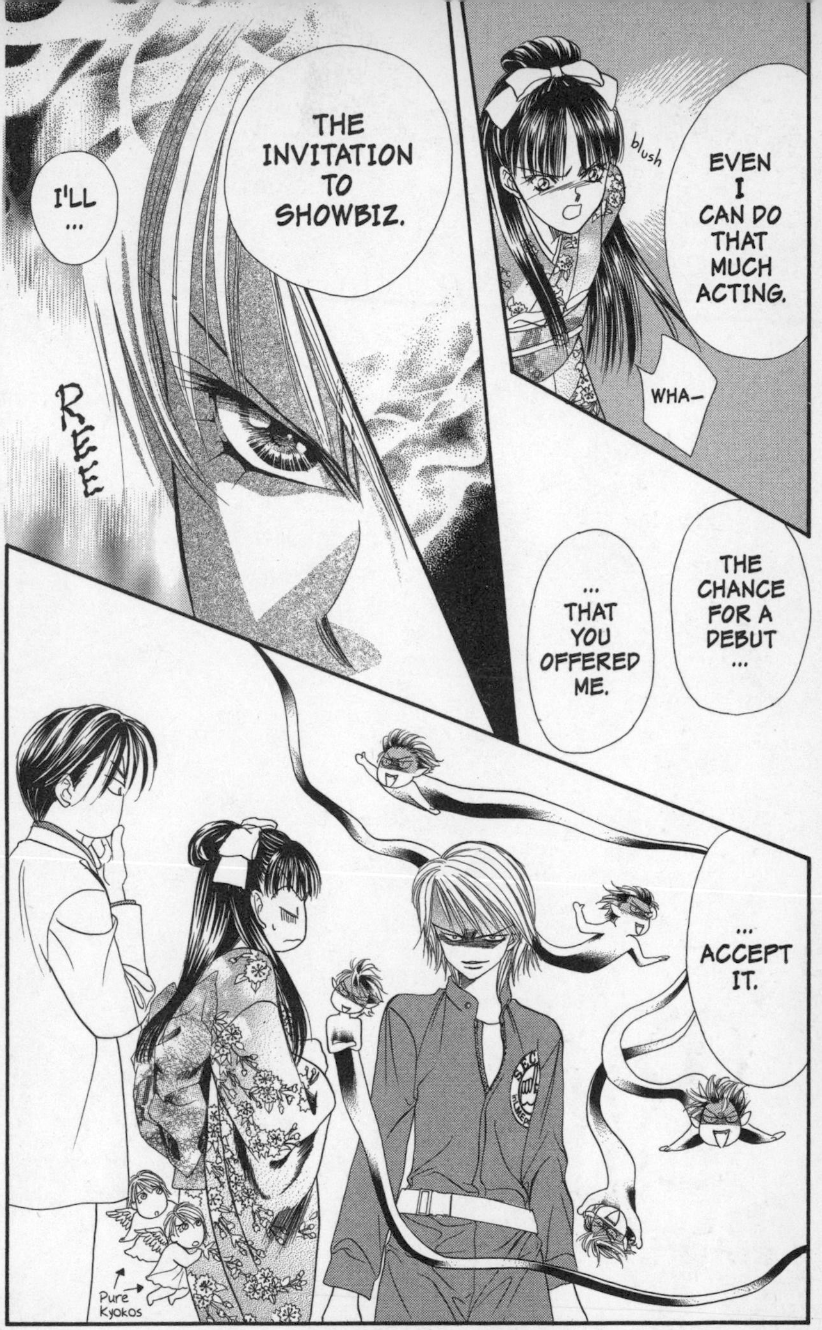
blush
EVEN I CAN DO THAT MUCH ACTING.
WHA-
THE INVITATION TO SHOWBIZ.
I'LL ...
REEE
THE CHANCE FOR A DEBUT ...
... THAT YOU OFFERED ME.
... ACCEPT IT.
Pure Kyokos

End of Act 10

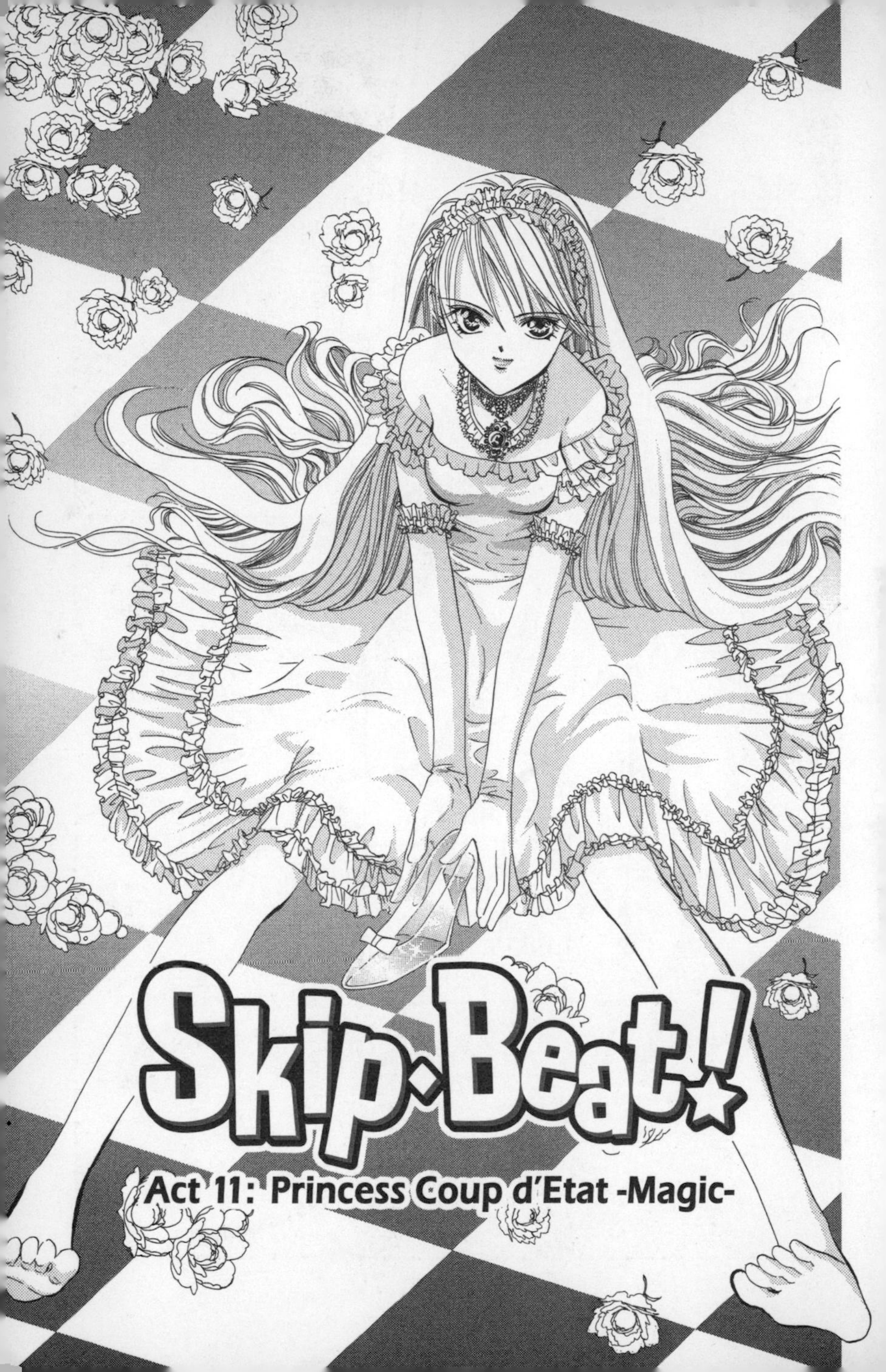
Skip·Beat!
Act 11: Princess Coup d'Etat -Magic-

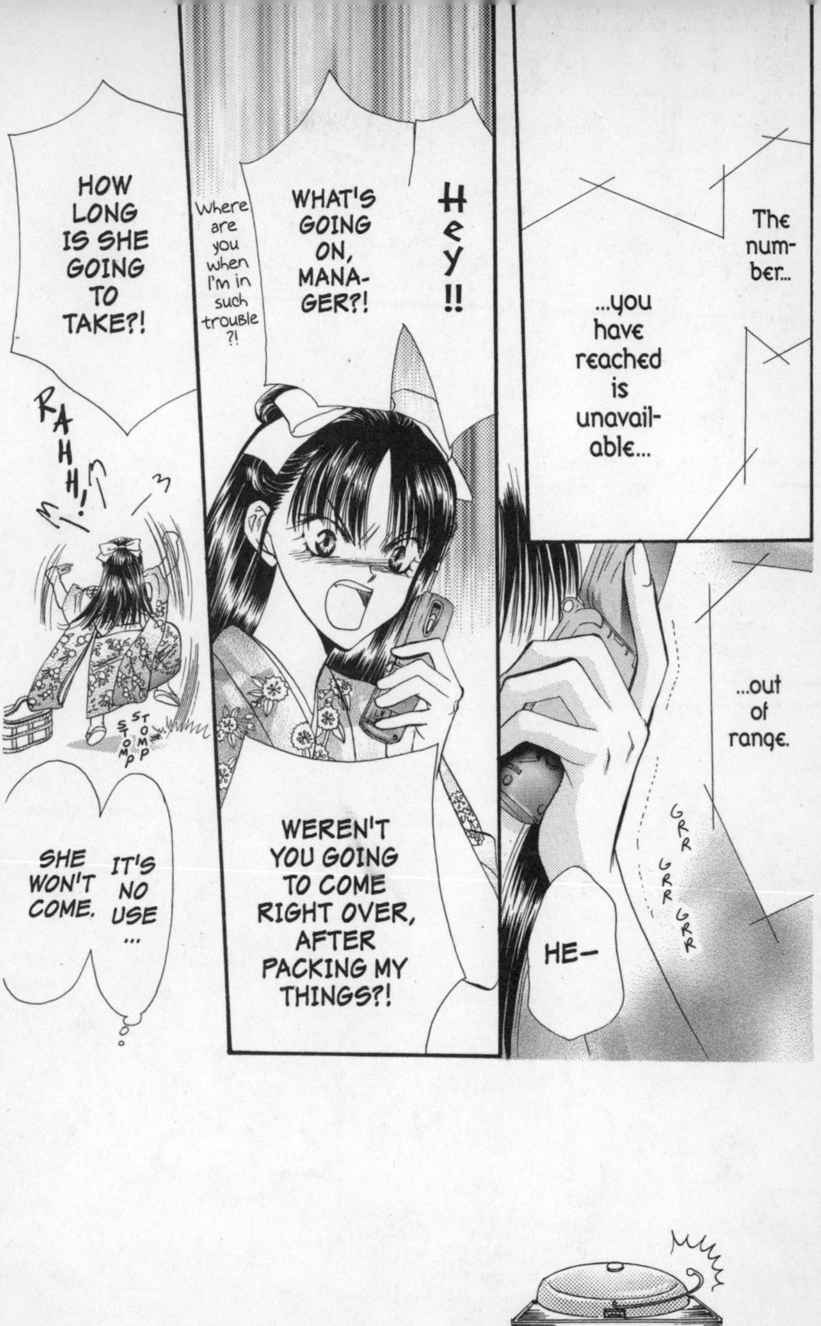
The number...
...you have reached is unavailable...
...out of range.
GRR GRR GRR GRR
HE-
HEY!!
WHAT'S GOING ON, MANAGER?!
Where are you when I'm in such trouble?!
WEREN'T YOU GOING TO COME RIGHT OVER, AFTER PACKING MY THINGS?!
HOW LONG IS SHE GOING TO TAKE?!
RAHH!!
STOMP STOMP
IT'S NO USE...
SHE WON'T COME.

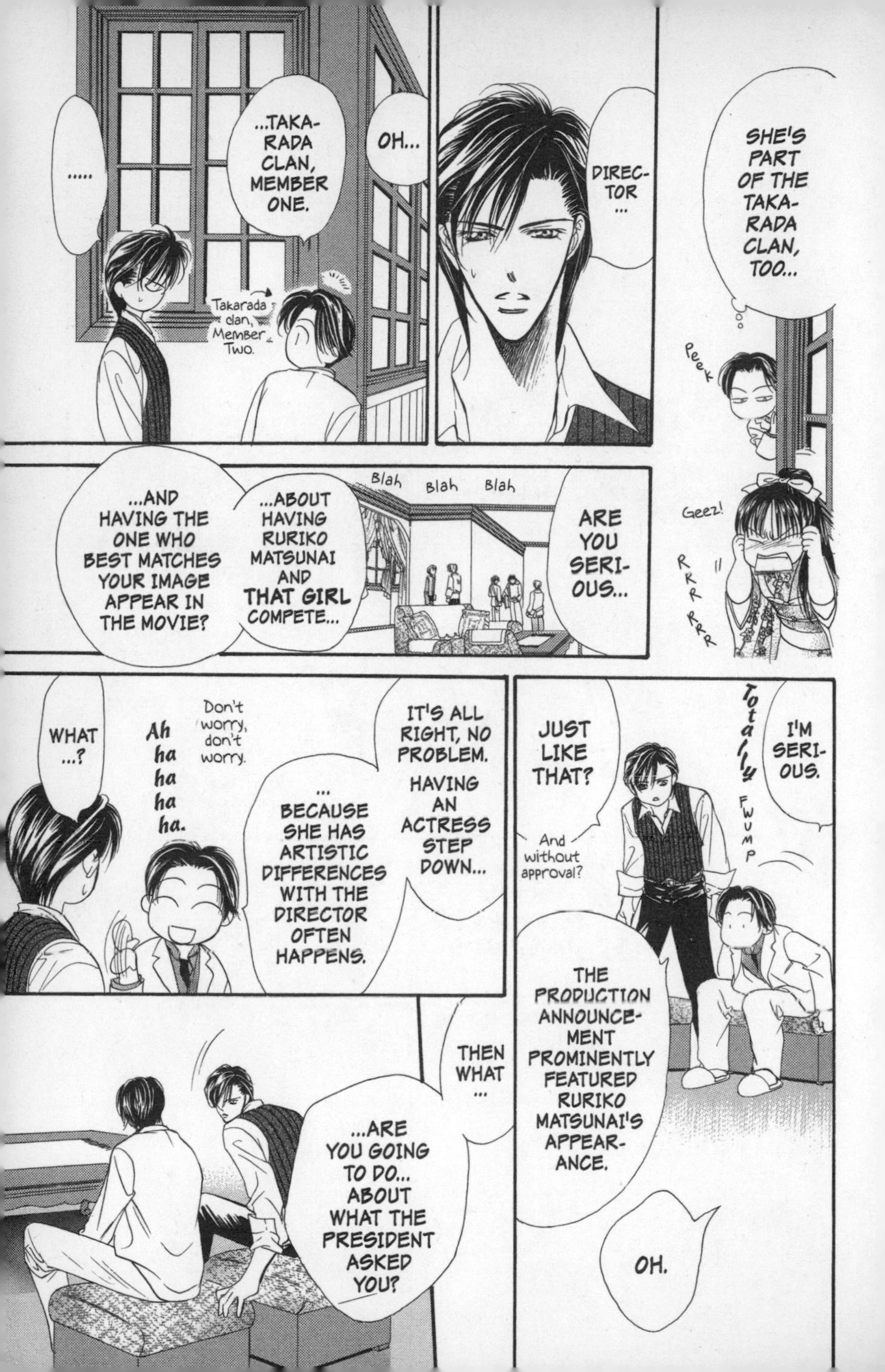
SHE'S PART OF THE TAKARADA CLAN, TOO...
Peek
Geez!
RRRRRR
DIRECTOR ...
OH...
...TAKARADA CLAN, MEMBER ONE.
Takarada clan, Member Two.
.....
ARE YOU SERIOUS...
Blah Blah Blah
...ABOUT HAVING RURIKO MATSUNAI AND THAT GIRL COMPETE...
...AND HAVING THE ONE WHO BEST MATCHES YOUR IMAGE APPEAR IN THE MOVIE?
I'M SERIOUS.
Totally
FWUMP
JUST LIKE THAT?
And without approval?
THE PRODUCTION ANNOUNCEMENT PROMINENTLY FEATURED RURIKO MATSUNAI'S APPEARANCE.
OH.
IT'S ALL RIGHT, NO PROBLEM.
HAVING AN ACTRESS STEP DOWN...
... BECAUSE SHE HAS ARTISTIC DIFFERENCES WITH THE DIRECTOR OFTEN HAPPENS.
Don't worry, don't worry.
Ah ha ha ha ha.
WHAT ...?
THEN WHAT ...
...ARE YOU GOING TO DO... ABOUT WHAT THE PRESIDENT ASKED YOU?

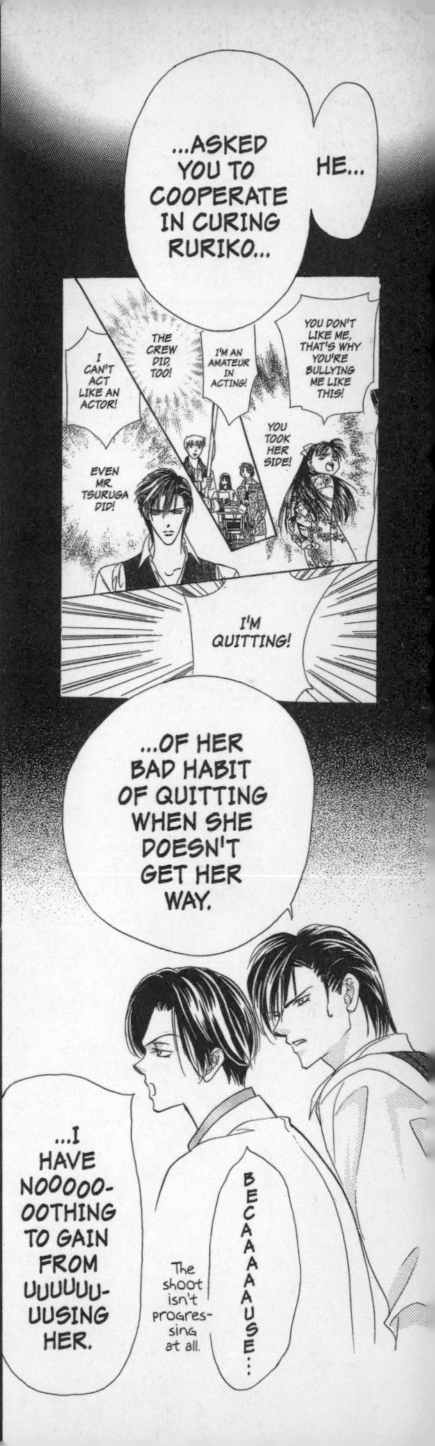
HE...
...ASKED YOU TO COOPERATE IN CURING RURIKO...
YOU DON'T LIKE ME, THAT'S WHY YOU'RE BULLYING ME LIKE THIS!
YOU TOOK HER SIDE!
I'M AN AMATEUR IN ACTING!
THE CREW DID, TOO!
I CAN'T ACT LIKE AN ACTOR!
EVEN MR. TSURUGA DID!
I'M QUITTING!
...OF HER BAD HABIT OF QUITTING WHEN SHE DOESN'T GET HER WAY.
BECAAAAAUSE...
The shoot isn't progres-sing at all.
...I HAVE NOOOOO-OOTHING TO GAIN FROM UUUUUU-UUSING HER.

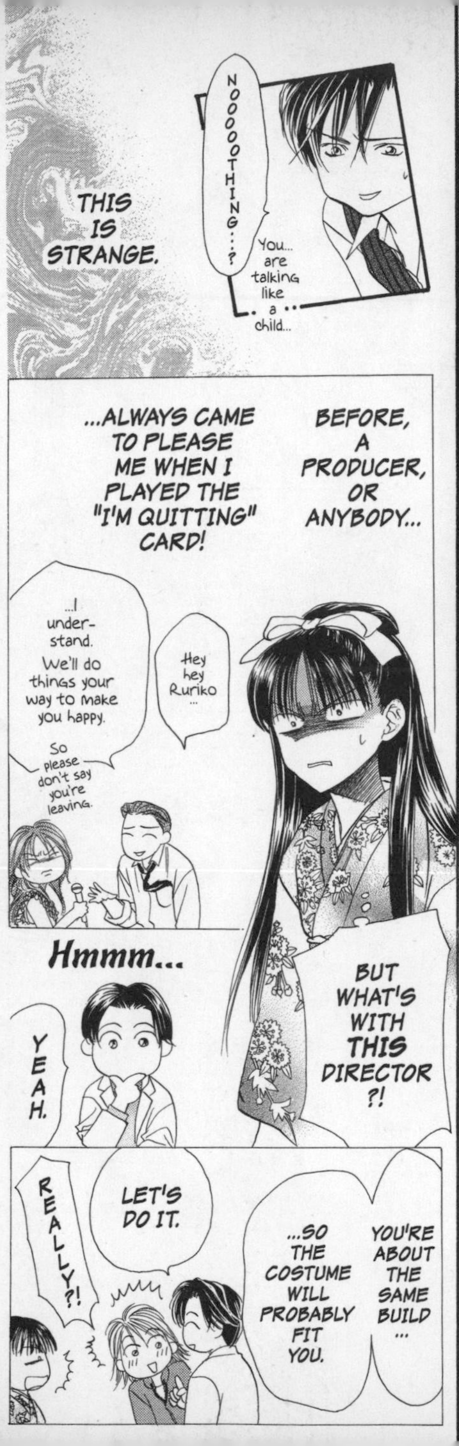
NOOOOOOTHING...?
You... are talking like a child...
THIS IS STRANGE.
BEFORE, A PRODUCER, OR ANYBODY...
...ALWAYS CAME TO PLEASE ME WHEN I PLAYED THE "I'M QUITTING" CARD!
Hey hey Ruriko ...
...I under-stand. We'll do things your way to make you happy.
So please don't say you're leaving.
BUT WHAT'S WITH THIS DIRECTOR?!
YEAH.
Hmmm...
YOU'RE ABOUT THE SAME BUILD ...
...SO THE COSTUME WILL PROBABLY FIT YOU.
LET'S DO IT.
REALLY?!

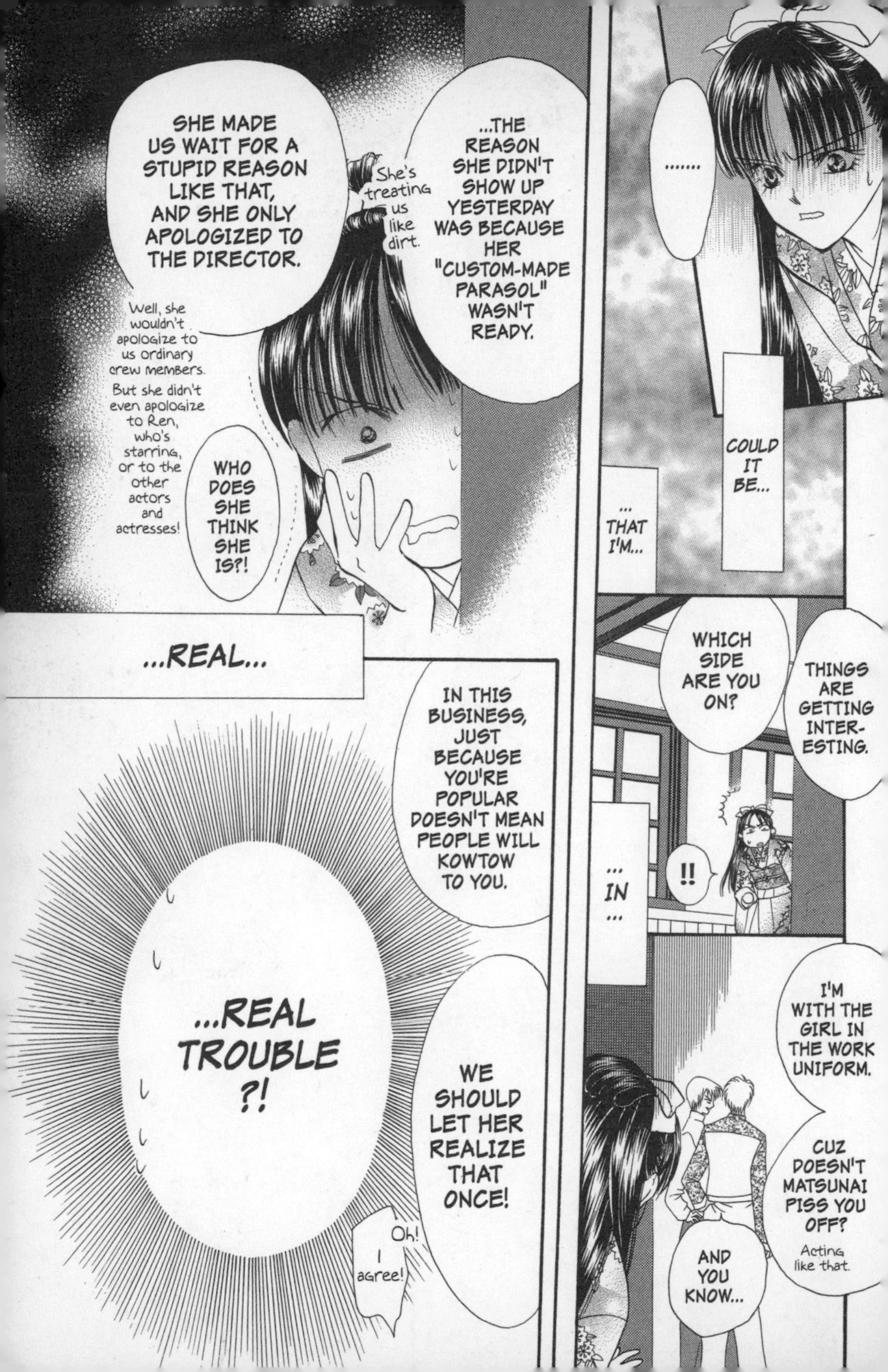

....
COULD IT BE...
...THAT I'M...
THINGS ARE GETTING INTER-ESTING.
WHICH SIDE ARE YOU ON?
!!
...IN...
I'M WITH THE GIRL IN THE WORK UNIFORM.
CUZ DOESN'T MATSUNAI PISS YOU OFF?
Acting like that.
AND YOU KNOW...
...THE REASON SHE DIDN'T SHOW UP YESTERDAY WAS BECAUSE HER "CUSTOM-MADE PARASOL" WASN'T READY.
She's treating us like dirt.
SHE MADE US WAIT FOR A STUPID REASON LIKE THAT, AND SHE ONLY APOLOGIZED TO THE DIRECTOR.
Well, she wouldn't apologize to us ordinary crew members. But she didn't even apologize to Ren, who's starring, or to the other actors and actresses!
WHO DOES SHE THINK SHE IS?!
...REAL...
IN THIS BUSINESS, JUST BECAUSE YOU'RE POPULAR DOESN'T MEAN PEOPLE WILL KOWTOW TO YOU.
WE SHOULD LET HER REALIZE THAT ONCE!
Oh! I agree!
...REAL TROUBLE?!

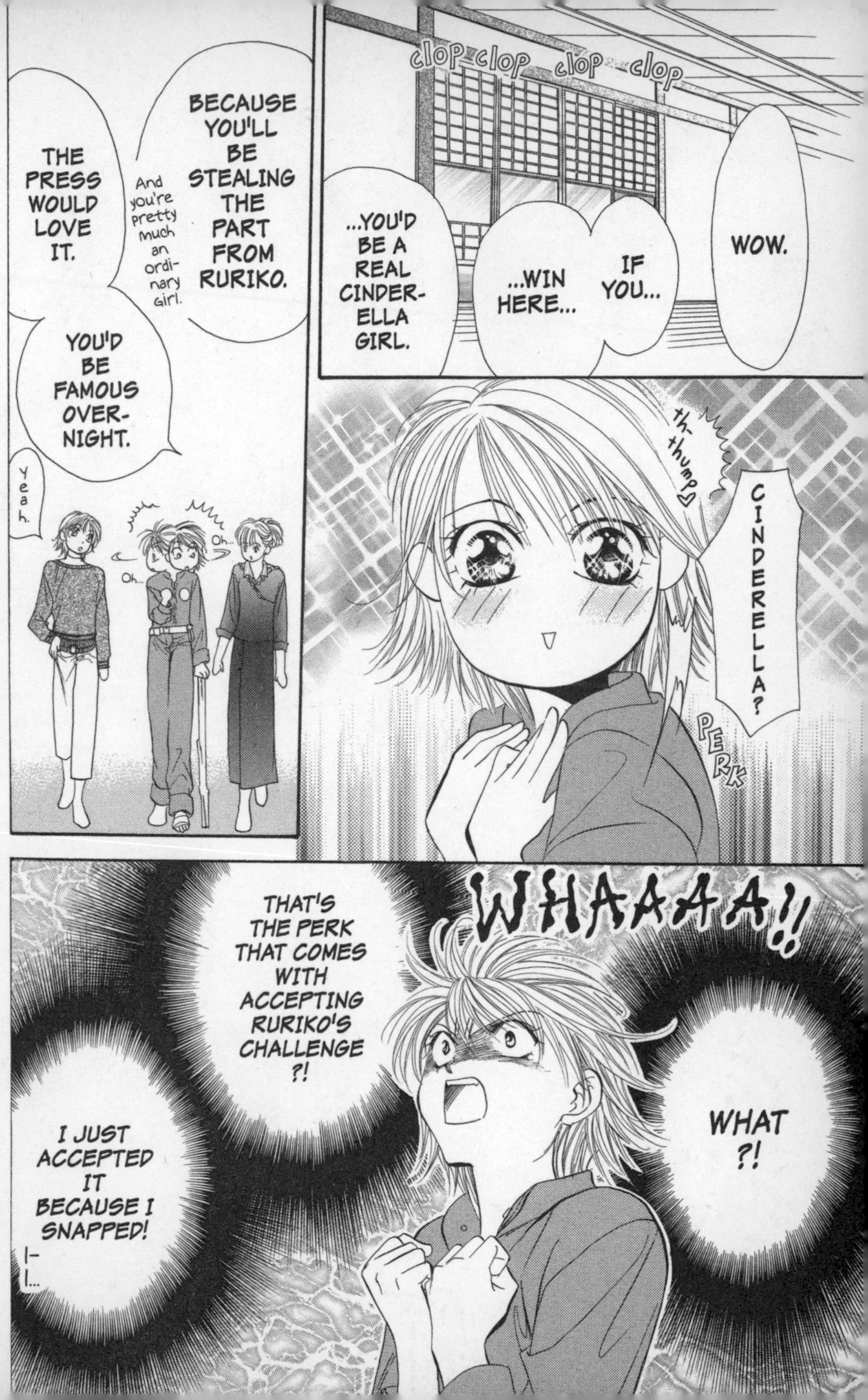
clop clop clop clop
WOW.
IF YOU...
...WIN HERE...
...YOU'D BE A REAL CINDERELLA GIRL.
th-thump
CINDERELLA?
PERK
BECAUSE YOU'LL BE STEALING THE PART FROM RURIKO.
And you're pretty much an ordinary girl.
THE PRESS WOULD LOVE IT.
YOU'D BE FAMOUS OVERNIGHT.
Oh...
Oh...
Yeah.
WHAAAA!!
WHAT?!
THAT'S THE PERK THAT COMES WITH ACCEPTING RURIKO'S CHALLENGE?!
I JUST ACCEPTED IT BECAUSE I SNAPPED!
I— I...

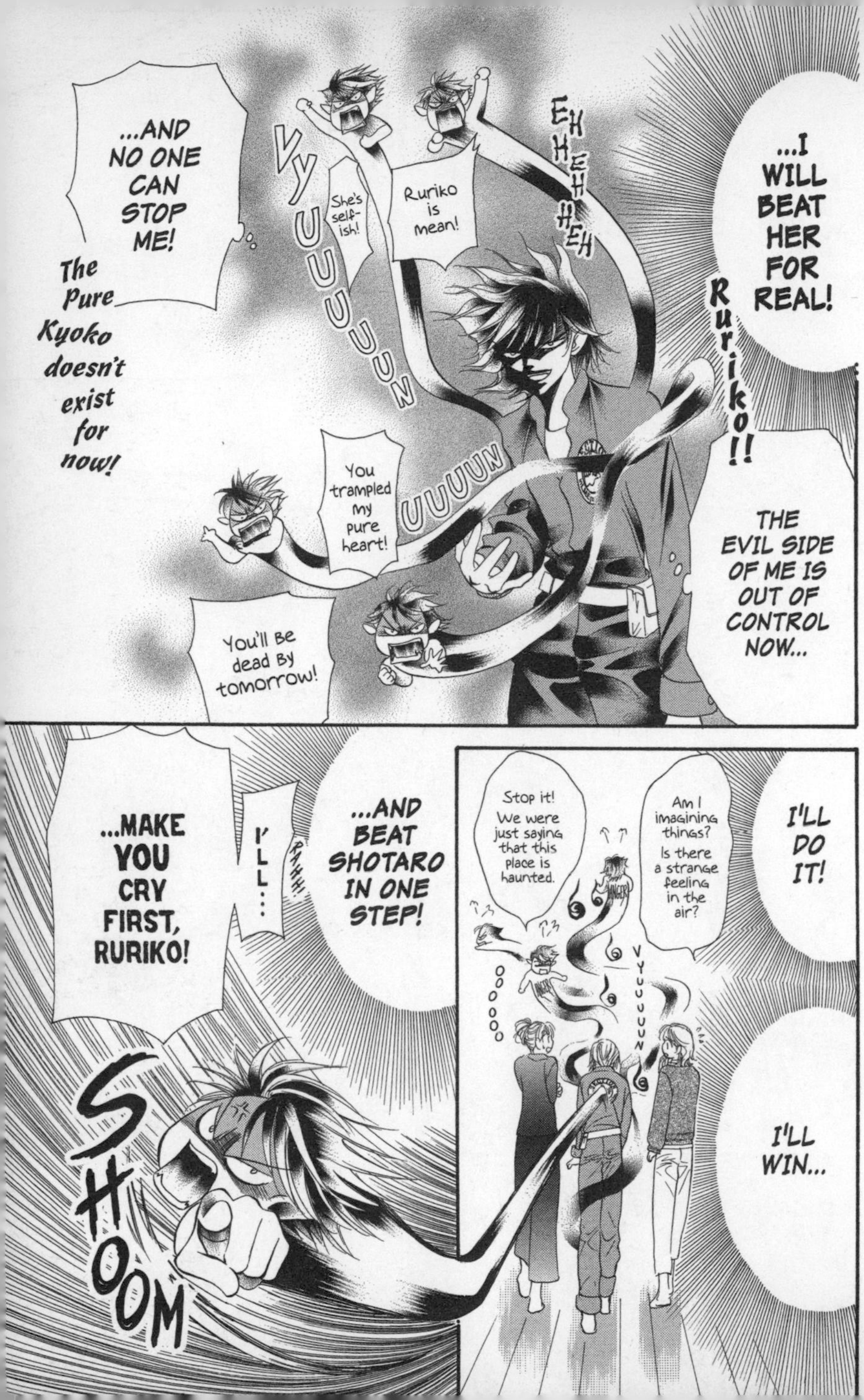
...I WILL BEAT HER FOR REAL!
Ruriko!!
EH HEH HEH
Ruriko is mean!
She's selfish!
VYUUUUUN
...AND NO ONE CAN STOP ME!
The Pure Kyoko doesn't exist for now!
THE EVIL SIDE OF ME IS OUT OF CONTROL NOW...
You trampled my pure heart!
UUUUN
You'll be dead by tomorrow!
I'LL DO IT!
Am I imagining things? Is there a strange feeling in the air?
Stop it! We were just saying that this place is haunted.
VYUUUUUN
OOOOOO
I'LL WIN...
...AND BEAT SHOTARO IN ONE STEP!
I'LL...
RAHH!
...MAKE YOU CRY FIRST, RURIKO!
SHOOOM

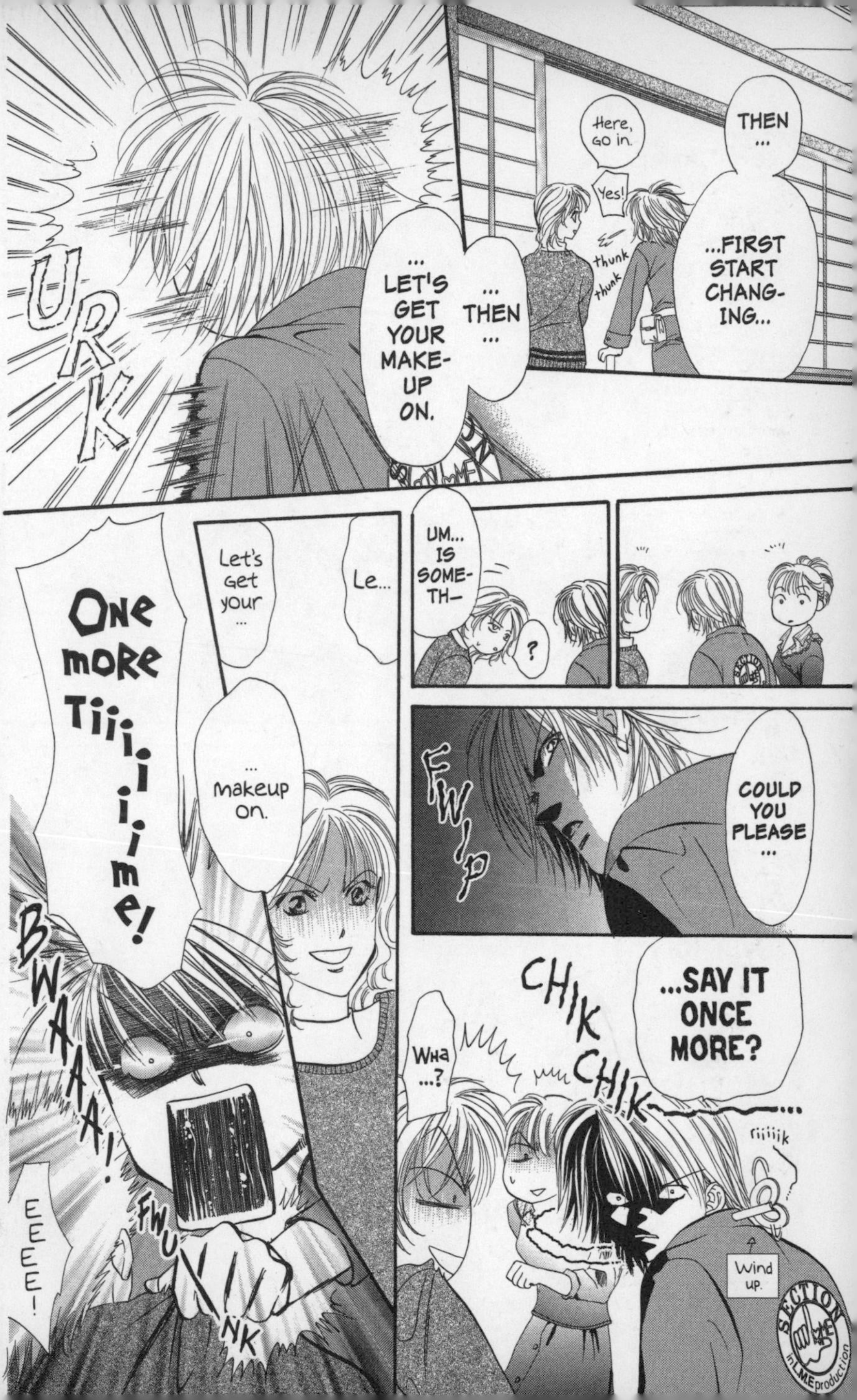
THEN ...
...FIRST START CHANGING...
Here, go in.
Yes!
thunk thunk
... THEN ...
... LET'S GET YOUR MAKE-UP ON.
URK
UM... IS SOMETH—
?
COULD YOU PLEASE ...
FWIP
...SAY IT ONCE MORE?
CHIK CHIK
Wha ...?
riiiiik
Wind up.
Le...
Let's get your ...
... makeup on.
One more Tiiiiiiime!
BWAAAA!
EEEE!
FWUNK

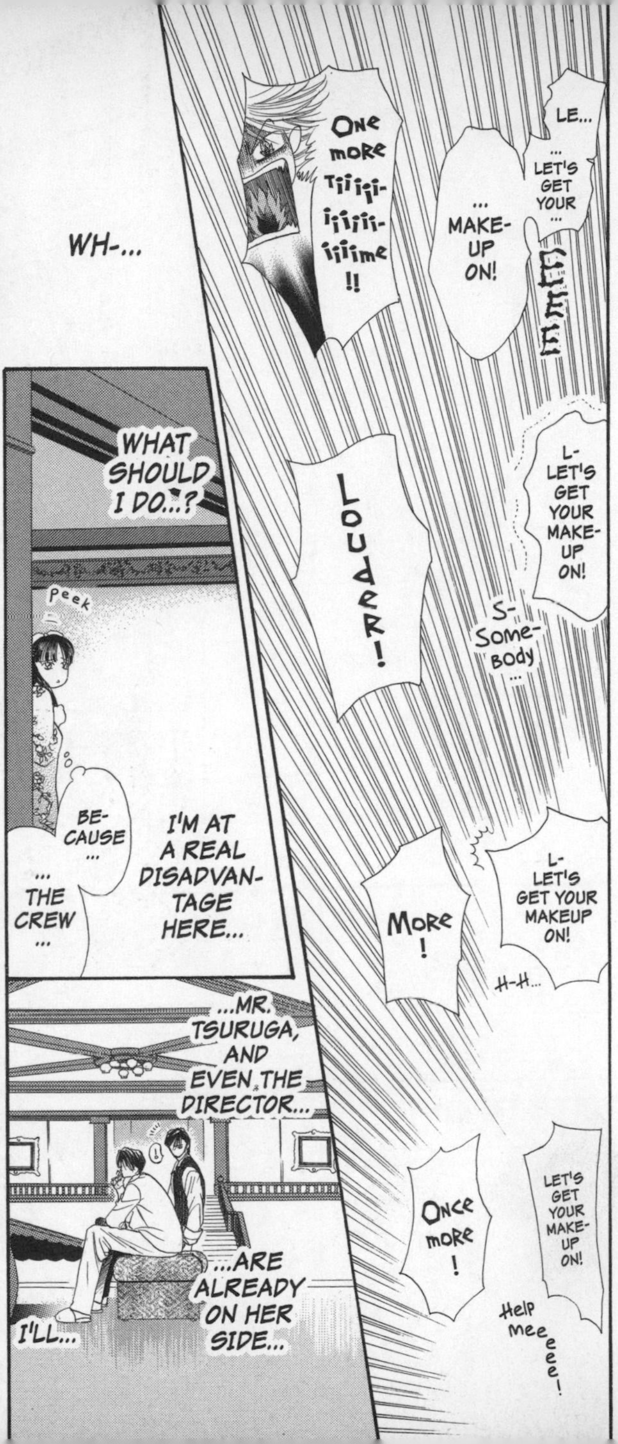
LE...
... LET'S GET YOUR ...
... MAKE-UP ON!
One more Tiiiii-iiiiii-iiiime!!
L- LET'S GET YOUR MAKE-UP ON!
S- Some-body ...
Louder!
L- LET'S GET YOUR MAKEUP ON!
H-H...
More!
LET'S GET YOUR MAKE-UP ON!
Help meeeeee!
Once more!
WH-...
WHAT SHOULD I DO...?
Peek
I'M AT A REAL DISADVANTAGE HERE...
BE-CAUSE ...
... THE CREW ...
...MR. TSURUGA, AND EVEN THE DIRECTOR...
...ARE ALREADY ON HER SIDE...
I'LL...

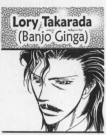

Lory Takarada
(Banjo Ginga)

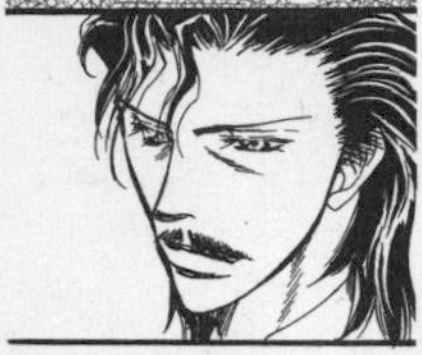

When I drew the scene where Lory first appears, I thought only Mr. Banjo Ginga could do him... Because I imagine that Lory has a really low voice that echoes in your stomach... Oh...but... I wrote "really low voice" in the FX once...

Takenori Sawara
(Tomoyuki Kono)

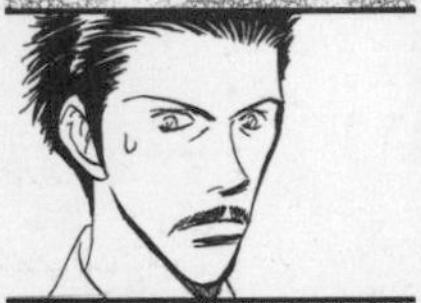

Kanae Kotonami
(Yukiko Tagami)

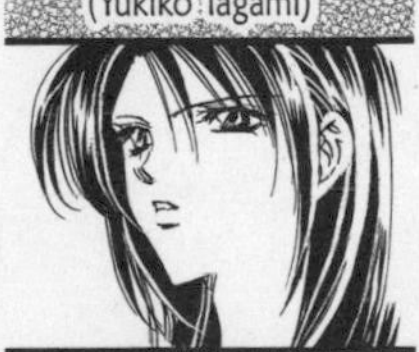

Darumaya Owners
(Masami Iwasaki)
(Mariko Nagahama)

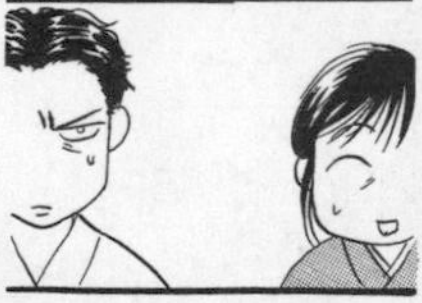

These are all the main cast. Thank you so much!!

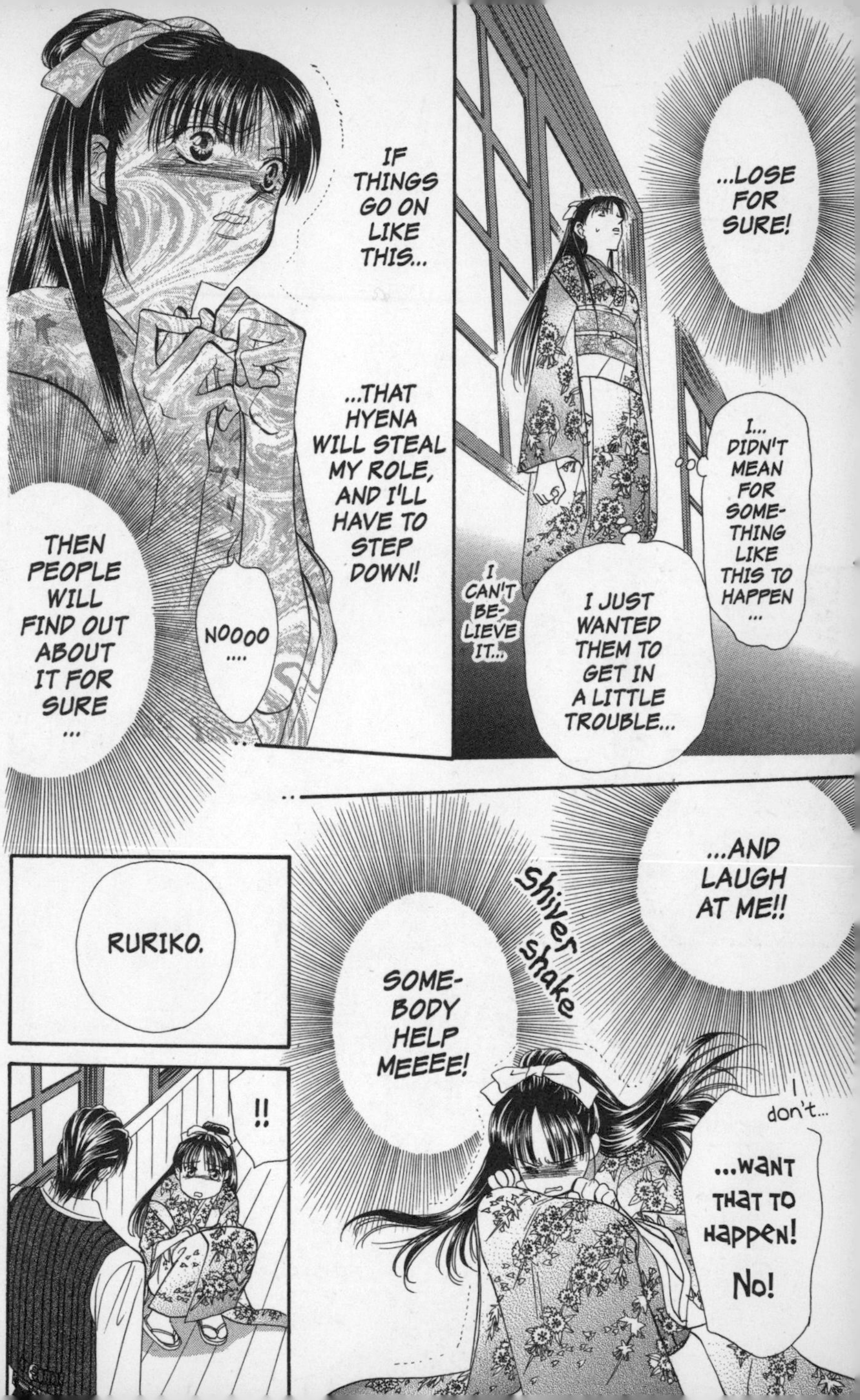
...LOSE FOR SURE!
I... DIDN'T MEAN FOR SOMETHING LIKE THIS TO HAPPEN...
I JUST WANTED THEM TO GET IN A LITTLE TROUBLE...
I CAN'T BELIEVE IT...
IF THINGS GO ON LIKE THIS...
...THAT HYENA WILL STEAL MY ROLE, AND I'LL HAVE TO STEP DOWN!
THEN PEOPLE WILL FIND OUT ABOUT IT FOR SURE...
NOOOO....
...AND LAUGH AT ME!!
Shiver shake
SOMEBODY HELP MEEEE!
I don't...
...want that to happen!
No!
RURIKO.
!!

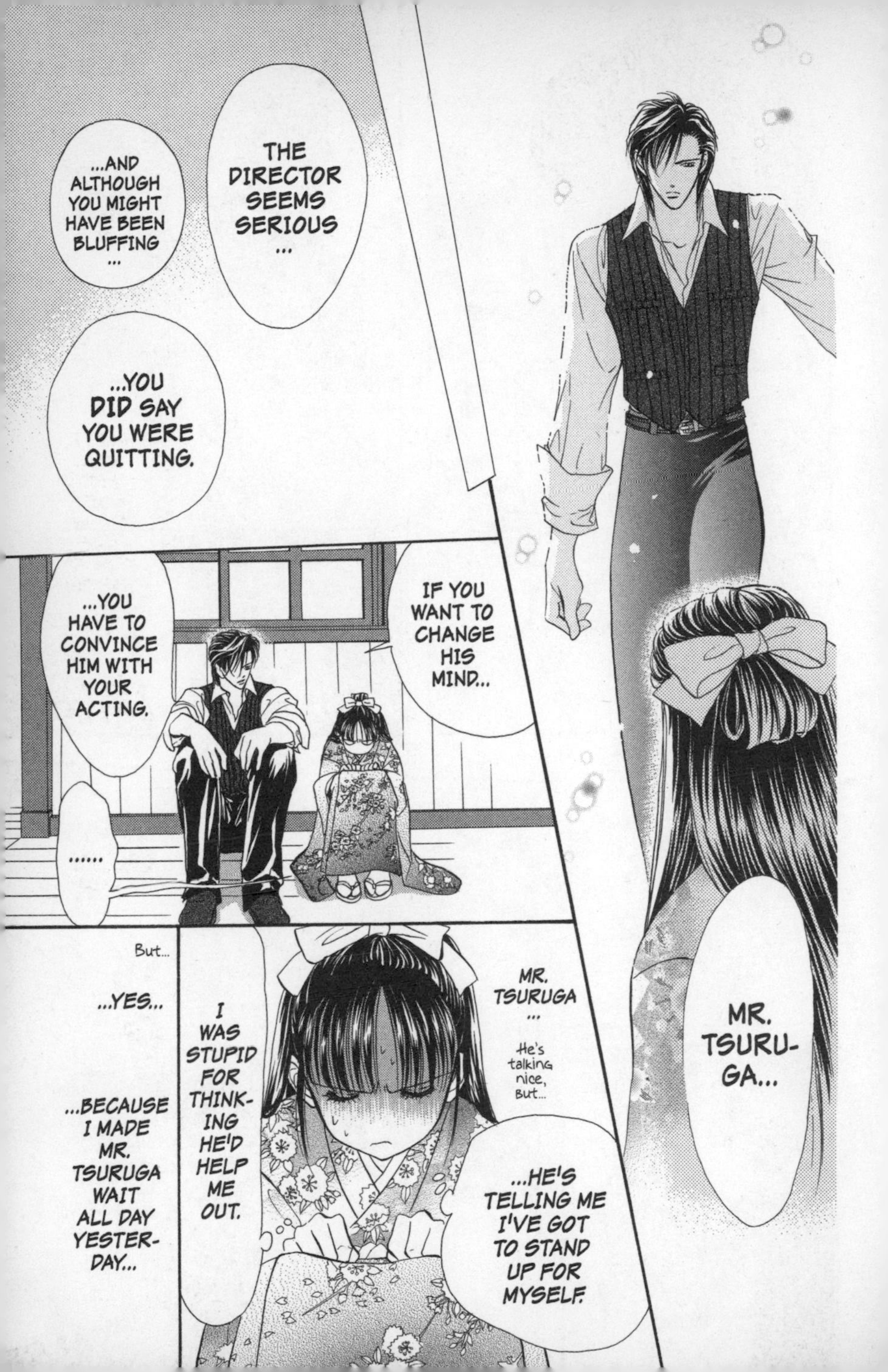
MR. TSURU-GA...
THE DIRECTOR SEEMS SERIOUS...
...AND ALTHOUGH YOU MIGHT HAVE BEEN BLUFFING...
...YOU DID SAY YOU WERE QUITTING.
IF YOU WANT TO CHANGE HIS MIND...
...YOU HAVE TO CONVINCE HIM WITH YOUR ACTING.
......
MR. TSURUGA...
He's talking nice, but...
...HE'S TELLING ME I'VE GOT TO STAND UP FOR MYSELF.
I WAS STUPID FOR THINK-ING HE'D HELP ME OUT.
But...
...YES...
...BECAUSE I MADE MR. TSURUGA WAIT ALL DAY YESTER-DAY...

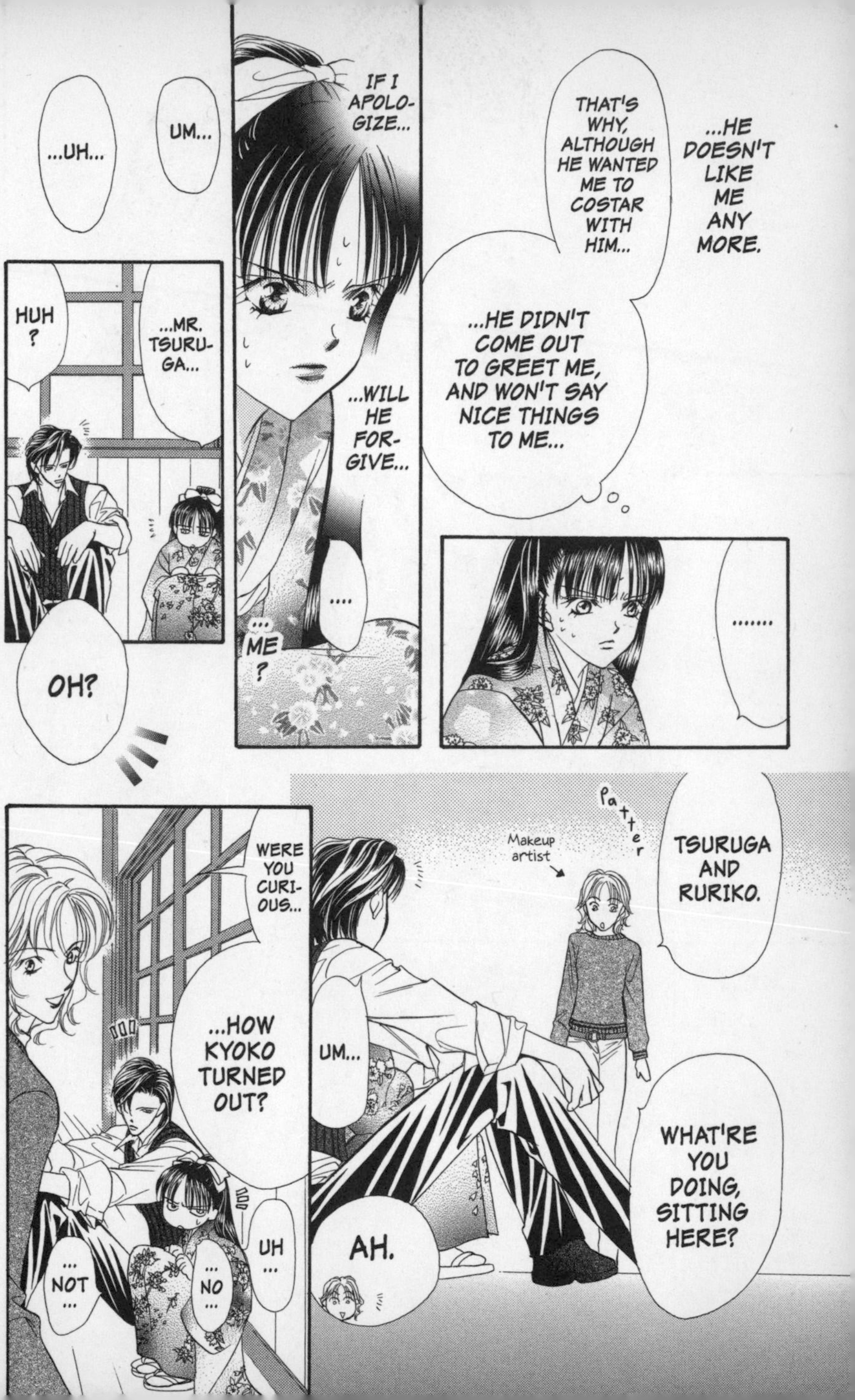

...HE DOESN'T LIKE ME ANY MORE.
THAT'S WHY, ALTHOUGH HE WANTED ME TO COSTAR WITH HIM...
...HE DIDN'T COME OUT TO GREET ME, AND WON'T SAY NICE THINGS TO ME...
....
IF I APOLOGIZE...
...WILL HE FORGIVE...
....
...ME?
UM...
...UH...
...MR. TSURUGA...
HUH?
OH?
TSURUGA AND RURIKO.
Patter
Makeup artist
WHAT'RE YOU DOING, SITTING HERE?
AH.
UM...
WERE YOU CURIOUS...
...HOW KYOKO TURNED OUT?
UH...
...NO...
...NOT...

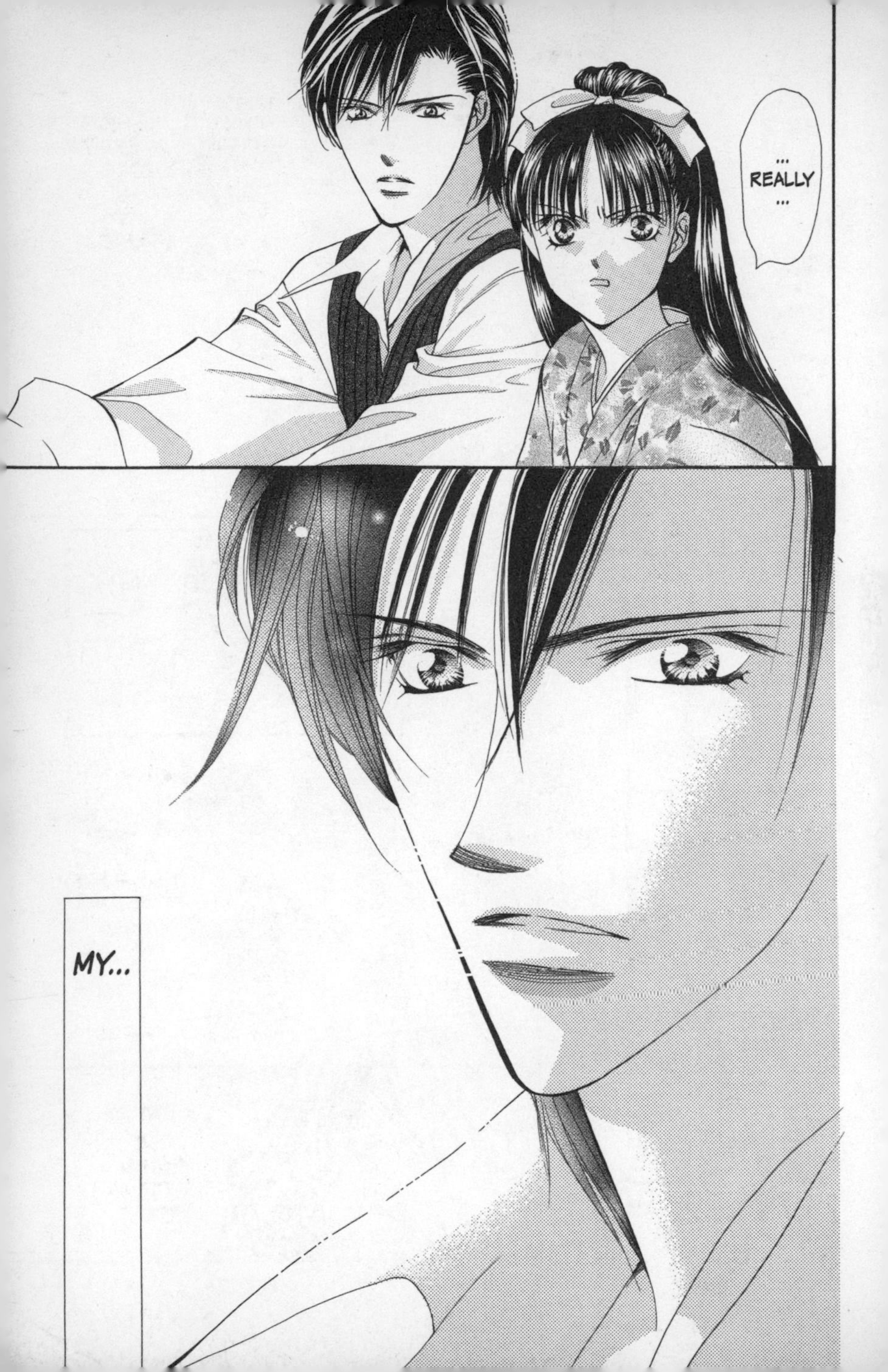
...
REALLY
...
MY...

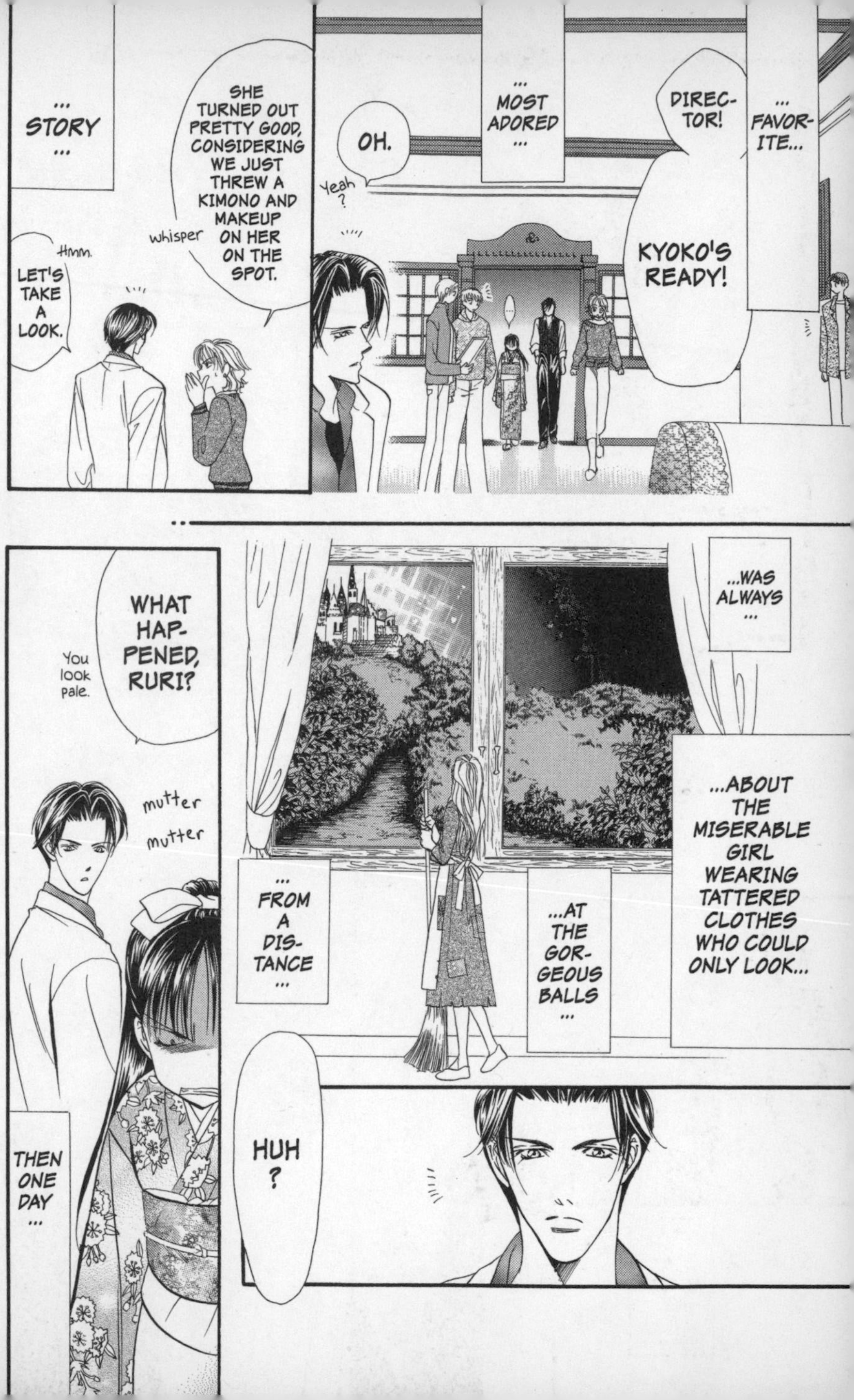
...FAVOR-ITE...
DIREC-TOR!
KYOKO'S READY!
... MOST ADORED ...
OH.
Yeah ?
... STORY ...
SHE TURNED OUT PRETTY GOOD, CONSIDERING WE JUST THREW A KIMONO AND MAKEUP ON HER ON THE SPOT.
whisper
Hmm.
LET'S TAKE A LOOK.
...WAS ALWAYS ...
...ABOUT THE MISERABLE GIRL WEARING TATTERED CLOTHES WHO COULD ONLY LOOK...
...AT THE GOR-GEOUS BALLS ...
... FROM A DIS-TANCE ...
HUH ?
WHAT HAP-PENED, RURI?
You look pale.
mutter
mutter
THEN ONE DAY ...

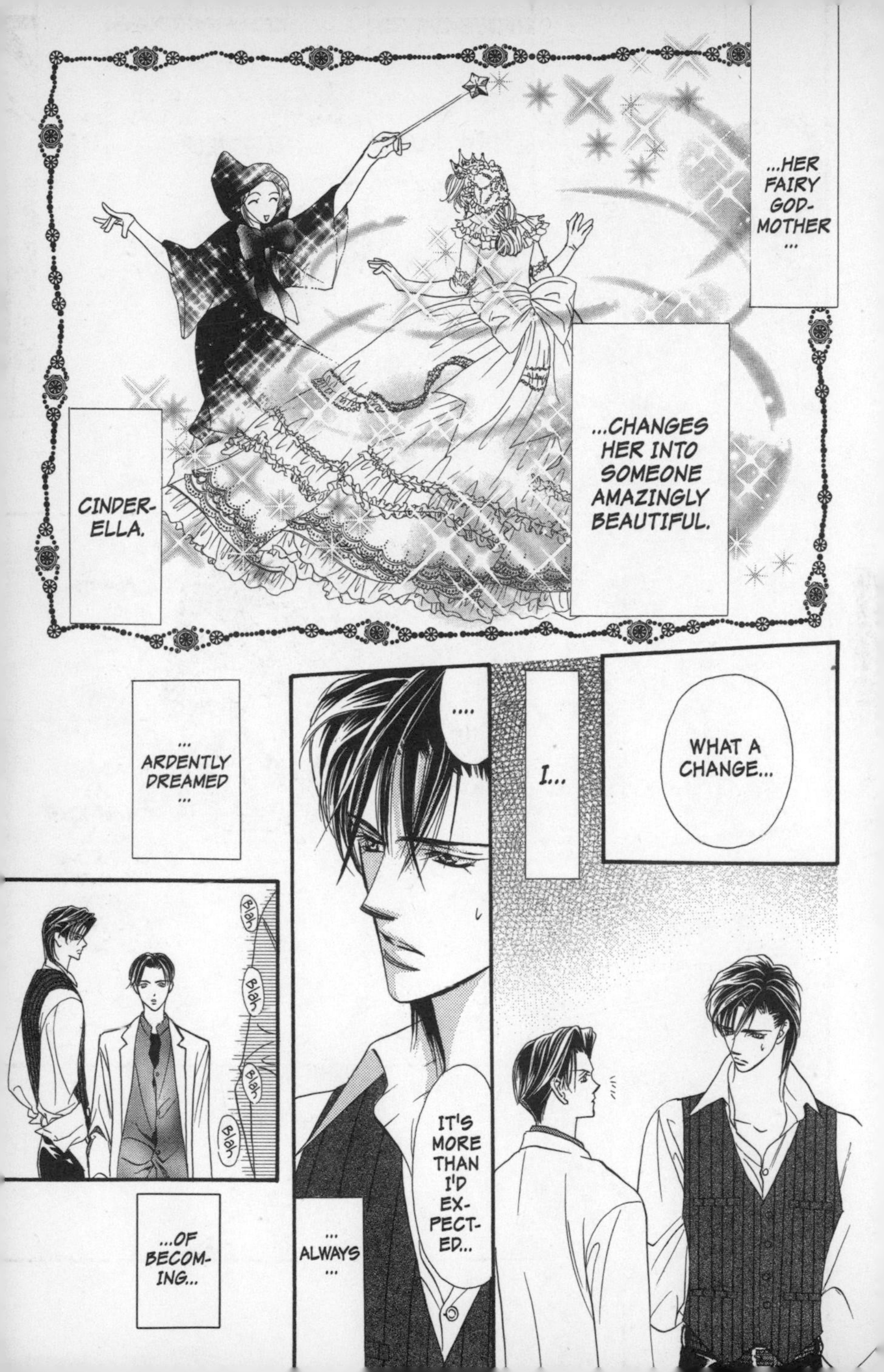
...HER FAIRY GOD-MOTHER...
...CHANGES HER INTO SOMEONE AMAZINGLY BEAUTIFUL.
CINDER-ELLA.
WHAT A CHANGE...
I...
....
IT'S MORE THAN I'D EX-PECT-ED...
...ALWAYS...
...ARDENTLY DREAMED...
Blah
Blah
Blah
Blah
...OF BECOM-ING...

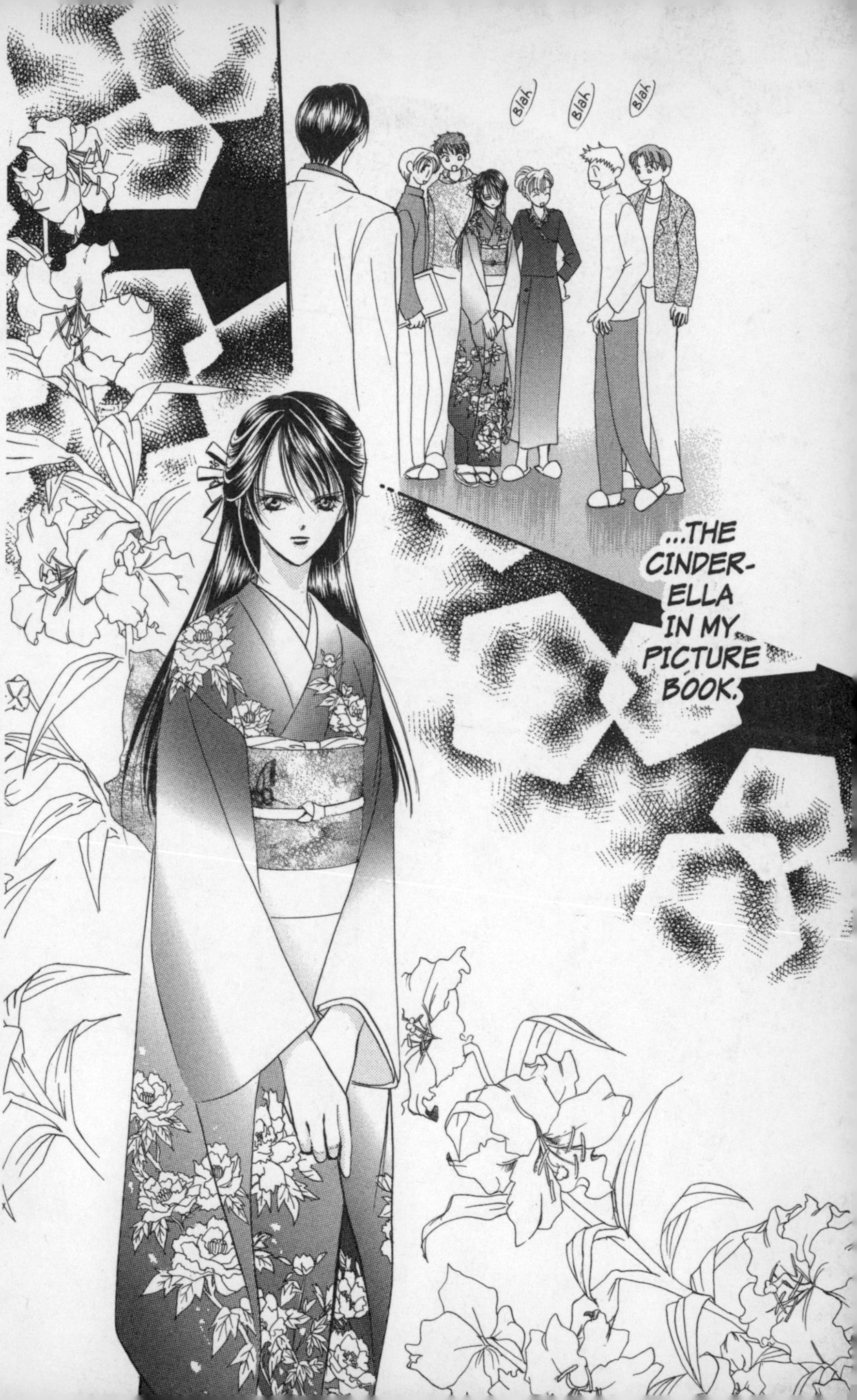
Blah
Blah
Blah
...THE CINDER-ELLA IN MY PICTURE BOOK.

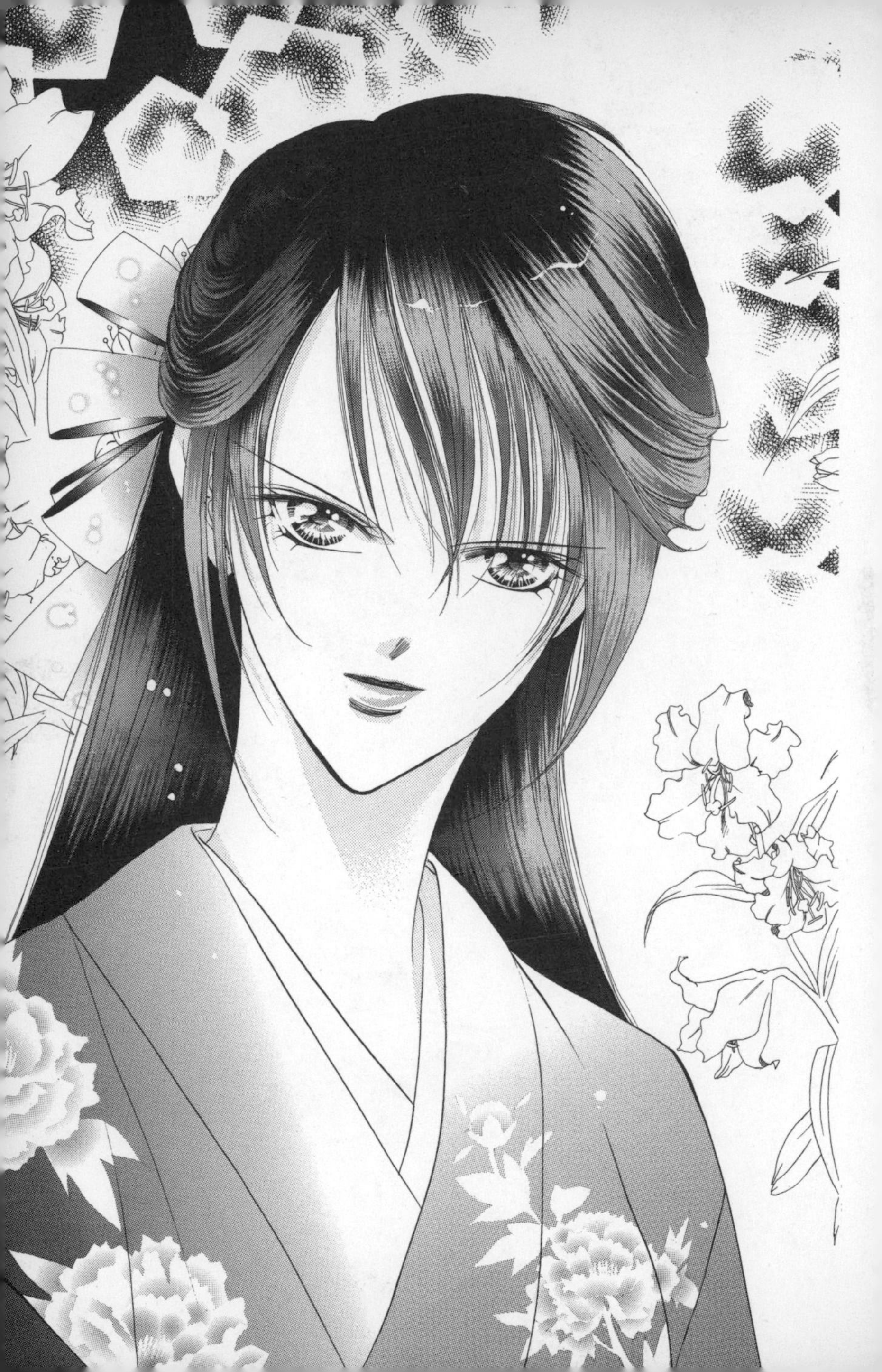

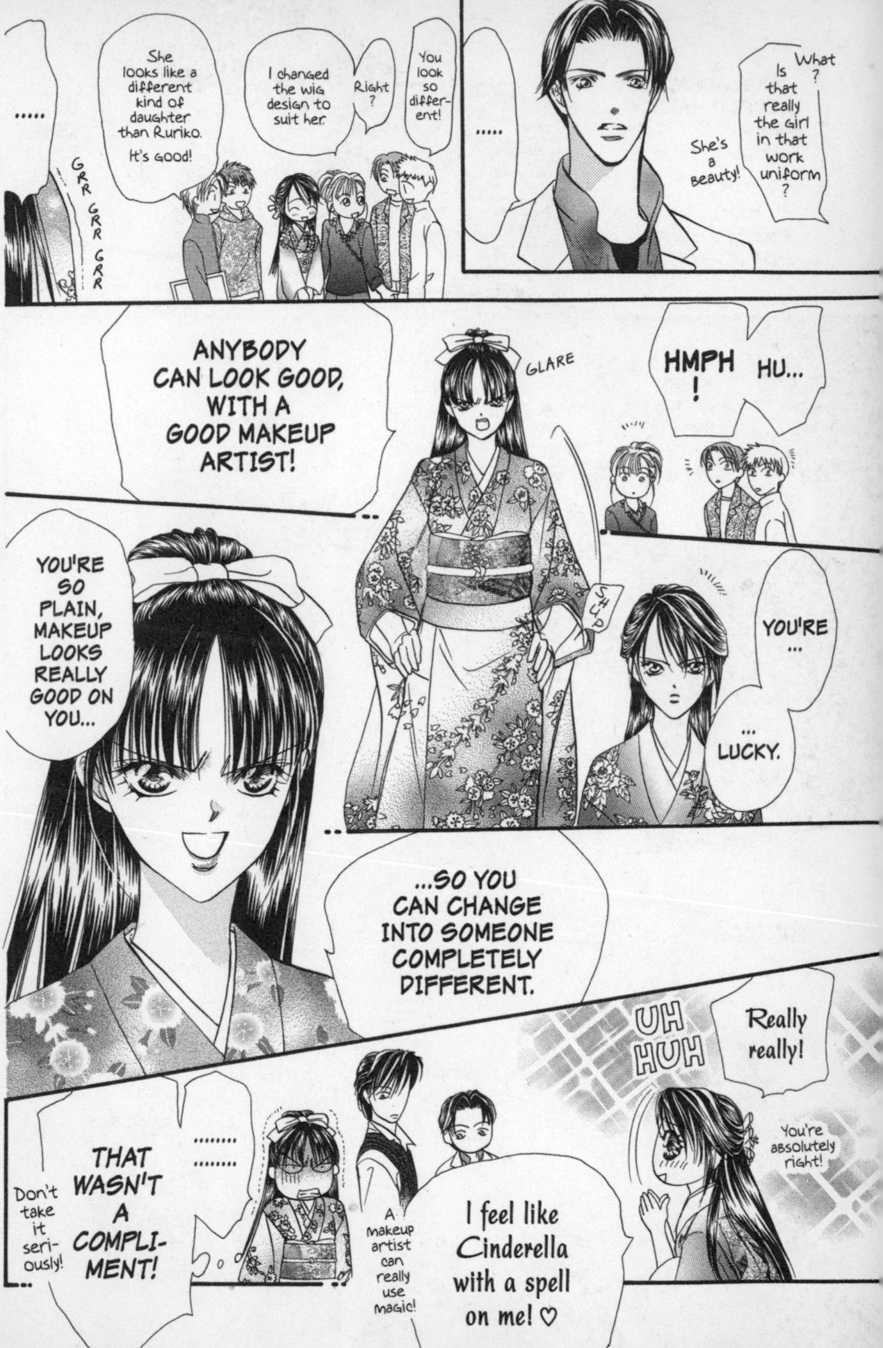
What?
Is that really the girl in that work uniform?
She's a beauty!
.....
You look so different!
Right?
I changed the wig design to suit her.
She looks like a different kind of daughter than Ruriko.
It's good!
.....
GRR GRR GRR
HMPH!
HU...
GLARE
ANYBODY CAN LOOK GOOD, WITH A GOOD MAKEUP ARTIST!
YOU'RE...
... LUCKY.
SHUP
YOU'RE SO PLAIN, MAKEUP LOOKS REALLY GOOD ON YOU...
...SO YOU CAN CHANGE INTO SOMEONE COMPLETELY DIFFERENT.
UH HUH
Really really!
You're absolutely right!
I feel like Cinderella with a spell on me! ♡
A makeup artist can really use magic!
....
....
THAT WASN'T A COMPLIMENT!
Don't take it seriously!

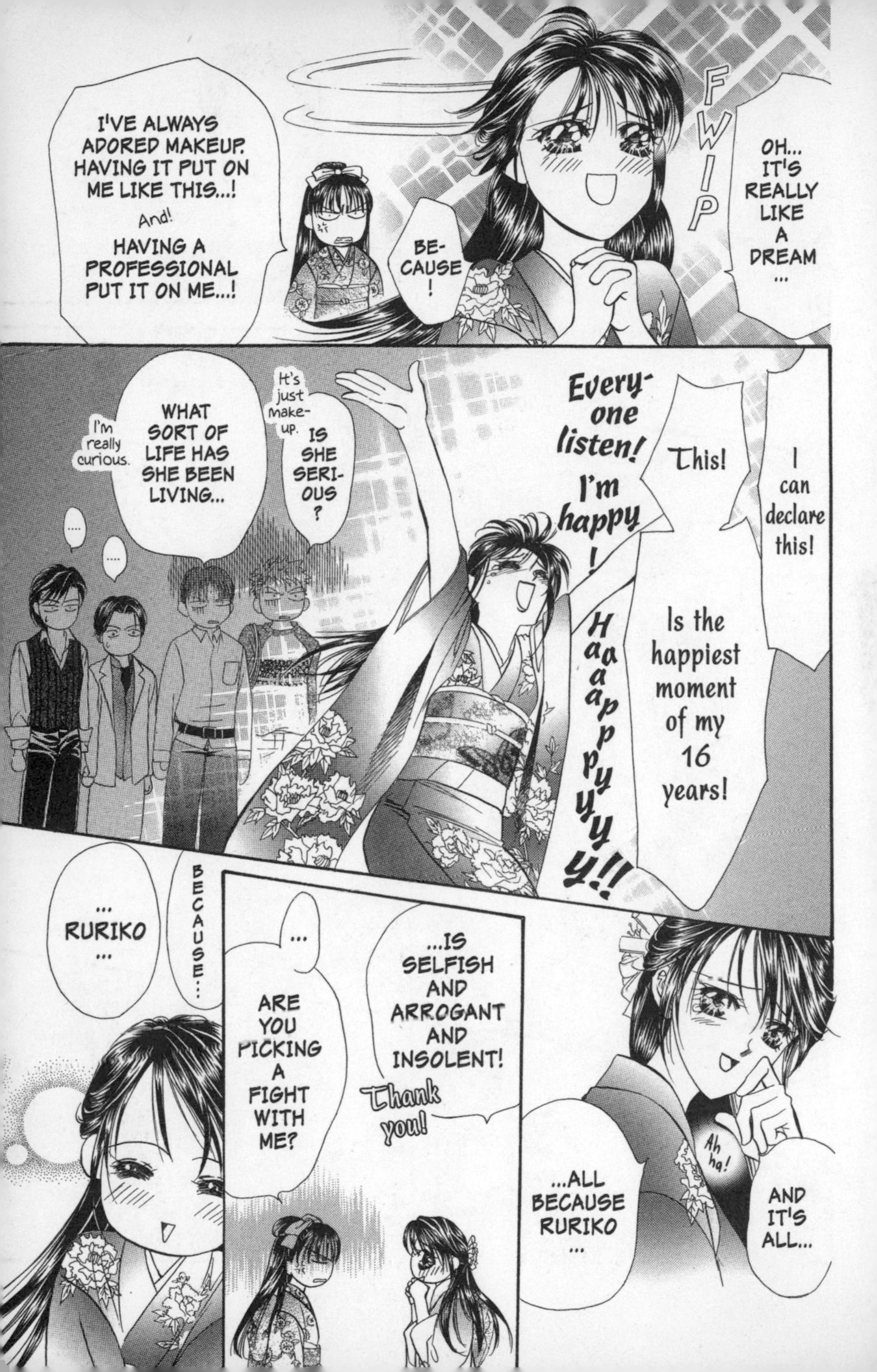
OH... IT'S REALLY LIKE A DREAM ...
FWIP
BE-CAUSE !
I'VE ALWAYS ADORED MAKEUP. HAVING IT PUT ON ME LIKE THIS...!
And!
HAVING A PROFESSIONAL PUT IT ON ME...!
I can declare this!
This!
Is the happiest moment of my 16 years!
Every-one listen! I'm happy!
Haaaappyyyy!!
It's just make-up.
IS SHE SERI-OUS?
WHAT SORT OF LIFE HAS SHE BEEN LIVING...
I'm really curious.
....
....
AND IT'S ALL...
Ah ha!
...ALL BECAUSE RURIKO ...
...IS SELFISH AND ARROGANT AND INSOLENT!
Thank you!
...
ARE YOU PICKING A FIGHT WITH ME?
BECAUSE...
... RURIKO ...

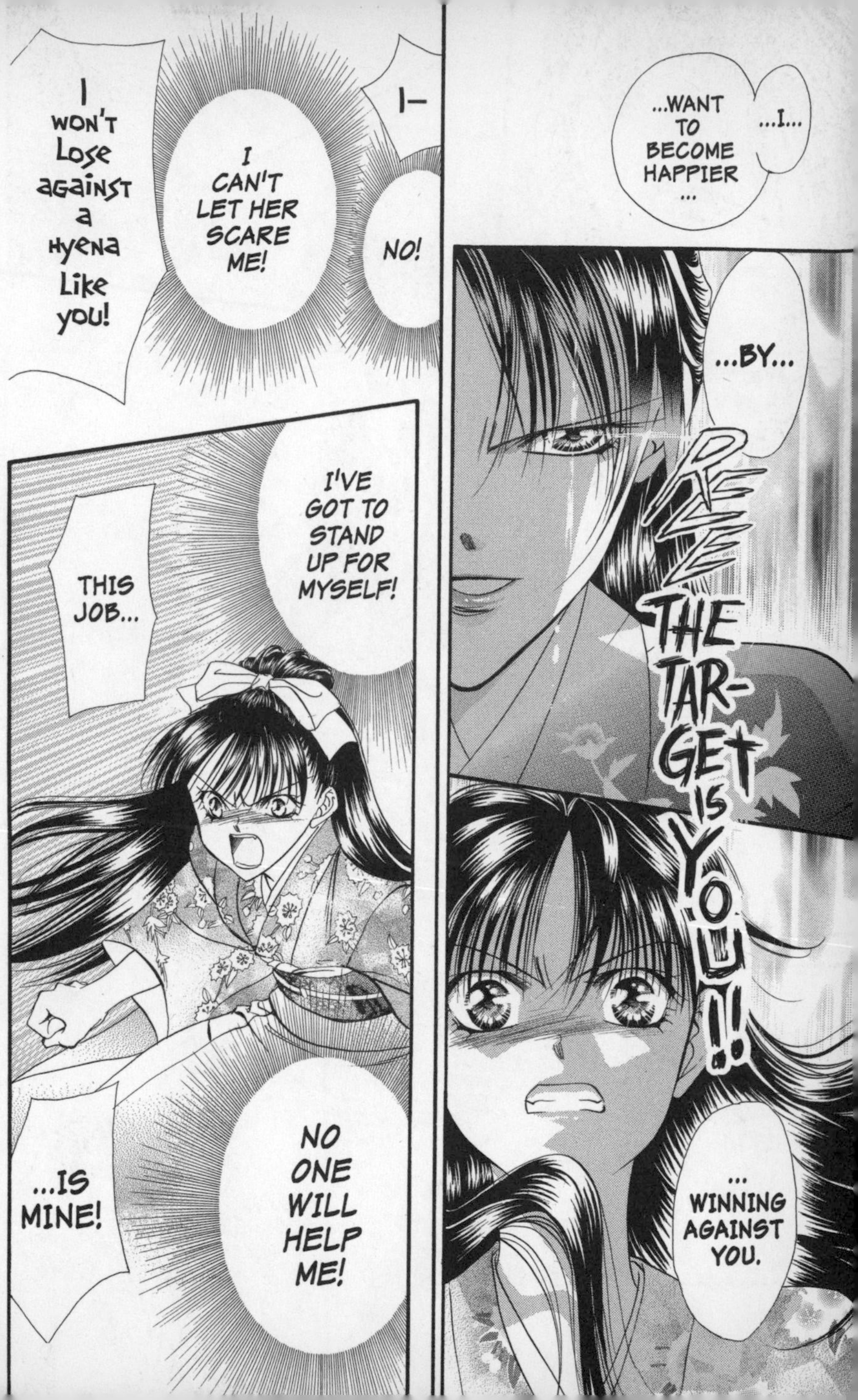
...I...
...WANT TO BECOME HAPPIER ...
...BY...
... WINNING AGAINST YOU.
THE TAR-GET IS YOU!!
I—
NO!
I CAN'T LET HER SCARE ME!
I WON'T LOSE AGAINST A HYENA LIKE YOU!
I'VE GOT TO STAND UP FOR MYSELF!
THIS JOB...
NO ONE WILL HELP ME!
...IS MINE!

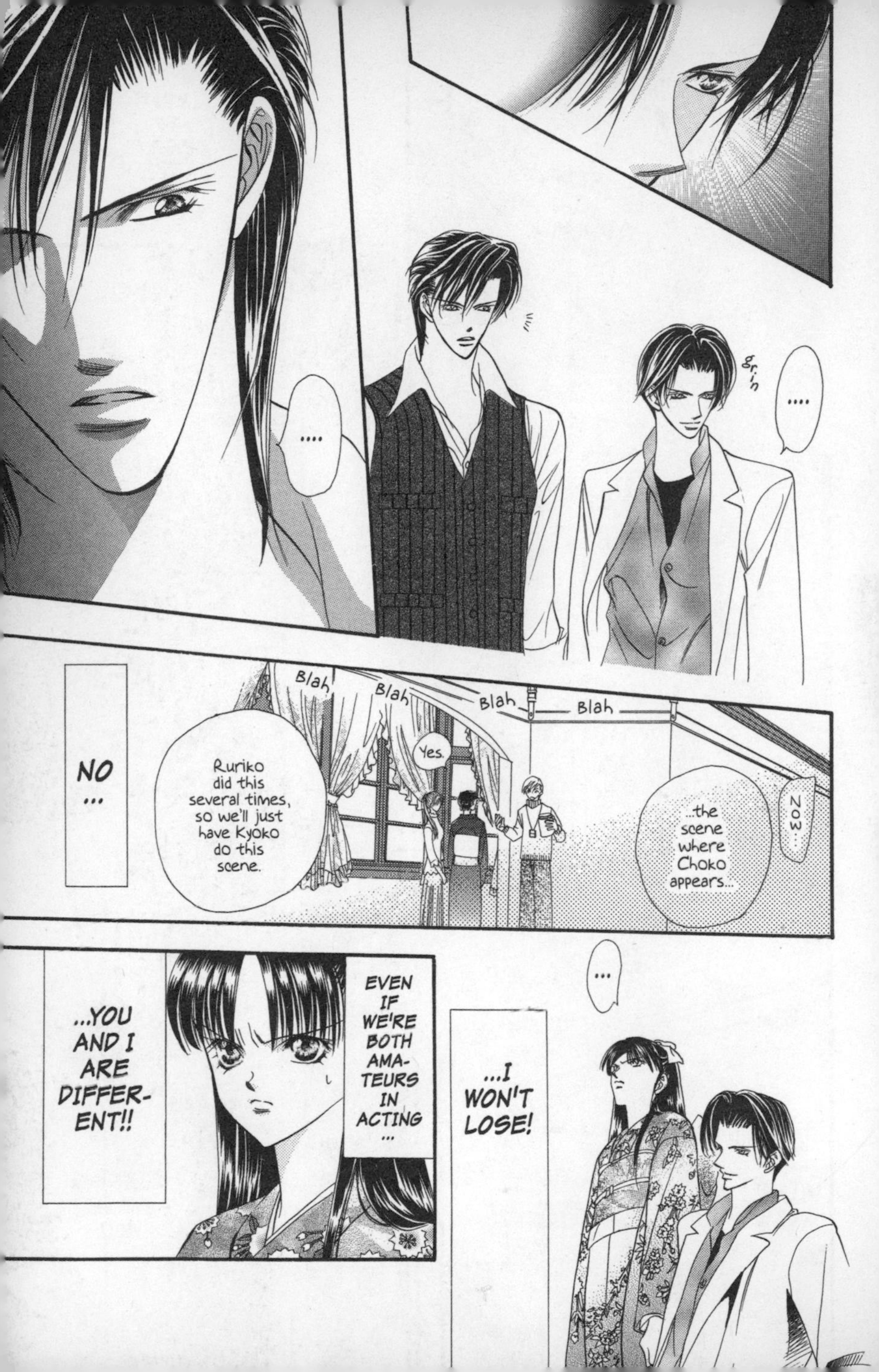
grin
....
....
Blah Blah Blah Blah
Now...
...the scene where Choko appears...
Yes.
Ruriko did this several times, so we'll just have Kyoko do this scene.
NO ...
...
...I WON'T LOSE!
EVEN IF WE'RE BOTH AMATEURS IN ACTING ...
...YOU AND I ARE DIFFERENT!!

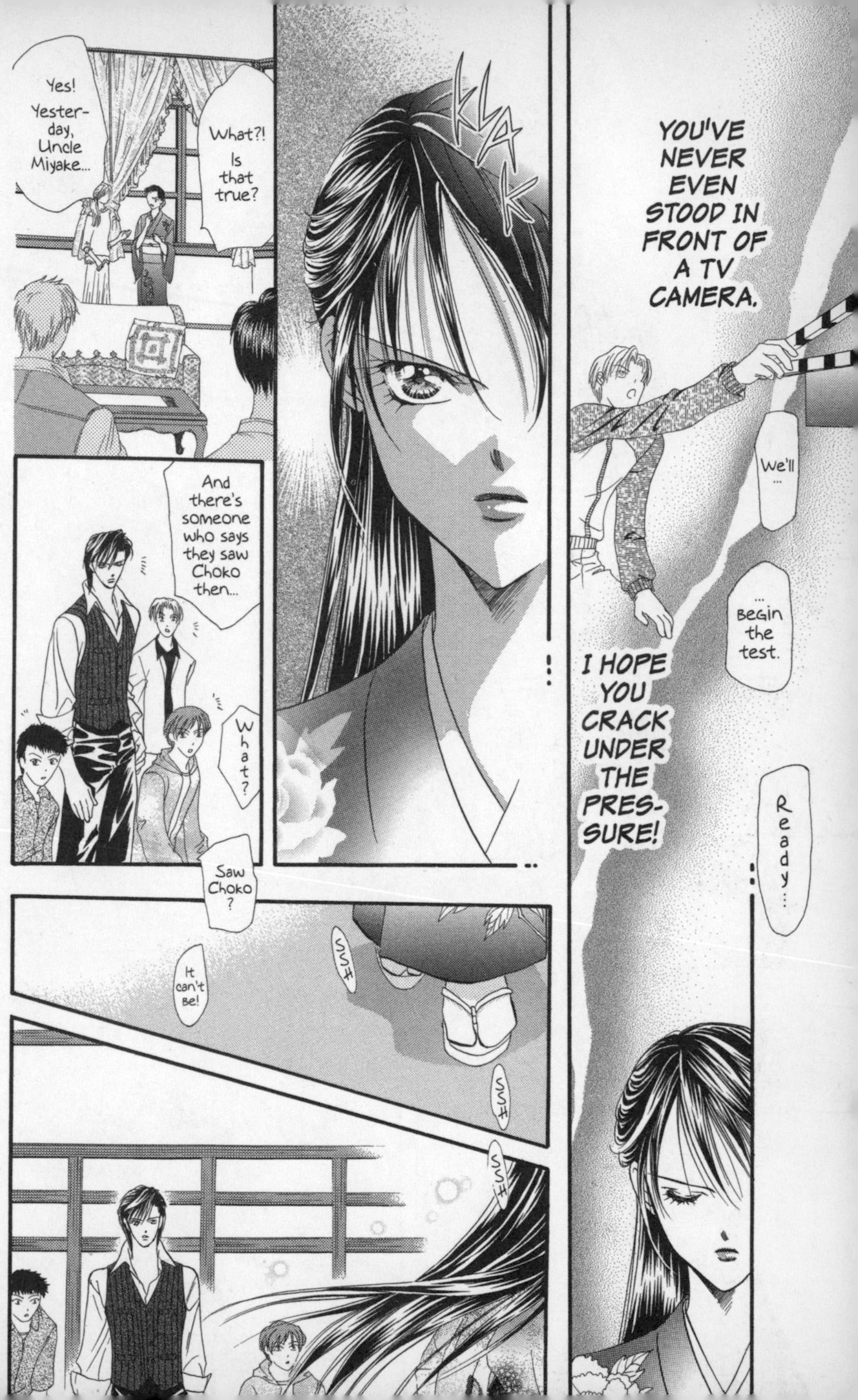
YOU'VE NEVER EVEN STOOD IN FRONT OF A TV CAMERA.
We'll ...
... Begin the test.
I HOPE YOU CRACK UNDER THE PRESSURE!
Ready...
KLAK
What?! Is that true?
Yes! Yesterday, Uncle Miyake...
And there's someone who says they saw Choko then...
What?
Saw Choko?
It can't be!
SSH
SSH
SSH

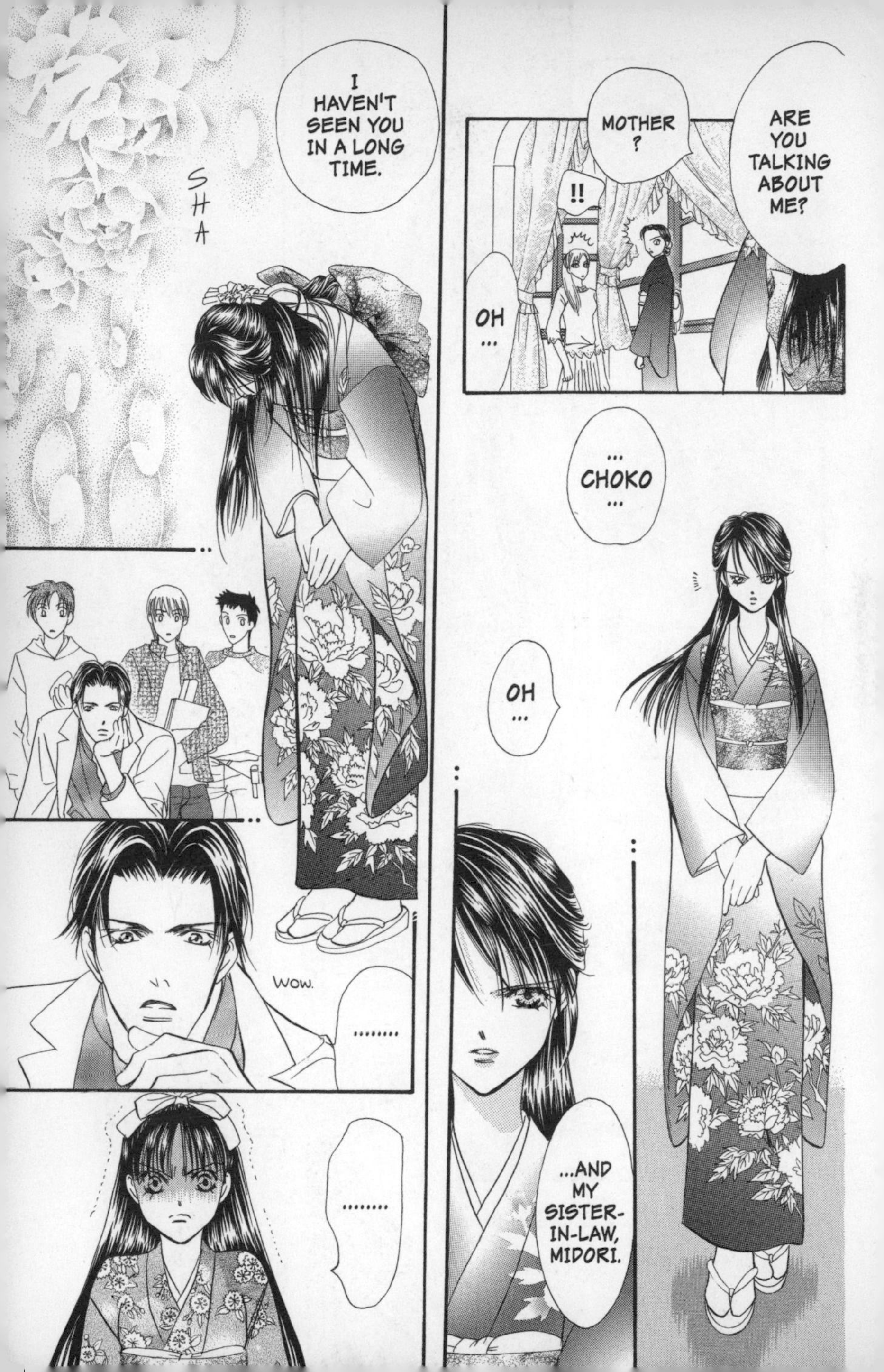
ARE YOU TALKING ABOUT ME?
MOTHER ?
!!
OH ...
... CHOKO ...
OH ...
...AND MY SISTER-IN-LAW, MIDORI.
I HAVEN'T SEEN YOU IN A LONG TIME.
SHA
WOW.
....
....

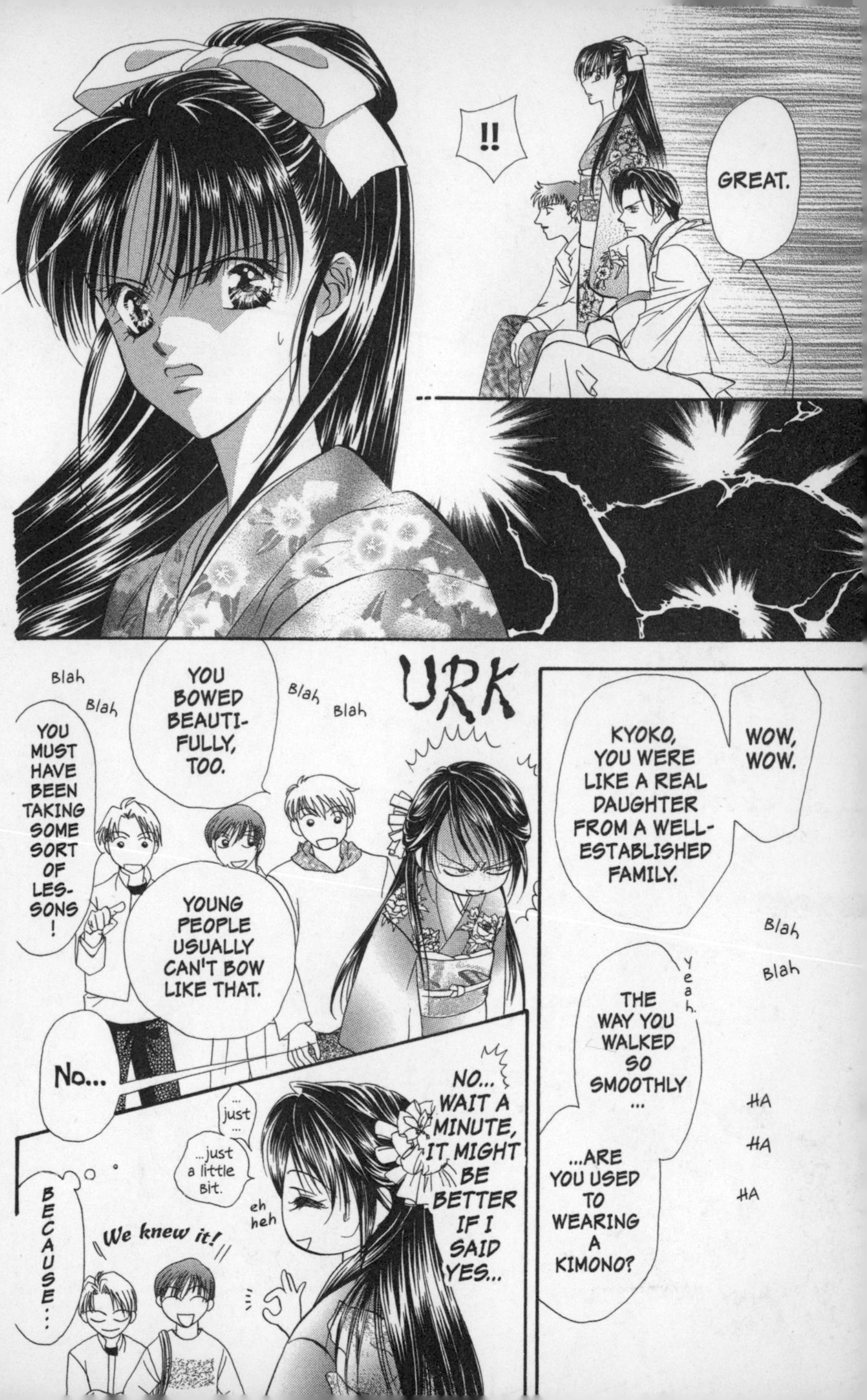
GREAT.
!!
WOW, WOW.
KYOKO, YOU WERE LIKE A REAL DAUGHTER FROM A WELL-ESTABLISHED FAMILY.
Blah
Blah
THE WAY YOU WALKED SO SMOOTHLY...
Yeah.
...ARE YOU USED TO WEARING A KIMONO?
HA
HA
HA
URK
Blah
Blah
YOU BOWED BEAUTIFULLY, TOO.
Blah
Blah
YOU MUST HAVE BEEN TAKING SOME SORT OF LESSONS!
YOUNG PEOPLE USUALLY CAN'T BOW LIKE THAT.
No...
NO... WAIT A MINUTE, IT MIGHT BE BETTER IF I SAID YES...
...just...
...just a little bit.
eh heh
We knew it!
BECAUSE...

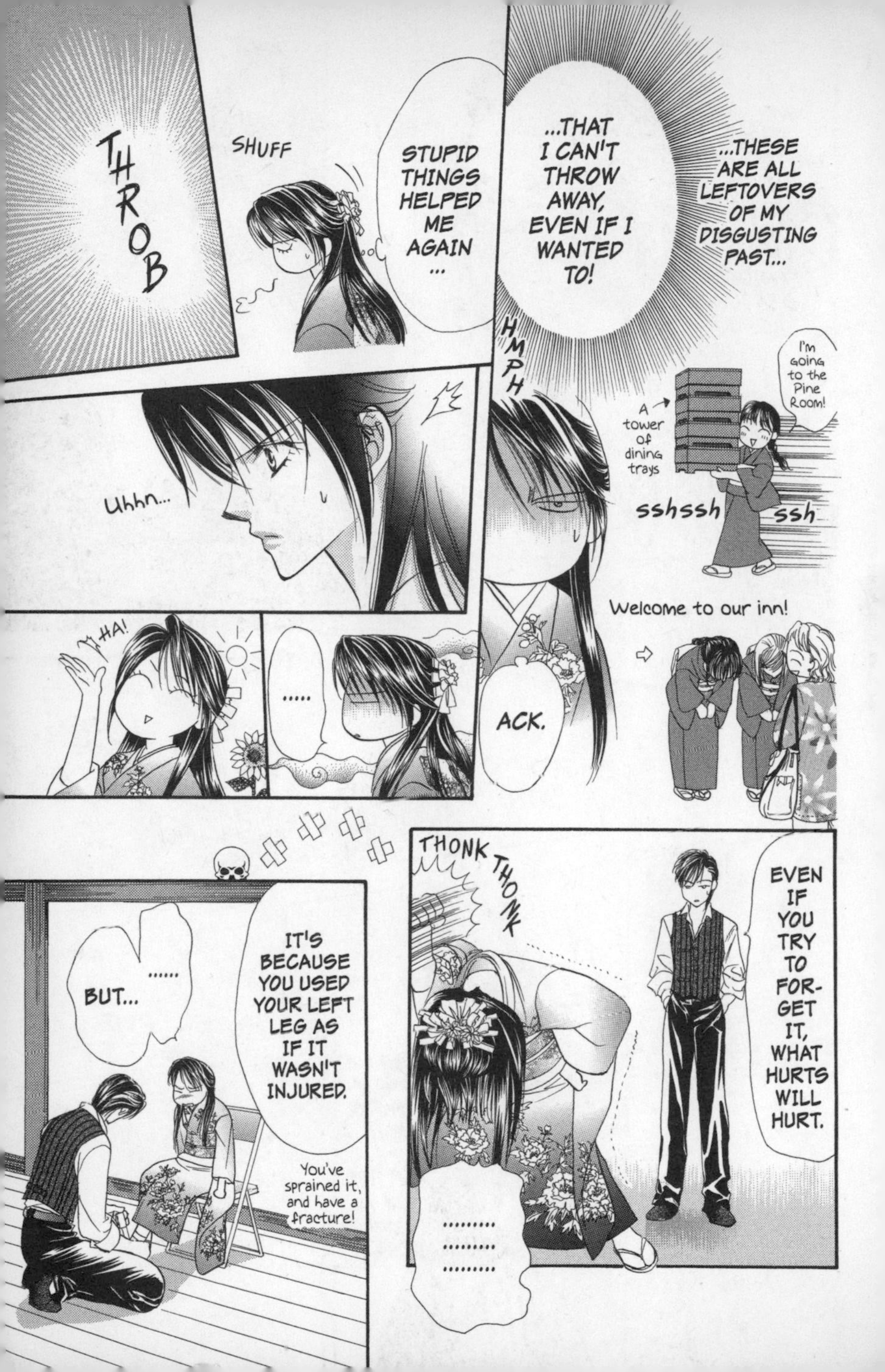
...THESE ARE ALL LEFTOVERS OF MY DISGUSTING PAST...
...THAT I CAN'T THROW AWAY, EVEN IF I WANTED TO!
STUPID THINGS HELPED ME AGAIN ...
SHUFF
THROB
HMPH
I'm going to the Pine Room!
A tower of dining trays
sshsssh
ssh
Welcome to our inn!
ACK.
Uhhn...
.....
HA!
EVEN IF YOU TRY TO FOR-GET IT, WHAT HURTS WILL HURT.
THONK THONK
....
....
....
IT'S BECAUSE YOU USED YOUR LEFT LEG AS IF IT WASN'T INJURED.
......
BUT...
You've sprained it, and have a fracture!

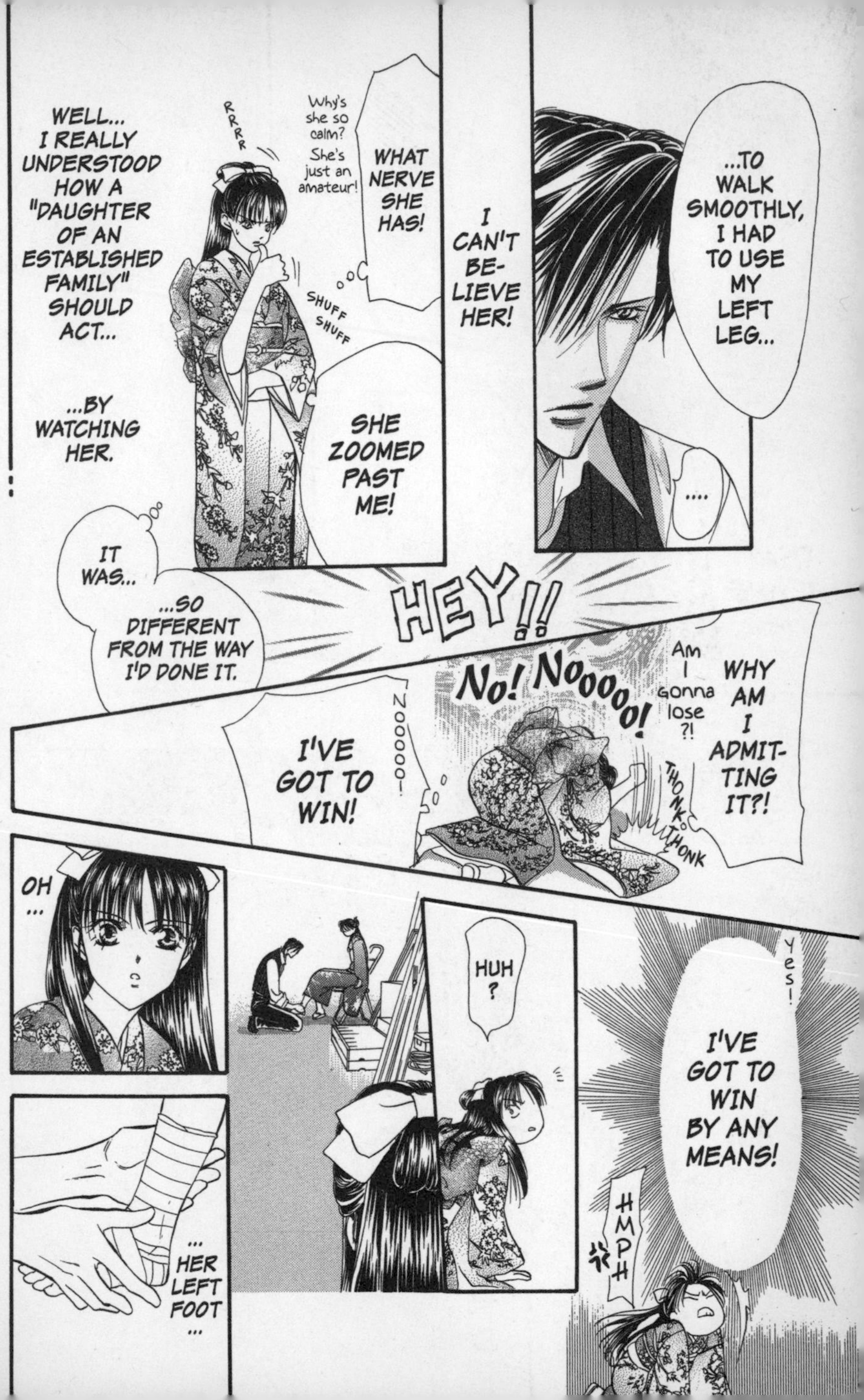
...TO WALK SMOOTHLY, I HAD TO USE MY LEFT LEG...
....
I CAN'T BE-LIEVE HER!
WHAT NERVE SHE HAS!
Why's she so calm? She's just an amateur!
RRRR
SHUFF SHUFF
SHE ZOOMED PAST ME!
WELL... I REALLY UNDERSTOOD HOW A "DAUGHTER OF AN ESTABLISHED FAMILY" SHOULD ACT...
...BY WATCHING HER.
IT WAS...
...SO DIFFERENT FROM THE WAY I'D DONE IT.
HEY!!
WHY AM I ADMIT-TING IT?!
Am I gonna lose ?!
No! Nooooo!
THONK THONK
I'VE GOT TO WIN!
NOOOOOO!
Yes!
I'VE GOT TO WIN BY ANY MEANS!
HMPH
HUH?
OH ...
... HER LEFT FOOT ...

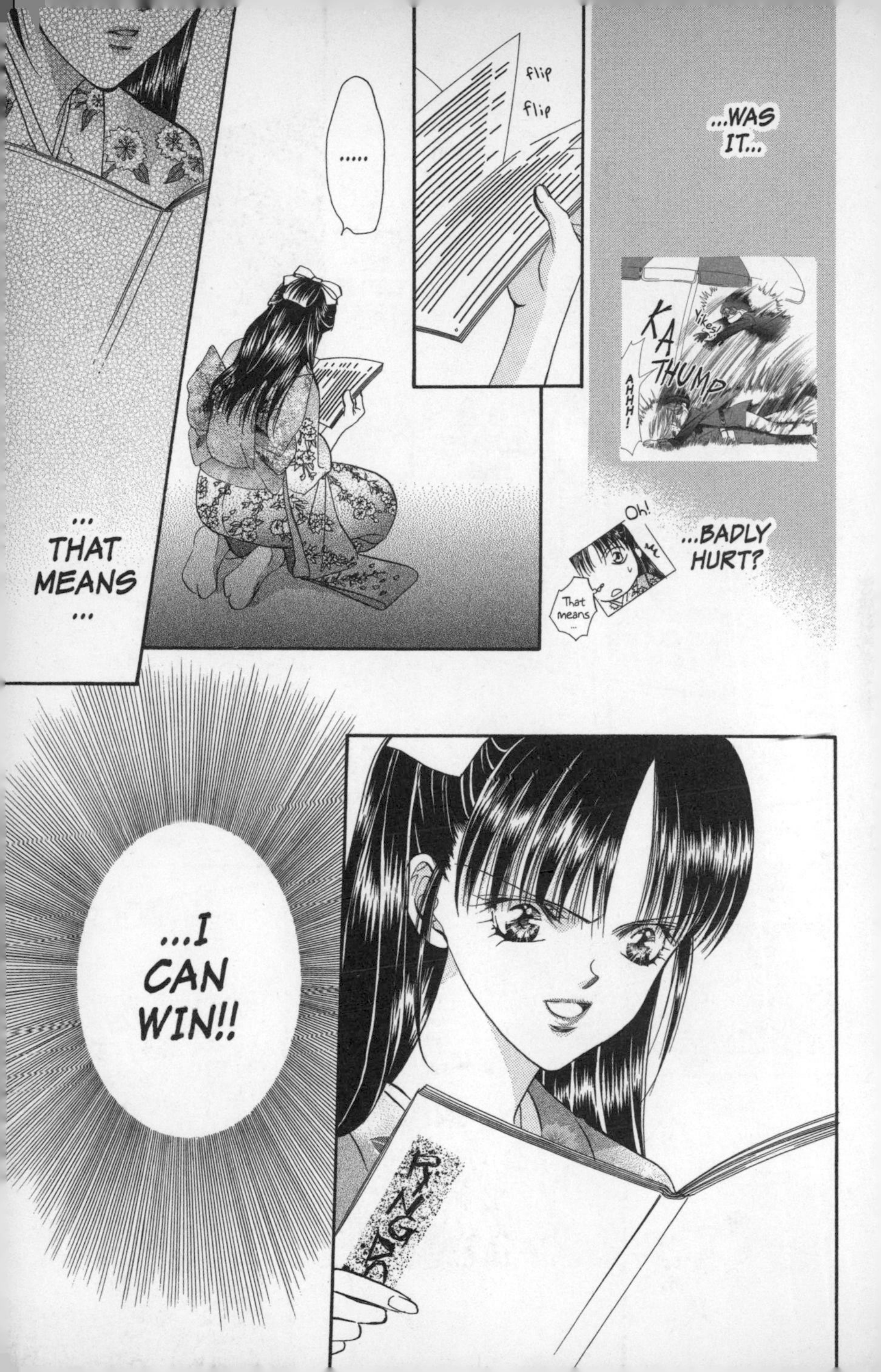
...WAS IT...
KA THUMP
Yikes!
AHHH!
...BADLY HURT?
Oh!
That means...
flip
flip
......
...THAT MEANS...
...I CAN WIN!!

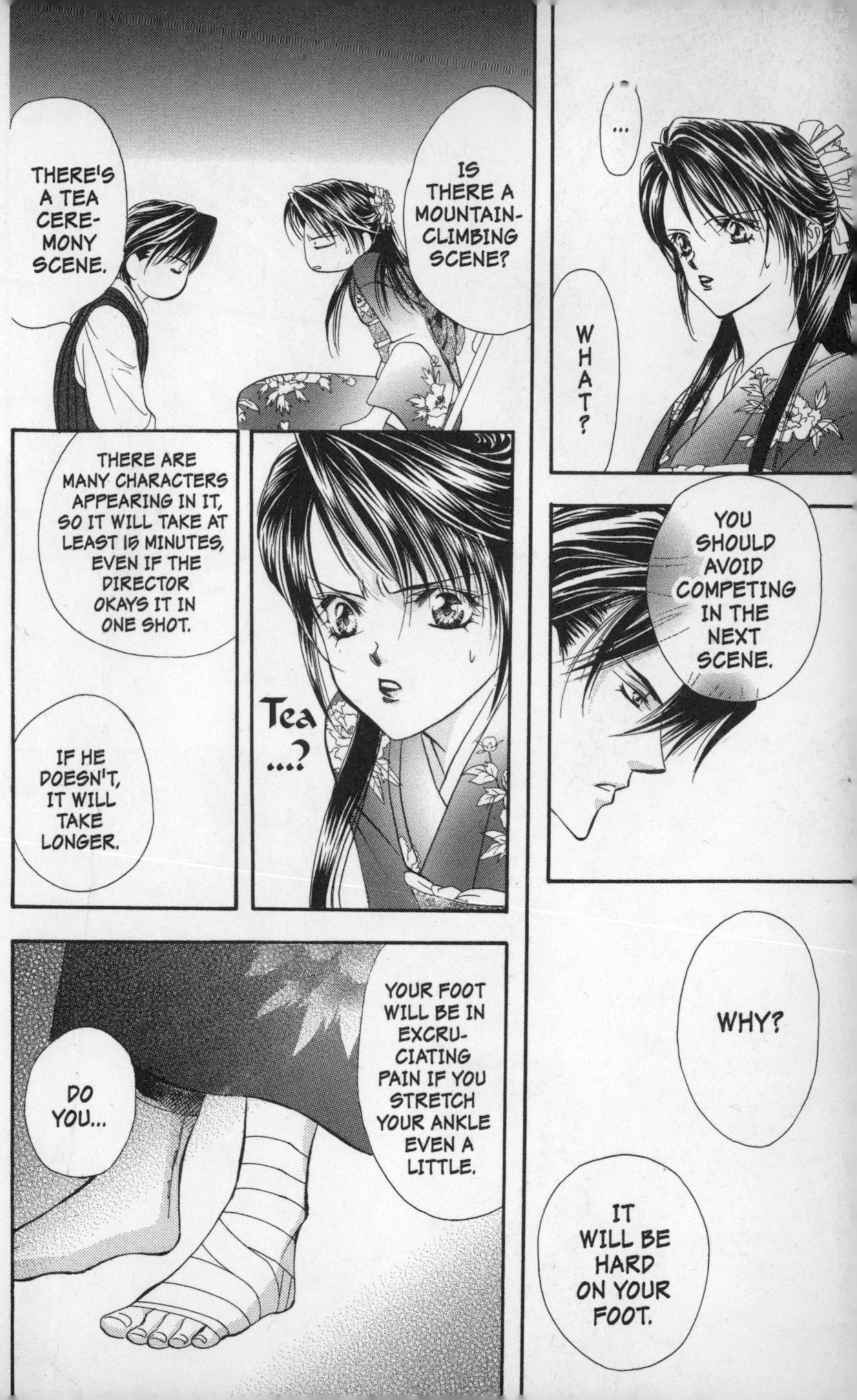
...
WHAT?
YOU SHOULD AVOID COMPETING IN THE NEXT SCENE.
WHY?
IT WILL BE HARD ON YOUR FOOT.
YOUR FOOT WILL BE IN EXCRU-CIATING PAIN IF YOU STRETCH YOUR ANKLE EVEN A LITTLE.
DO YOU...
IS THERE A MOUNTAIN-CLIMBING SCENE?
THERE'S A TEA CERE-MONY SCENE.
Tea ...?
THERE ARE MANY CHARACTERS APPEARING IN IT, SO IT WILL TAKE AT LEAST 15 MINUTES, EVEN IF THE DIRECTOR OKAYS IT IN ONE SHOT.
IF HE DOESN'T, IT WILL TAKE LONGER.

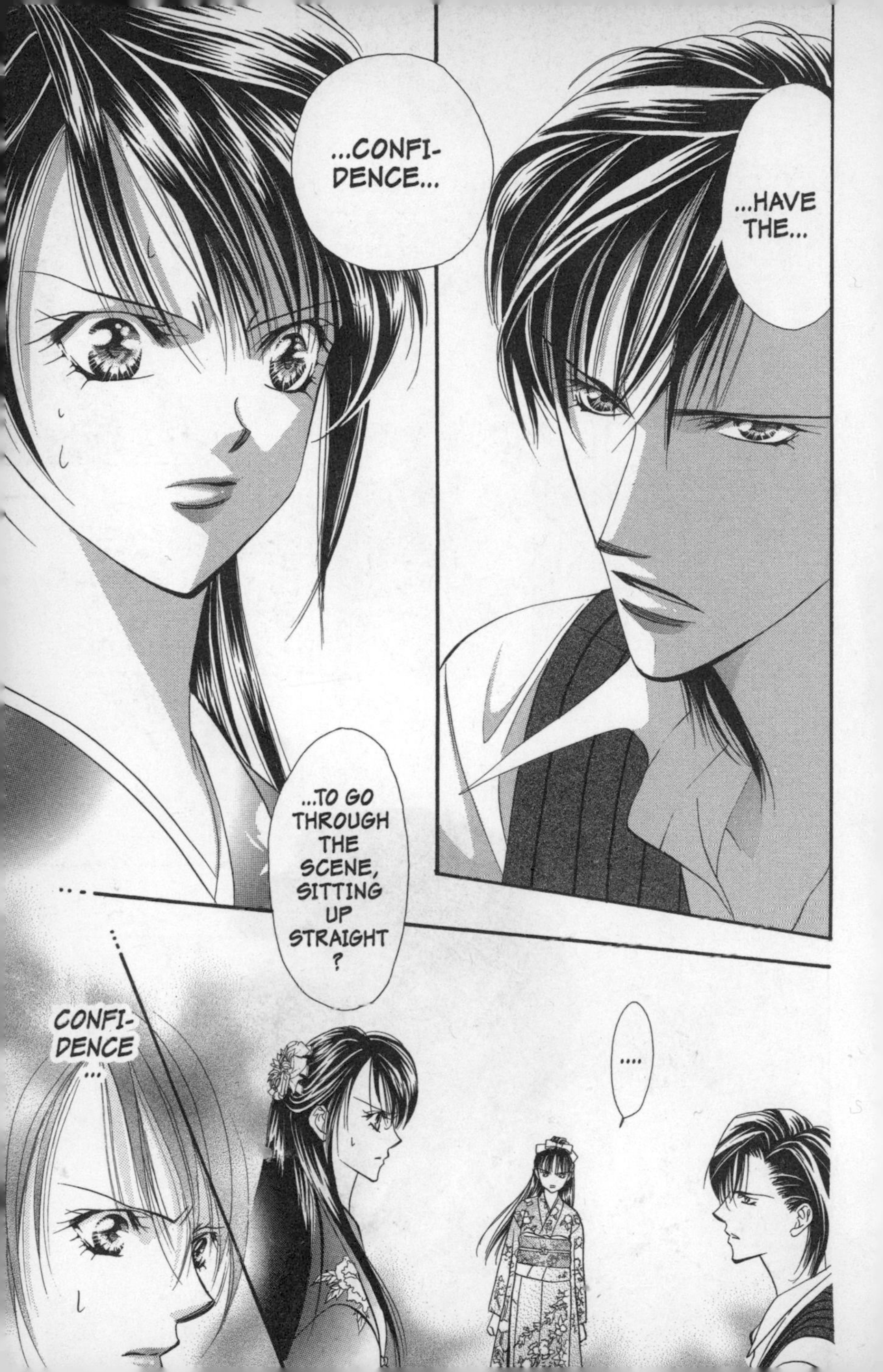
...HAVE THE...
...CONFIDENCE...
...TO GO THROUGH THE SCENE, SITTING UP STRAIGHT?
....
CONFIDENCE ...

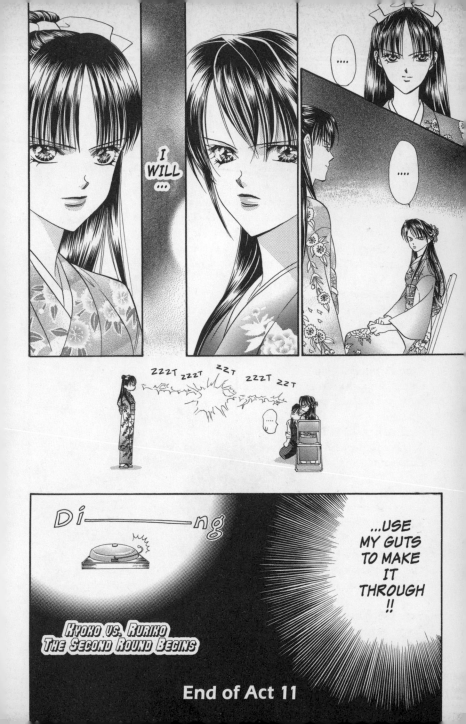

I WILL ...

....

....

ZZZT ZZZT ZZZT ZZZT ZZT

Di————ng

...USE
MY GUTS
TO MAKE
IT
THROUGH
!!

Kyoko vs. Ruriko
The Second Round Begins

End of Act 11

Skip·Beat! End Notes
Everyone knows how to be a fan, but sometimes cool things
from other cultures need a little help crossing the language barrier.

Page 40, panel 3: Draw an eye on the daruma
People draw an eye on a daruma (usually the left eye) when they have a major
goal or wish they want to achieve. The other eye is added when they reach
their goal, and the daruma is placed in a shrine as a thank-you. At election
time, many politicians can be seen drawing on the second eye when they win.

Page 42, panel 1: Tsuzumi
Hand drums used in traditional Japanese court music, Noh, and kabuki.
Kotsuzumi are played on the shoulder, while *otsuzumi* are played at the hip.
Both drums are played with the hand instead of sticks.

Page 42, panel 2: Pon
One of the sounds from the kotsuzumi, produced by hitting
the center of the drumhead.

Page 108, panel 7: Tsuru
This is a play on *Tsuruga*. *Tsuru* can mean crane, but it is spelled with
a different kanji than Ren's last name.

Page 108, panel 8: Renga
Renga means bricks. In her shock, Kyoko has temporarily gone batty, and is
mixing up Ren's name…much to her own confusion.

Page 146, panel 8: Shabadaba
This isn't just a snappy tune, it's a play on words using yakuza slang. The way
shaba is spelled in the original Japanese means "the world outside prison."

Page 159, panel 6: Tengu Nose
Tengu are mountain spirits with wings and long noses. People who are being
vain and boastful are often described as Tengu. Kyoko had a Tengu nose herself,
back on page 11 of Volume 1.

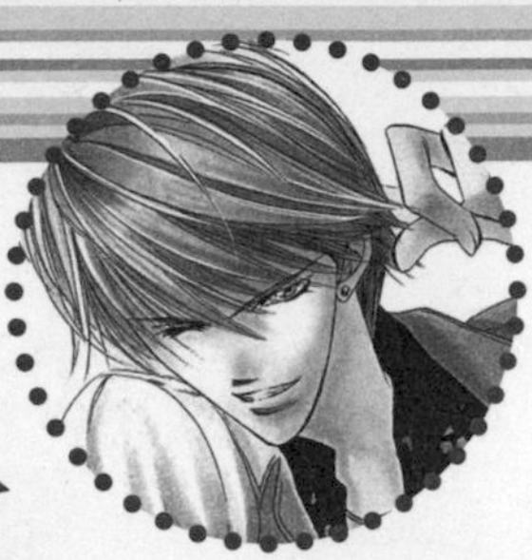

Yoshiki Nakamura is originally from Tokushima prefecture. She started drawing manga in elementary school, which eventually led to her 1993 debut of *Yume de Au yori Suteki* (Better than Seeing in a Dream) in *Hana to Yume* magazine. Her other works include the basketball series *Saint Love, MVP wa Yuzurenai* (Can't Give Up MVP), *Blue Wars*, and *Tokyo Crazy Paradise*, a series about a female bodyguard in 2020 Tokyo.

SKIP·BEAT!

Vol. 2

The Shojo Beat Manga Edition

STORY AND ART BY YOSHIKI NAKAMURA

English Translation & Adaptation/Tomo Kimura
Touch-up Art & Lettering/Sabrina Heep
Design/Yukiko Whitley
Editor/Pancha Diaz

Editor in Chief, Books/Alvin Lu
Editor in Chief, Magazines/Marc Weidenbaum
VP, Publishing Licensing/Rika Inouye
VP, Sales & Product Marketing/Gonzalo Ferreyra
VP, Creative/Linda Espinosa
Publisher/Hyoe Narita

Printed in Canada

Published by VIZ Media, LLC
P.O. Box 77010
San Francisco, CA 94107

Shojo Beat Manga Edition
10 9 8 7 6 5 4 3
First printing, September 2006
Third printing, September 2008

store.viz.com

RATED T FOR TEEN

PARENTAL ADVISORY
SKIP•BEAT! is rated T for Teen and is recommended for ages 13 and up. This volume contains suggestive themes.

ratings.viz.com

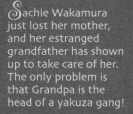

I·O·N

By **Arina Tanemura**,
creator of *Full Moon*
and *The Gentlemen's
Alliance* †

Ion Tsuburagi is a normal junior high girl with normal junior high problems. But when a mysterious substance grants her telekinetic powers, she finds herself struggling to keep everything together! Are her new abilities a blessing...or a curse?

Find out in *I·O·N*—manga on sale now!

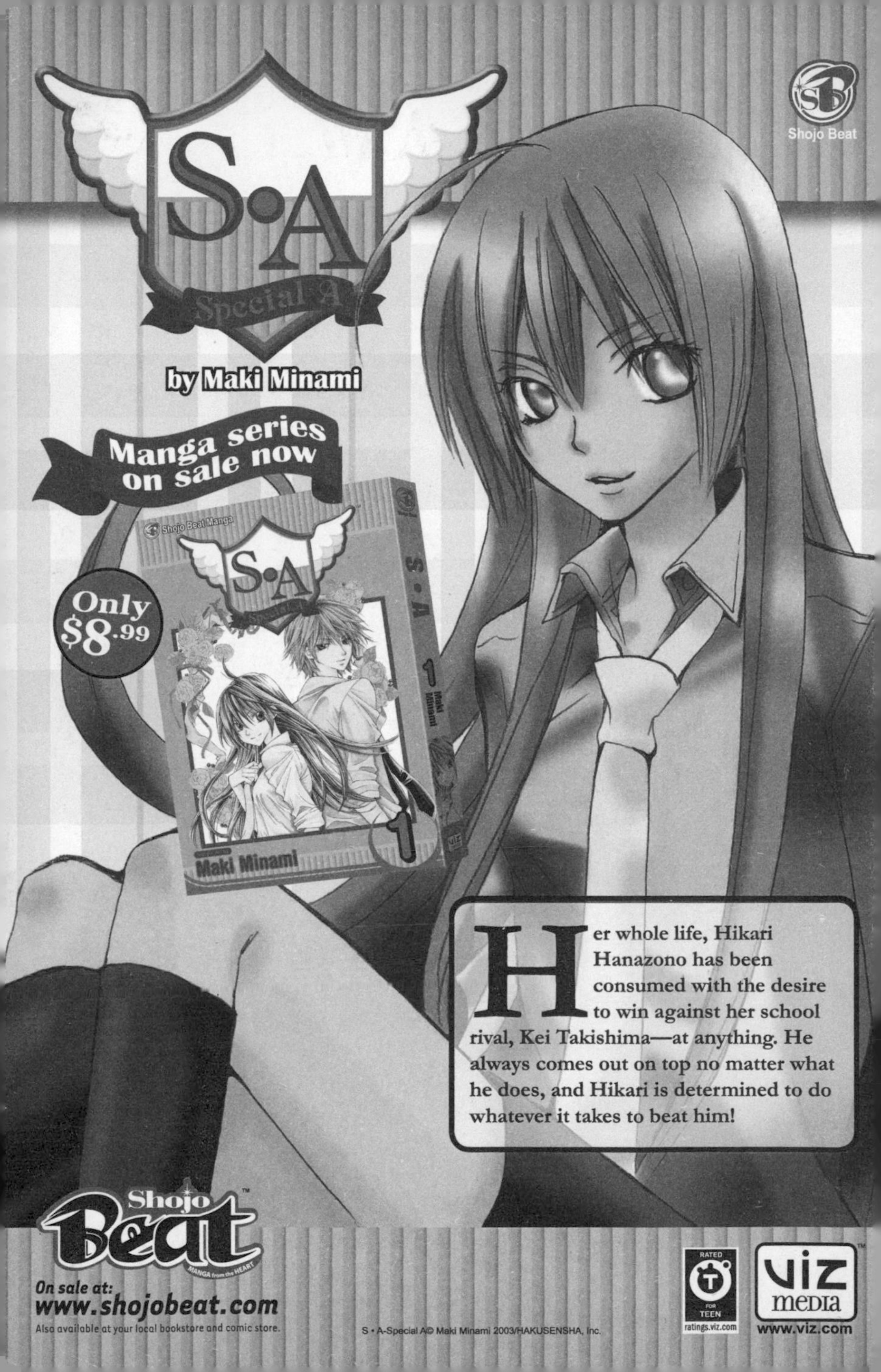
S•A
Special A
Shojo Beat
by Maki Minami
Manga series on sale now
Only $8.99
Shojo Beat Manga
S•A
1
Maki Minami
Her whole life, Hikari Hanazono has been consumed with the desire to win against her school rival, Kei Takishima—at anything. He always comes out on top no matter what he does, and Hikari is determined to do whatever it takes to beat him!
Shojo Beat™
MANGA from the HEART
On sale at:
www.shojobeat.com
Also available at your local bookstore and comic store.
S • A-Special A© Maki Minami 2003/HAKUSENSHA, Inc.
RATED T FOR TEEN
ratings.viz.com
VIZ media™
www.viz.com

Tell us what you think about Shojo Beat Manga!

Our survey is now available online. Go to:

shojobeat.com/mangasurvey

Help us make our product offerings better!